FIRE PUNCH

4

STORY AND ART BY
TATSUKI FUJIMOTO

TOGATA

A mysterious
girl who is trying
to film a movie
starring Agni.

AGNI

A Blessed with the power of
regeneration, his little sister is killed
by Doma, who engulfs Agni in flames
that will never extinguish.

JUDAH

A soldier of
Behemdorg
who is a
Blessed with
the power of
regeneration.

NENETO

A girl
taken to
Behemdorg
with Sun.

SUN

A Blessed with the power of electricity. Agni saves his life.

ICE WITCH

An unidentified person who has appeared out of nowhere claiming to be the Ice Witch.

...sess unique powers are called Blessed, and two such Blessed, Agni ...a world frozen over by the Ice Witch. One day, Agni and Luna's village ...chemdorg soldier named Doma, who's a Blessed whose flames won't ...hey've completely consumed their fuel. Luna loses her life, but Agni ...a living hell of trying to master the art of controlling the flames that ...e him. He seeks revenge on Doma but doesn't realize that Togata, the ...m to get his revenge, has instead schemed to get him killed. When ...emdorg, he's forced to battle three ruthless death row criminals. He's ...olute limit, but he manages to kill two of them and drive one away. ...upe of Agni's followers, led by their boss, show up and concoct a plan ...n, taking the freed slaves with them. Left behind, Agni exchanges words ...seemingly out of nowhere, a person identifying themselves as the Ice

STORY

FIRE PUNCH

STORY AND ART BY
TATSUKI FUJIMOTO

CHAPTER 29

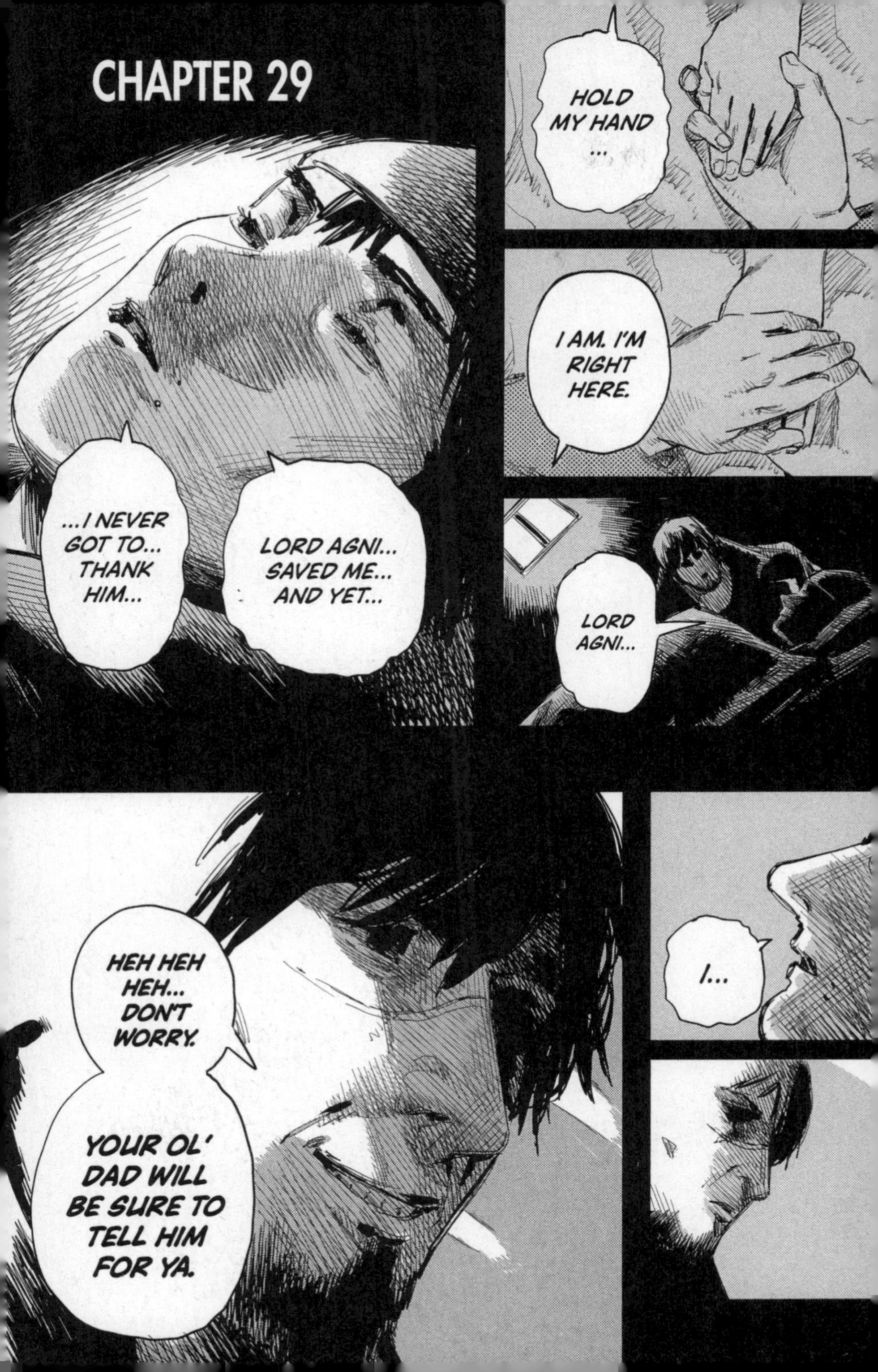
HOLD MY HAND ...
I AM. I'M RIGHT HERE.
LORD AGNI...
LORD AGNI... SAVED ME... AND YET...
...I NEVER GOT TO... THANK HIM...
I...
HEH HEH HEH... DON'T WORRY.
YOUR OL' DAD WILL BE SURE TO TELL HIM FOR YA.

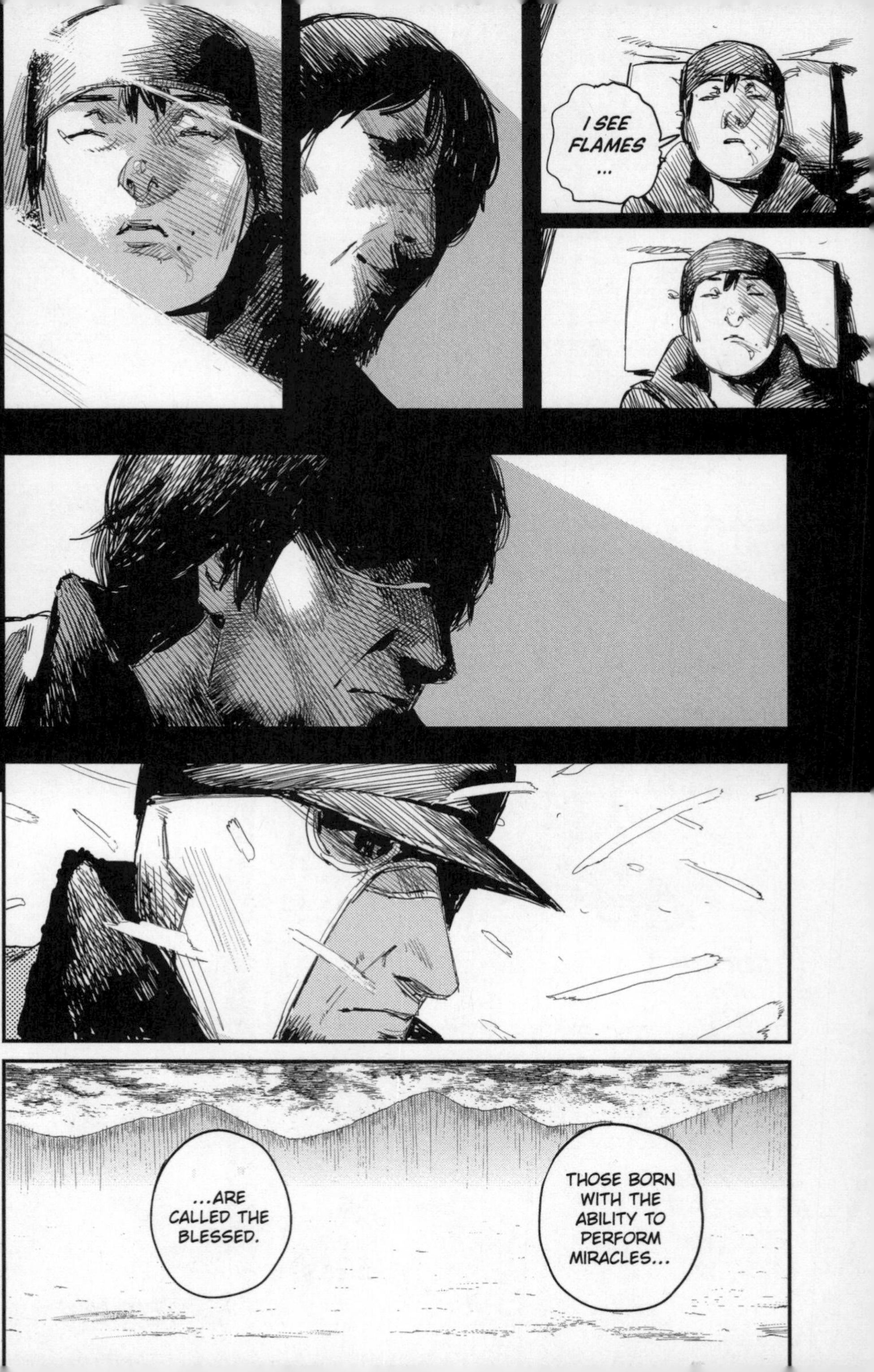
I SEE FLAMES ...
THOSE BORN WITH THE ABILITY TO PERFORM MIRACLES...
...ARE CALLED THE BLESSED.

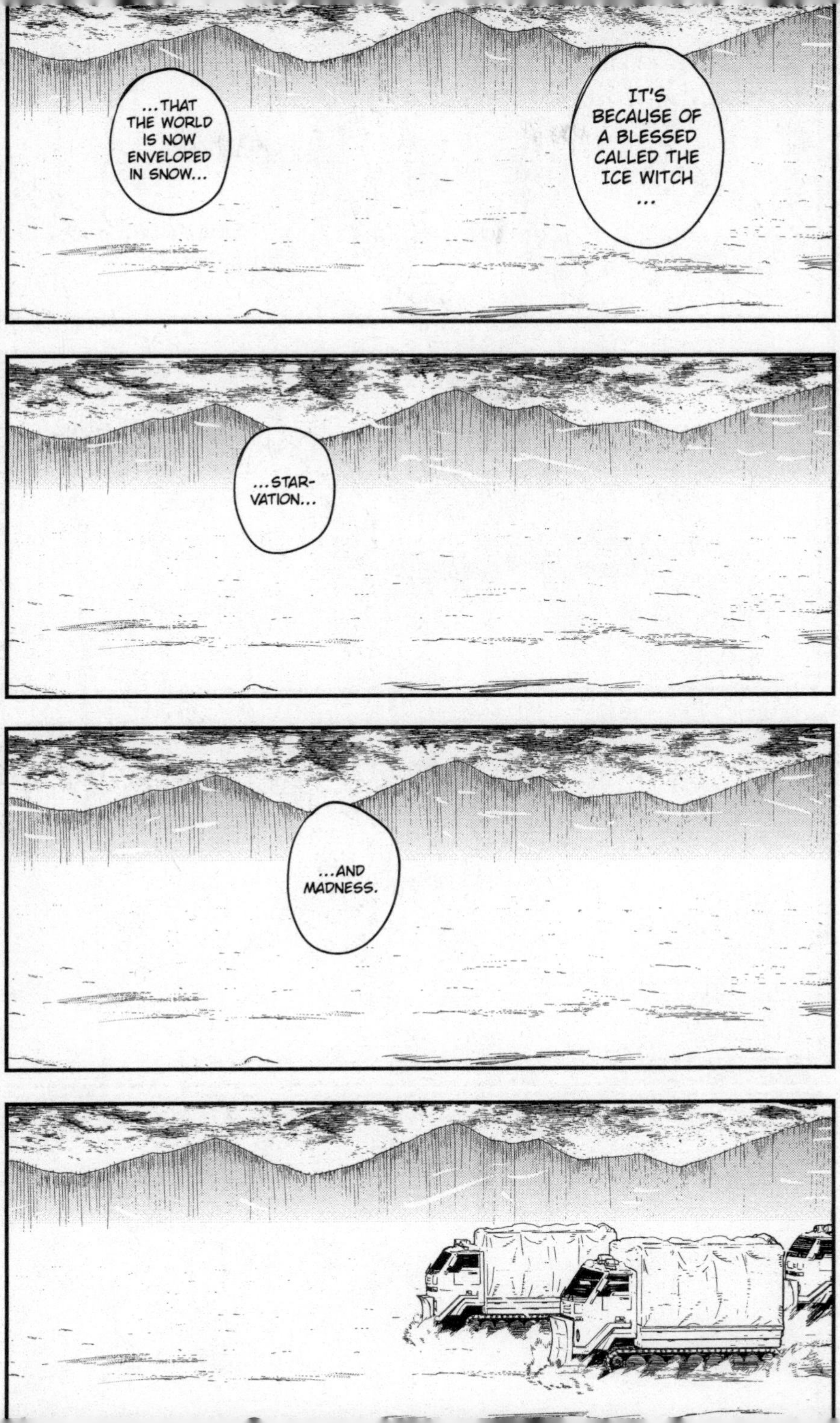
IT'S BECAUSE OF A BLESSED CALLED THE ICE WITCH ...
...THAT THE WORLD IS NOW ENVELOPED IN SNOW...
...STAR-VATION...
...AND MADNESS.

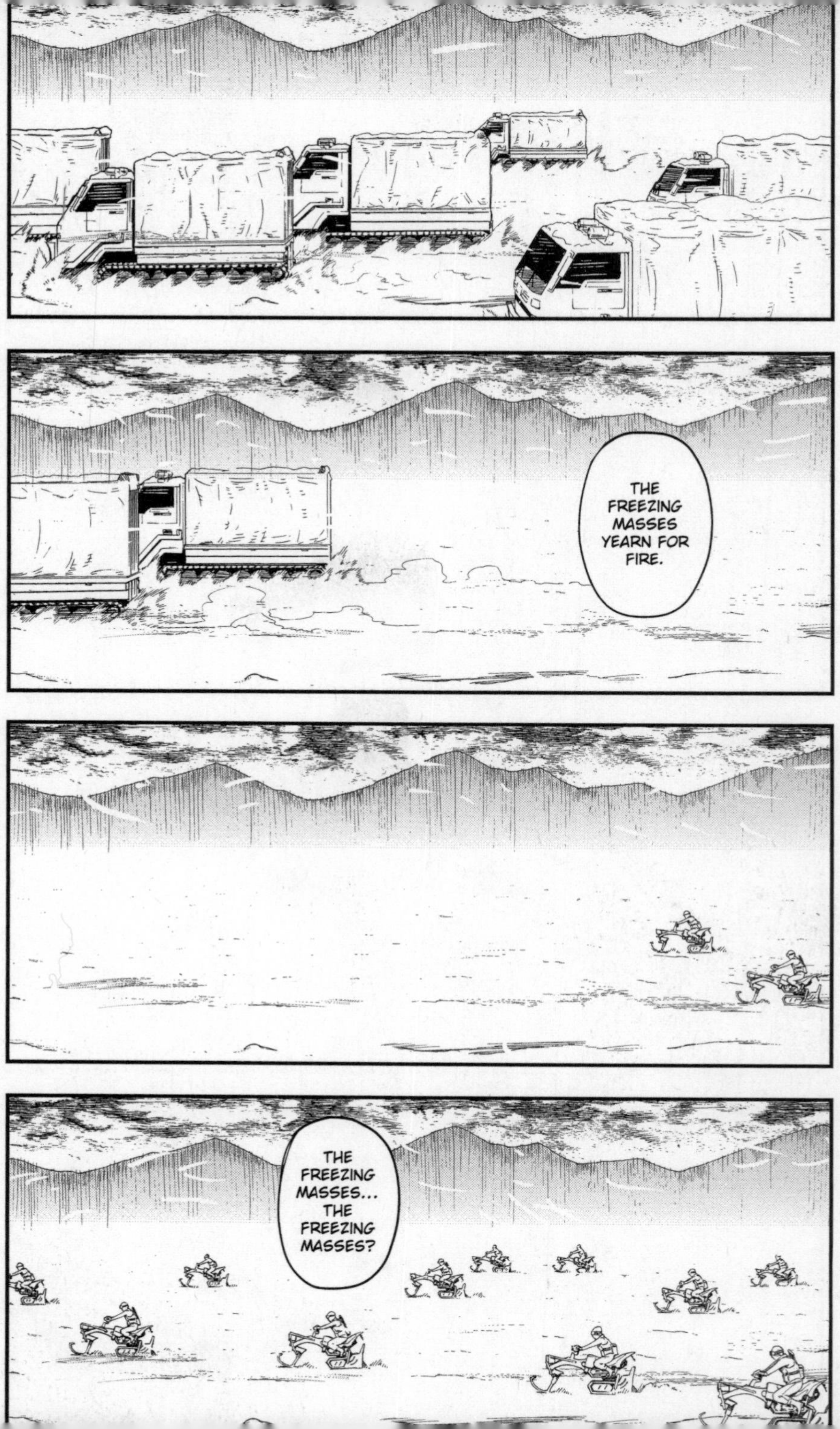
THE FREEZING MASSES YEARN FOR FIRE.
THE FREEZING MASSES... THE FREEZING MASSES?

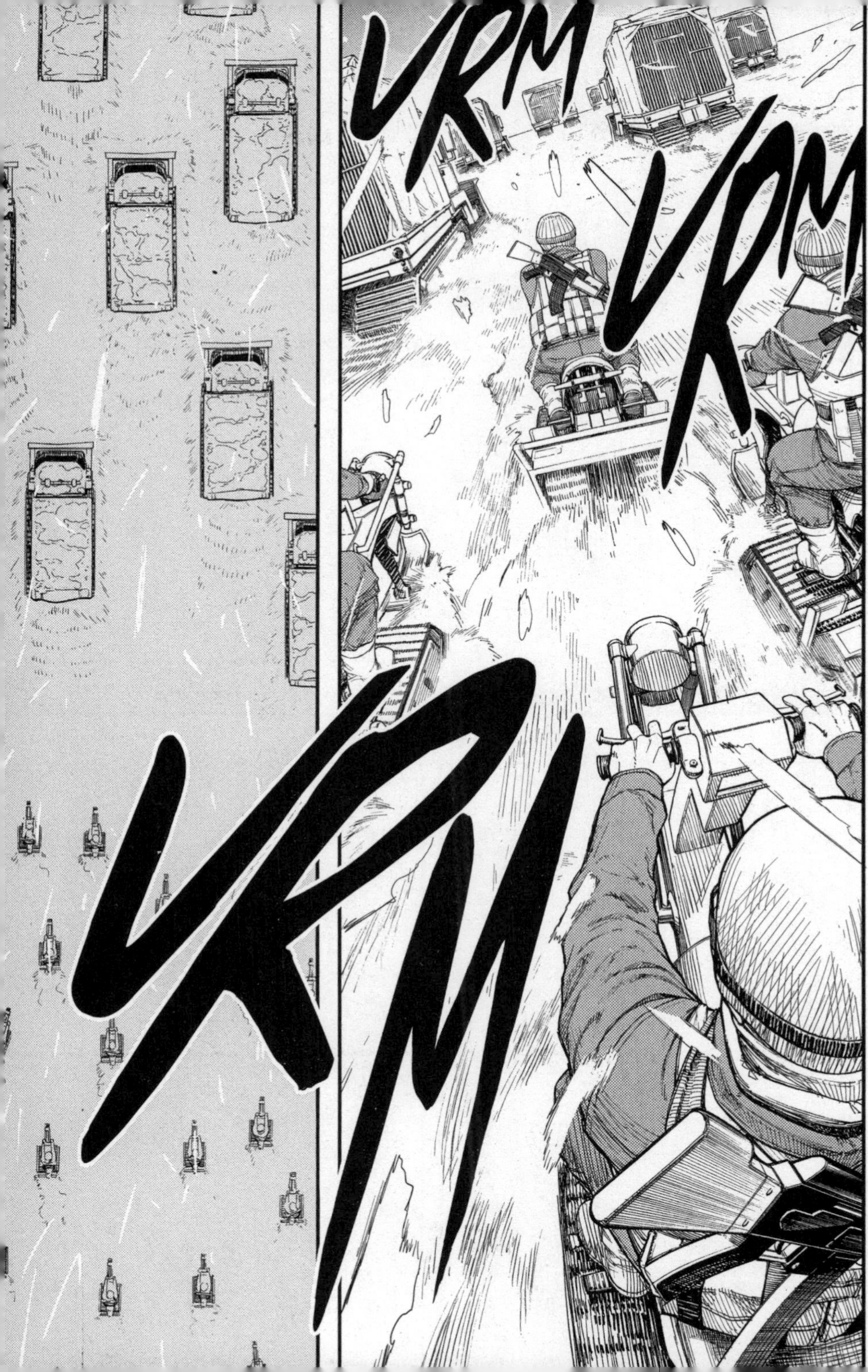
VRM
VRM
VRM

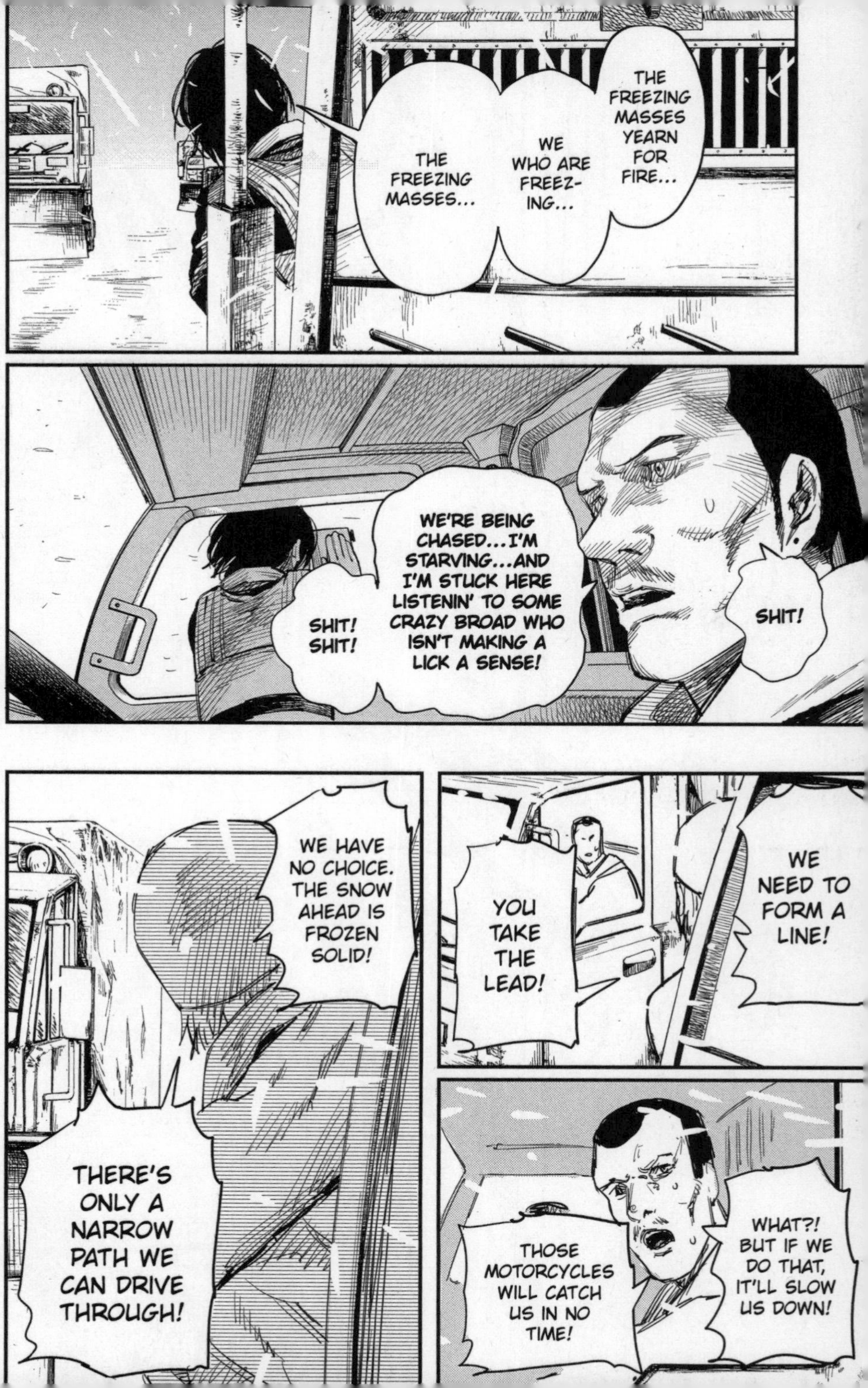
THE FREEZING MASSES YEARN FOR FIRE...
WE WHO ARE FREEZ-ING...
THE FREEZING MASSES...
SHIT!
WE'RE BEING CHASED...I'M STARVING...AND I'M STUCK HERE LISTENIN' TO SOME CRAZY BROAD WHO ISN'T MAKING A LICK A SENSE!
SHIT! SHIT!
WE NEED TO FORM A LINE!
YOU TAKE THE LEAD!
WHAT?! BUT IF WE DO THAT, IT'LL SLOW US DOWN!
THOSE MOTORCYCLES WILL CATCH US IN NO TIME!
WE HAVE NO CHOICE. THE SNOW AHEAD IS FROZEN SOLID!
THERE'S ONLY A NARROW PATH WE CAN DRIVE THROUGH!

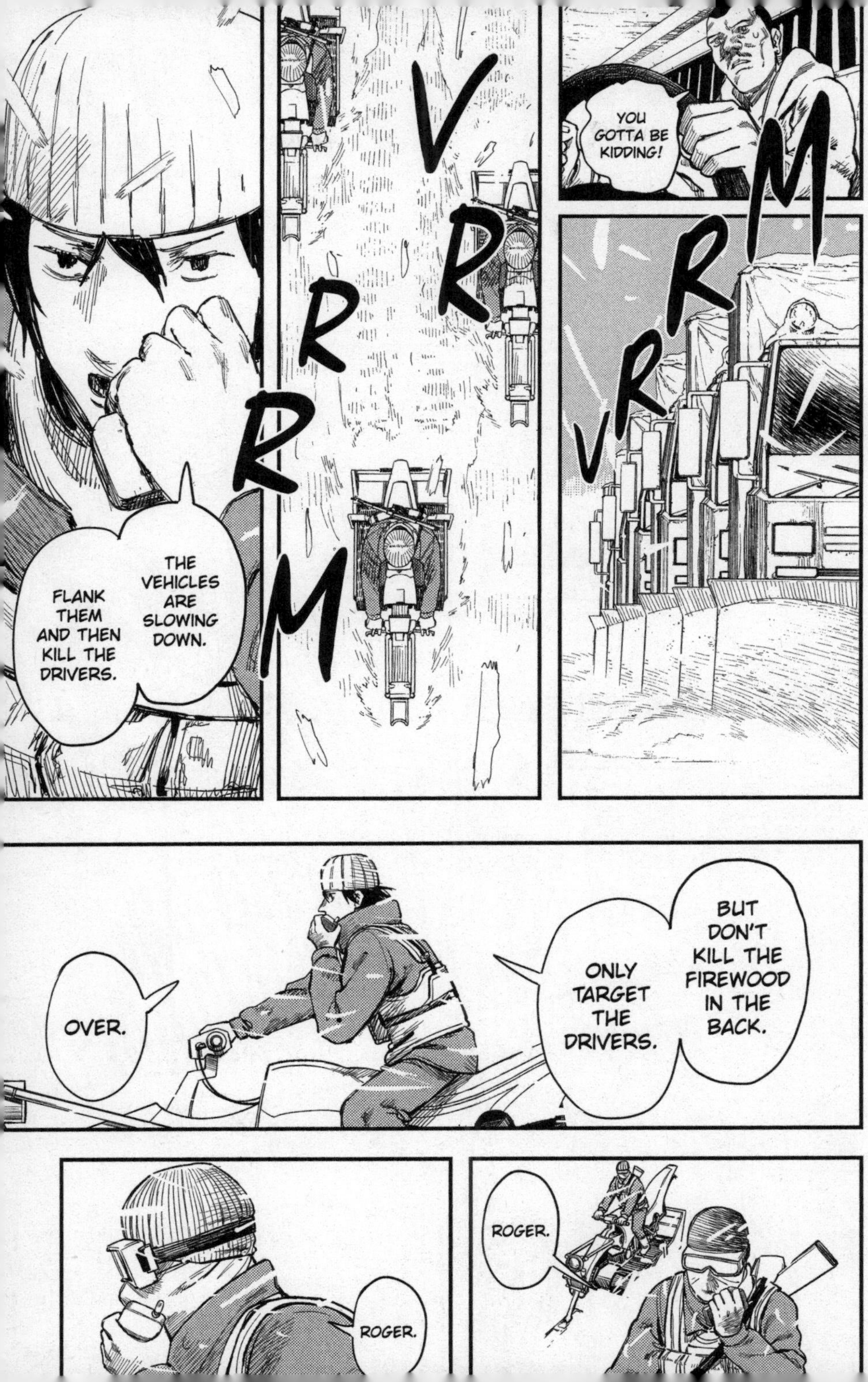
YOU GOTTA BE KIDDING!
VRRRM
VRRRM
THE VEHICLES ARE SLOWING DOWN.
FLANK THEM AND THEN KILL THE DRIVERS.
BUT DON'T KILL THE FIREWOOD IN THE BACK.
ONLY TARGET THE DRIVERS.
OVER.
ROGER.
ROGER.

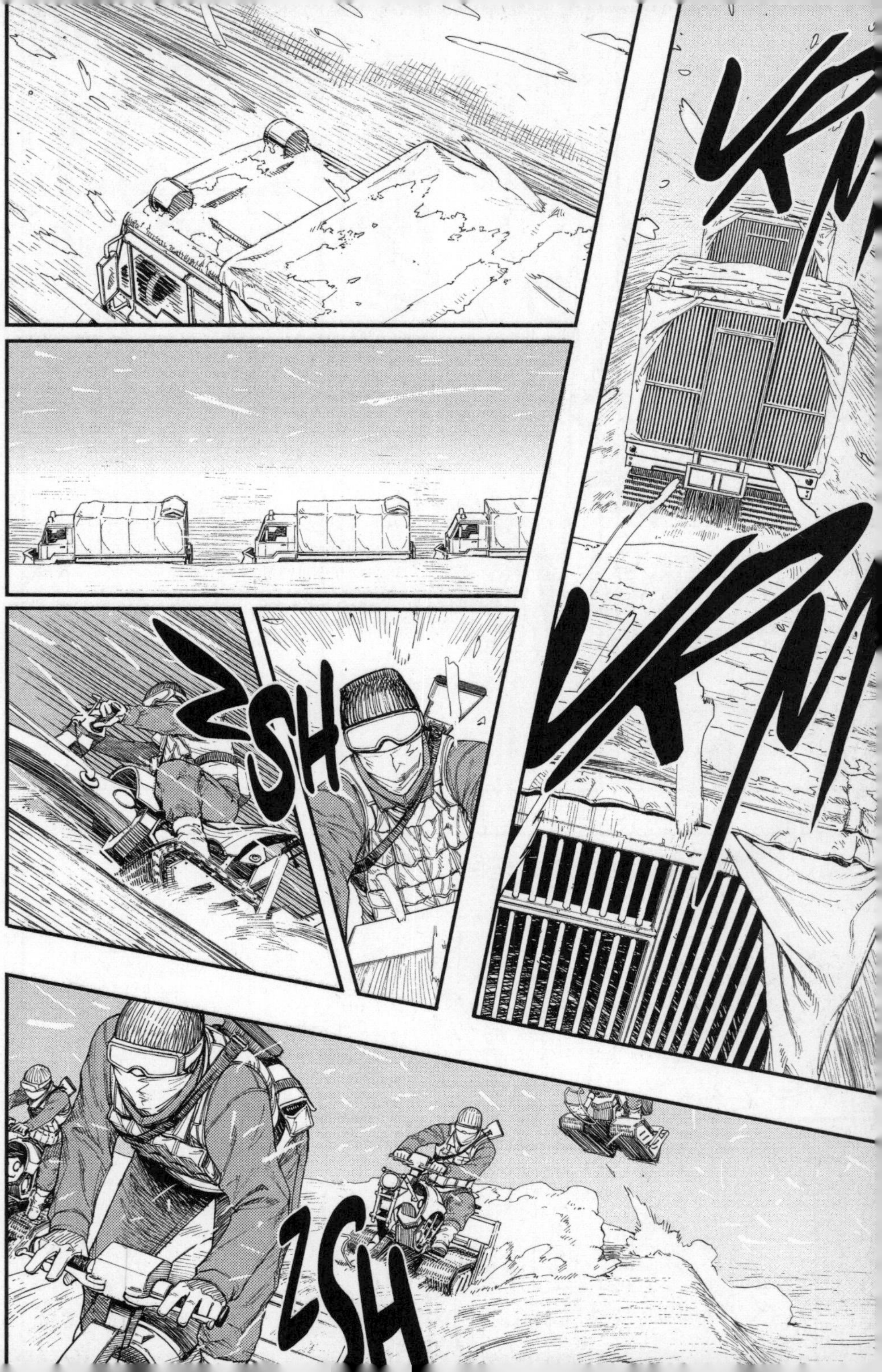
ZSH
ZSH

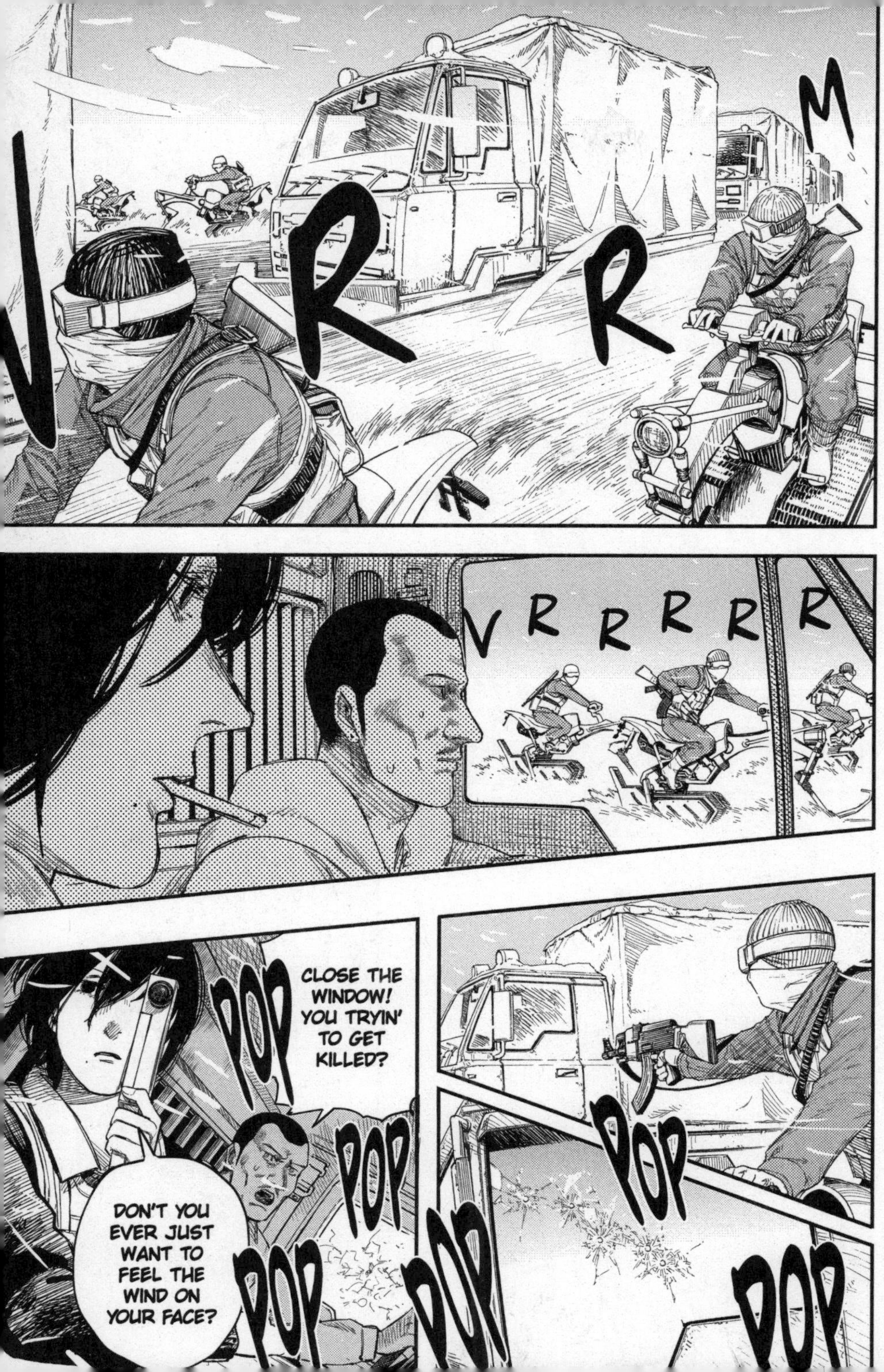
VRRRM
VRRRRR
POP
POP
POP
CLOSE THE WINDOW! YOU TRYIN' TO GET KILLED?
DON'T YOU EVER JUST WANT TO FEEL THE WIND ON YOUR FACE?
POP
POP
POP
POP
POP

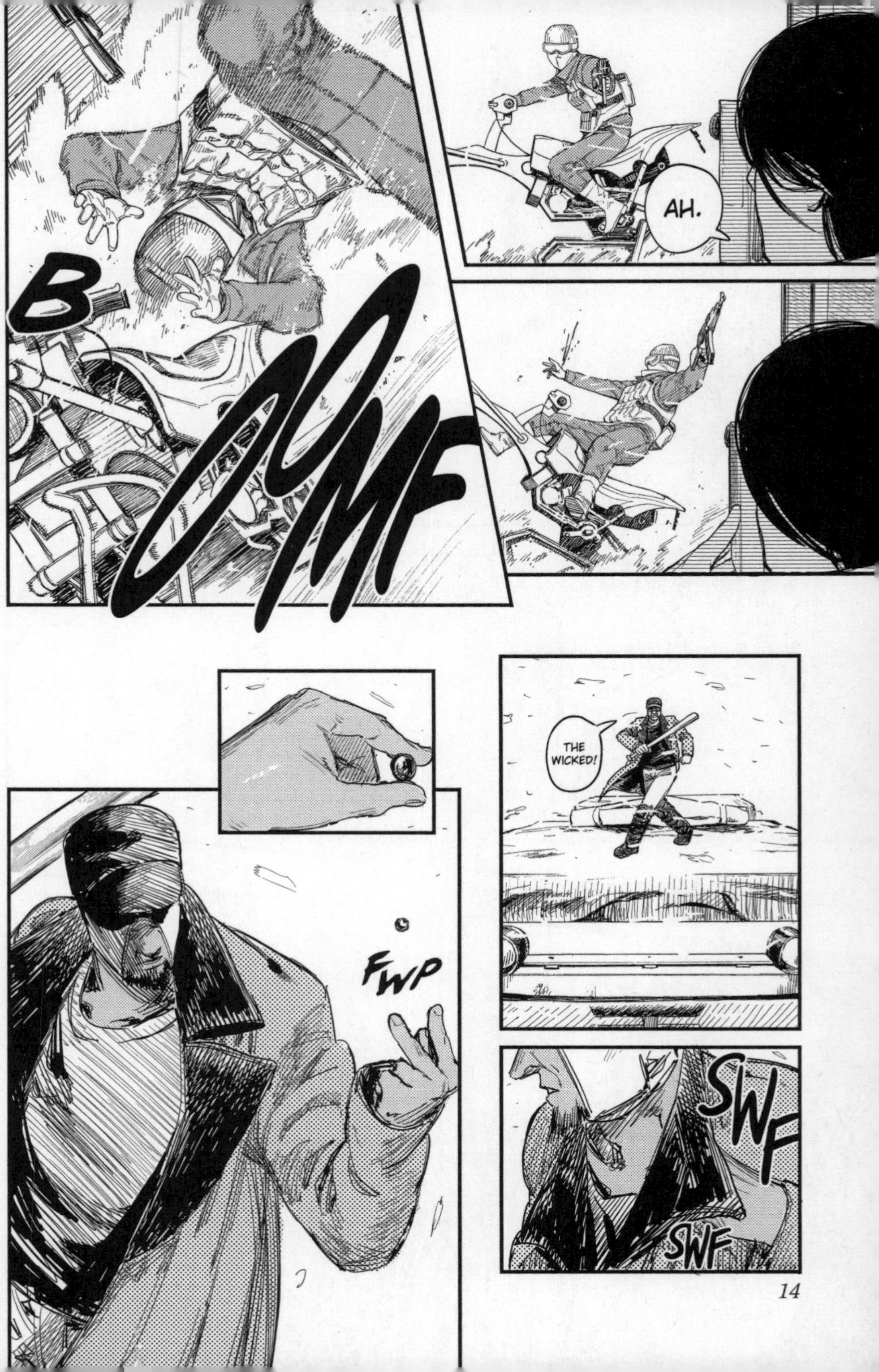
AH.
BOMF
THE WICKED!
SWF
SWF
FWP

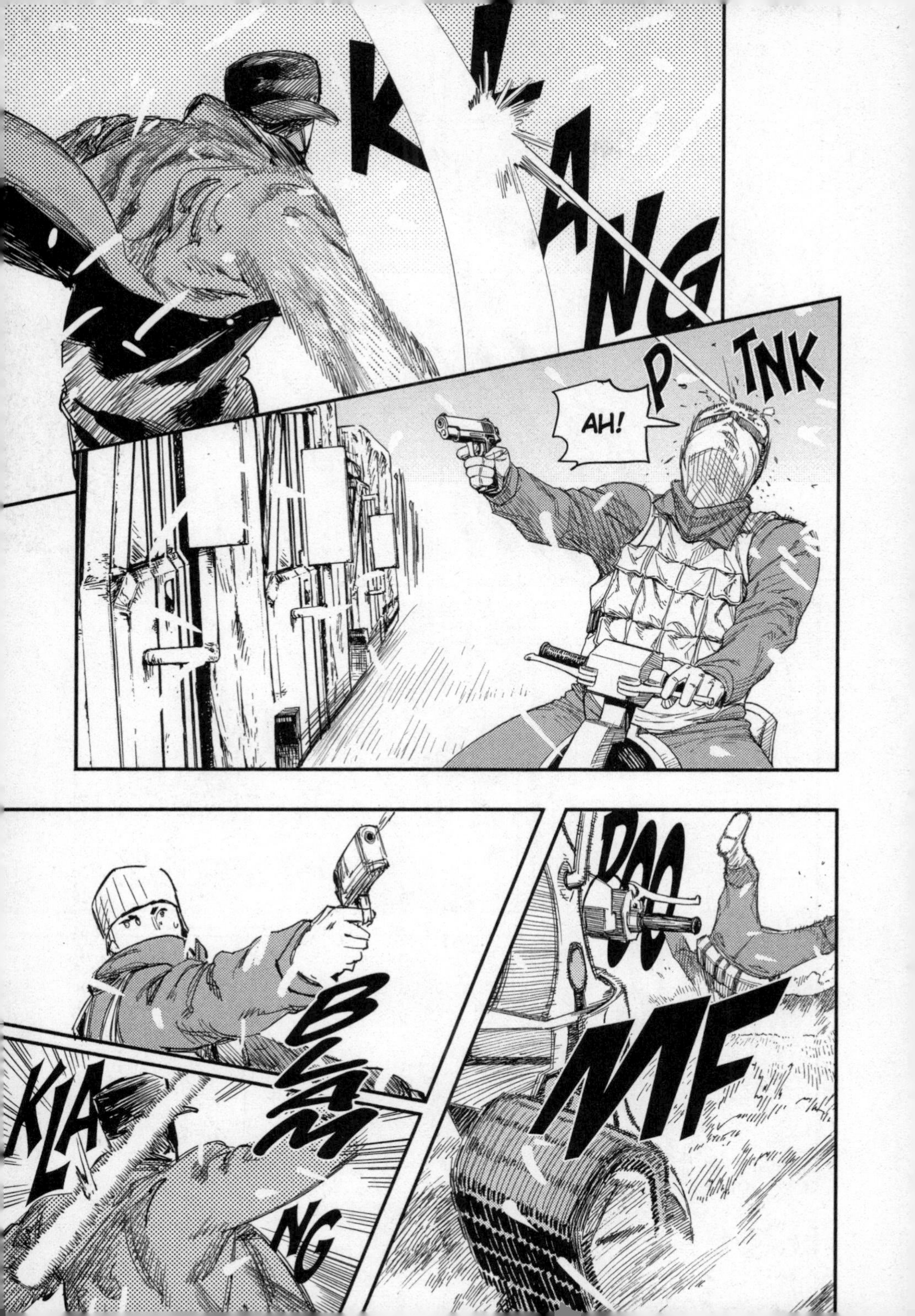
KLANG
TNK
P
AH!
DOOOMF
BLAM
KLANG

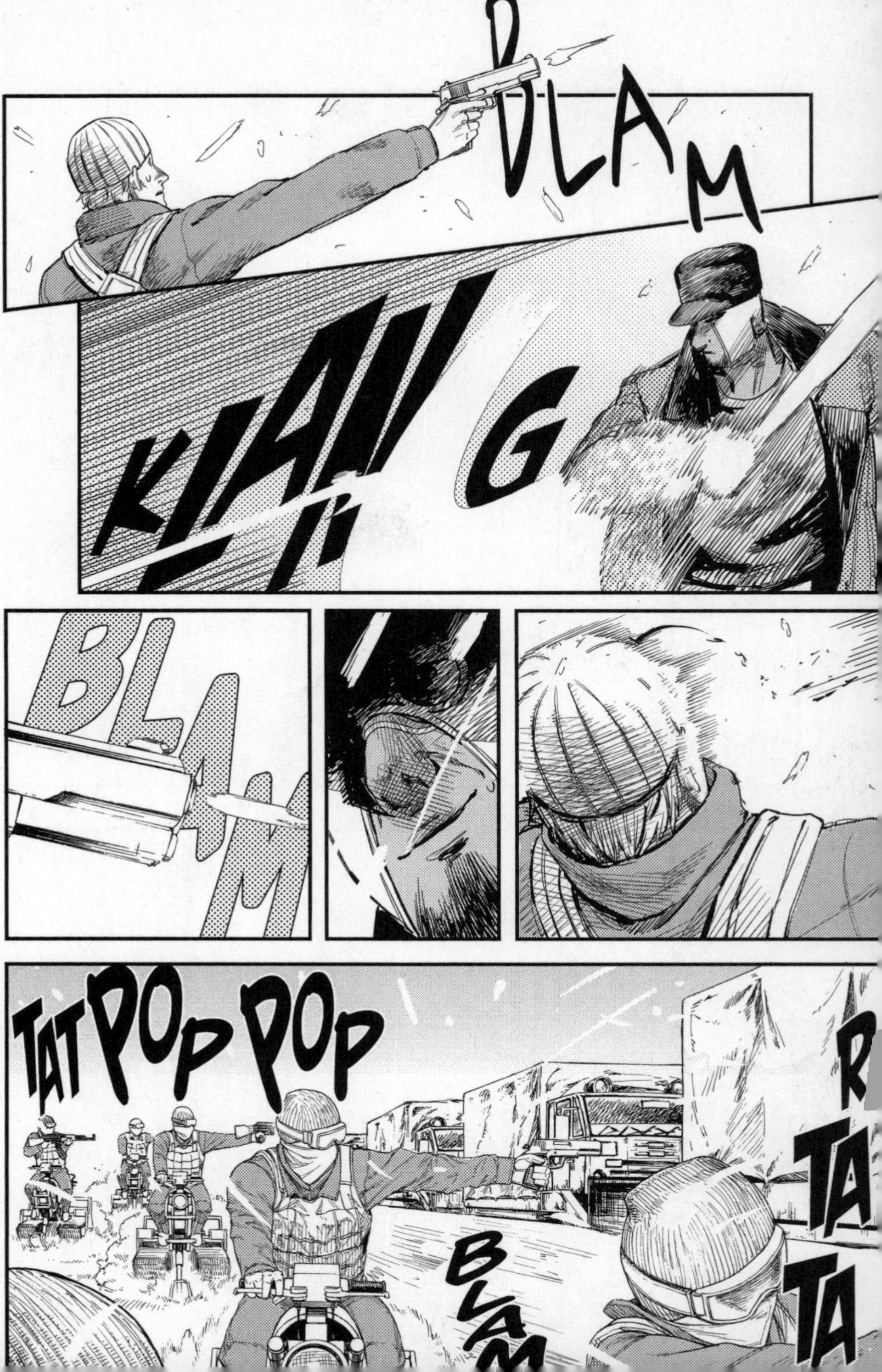
BLAM
KLANG
BLAM
RATATA
BLAM
TAT POP POP POP

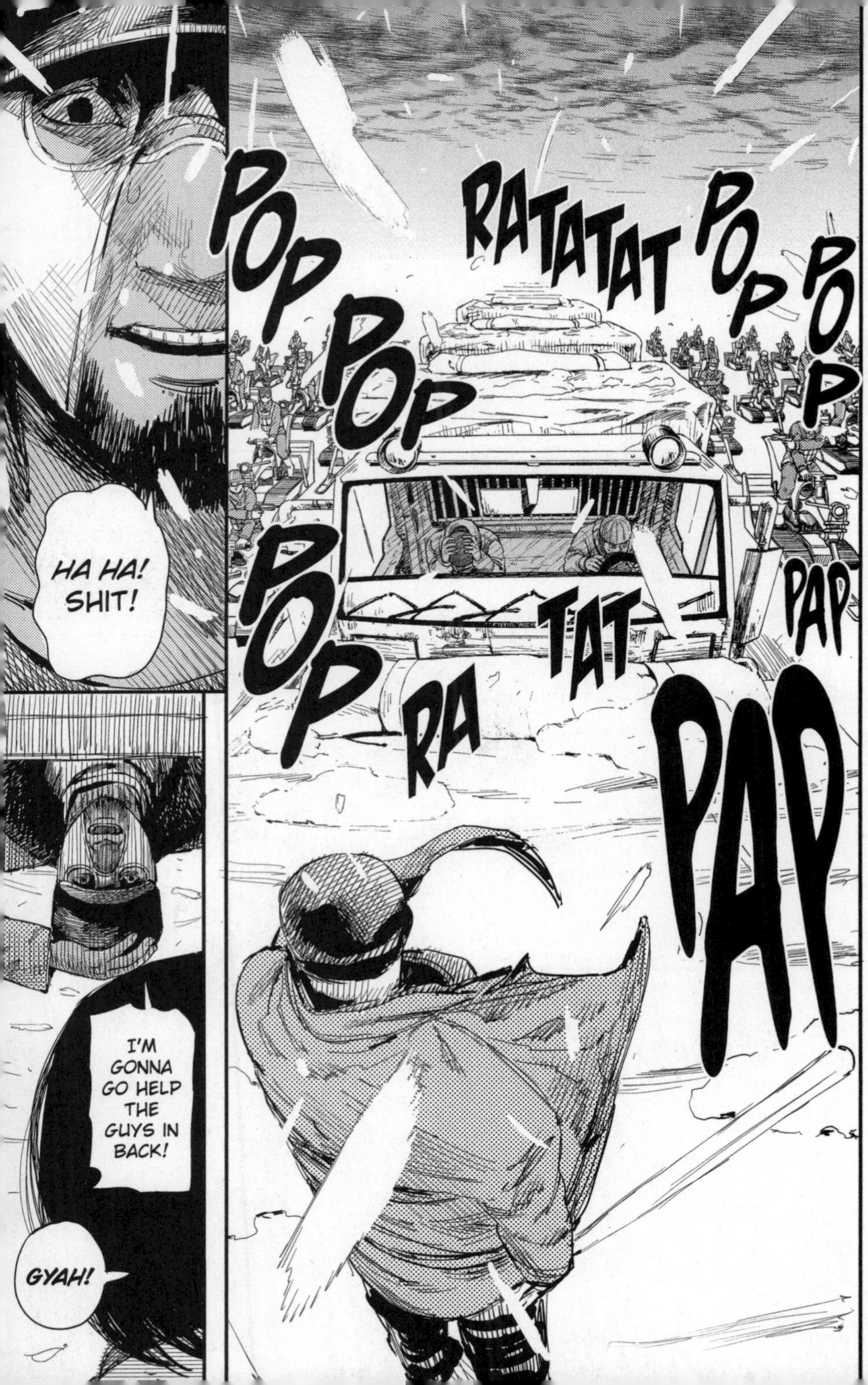
POP POP
RATATAT
POP POP
POP POP
POP POP
PAP
TAT
RA
PAP
HA HA! SHIT!
I'M GONNA GO HELP THE GUYS IN BACK!
GYAH!

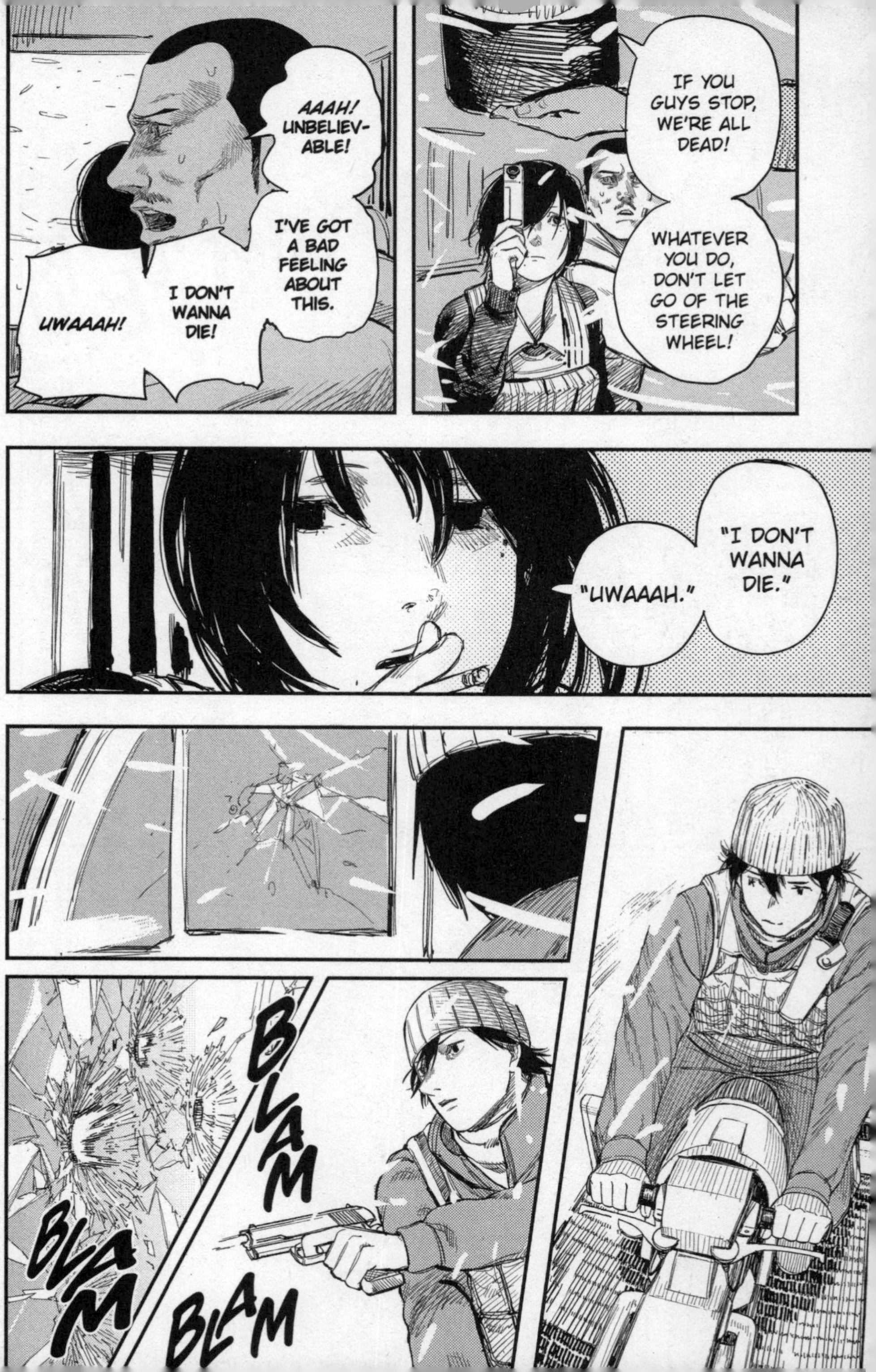
IF YOU GUYS STOP, WE'RE ALL DEAD!
WHATEVER YOU DO, DON'T LET GO OF THE STEERING WHEEL!
AAAH! UNBELIEV-ABLE!
I'VE GOT A BAD FEELING ABOUT THIS.
I DON'T WANNA DIE!
UWAAAH!
"I DON'T WANNA DIE."
"UWAAAH."
BLAM
BLAM
BLAM
BLAM

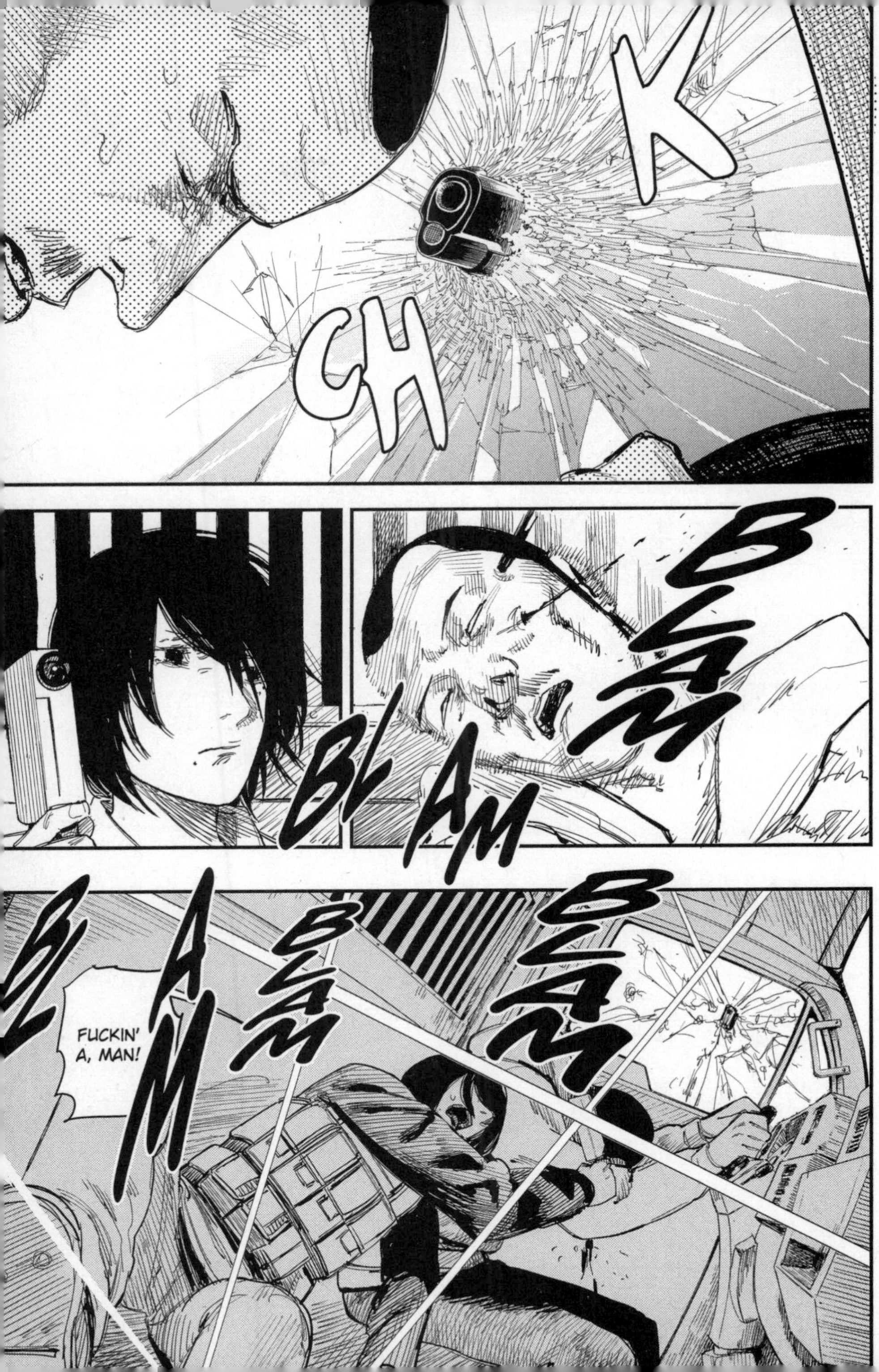

CHK
BLAM
BLAM
BLAM
BLAM
FUCKIN' A, MAN!
BLAM

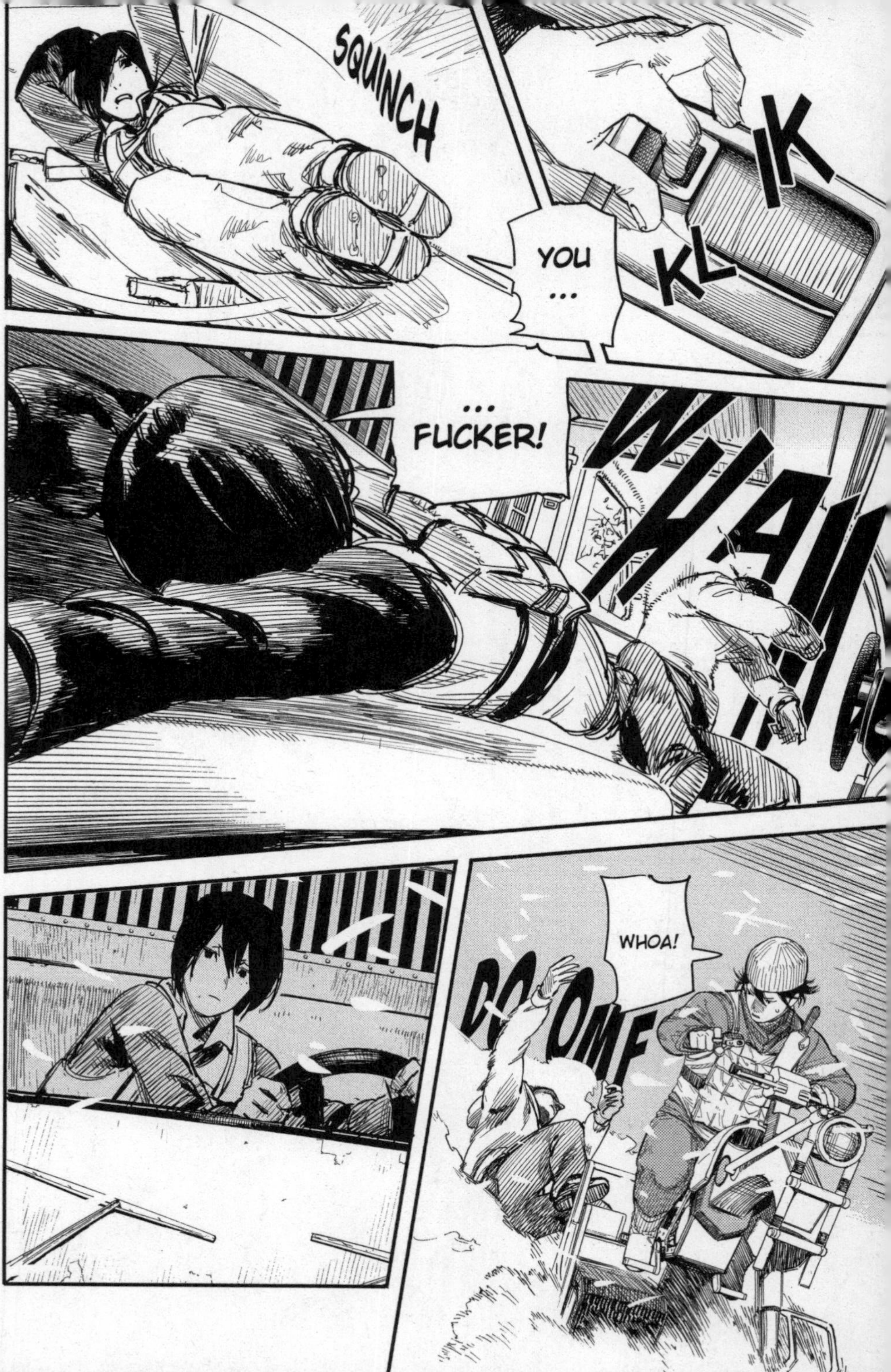
KLIK
YOU ...
SQUINCH
... FUCKER!
WHA
WHOA!
DOOMF

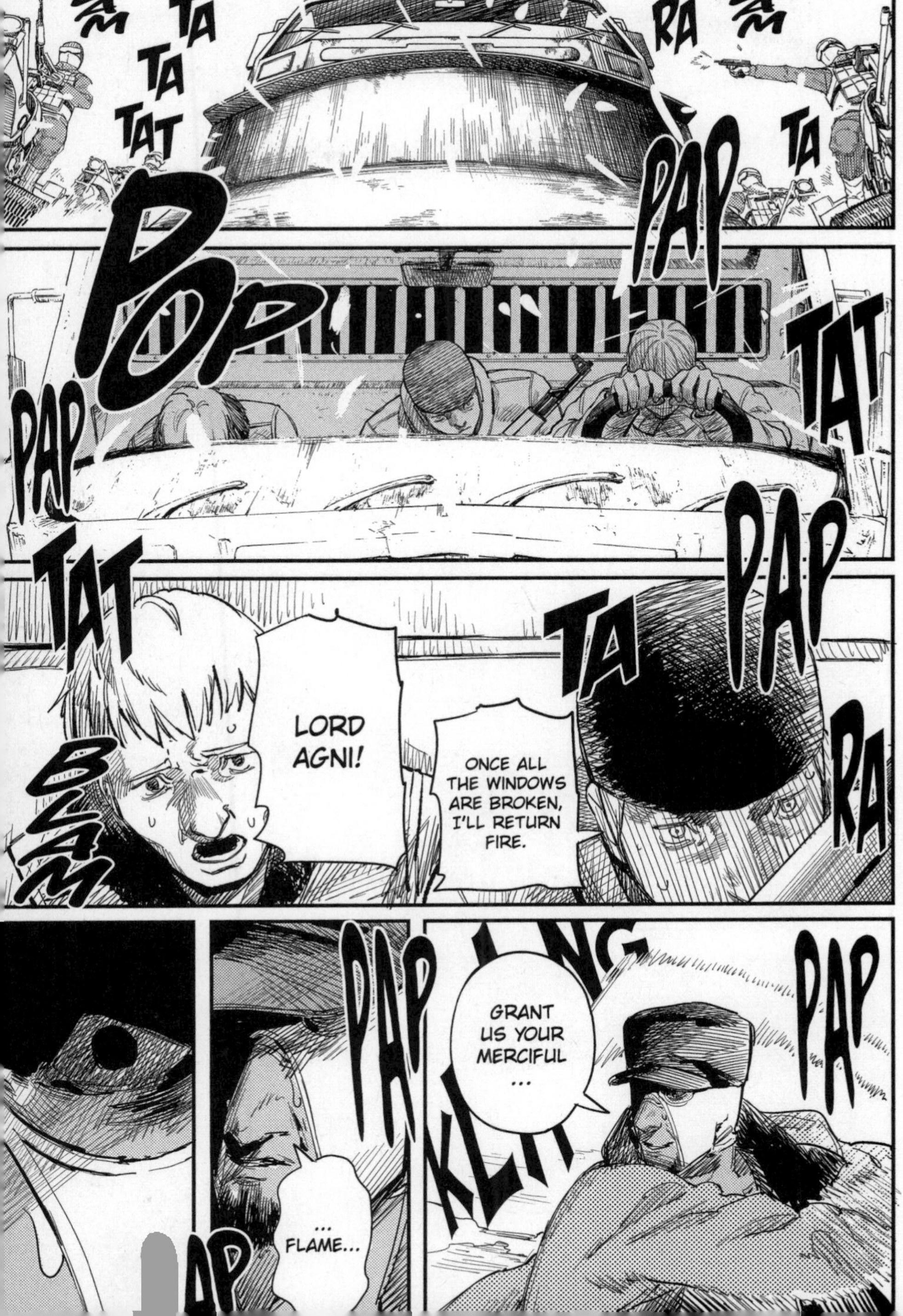
BLAM
RA
PAP
TA
BLAM
TA
TA
TAT
POP
TAT
PAP
TA
PAP
PAP
RA
ONCE ALL THE WINDOWS ARE BROKEN, I'LL RETURN FIRE.
LORD AGNI!
TAT
BLAM
PAP
GRANT US YOUR MERCIFUL ...
PAP
... FLAME...
AP

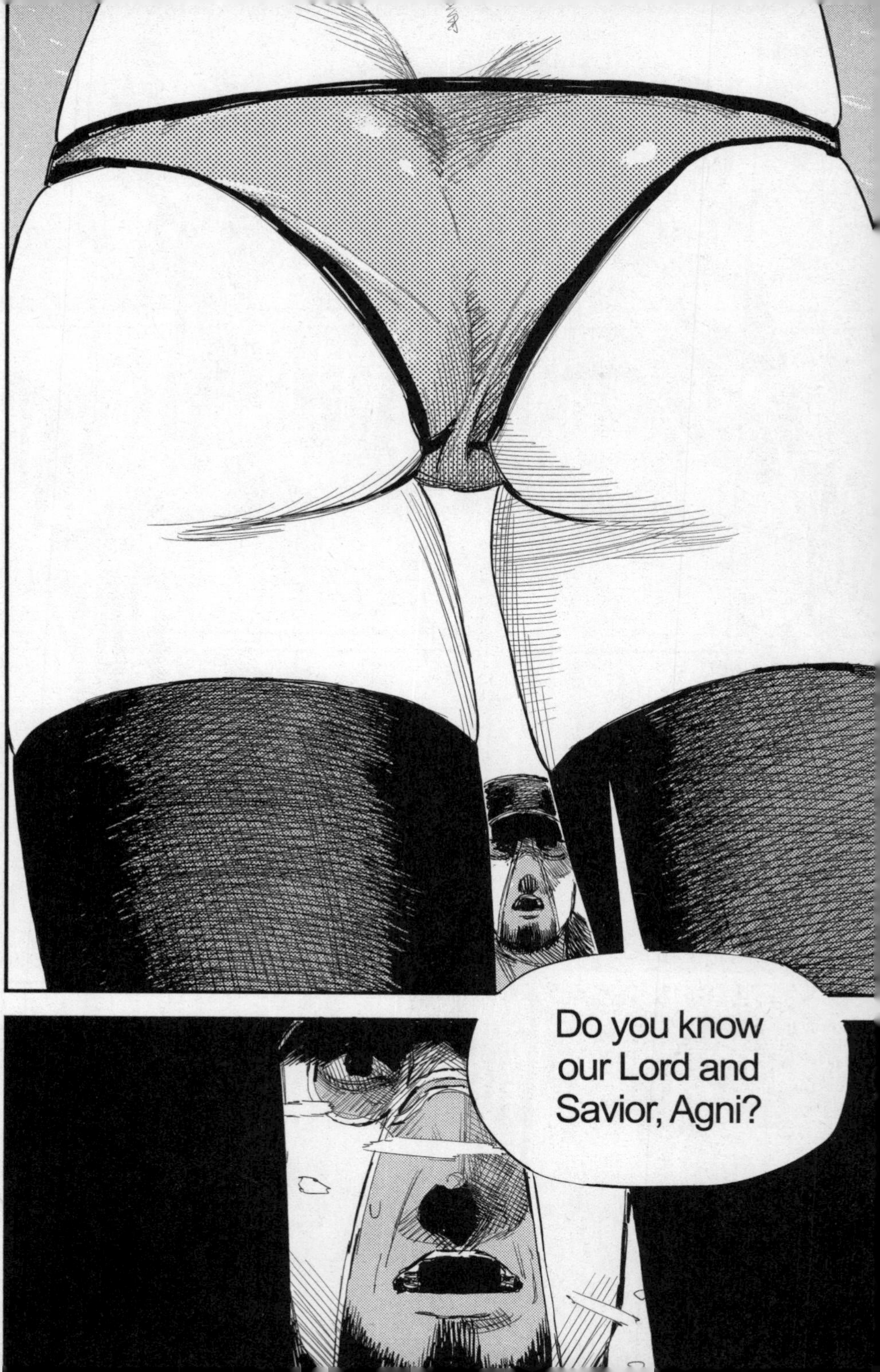
Do you know our Lord and Savior, Agni?

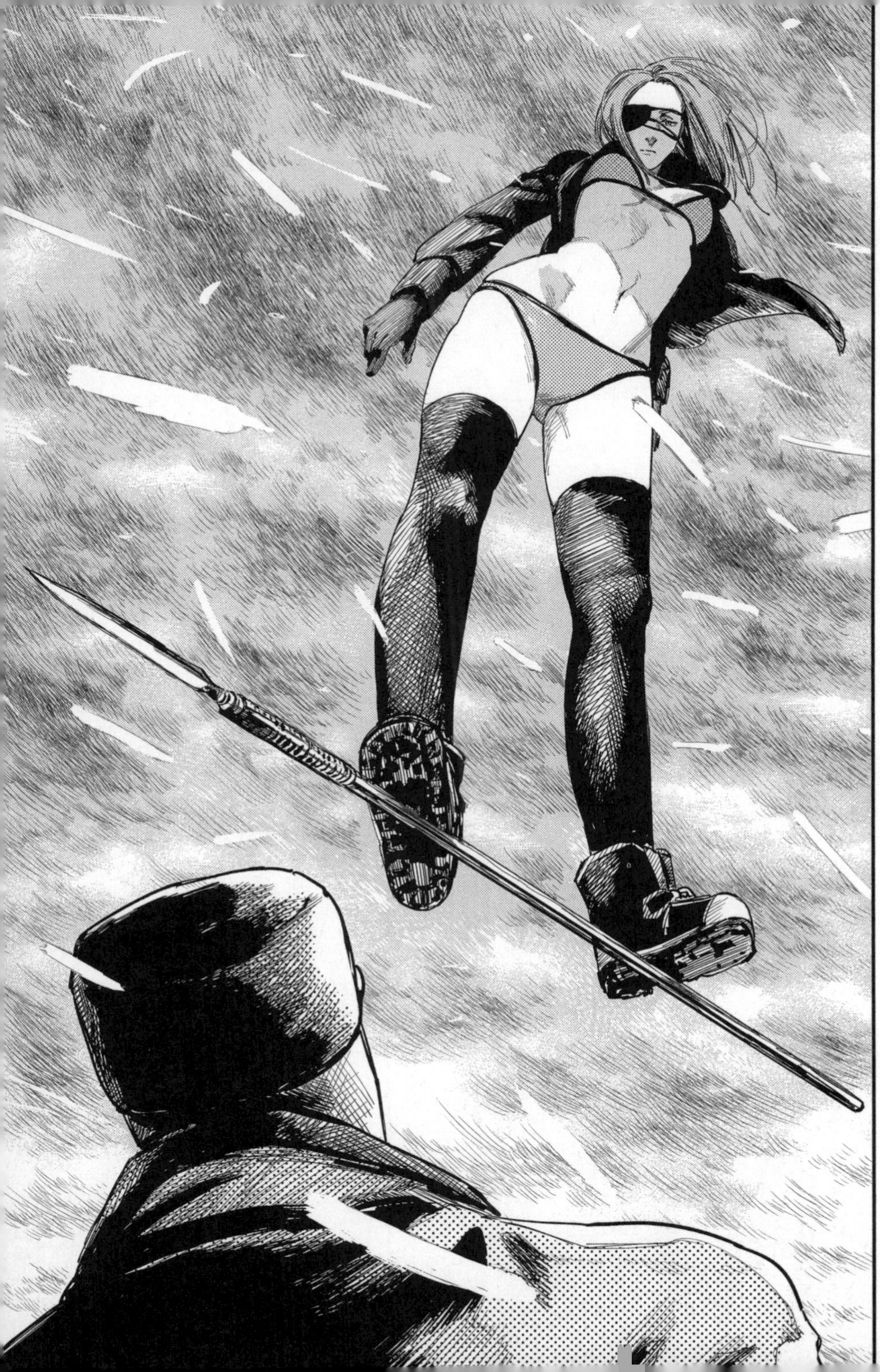

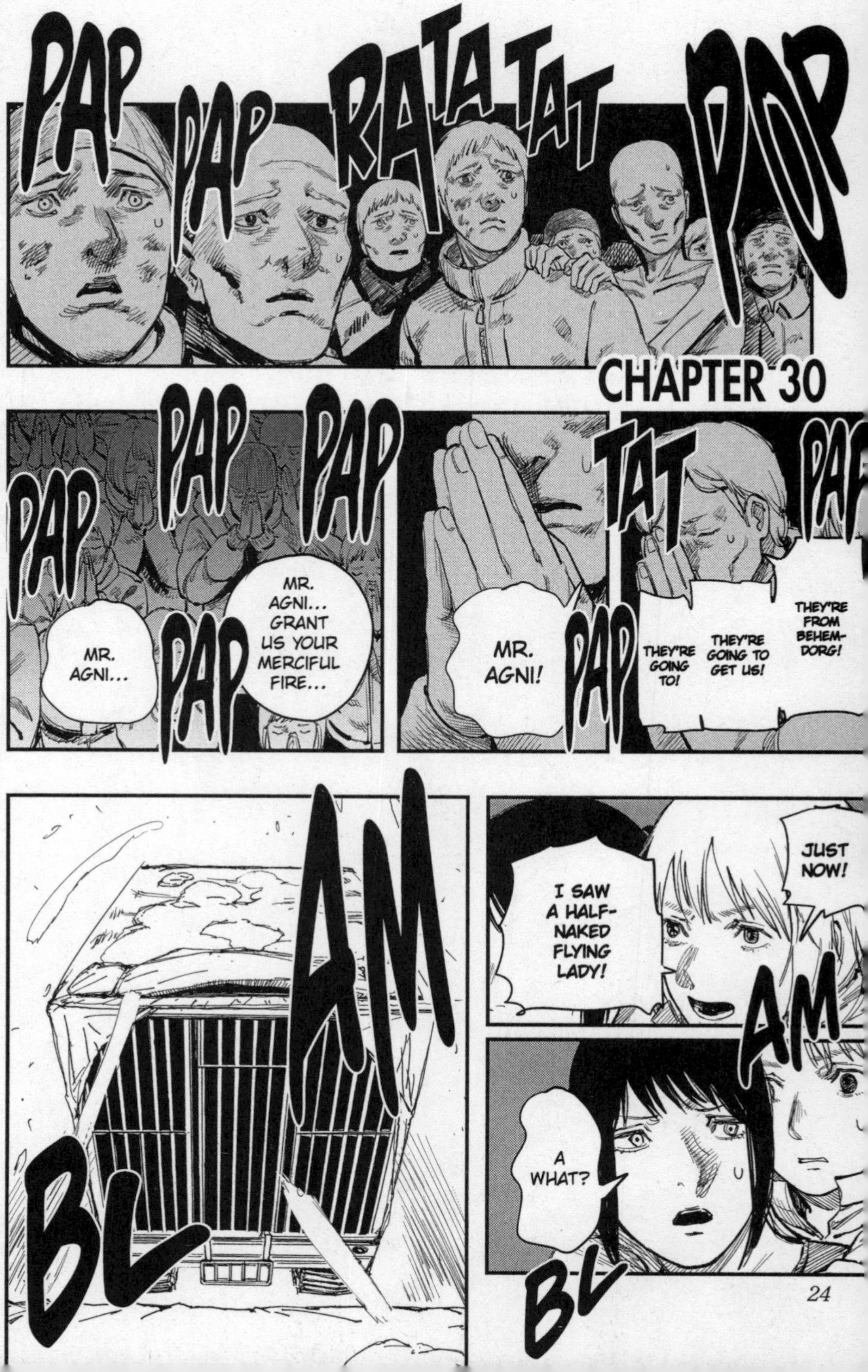
PAP
TAT
RATA
PAP
PAP
CHAPTER 30
PAP
TAT
THEY'RE FROM BEHEMDORG!
THEY'RE GOING TO GET US!
THEY'RE GOING TO!
PAP
MR. AGNI!
PAP
PAP
MR. AGNI... GRANT US YOUR MERCIFUL FIRE...
PAP
PAP
MR. AGNI...
JUST NOW!
I SAW A HALF-NAKED FLYING LADY!
AM
BL
A WHAT?
BLAM

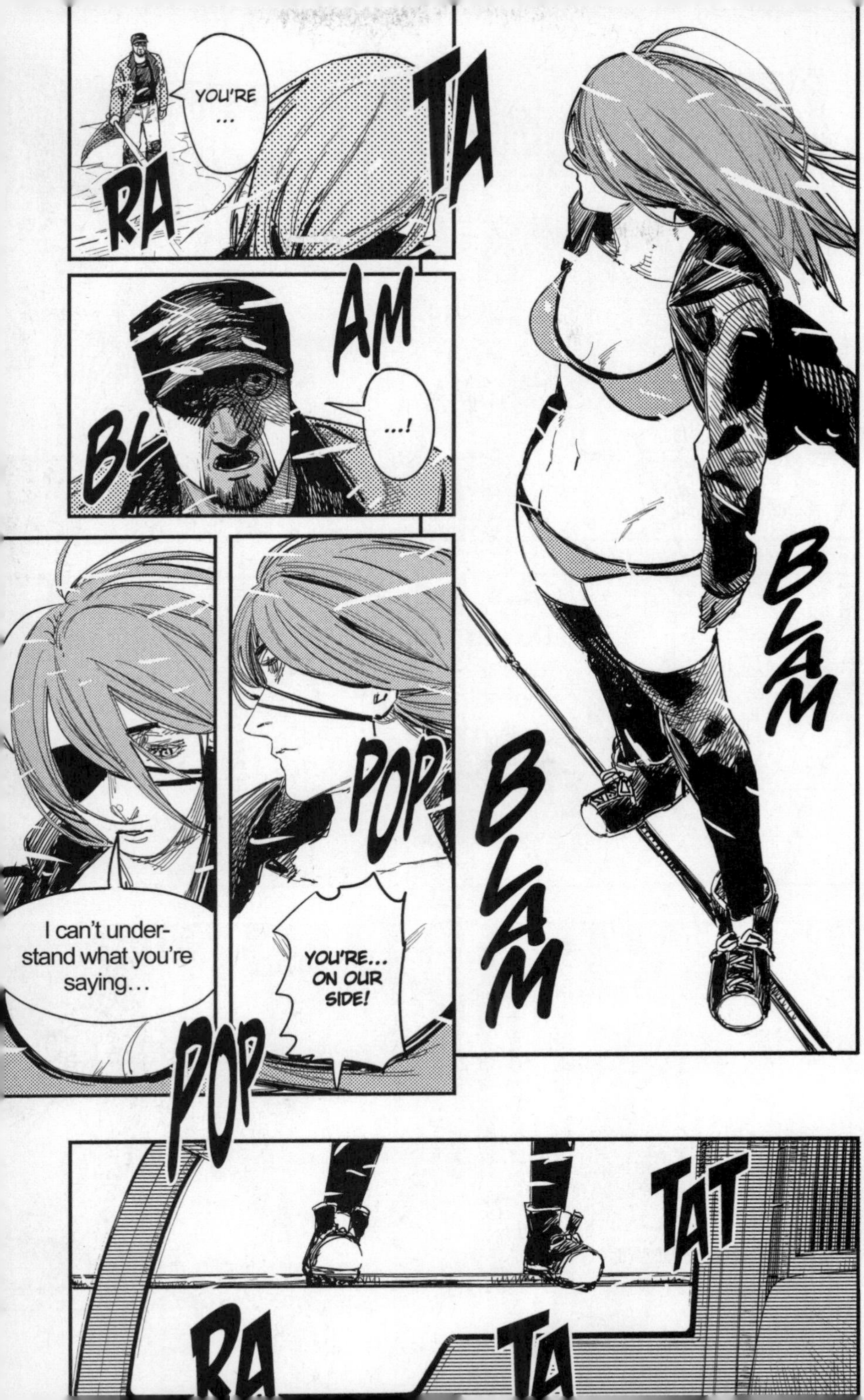
BLAM
BLAM
RA
TA
YOU'RE ...
BL
AM
...!
YOU'RE... ON OUR SIDE!
POP
POP
I can't under-stand what you're saying...
POP
TAT
TA
RA

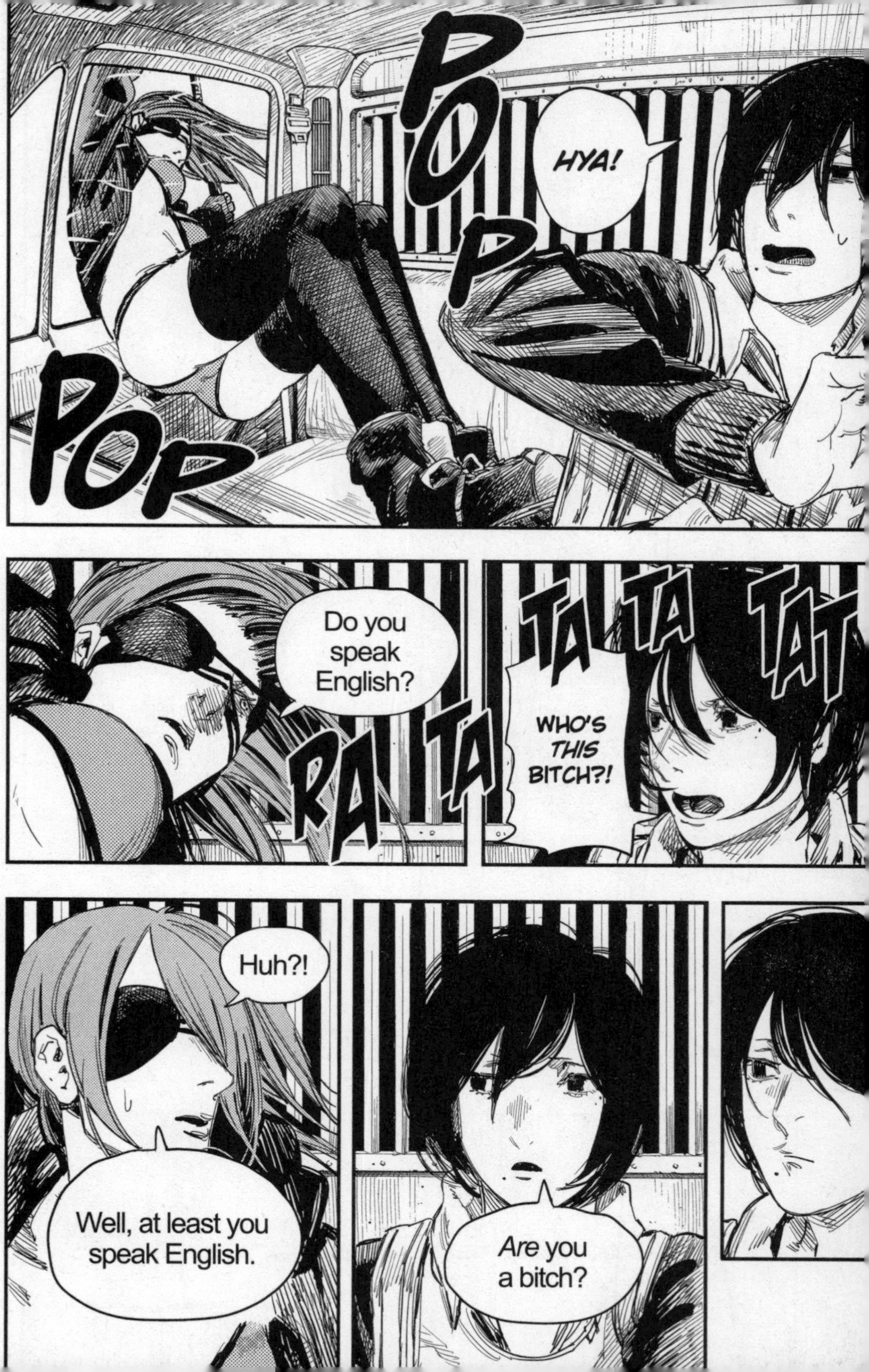
POP
HYA!
POP
TA TA TAT
WHO'S THIS BITCH?!
RA TA
Do you speak English?
Are you a bitch?
Huh?!
Well, at least you speak English.

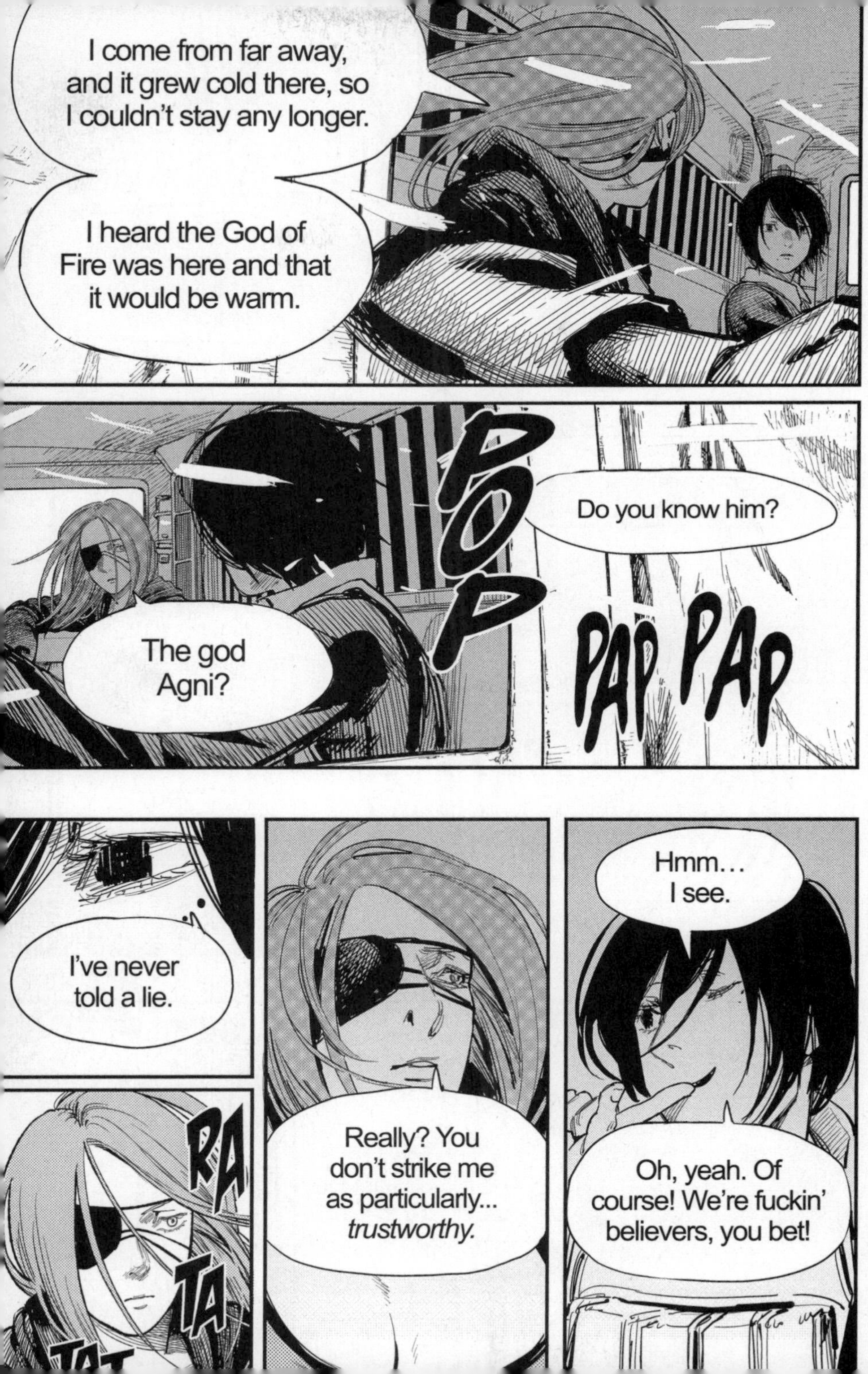
I come from far away, and it grew cold there, so I couldn't stay any longer.
I heard the God of Fire was here and that it would be warm.
Do you know him?
PAP PAP
POP
The god Agni?
Hmm... I see.
Oh, yeah. Of course! We're fuckin' believers, you bet!
Really? You don't strike me as particularly... *trustworthy.*
I've never told a lie.
RA TA TAT

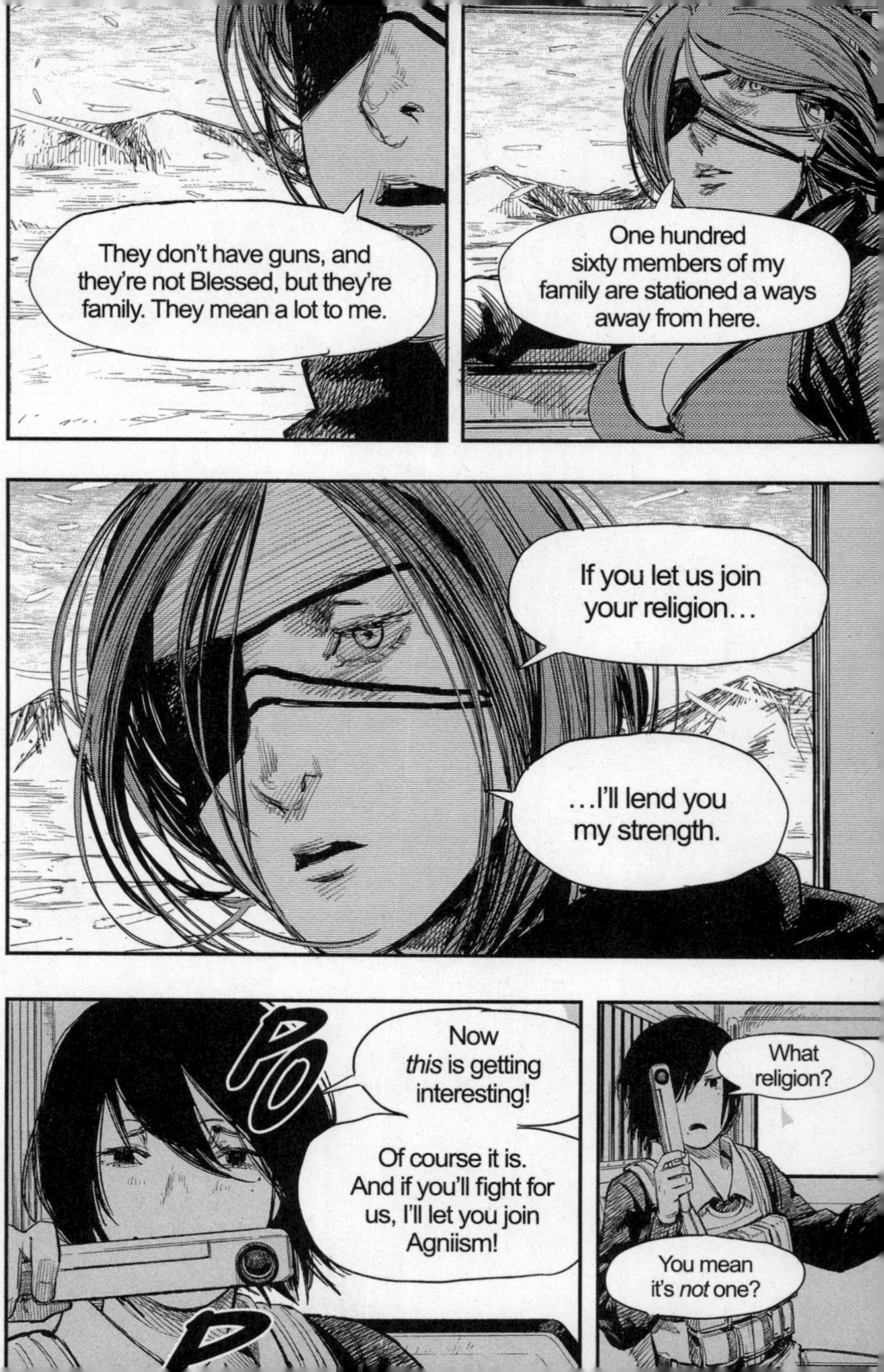
One hundred sixty members of my family are stationed a ways away from here.
They don't have guns, and they're not Blessed, but they're family. They mean a lot to me.
If you let us join your religion…
…I'll lend you my strength.
What religion?
You mean it's *not* one?
PO
Now *this* is getting interesting!
Of course it is. And if you'll fight for us, I'll let you join Agniism!

TAPOP

RATA

TAT

Hey... Aren't you freezing your nips off in that?

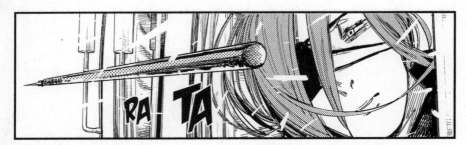

RATA

BL

AM

HM?

I have a really fast metabolism.

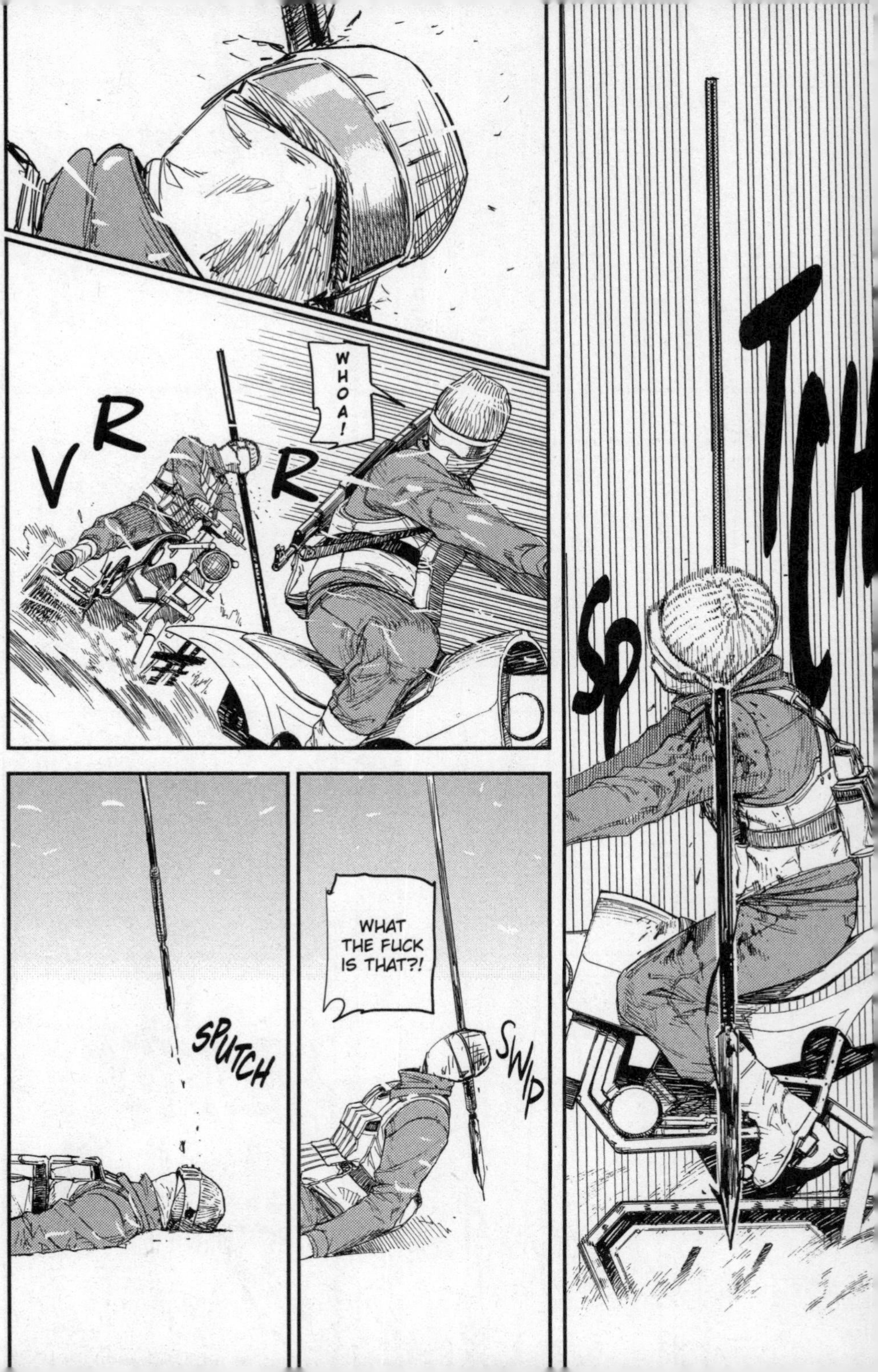
TCH
SP
WHOA!
VRR
WHAT THE FUCK IS THAT?!
SWIP
SPUTCH

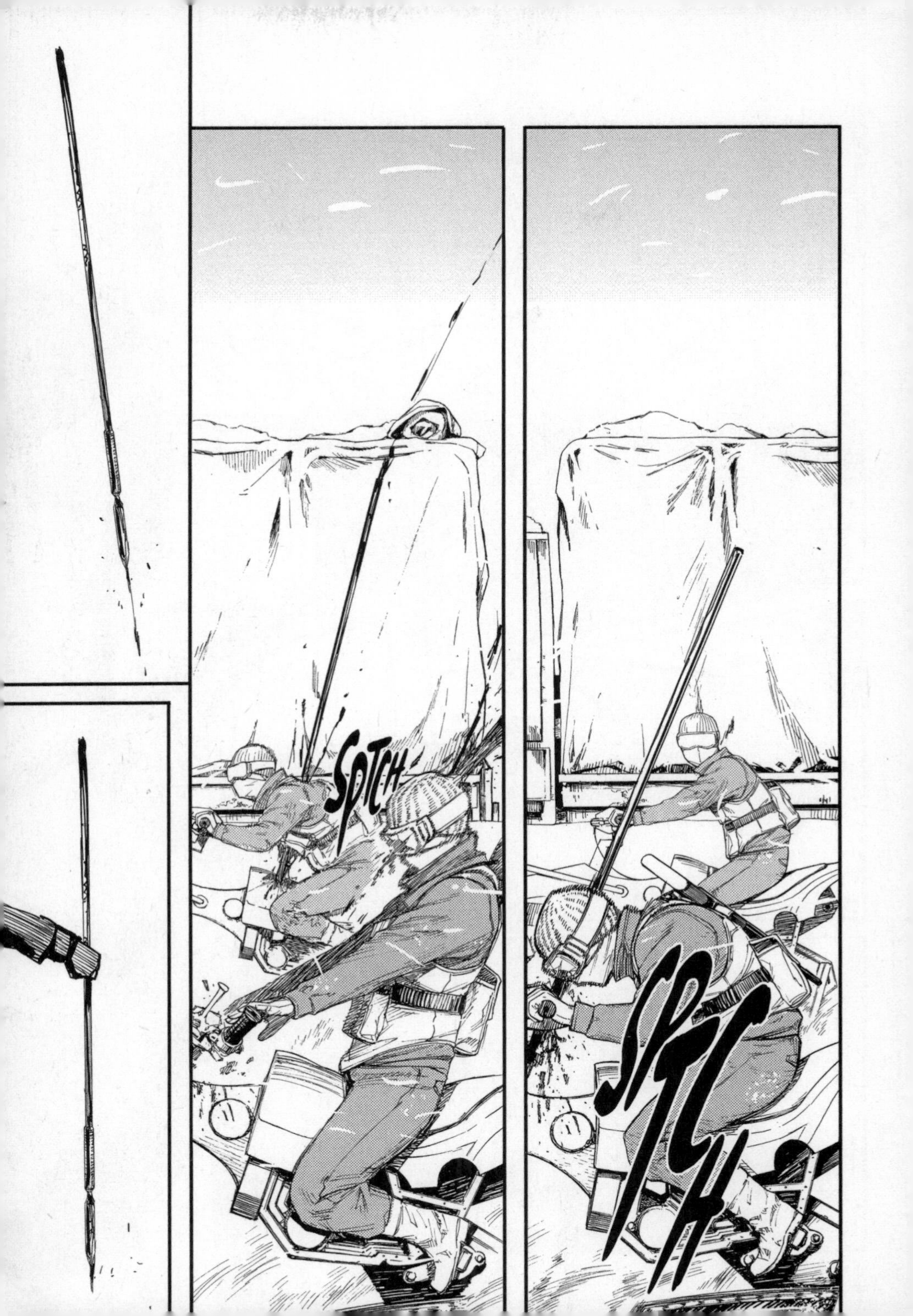
SPTCH
SPTCH

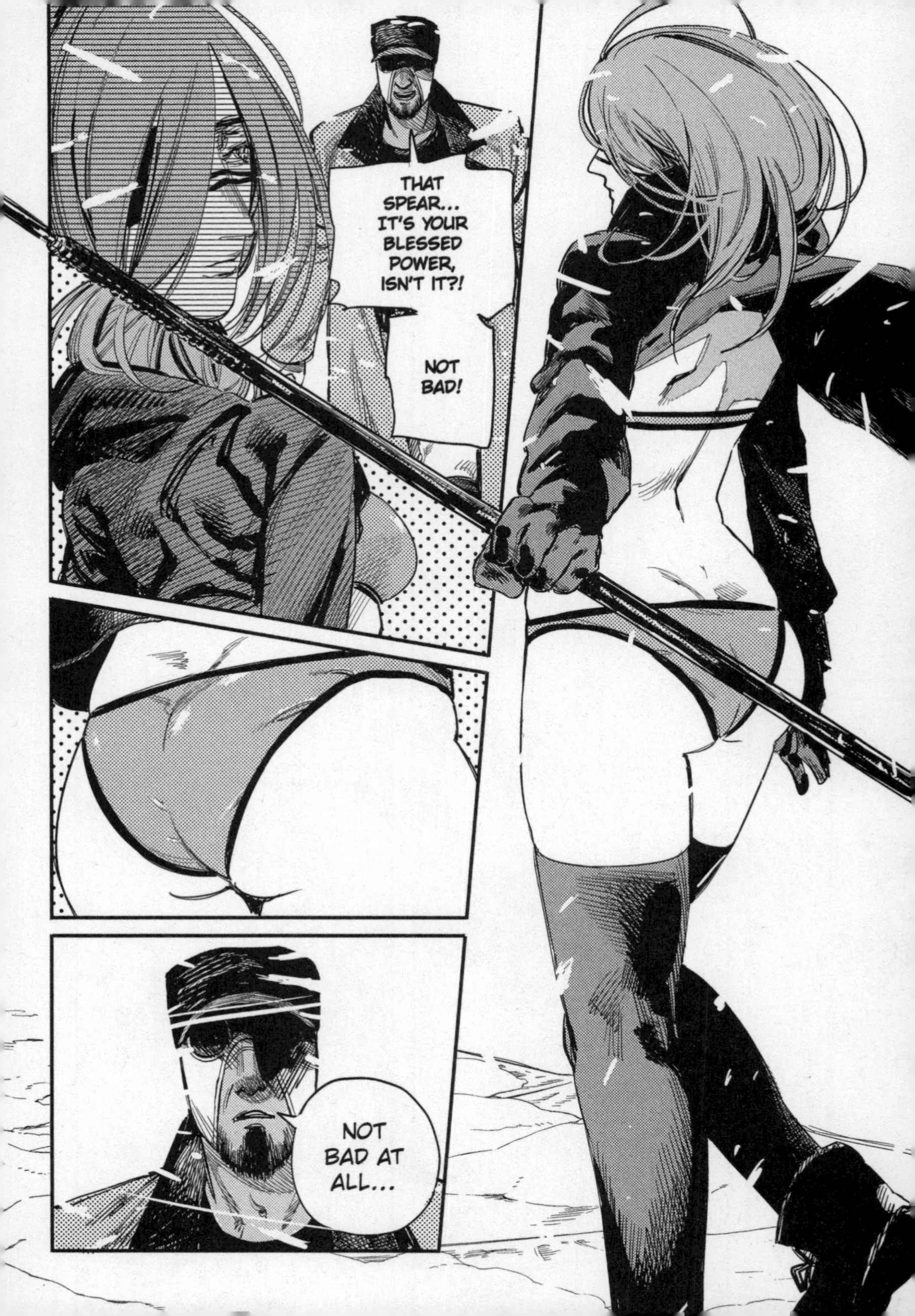
THAT SPEAR... IT'S YOUR BLESSED POWER, ISN'T IT?!
NOT BAD!
NOT BAD AT ALL...

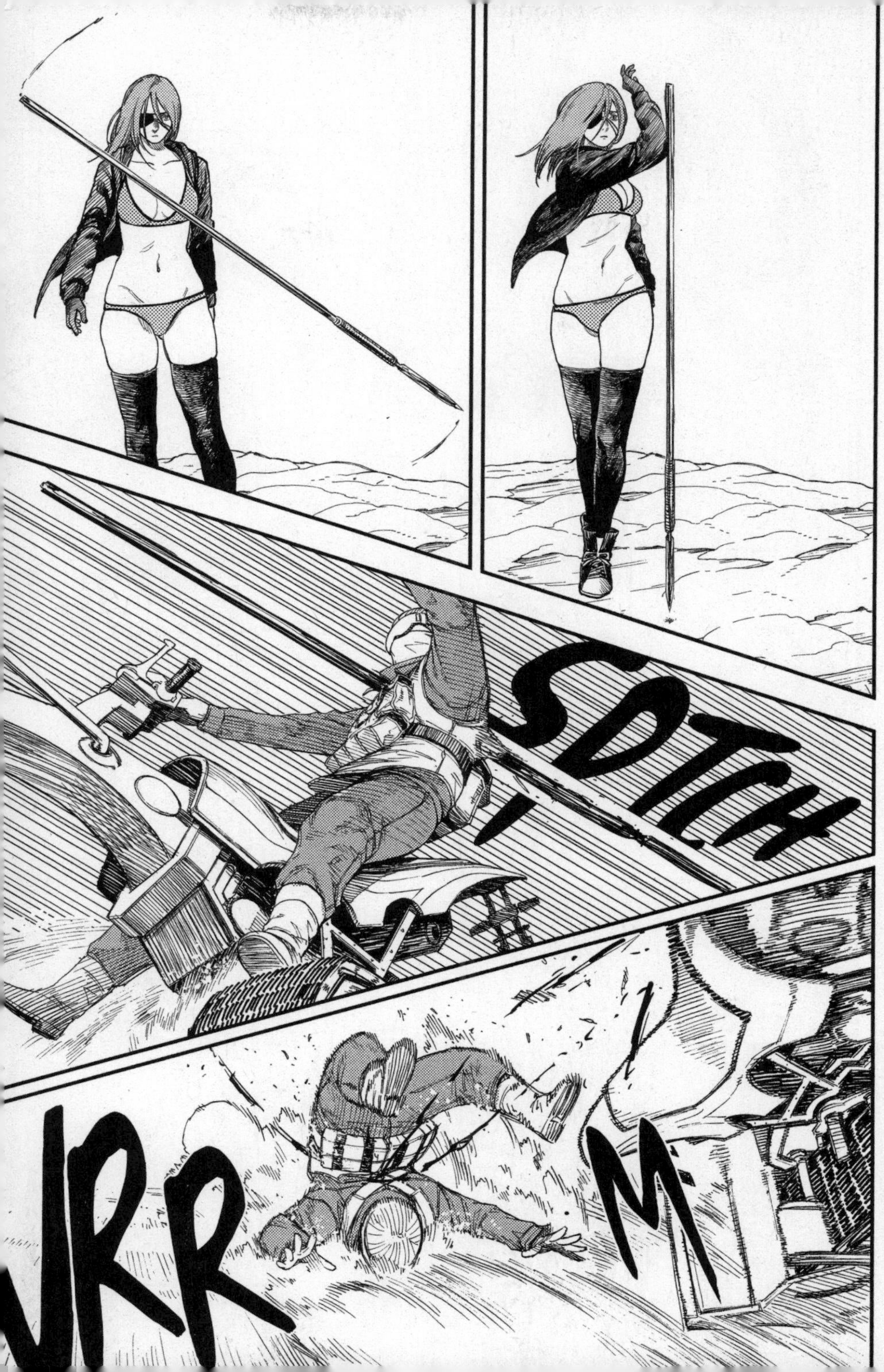
SPTCH
VRR
M

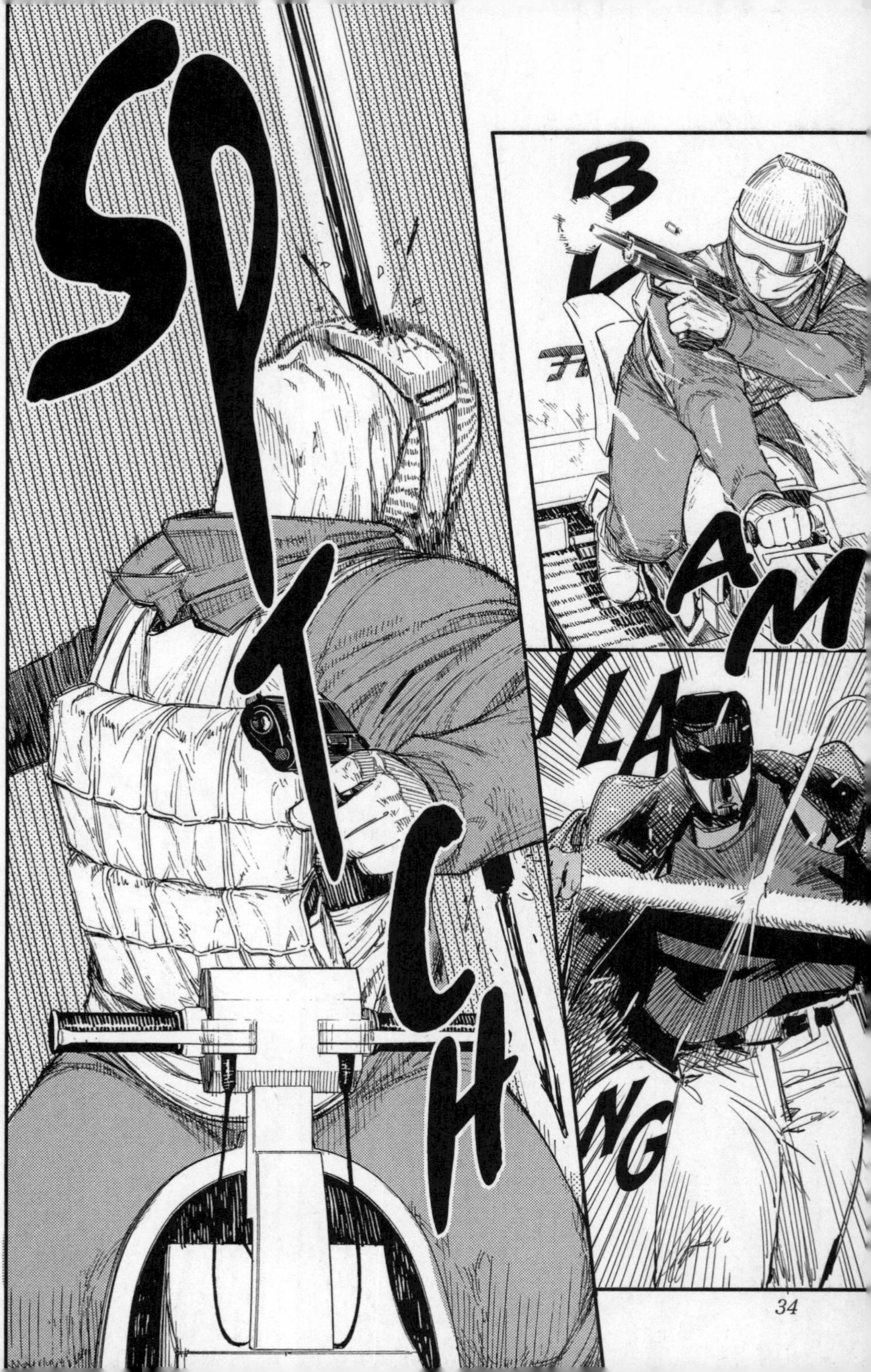
SPLITCH
BLAM
KLANG

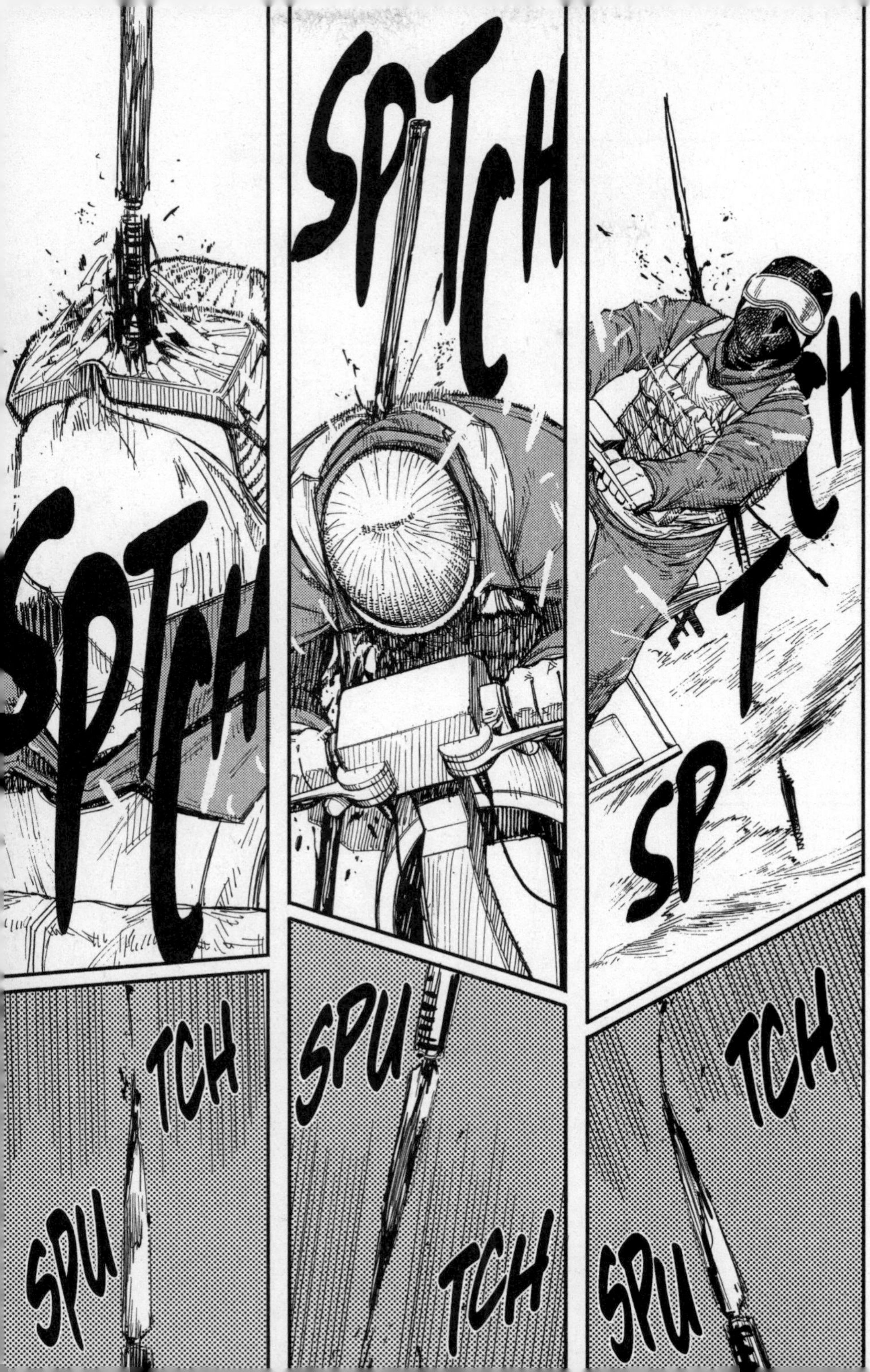
SPTCH
SPTCH
SPTCH
SPU TCH
SPU TCH
SPU TCH

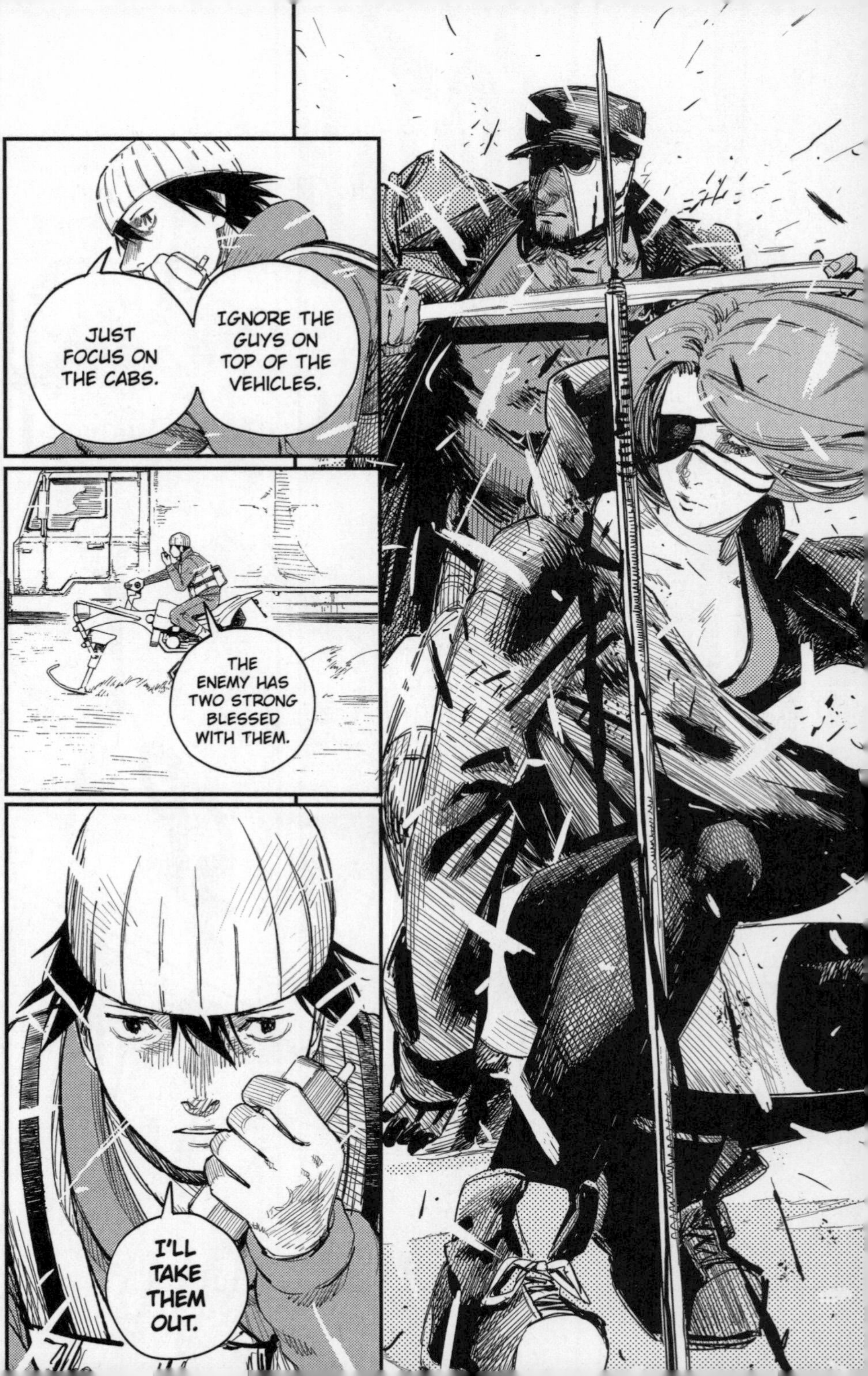
IGNORE THE GUYS ON TOP OF THE VEHICLES.
JUST FOCUS ON THE CABS.
THE ENEMY HAS TWO STRONG BLESSED WITH THEM.
I'LL TAKE THEM OUT.

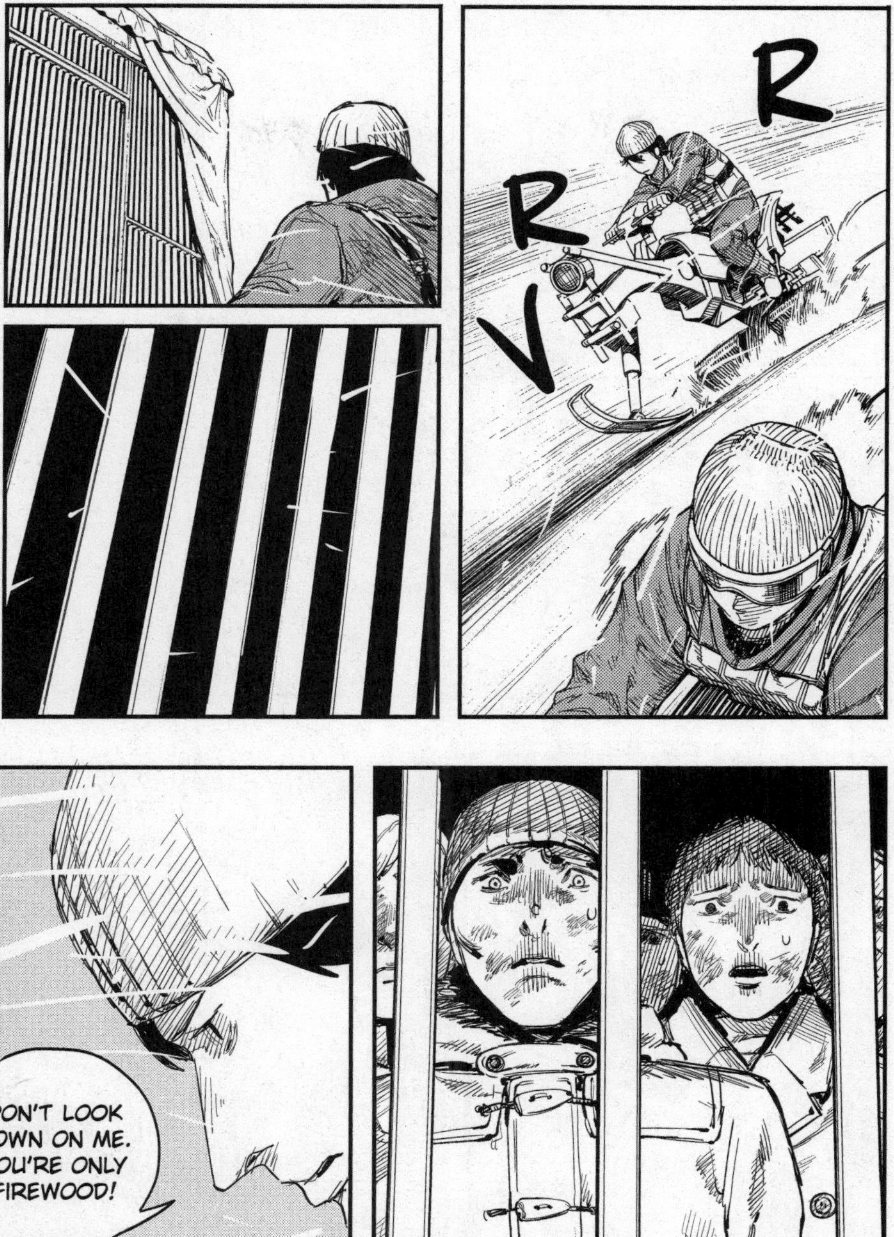
R
R
V
DON'T LOOK DOWN ON ME. YOU'RE ONLY FIREWOOD!

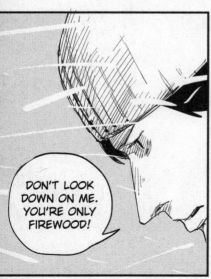

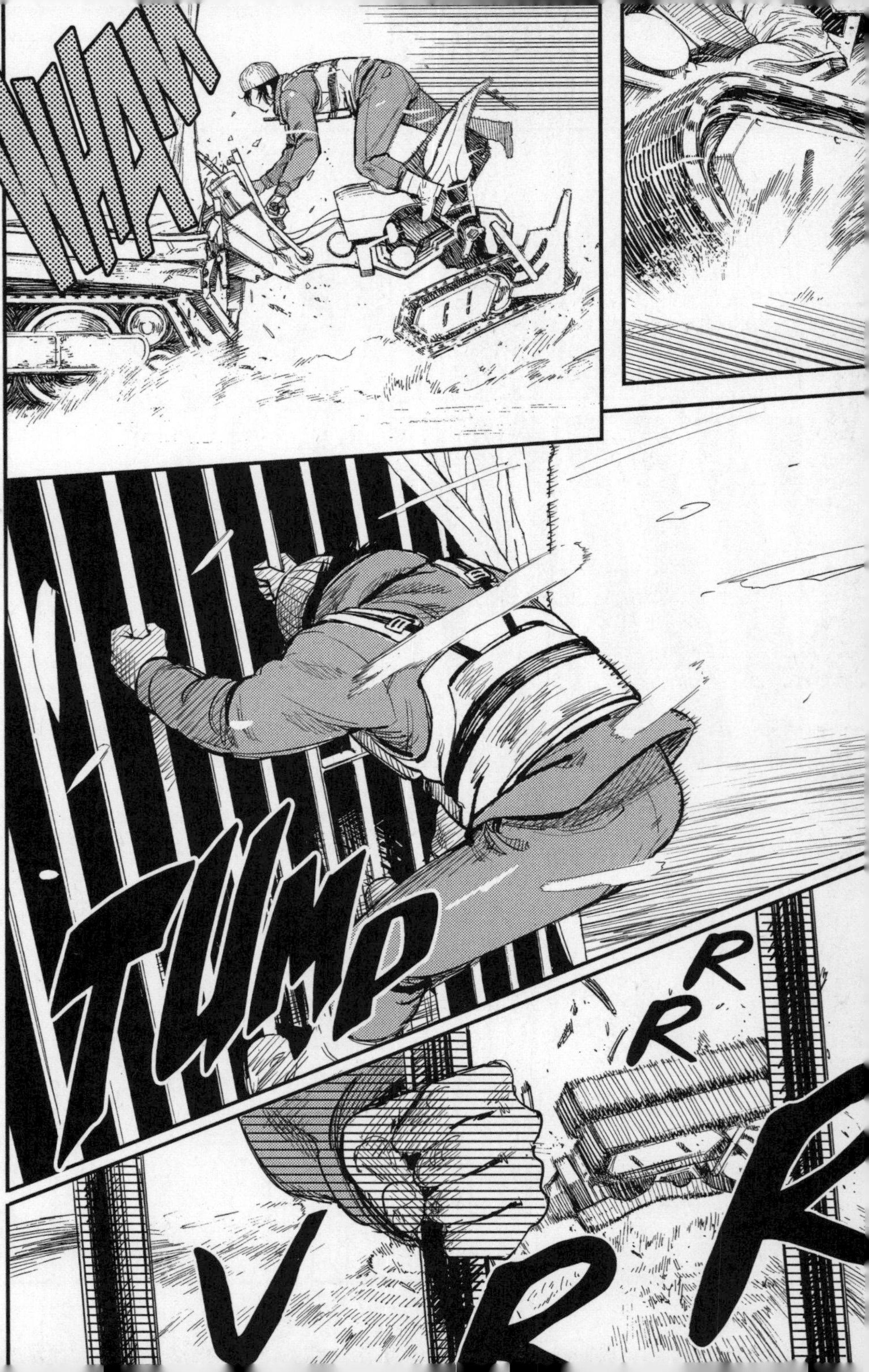
WHAM
TUMP
RRR
VRRR

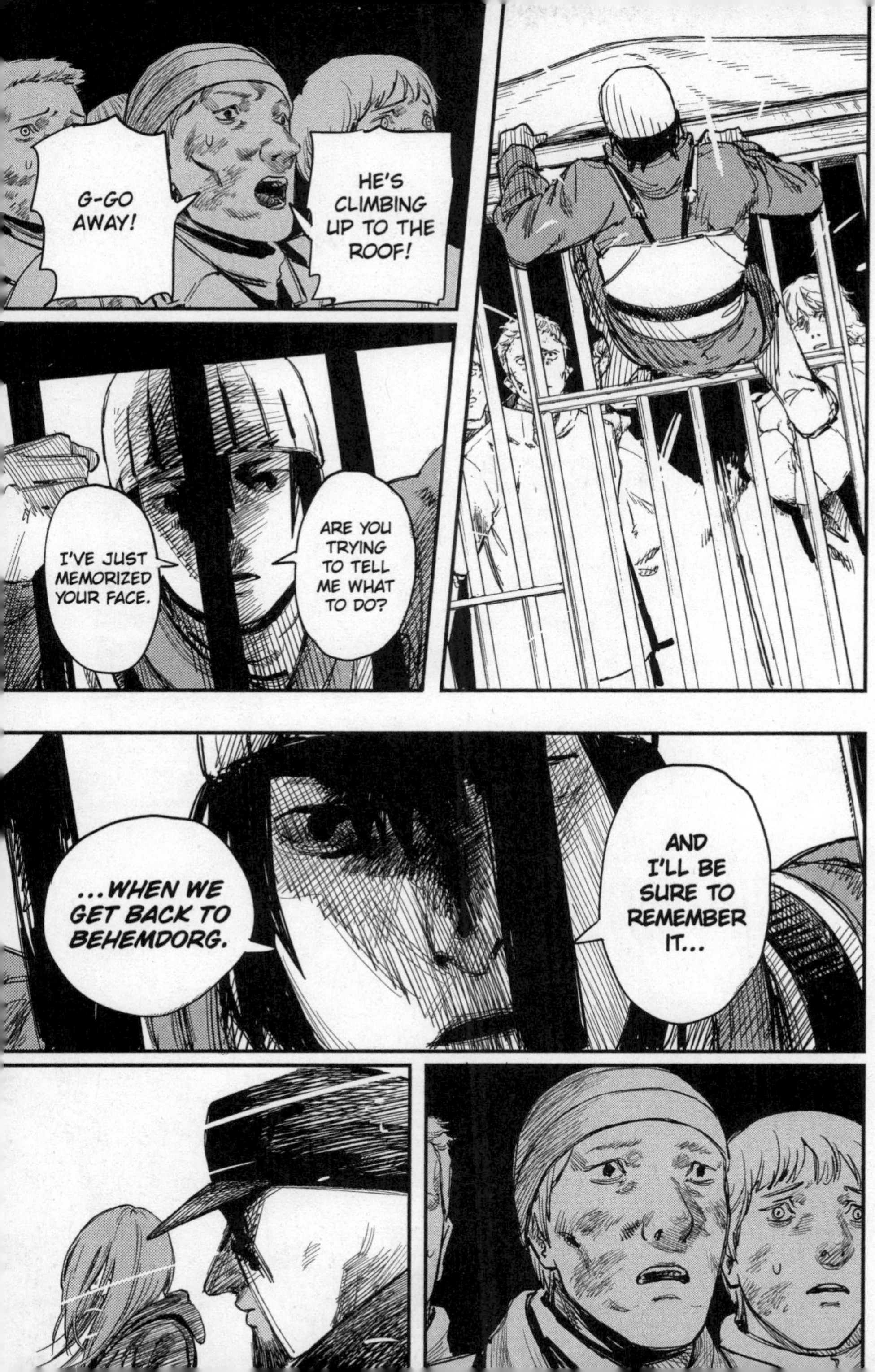
HE'S CLIMBING UP TO THE ROOF!
G-GO AWAY!
ARE YOU TRYING TO TELL ME WHAT TO DO?
I'VE JUST MEMORIZED YOUR FACE.
AND I'LL BE SURE TO REMEMBER IT...
...WHEN WE GET BACK TO BEHEMDORG.

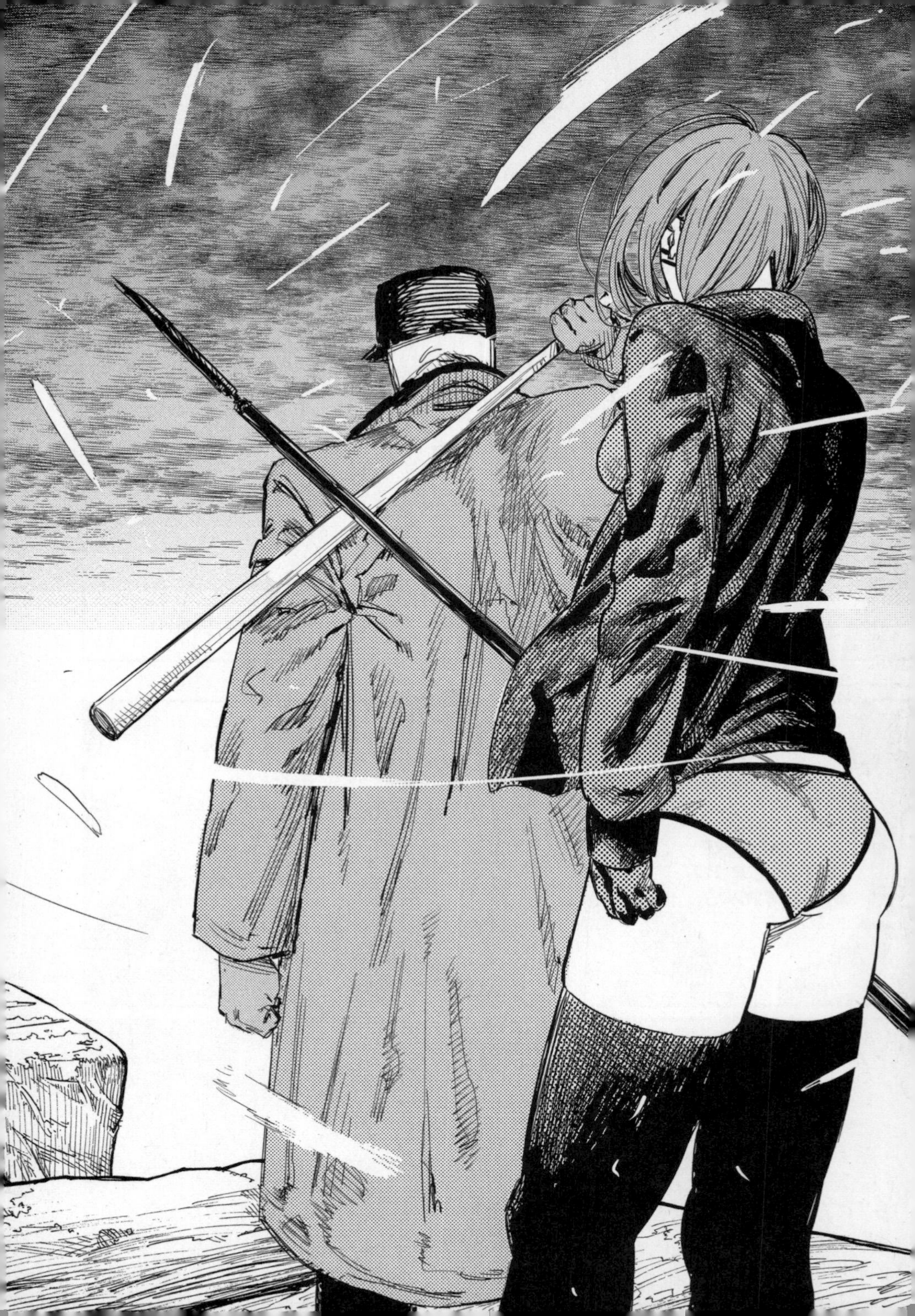

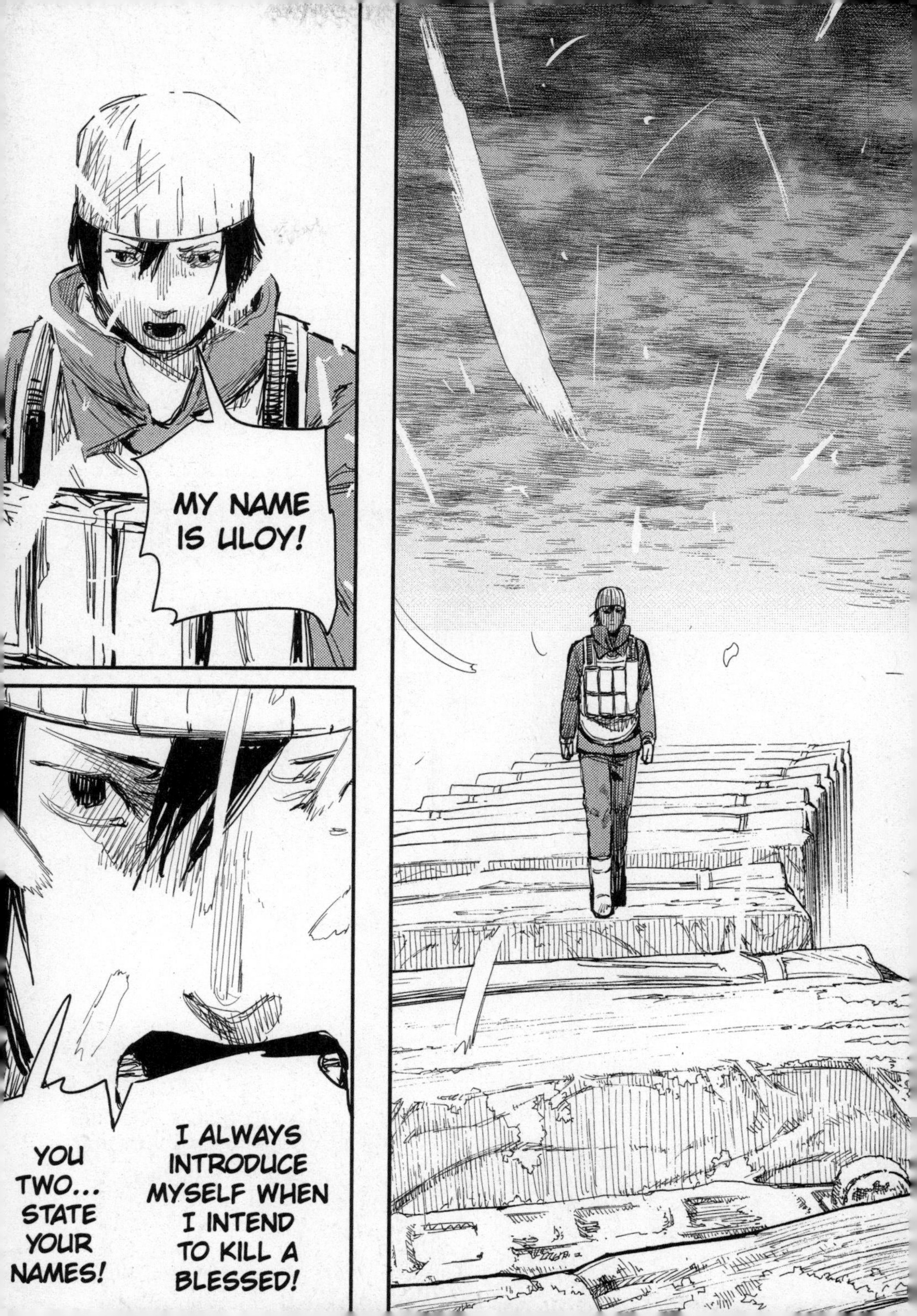
MY NAME IS ULOY!
I ALWAYS INTRODUCE MYSELF WHEN I INTEND TO KILL A BLESSED!
YOU TWO... STATE YOUR NAMES!

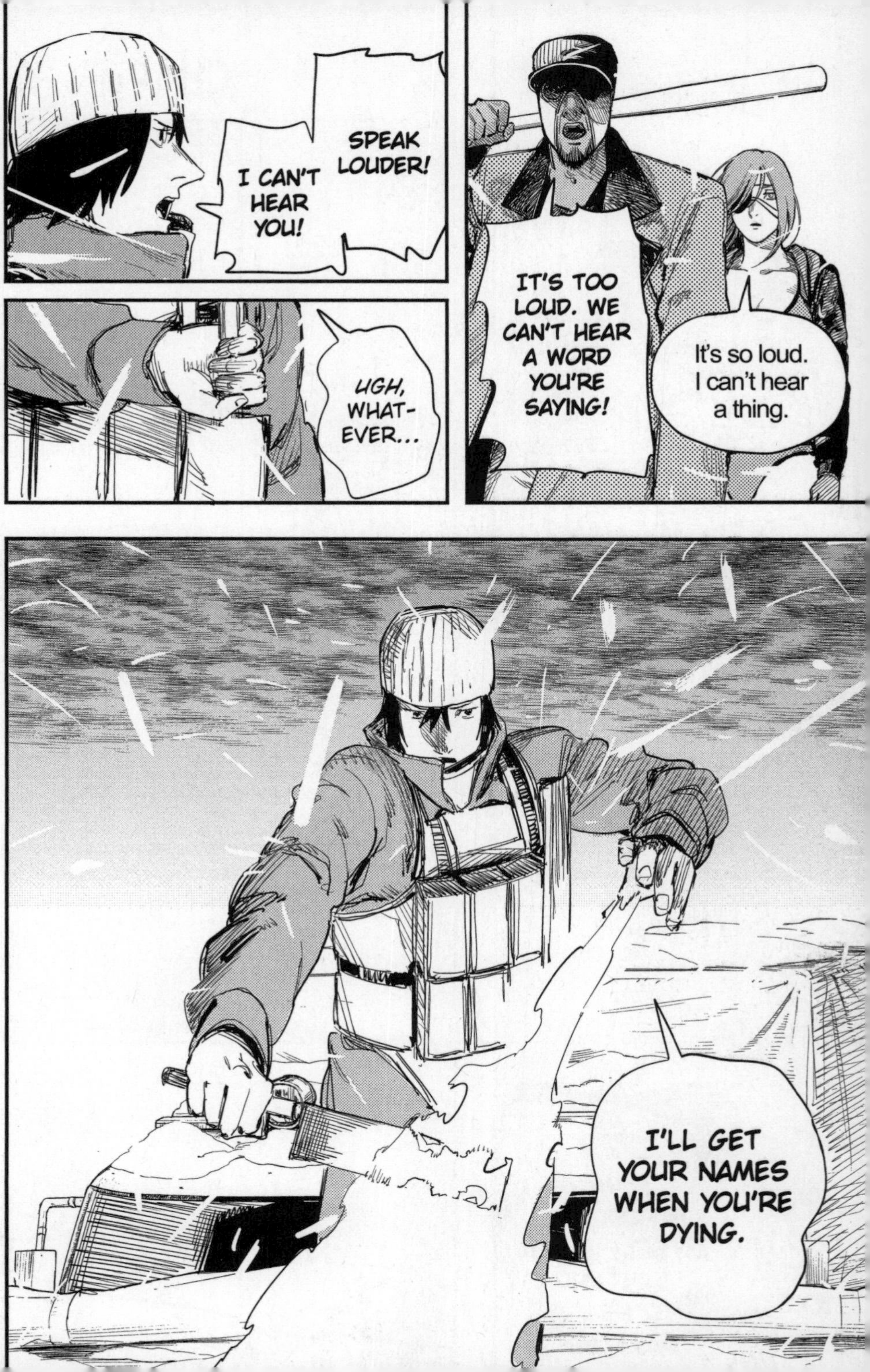
IT'S TOO LOUD. WE CAN'T HEAR A WORD YOU'RE SAYING!
It's so loud. I can't hear a thing.
SPEAK LOUDER!
I CAN'T HEAR YOU!
UGH, WHATEVER...
I'LL GET YOUR NAMES WHEN YOU'RE DYING.

CHAPTER 31

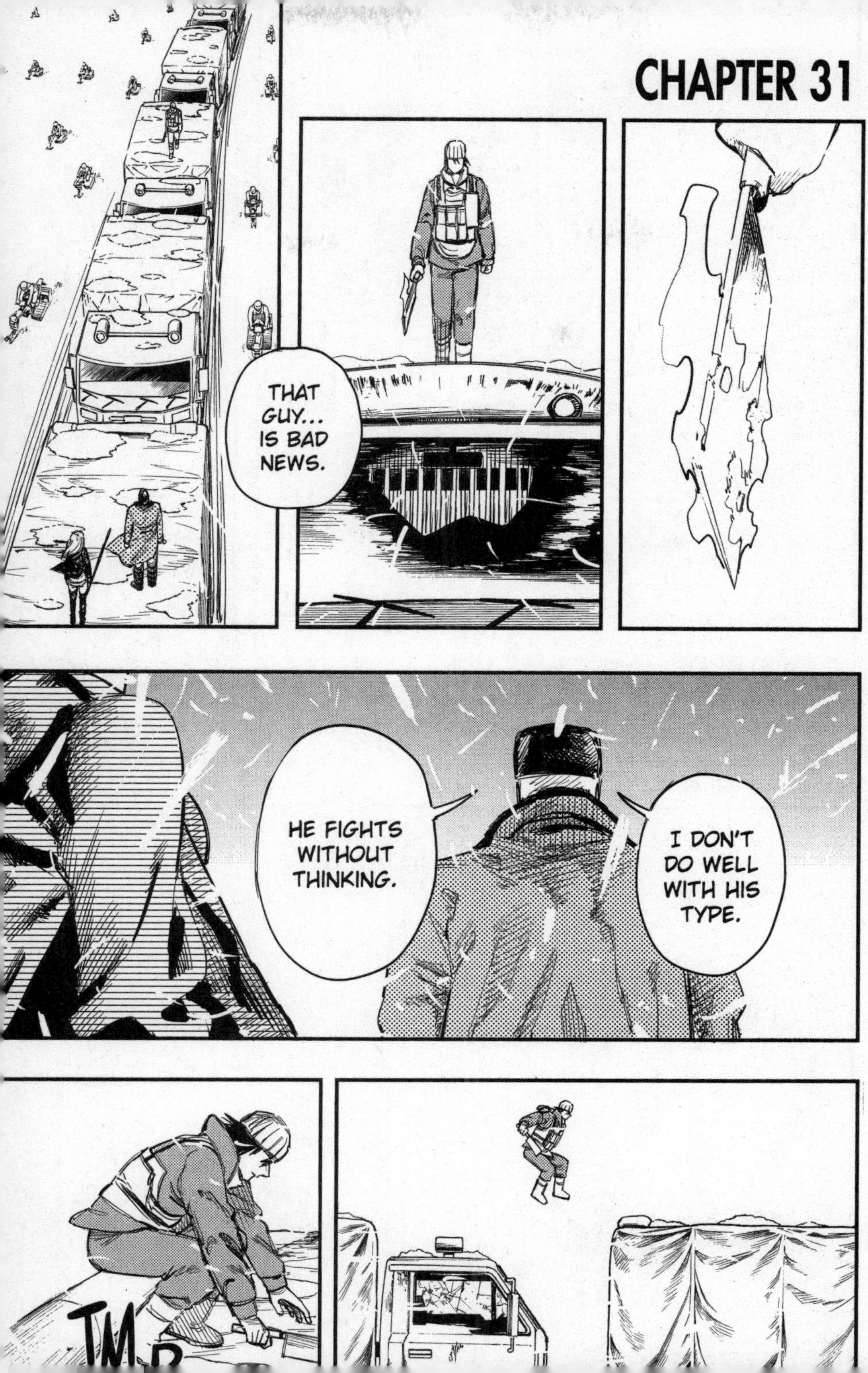
THAT GUY... IS BAD NEWS.
I DON'T DO WELL WITH HIS TYPE.
HE FIGHTS WITHOUT THINKING.

KSIING

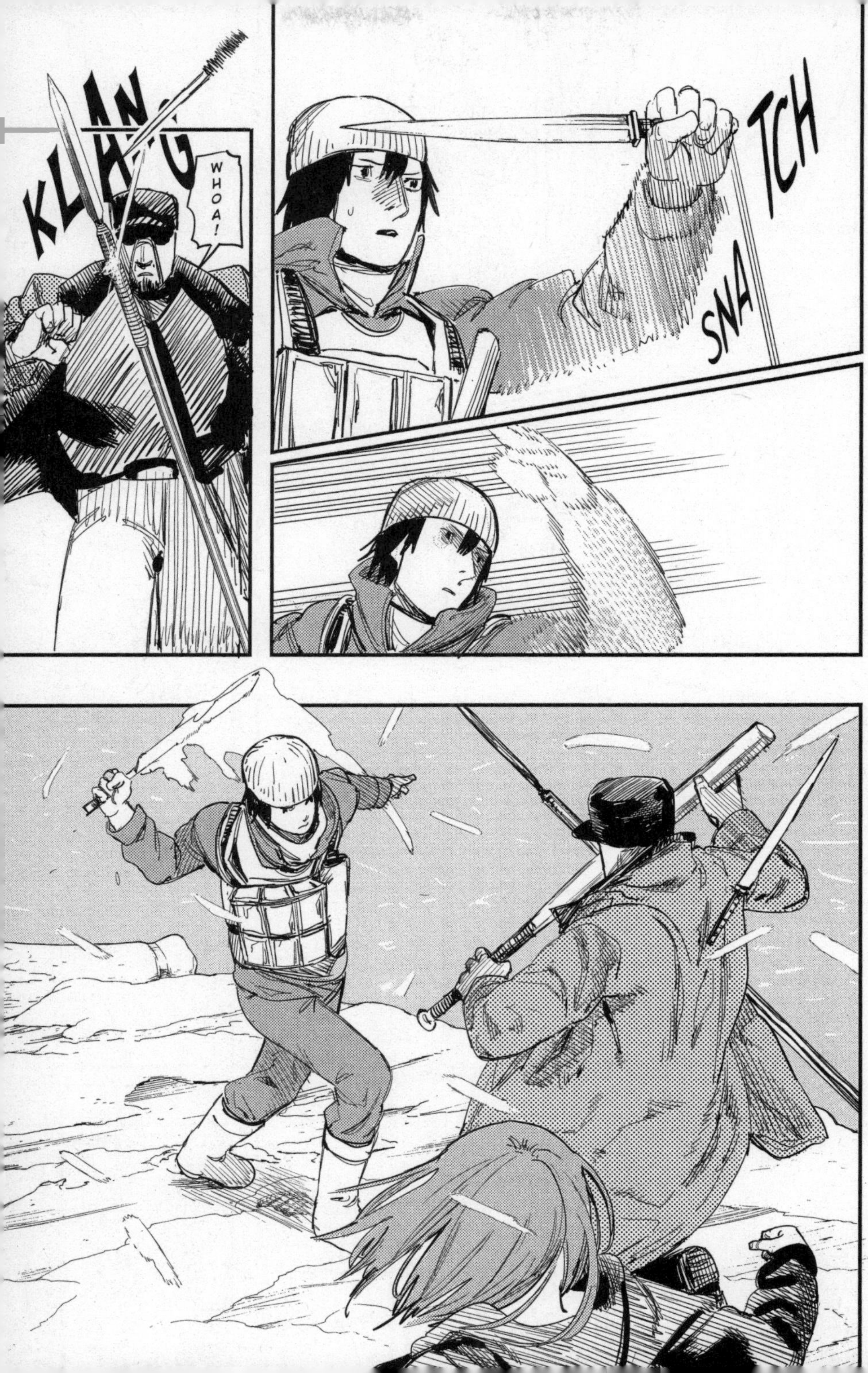
SNATCH
KLANG
WHOA!

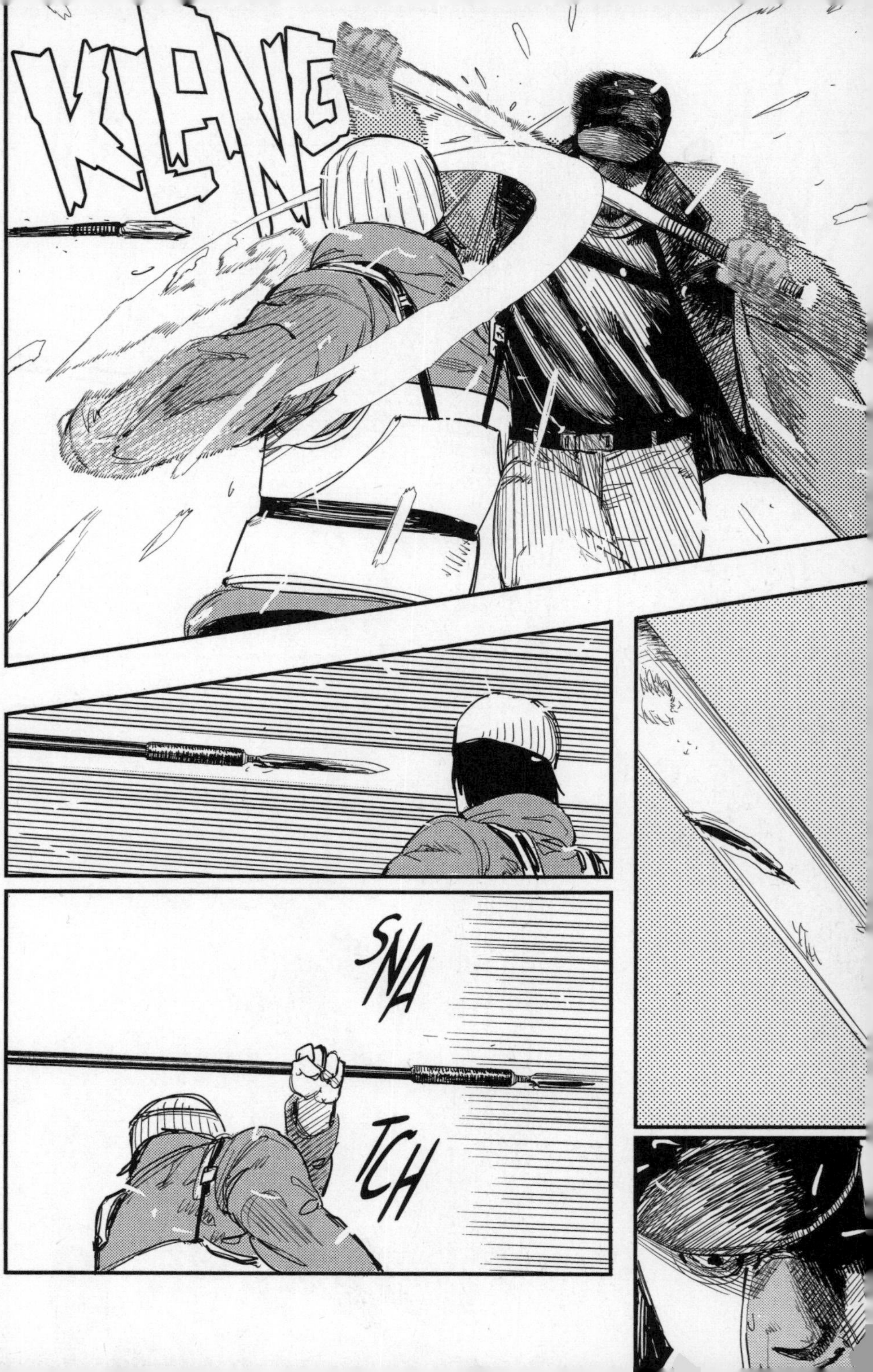
KLANG
SNATCH

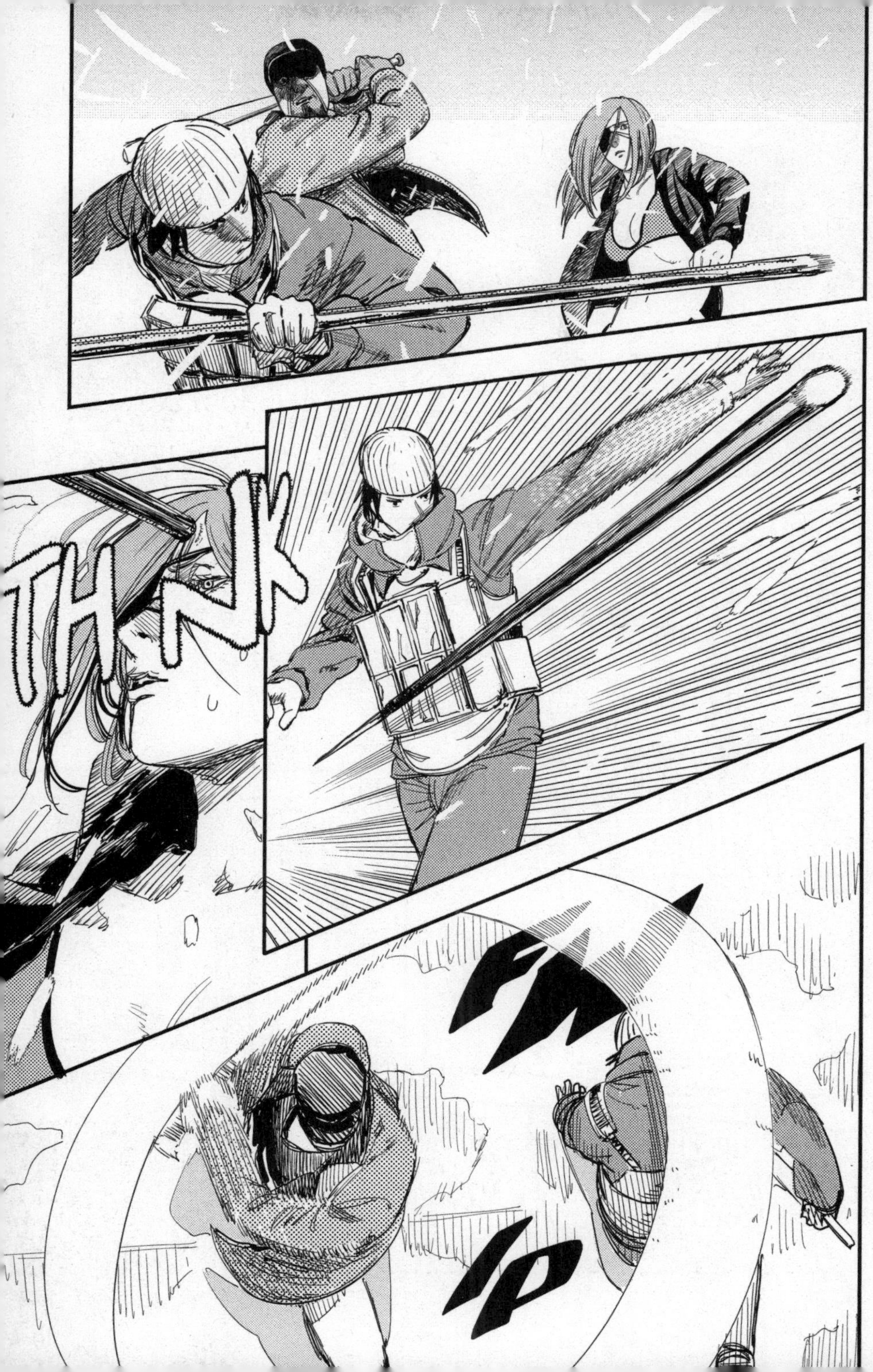
THNK
FWIP

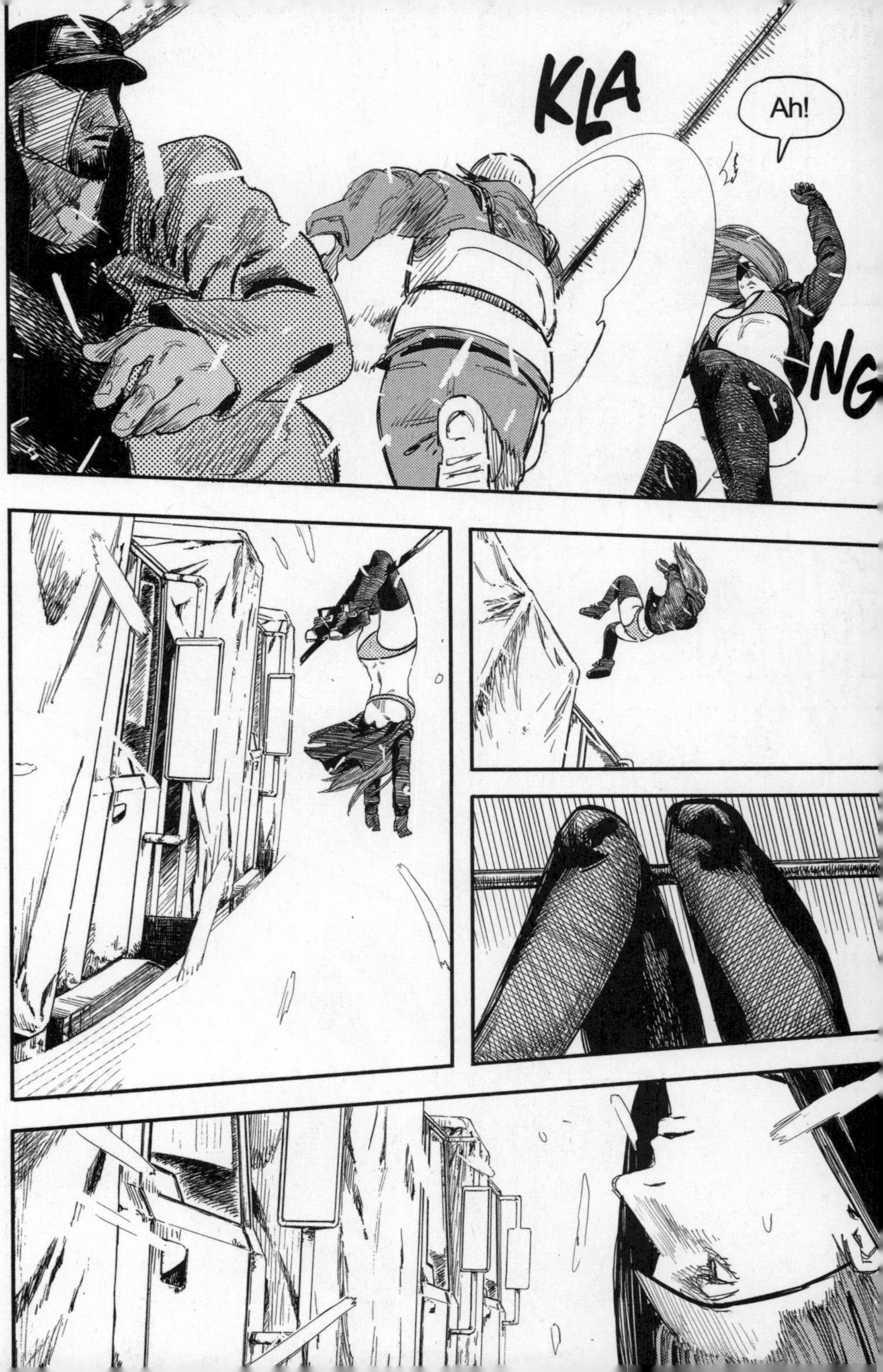
KLA
NG
Ah!

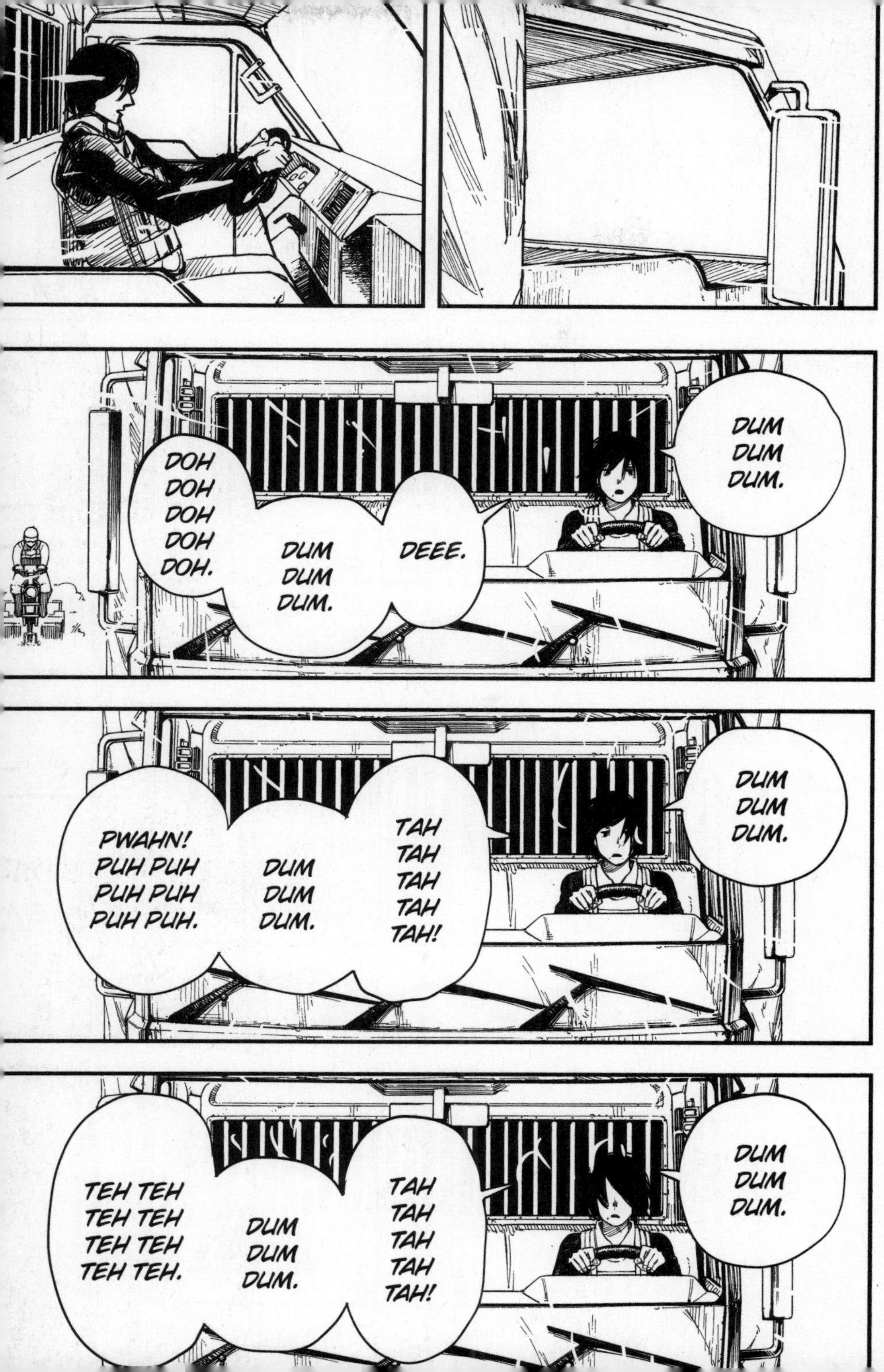
DUM DUM DUM.
DEEE.
DUM DUM DUM.
DOH DOH DOH DOH DOH.
DUM DUM DUM.
TAH TAH TAH TAH TAH!
DUM DUM DUM.
PWAHN! PUH PUH PUH PUH PUH PUH.
DUM DUM DUM.
TAH TAH TAH TAH TAH!
DUM DUM DUM.
TEH TEH TEH TEH TEH TEH TEH TEH.

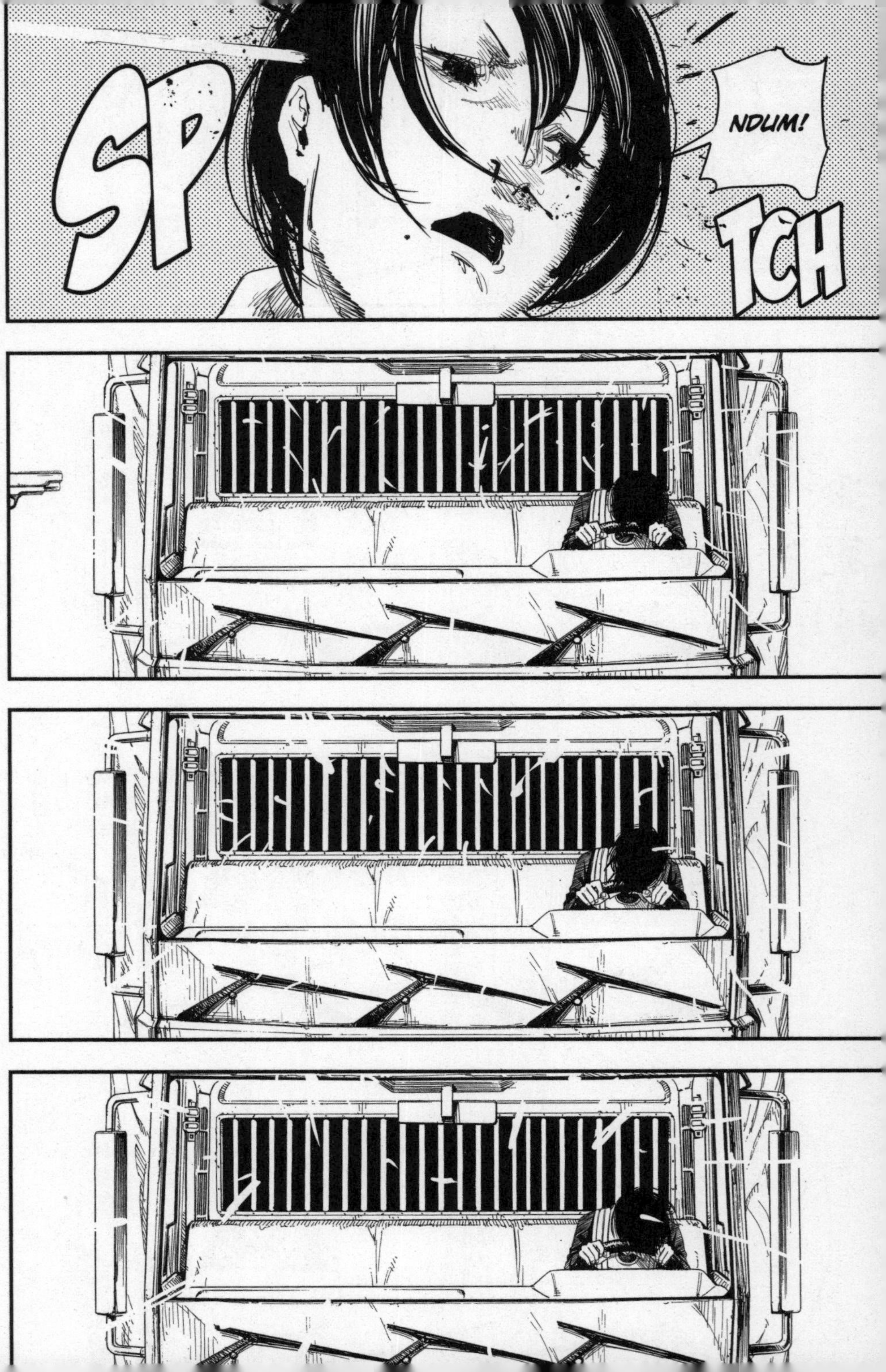
NDUM!
SP
TCH

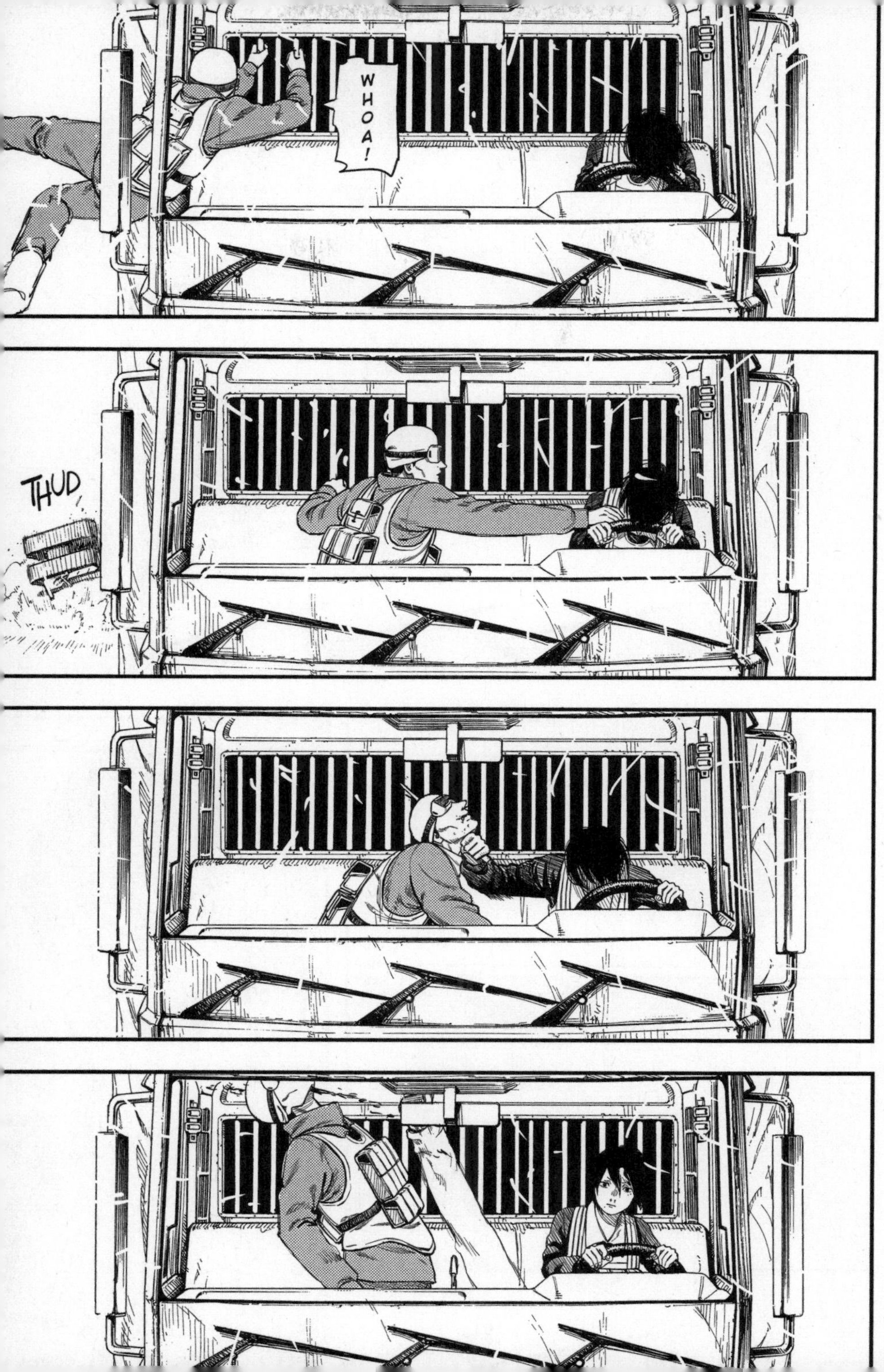
WHOA!
THUD

HM.

LIGHTER
...

LIGHTER
...

BOOYAH!

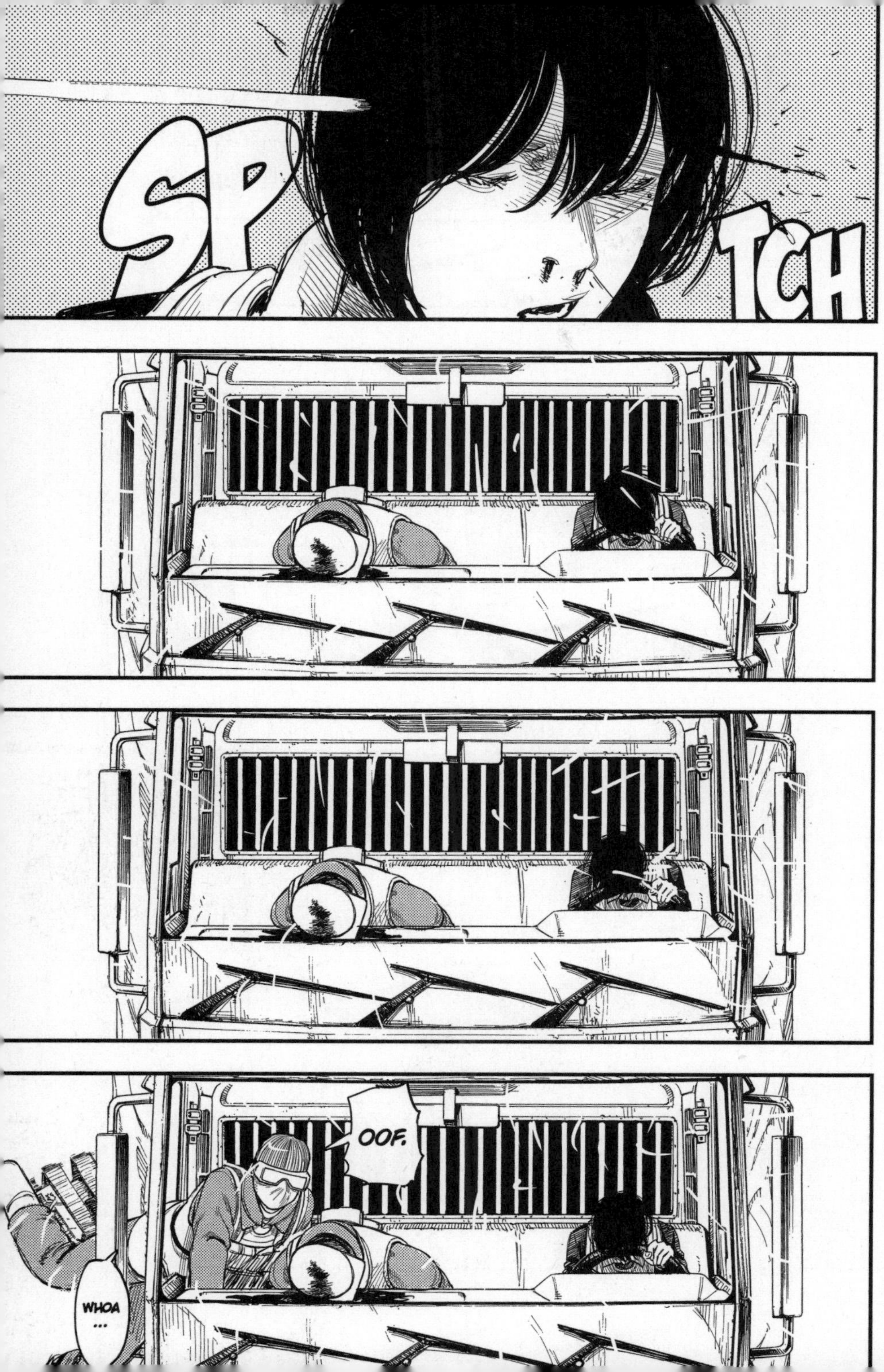
SP
TCH
OOF.
WHOA ...

I'VE AVENGED YOU, MY FRIEND.
BLAM

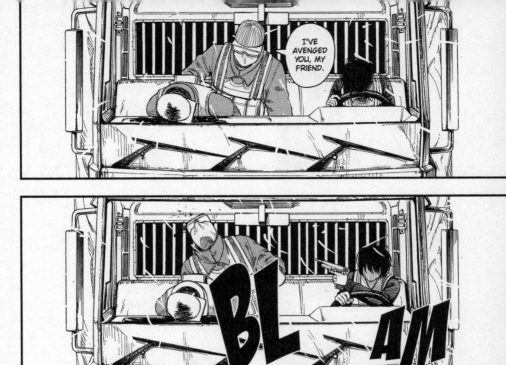

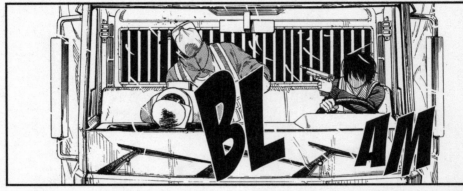

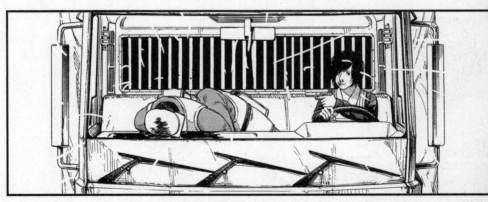

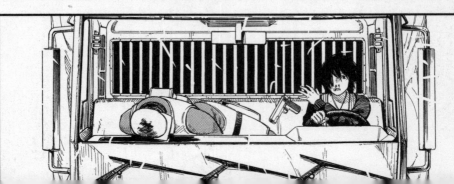

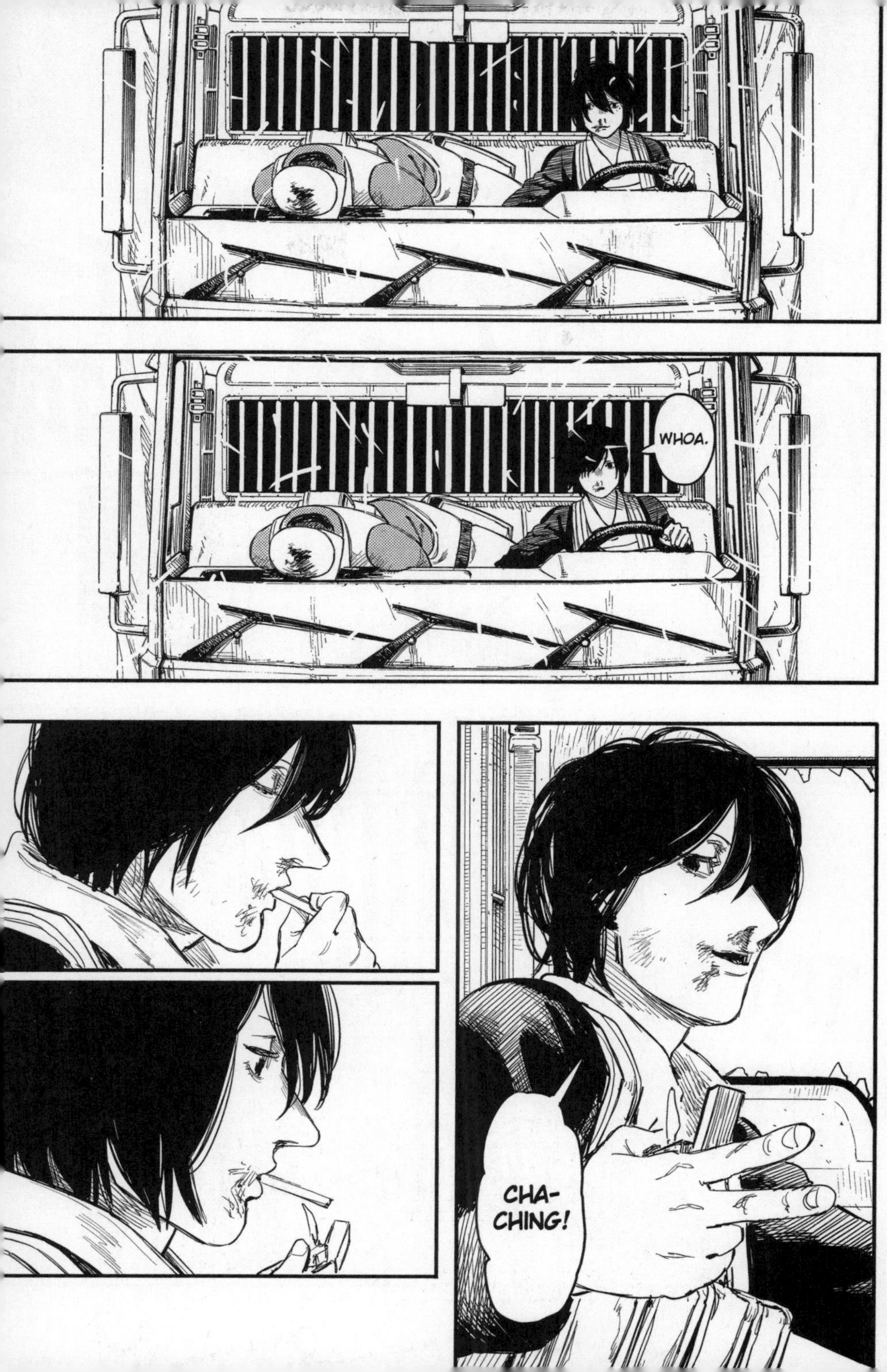
WHOA.
CHA-
CHING!

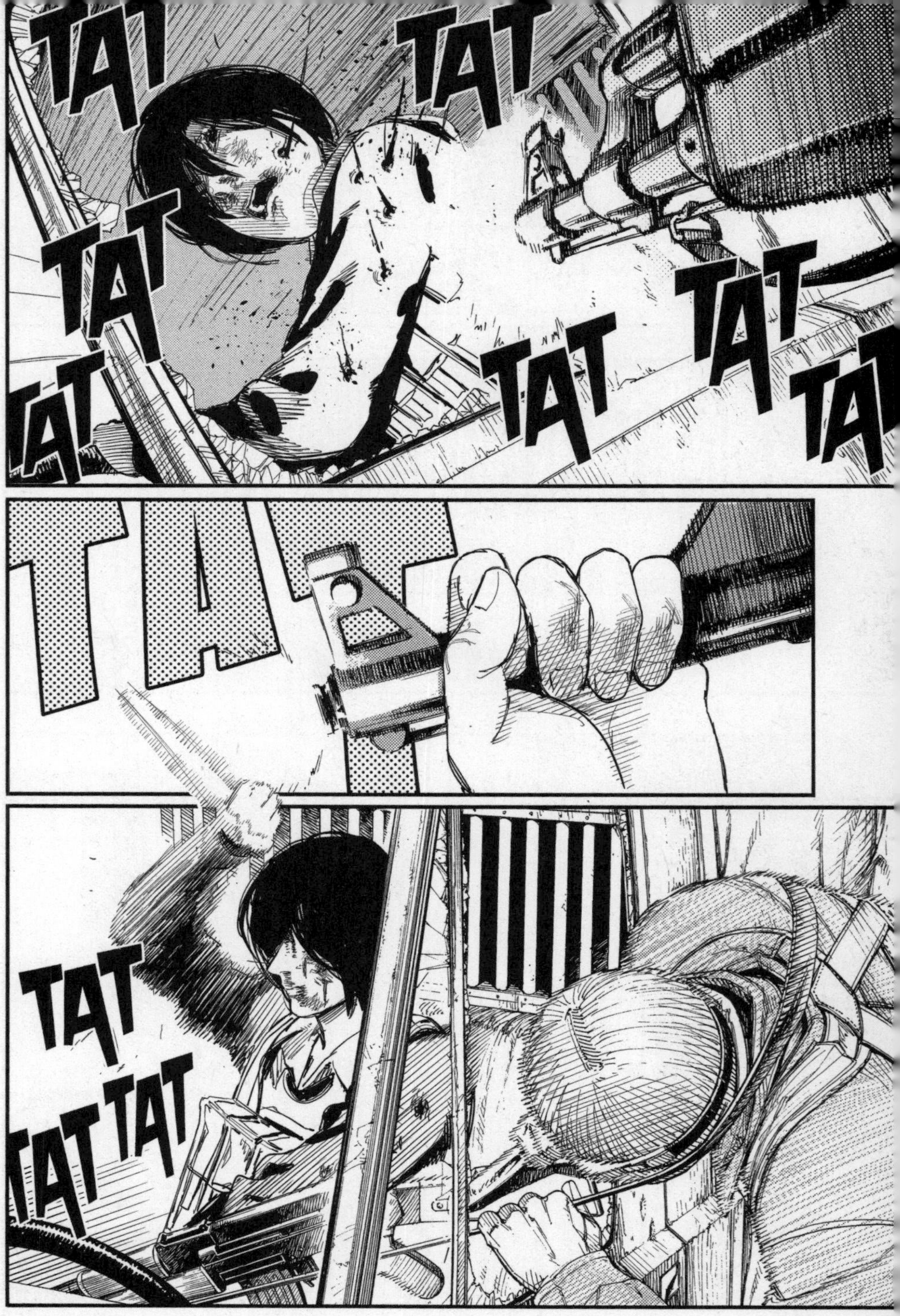
TAT
TAT
TAT TAT TAT
TAT
TAT TAT
TAT
TAT TAT TAT

HM?

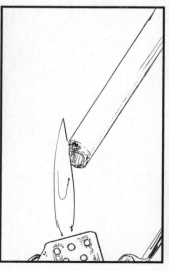

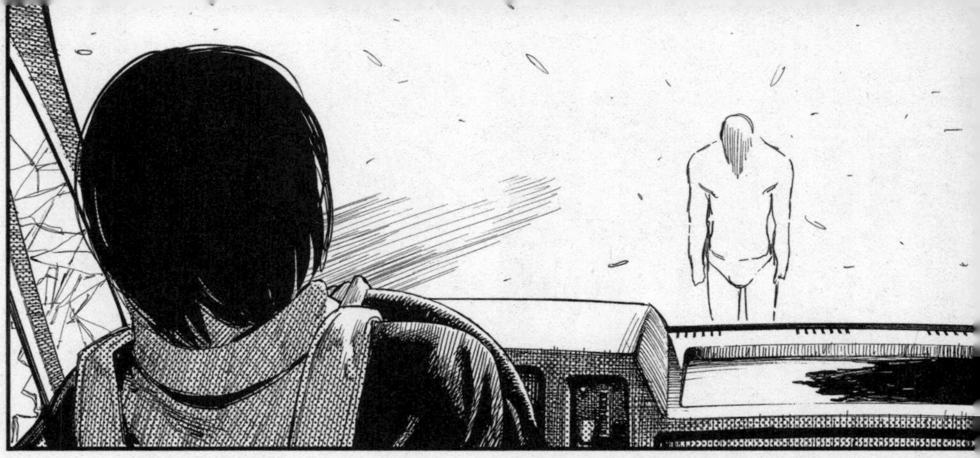

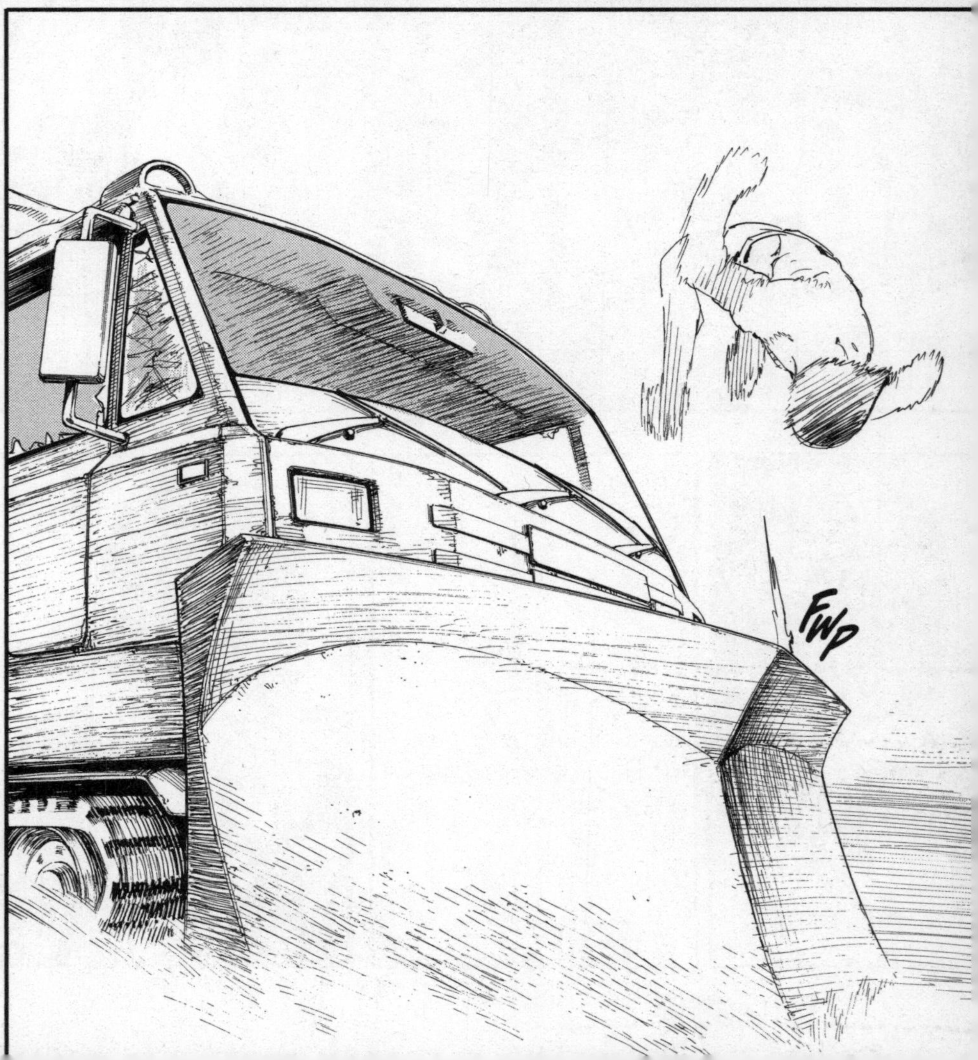
FWP

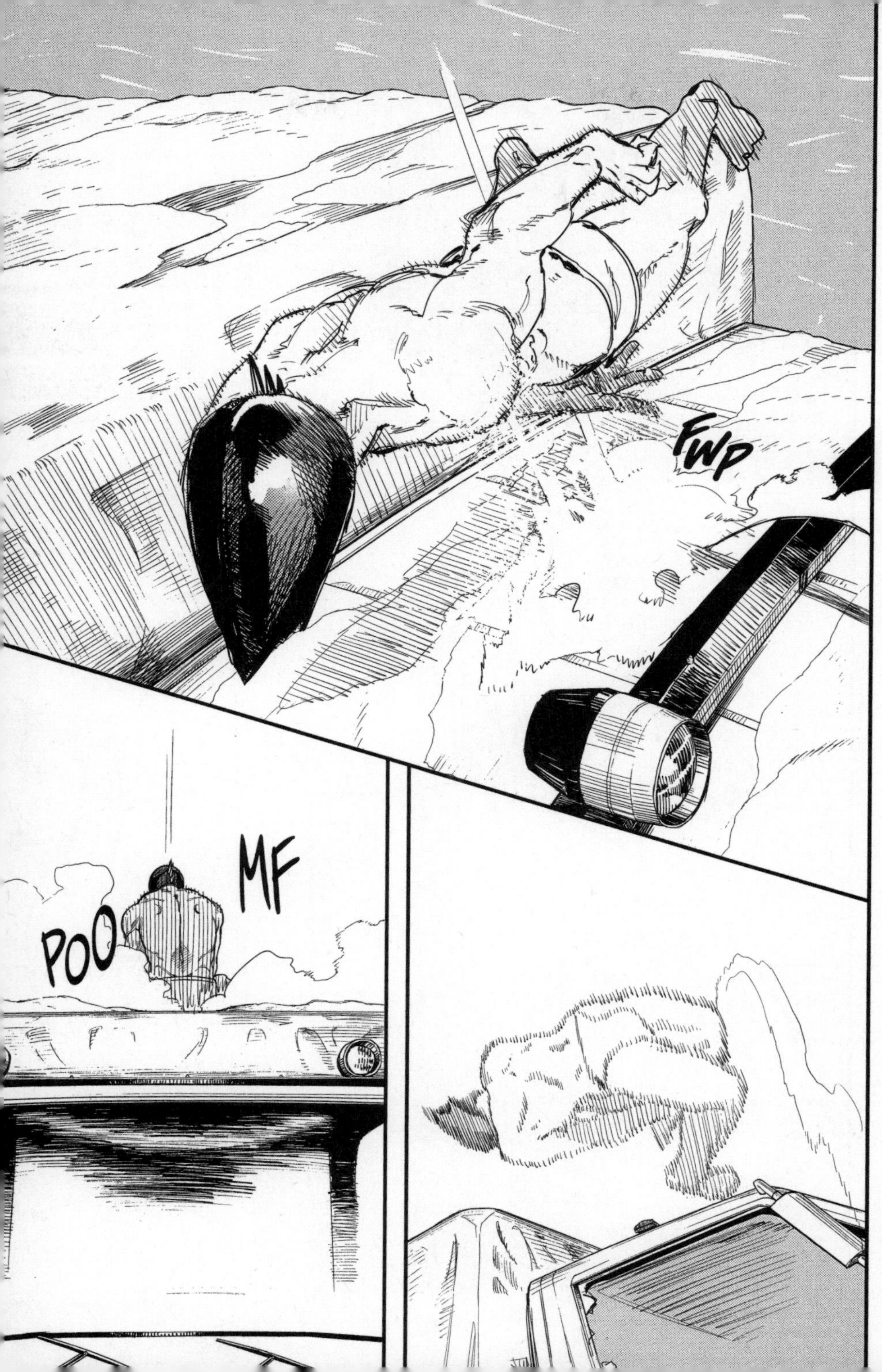
FWP
POOMF

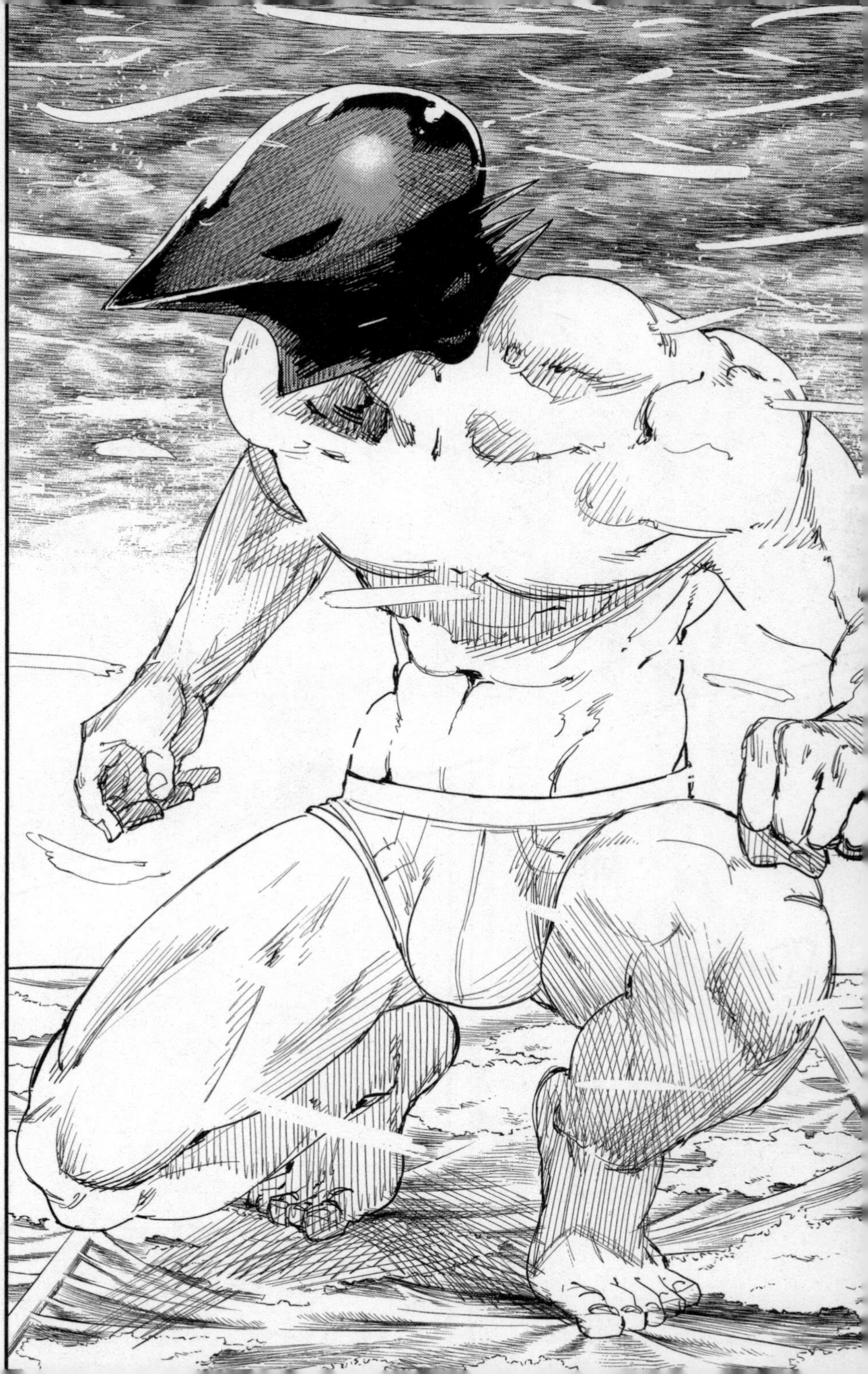

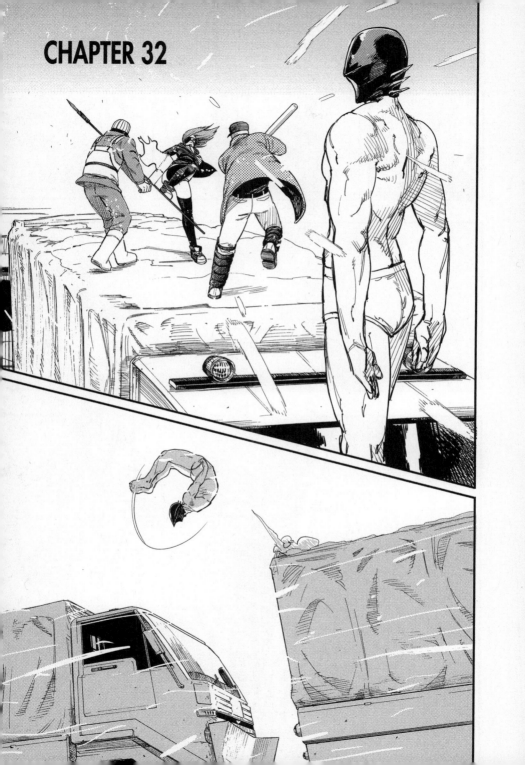

CHAPTER 32

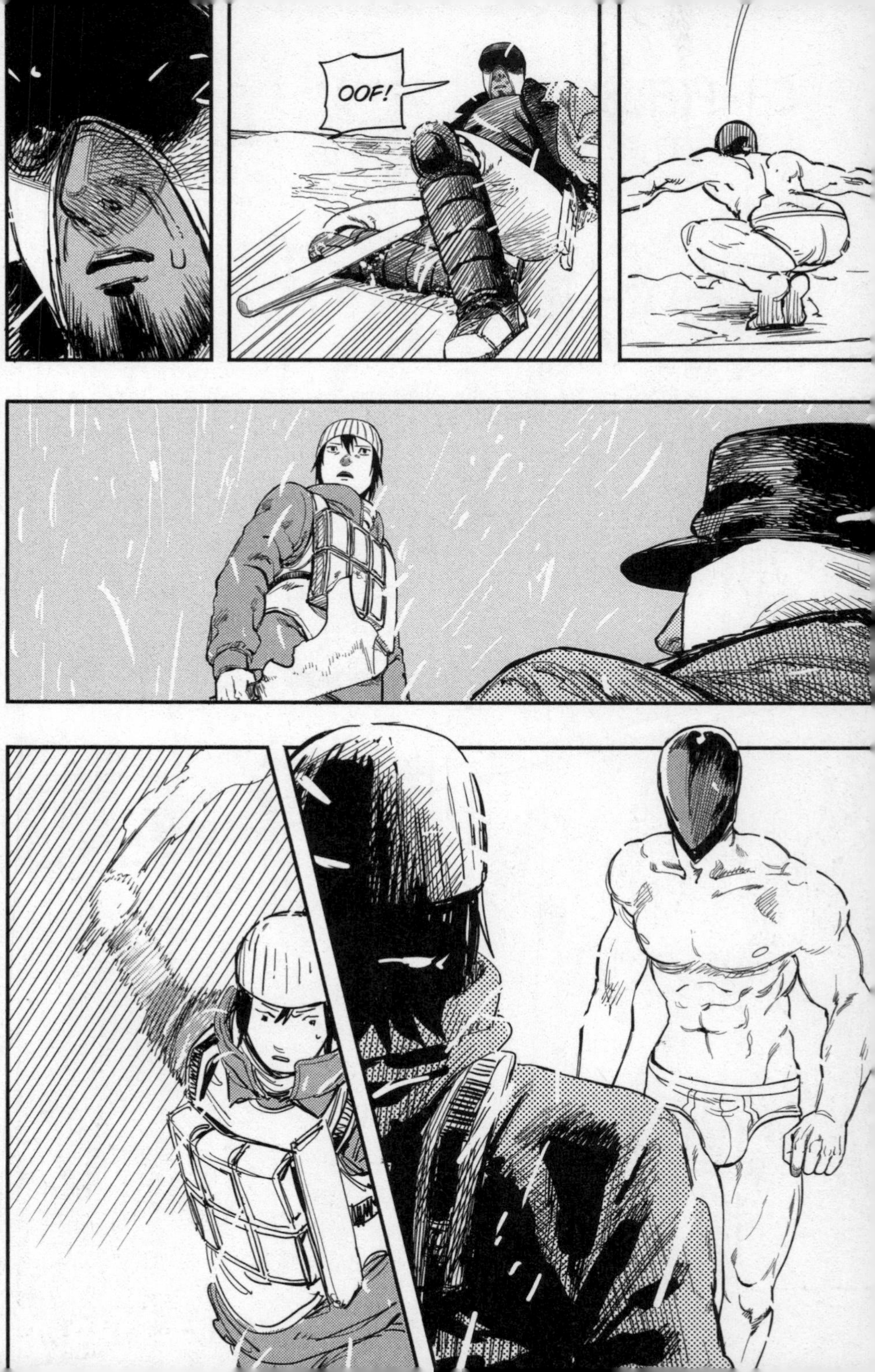
OOF!

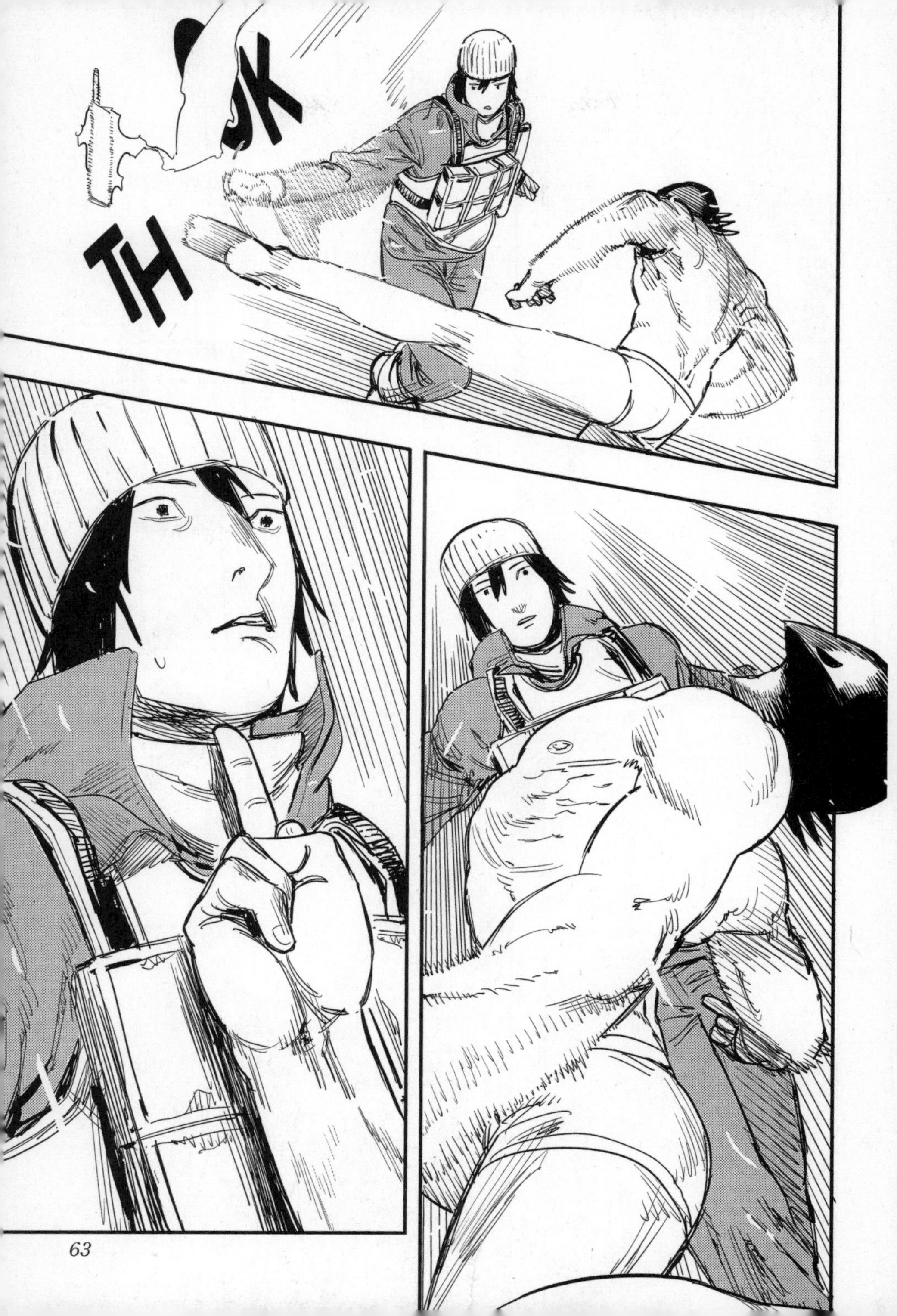
TH

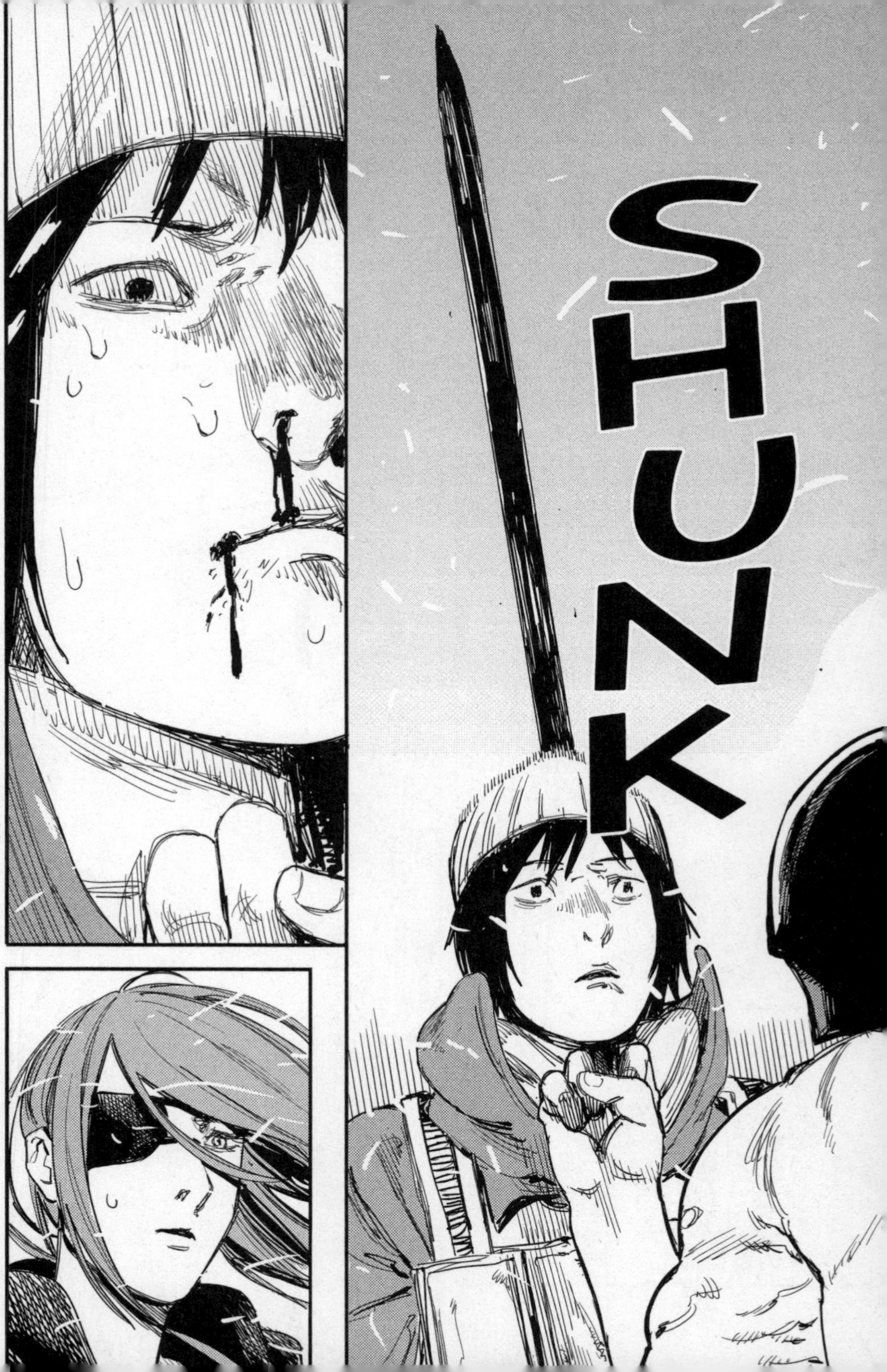
SHUNK

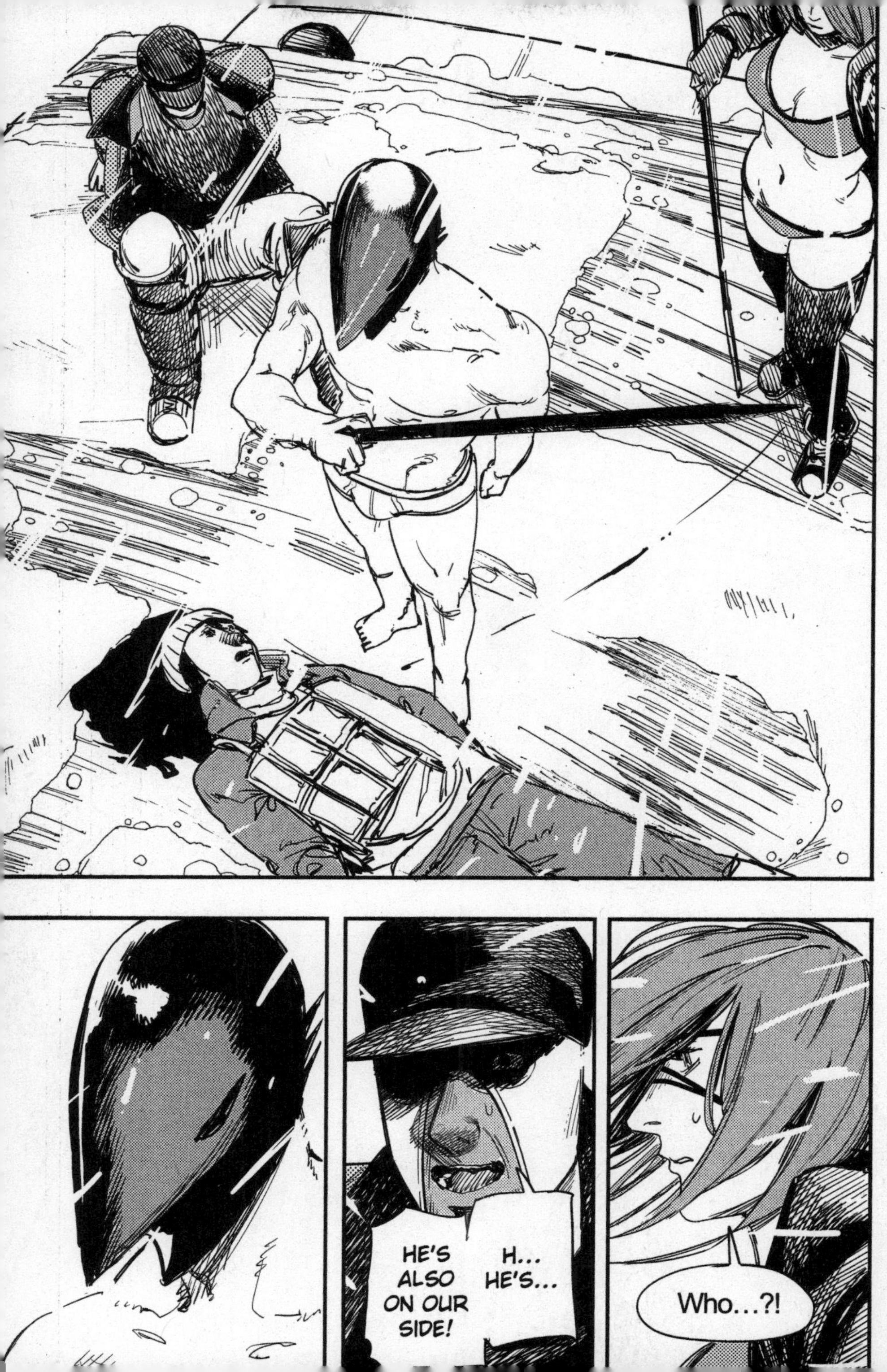
Who…?!
H… HE'S…
HE'S ALSO ON OUR SIDE!

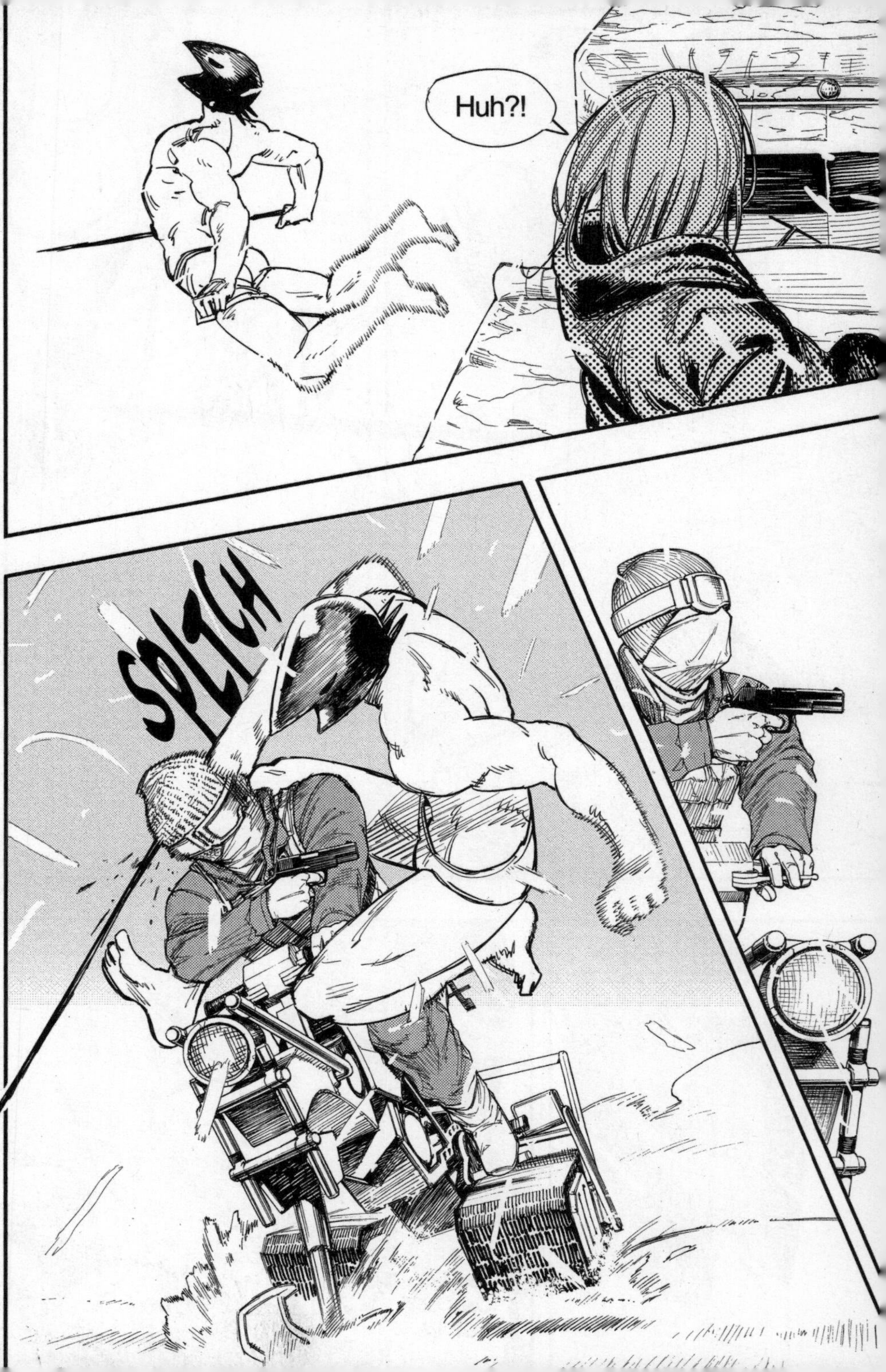
Huh?!
SPLTCH

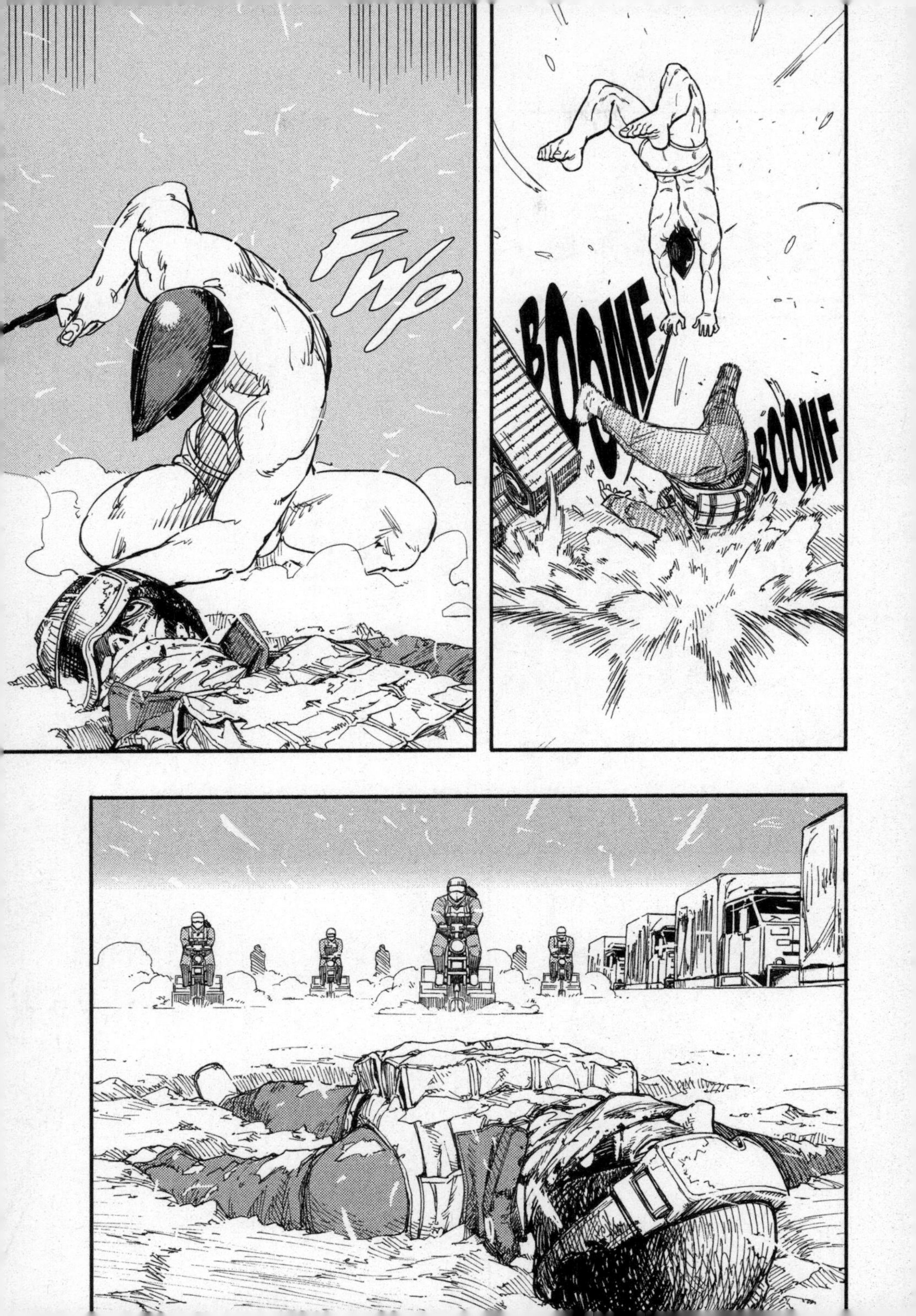
BOOMF
BOOMF
FWP

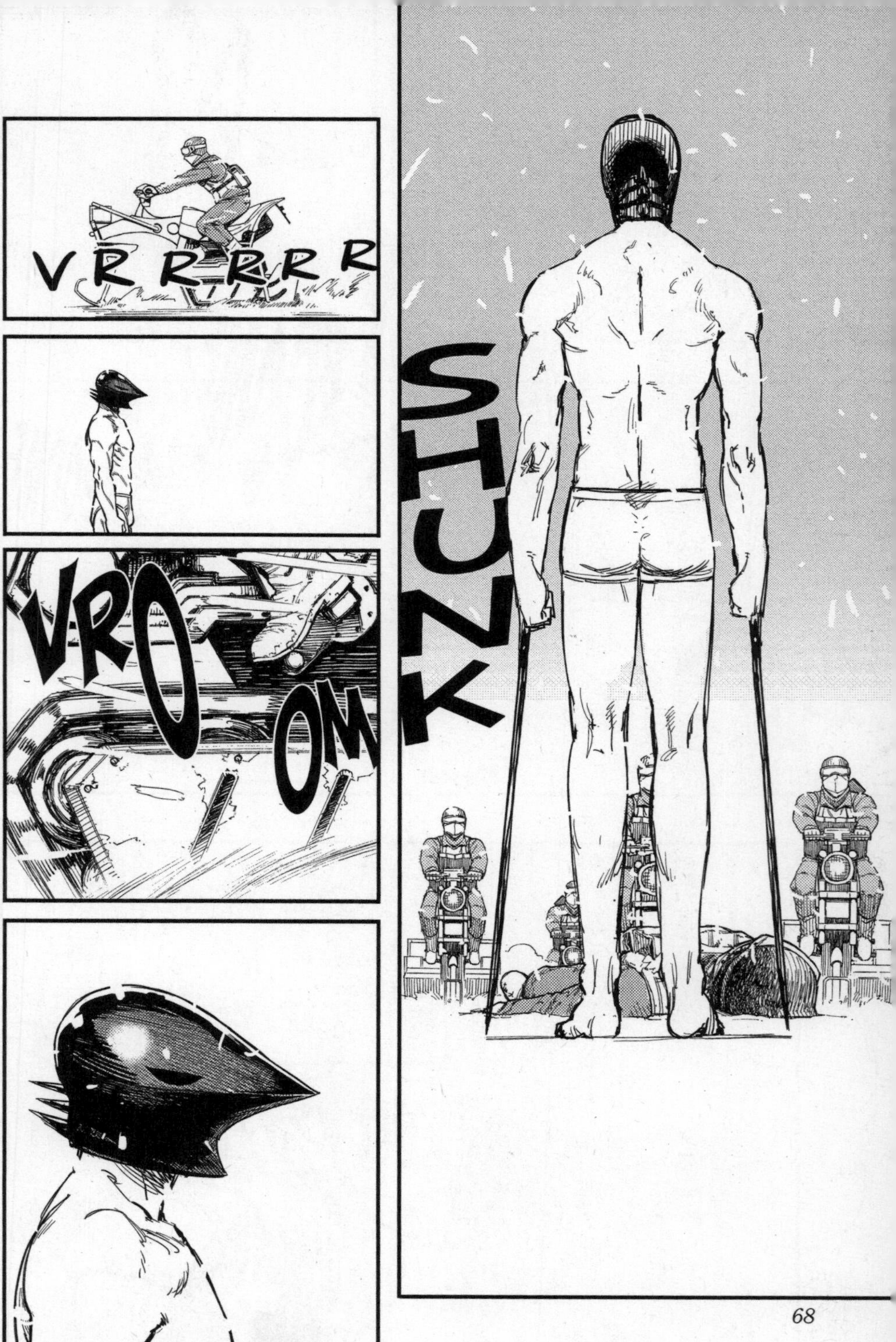
SHUNK
VRRRRR
VROOOM

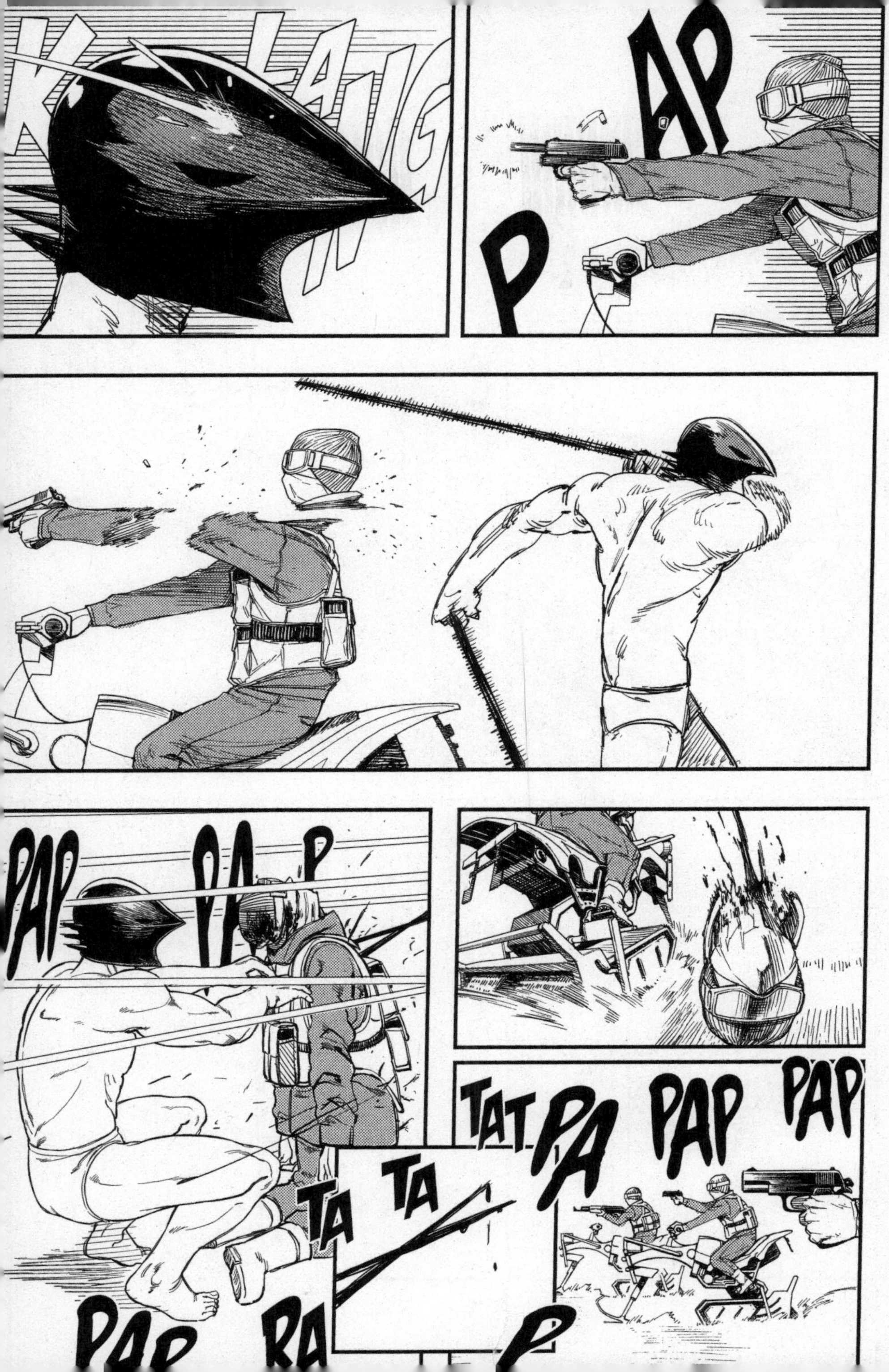
AP
P
KLANG
PAP
PAP
TAT
PA
P
PA
PAP
TA TA
PAP
RA
P

THOK
THOK
FMP

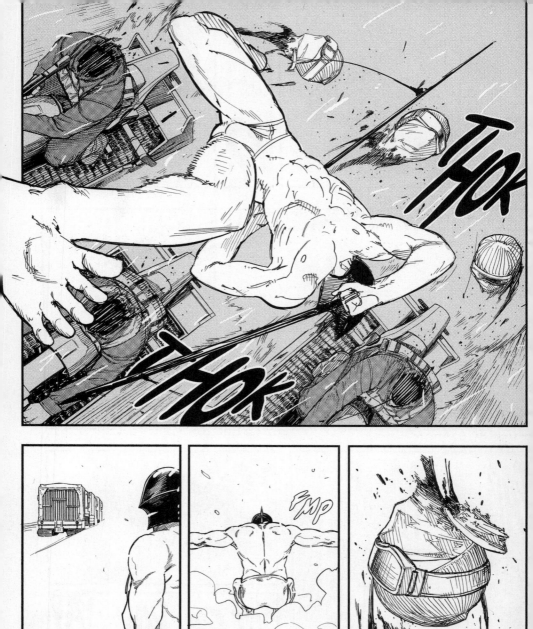

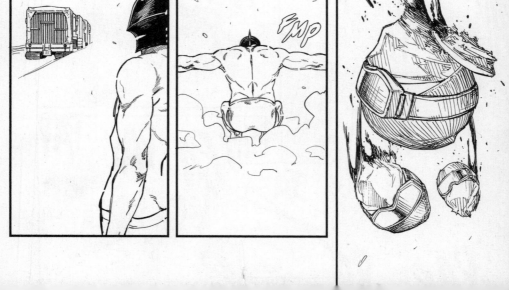

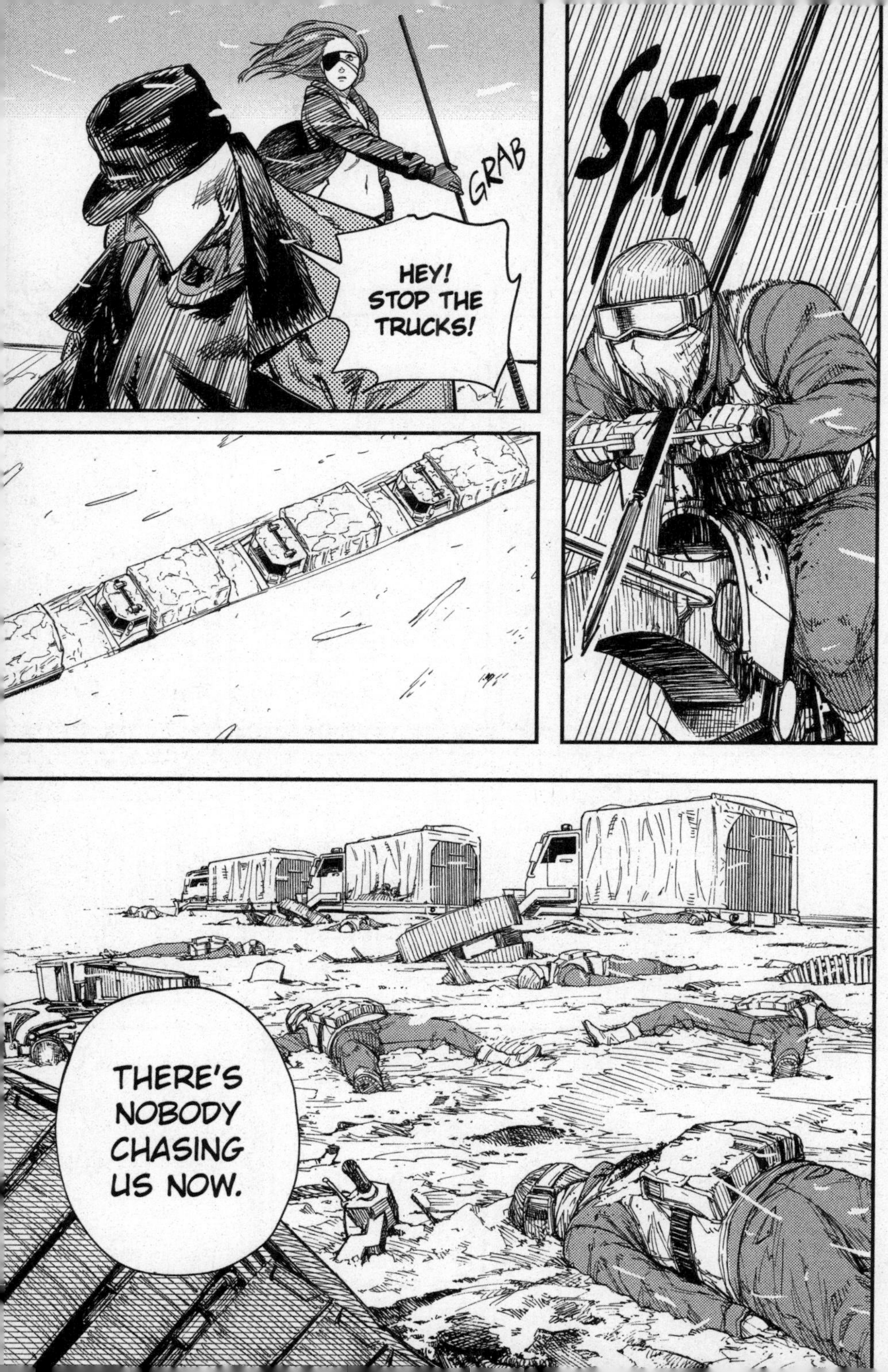
SPTCH
GRAB
HEY! STOP THE TRUCKS!
THERE'S NOBODY CHASING US NOW.

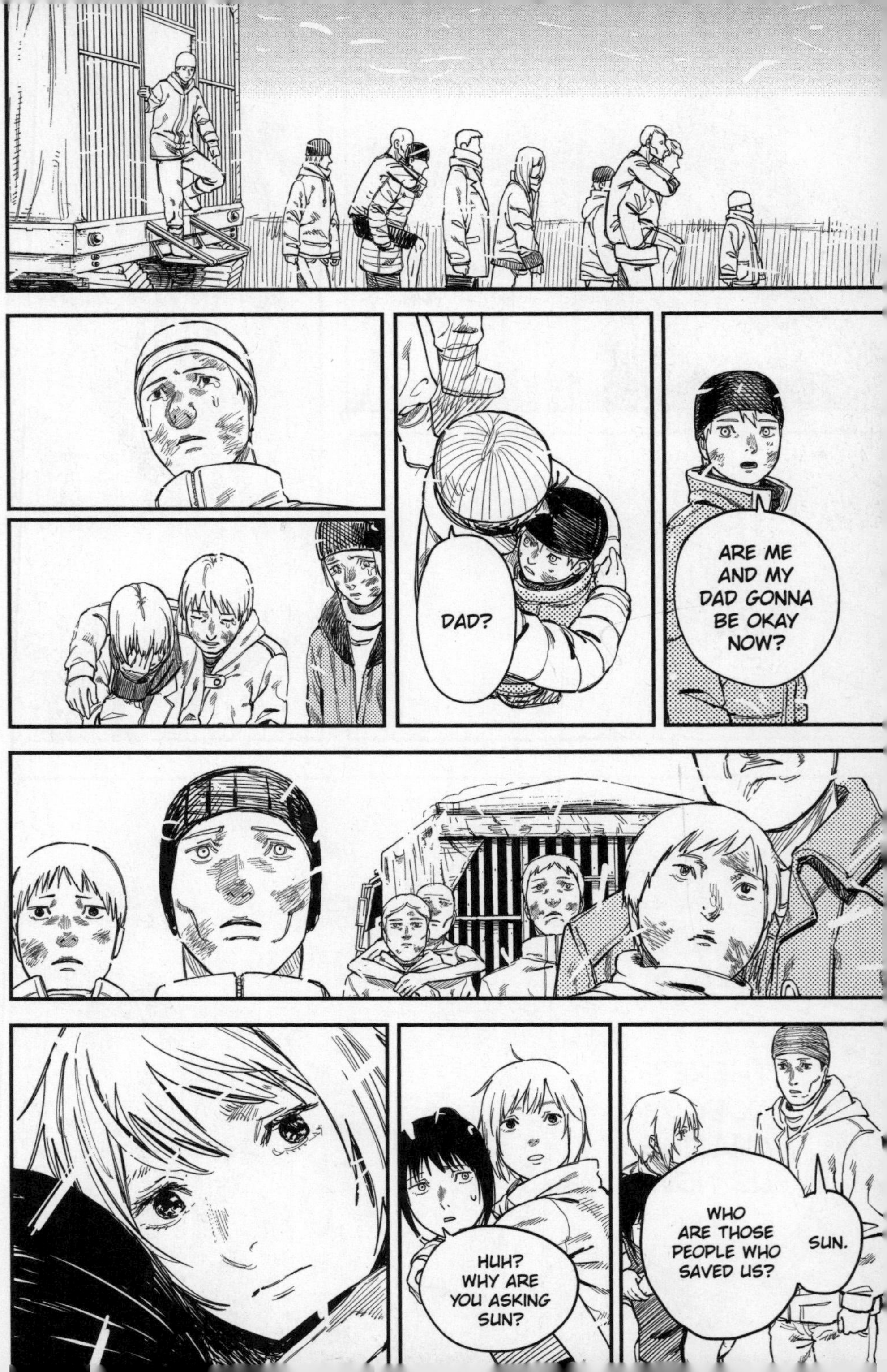
ARE ME AND MY DAD GONNA BE OKAY NOW?
DAD?
SUN.
WHO ARE THOSE PEOPLE WHO SAVED US?
HUH? WHY ARE YOU ASKING SUN?

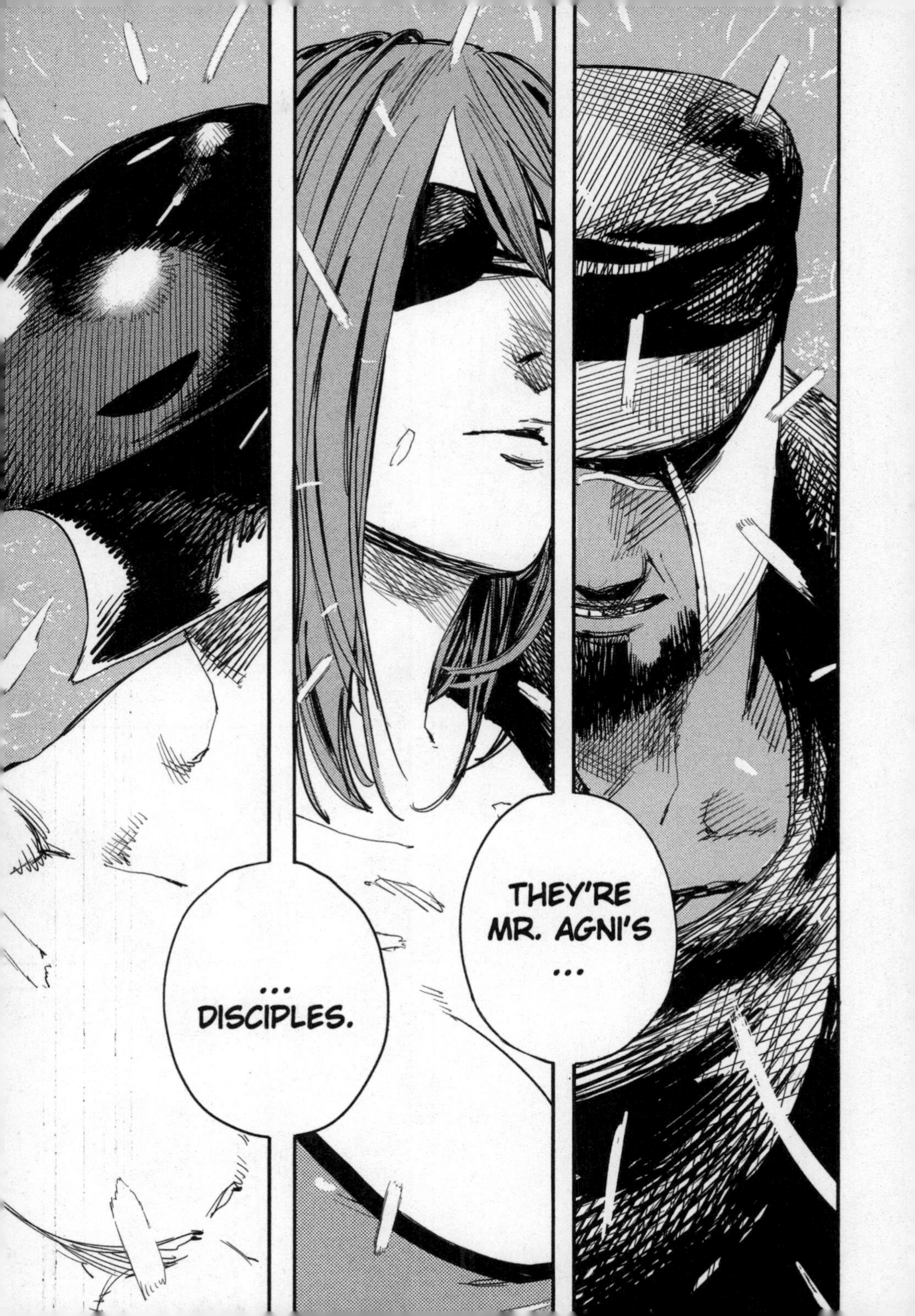
THEY'RE MR. AGNI'S ...
... DISCIPLES.

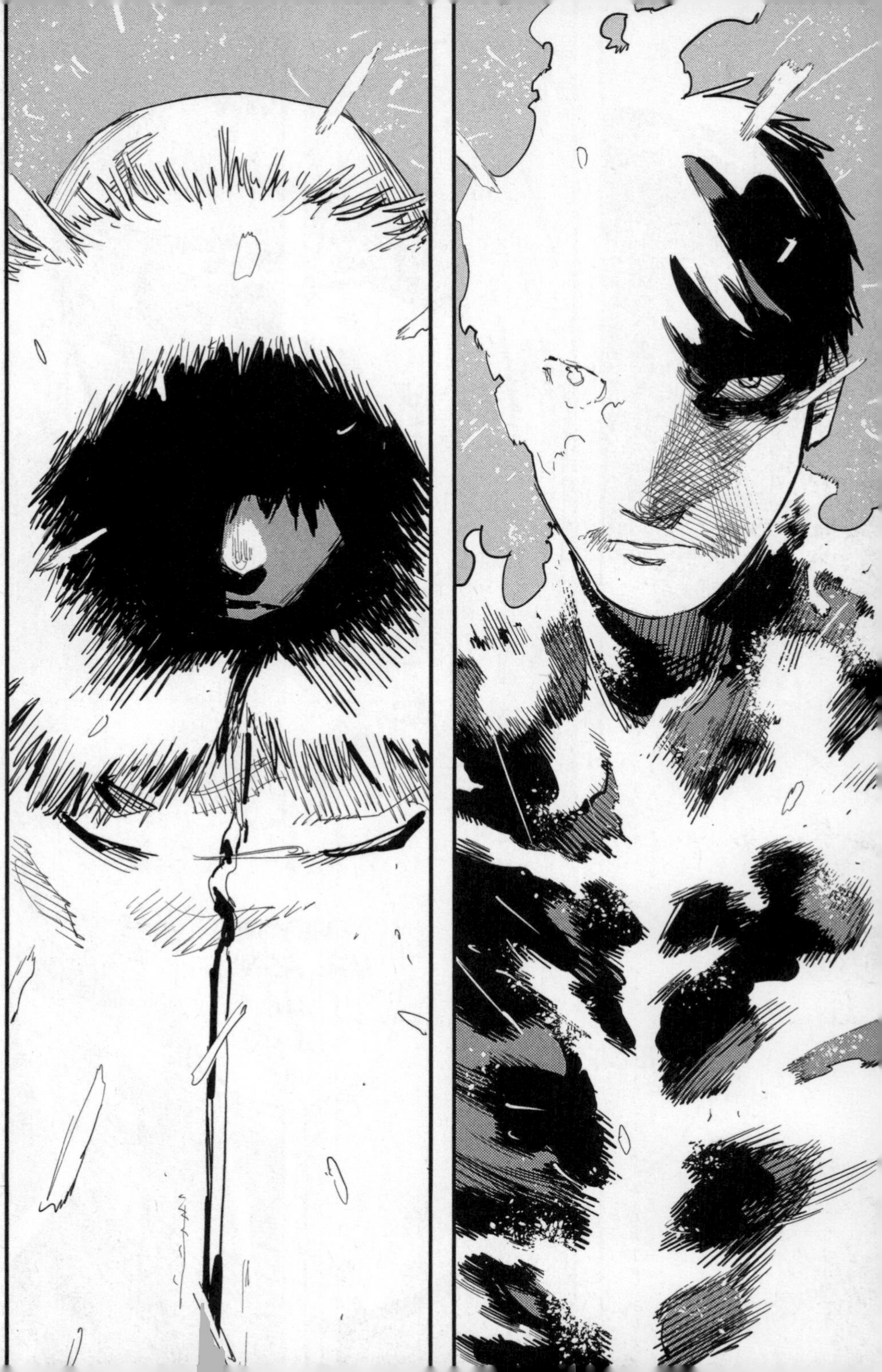

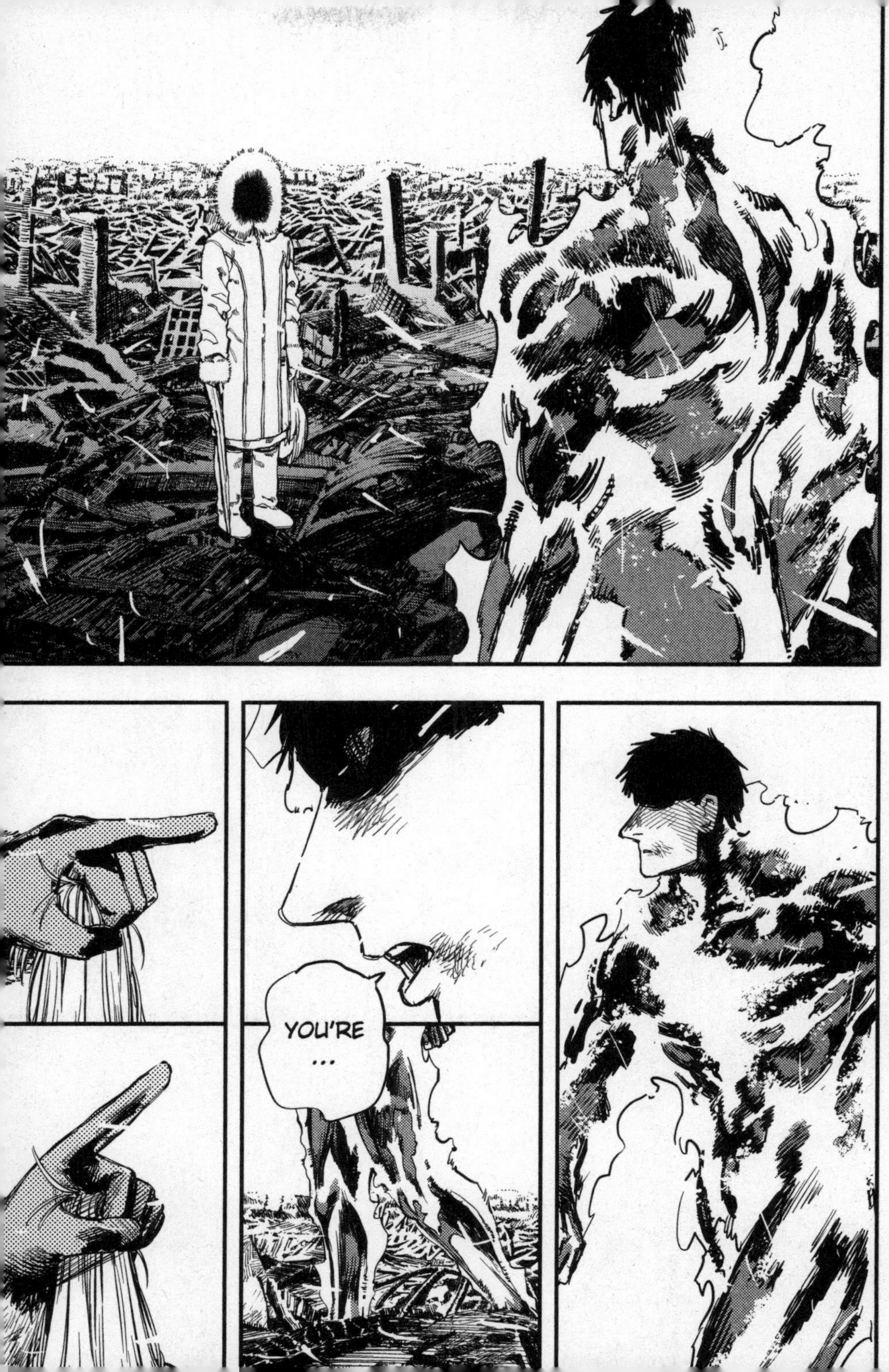
YOU'RE ...

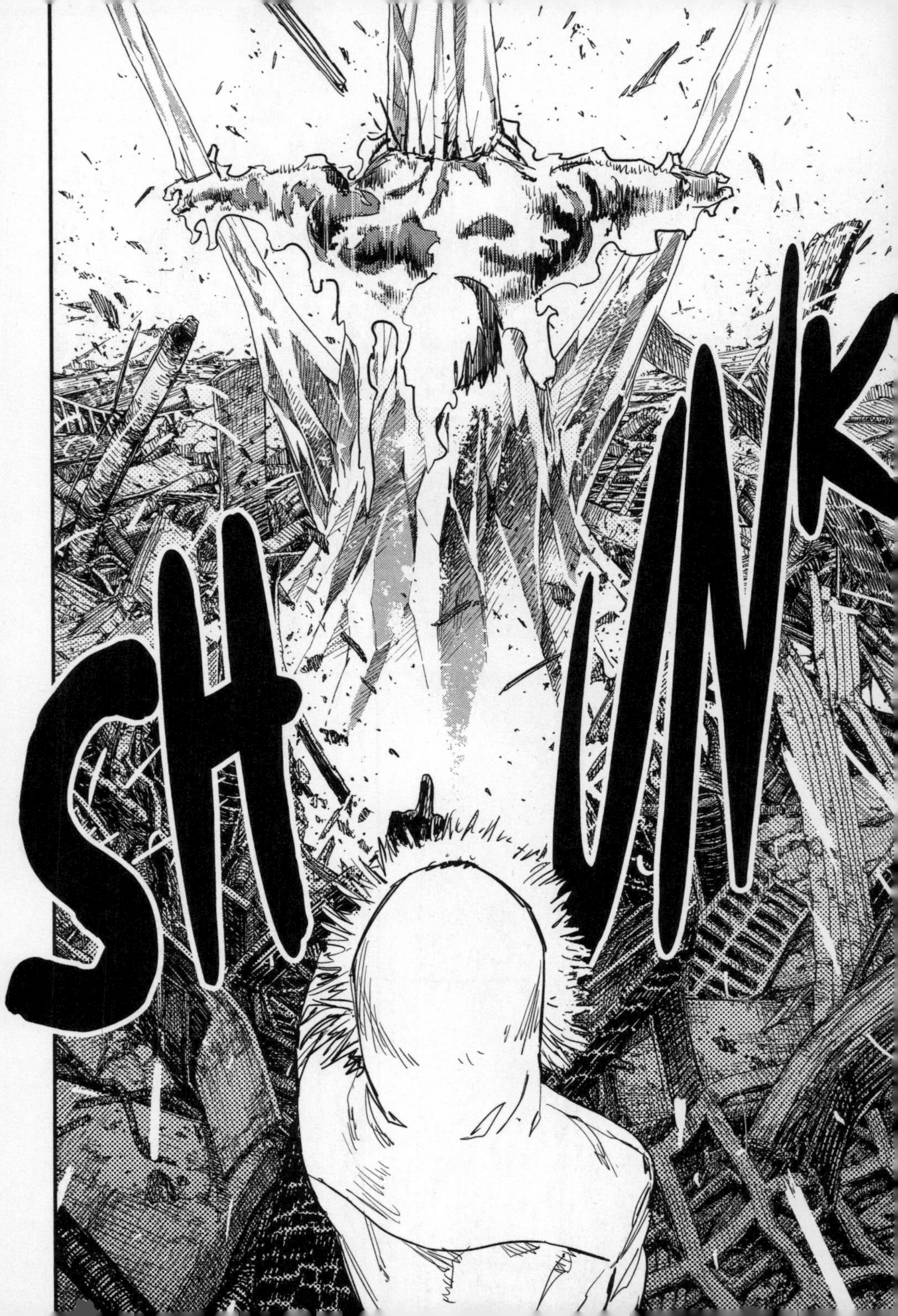
SHUNK

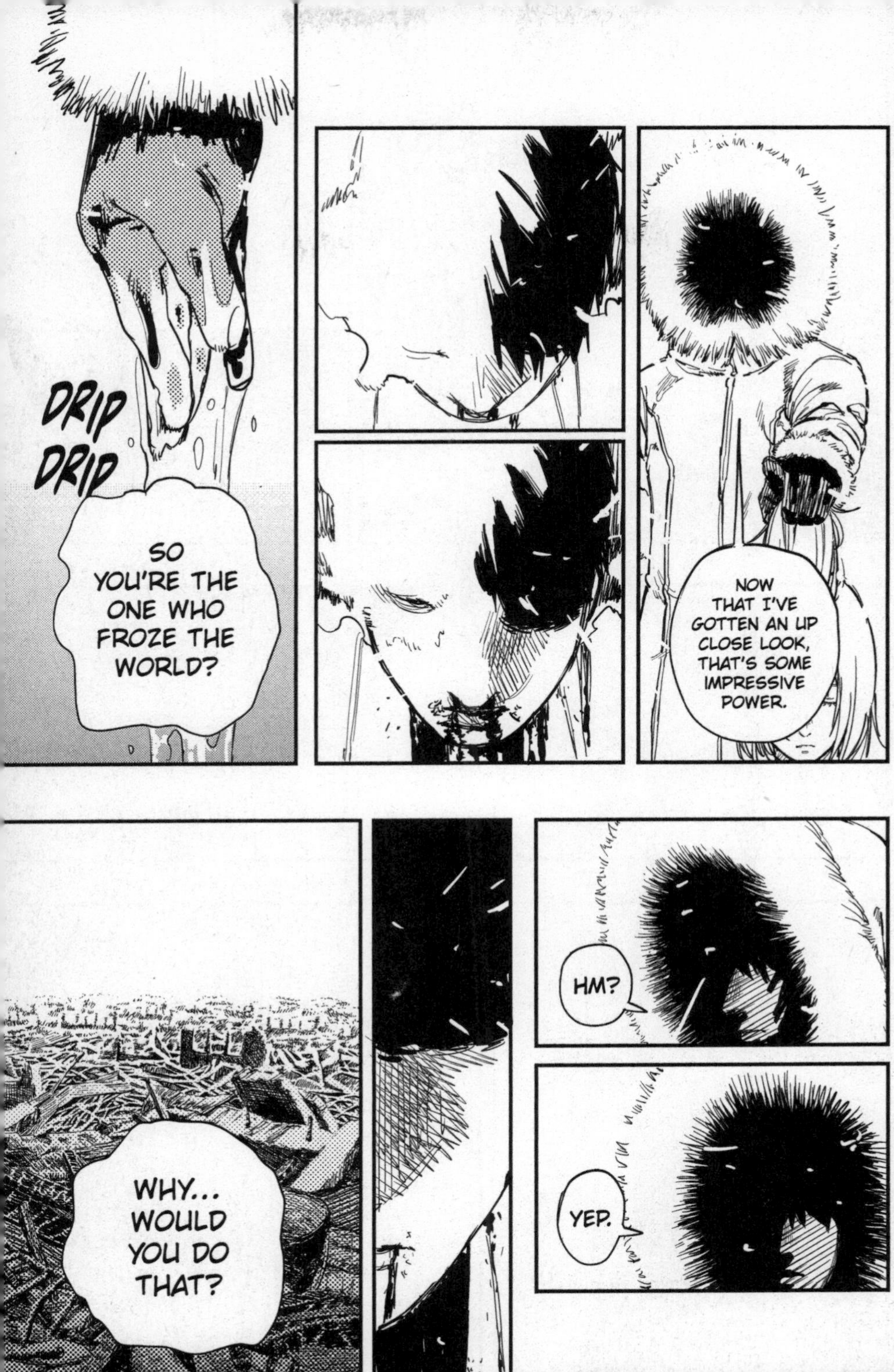
NOW THAT I'VE GOTTEN AN UP CLOSE LOOK, THAT'S SOME IMPRESSIVE POWER.
DRIP DRIP
SO YOU'RE THE ONE WHO FROZE THE WORLD?
HM?
YEP.
WHY... WOULD YOU DO THAT?

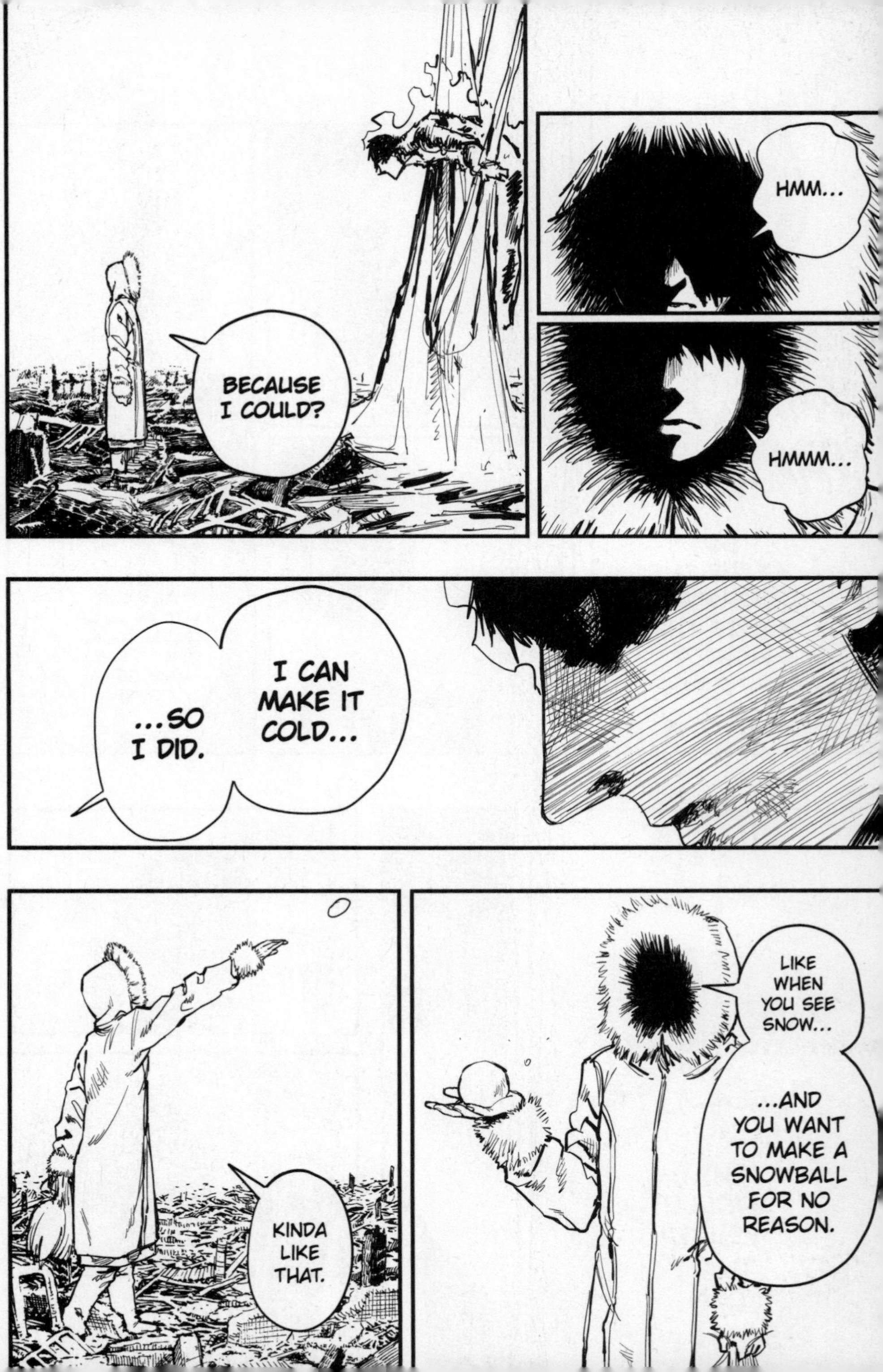
HMM...
HMMM...
BECAUSE I COULD?
I CAN MAKE IT COLD...
...SO I DID.
LIKE WHEN YOU SEE SNOW...
...AND YOU WANT TO MAKE A SNOWBALL FOR NO REASON.
KINDA LIKE THAT.

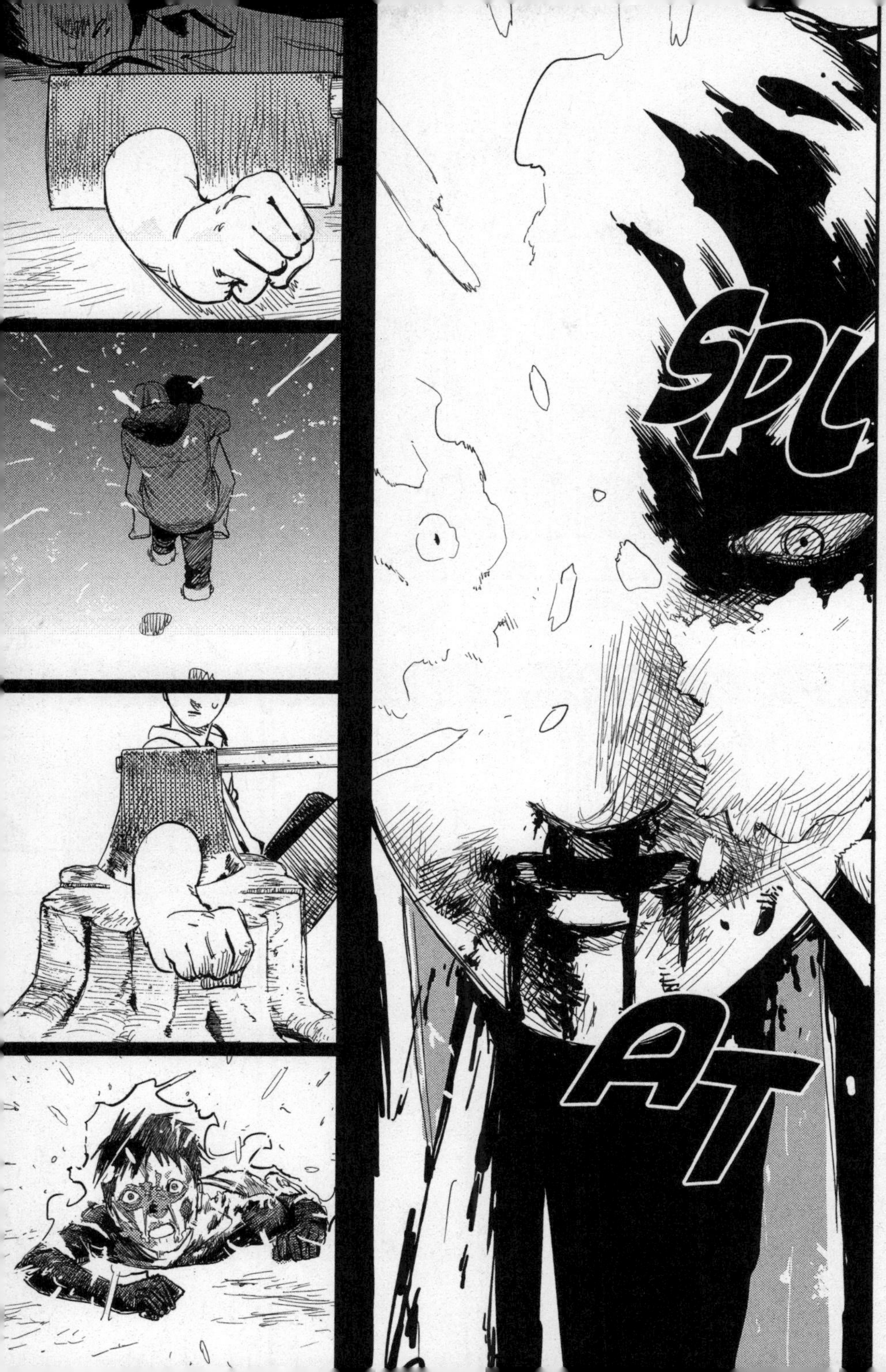
SPLAT

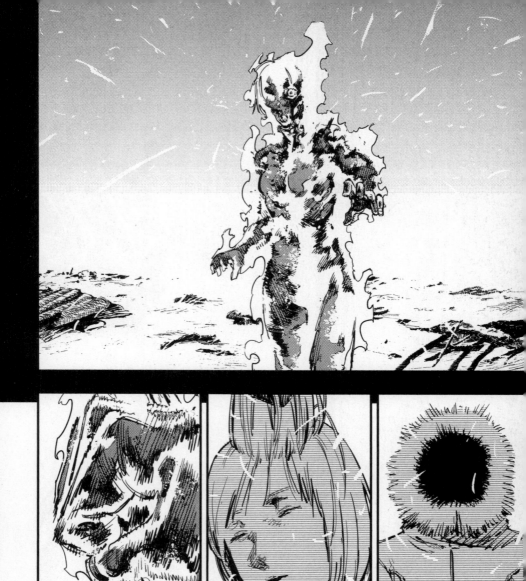

...
SECOND.

...A
SINGLE...

I CAN'T
WASTE...

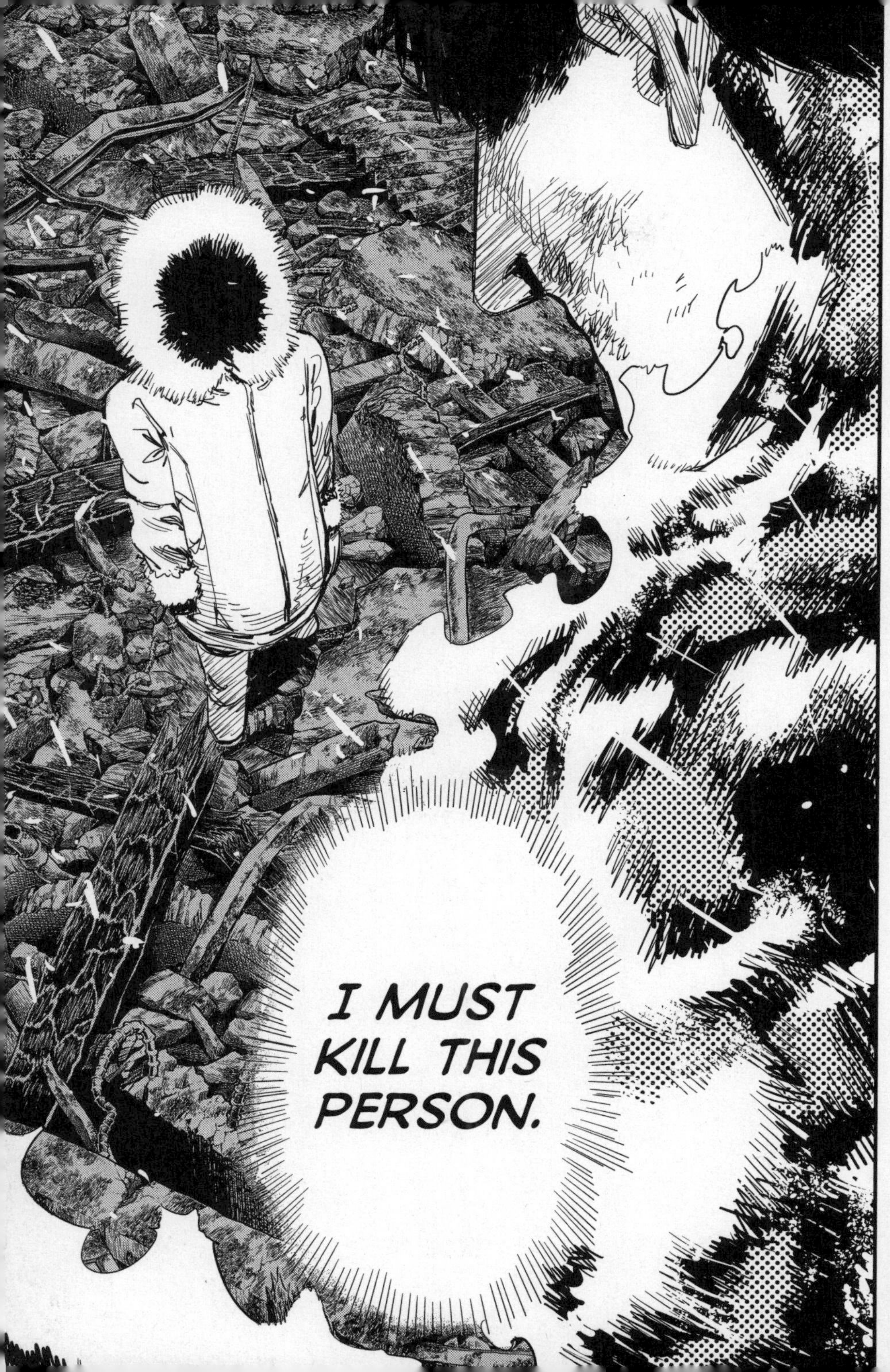
I MUST
KILL THIS
PERSON.

FIRE PUNCH

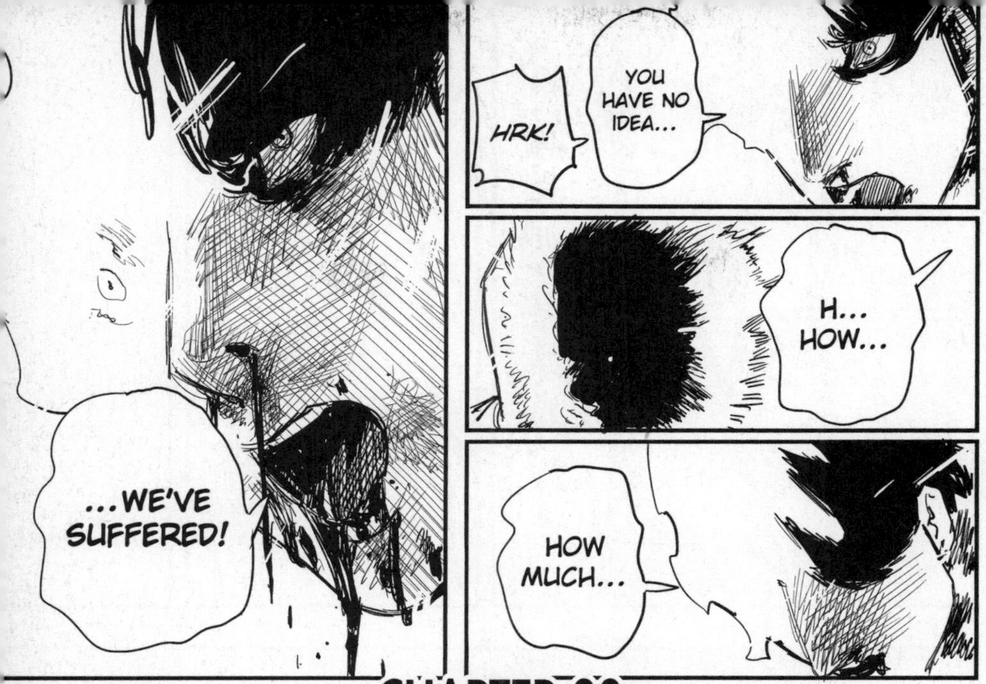
YOU HAVE NO IDEA...
HRK!
H... HOW...
HOW MUCH...
...WE'VE SUFFERED!

CHAPTER 33

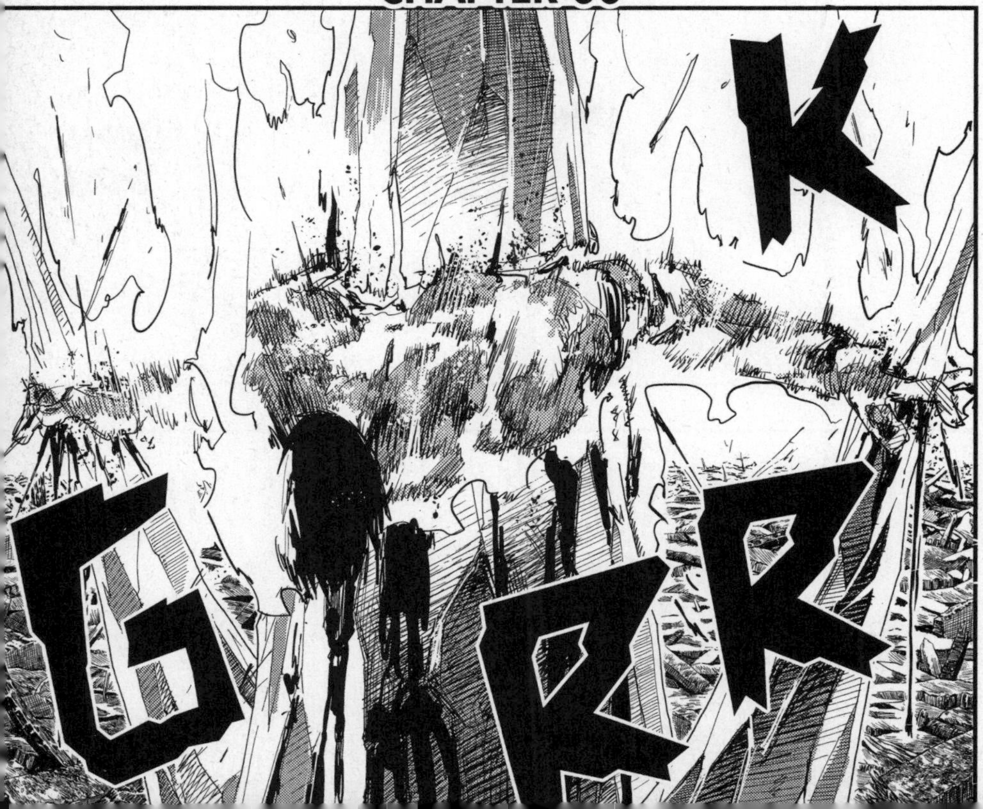
GRRK

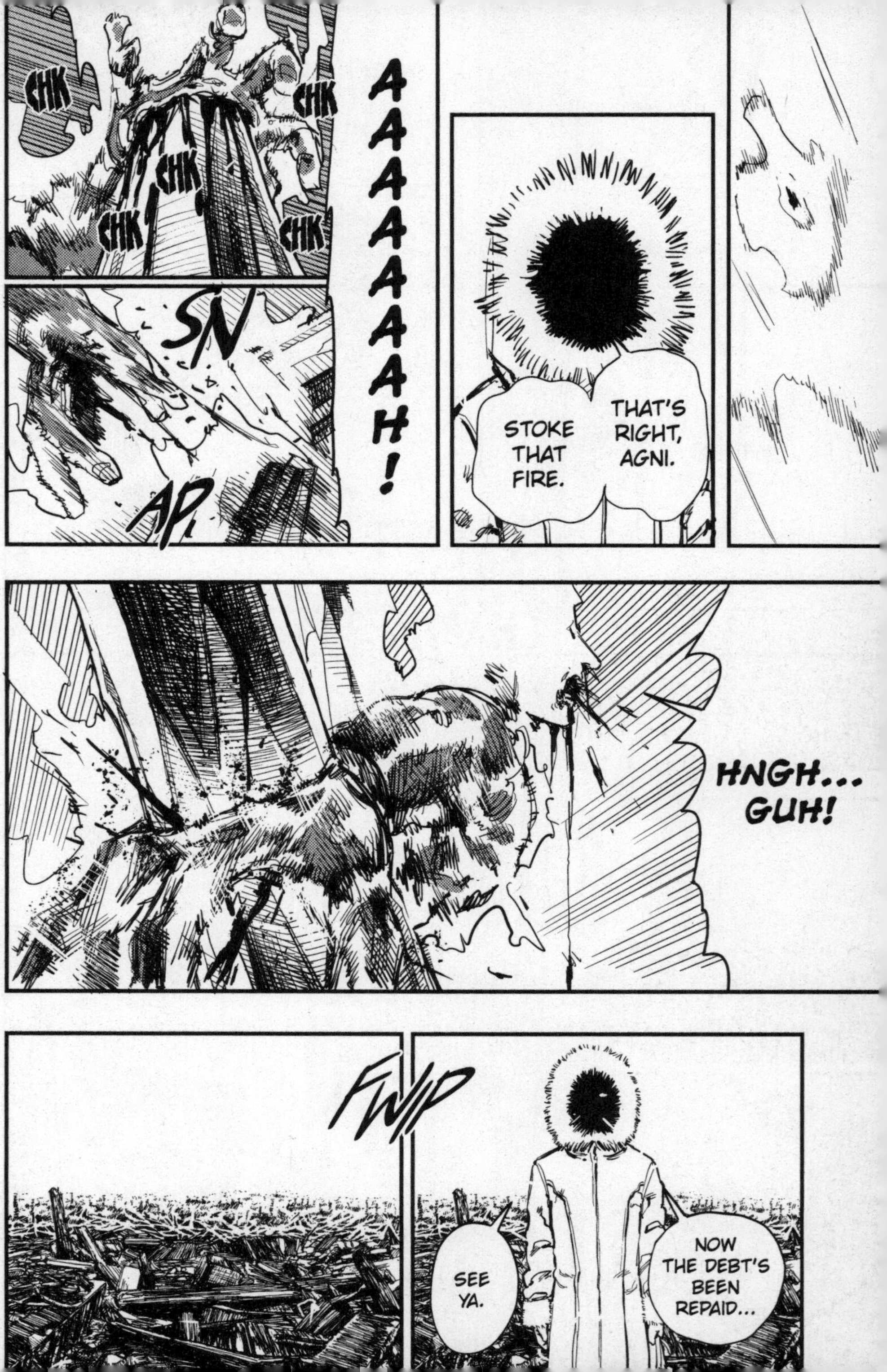
THAT'S RIGHT, AGNI.
STOKE THAT FIRE.
CHK
CHK
CHK
CHK
CHK
AAAAAAAAH!
SNAP
HNGH... GUH!
FWIP
NOW THE DEBT'S BEEN REPAID...
SEE YA.

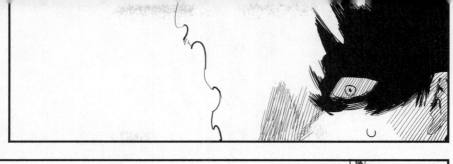

KLSHT

SN

AP

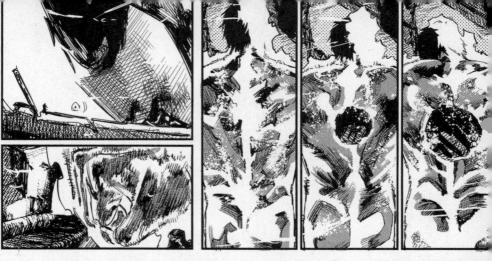

DAMN IT...

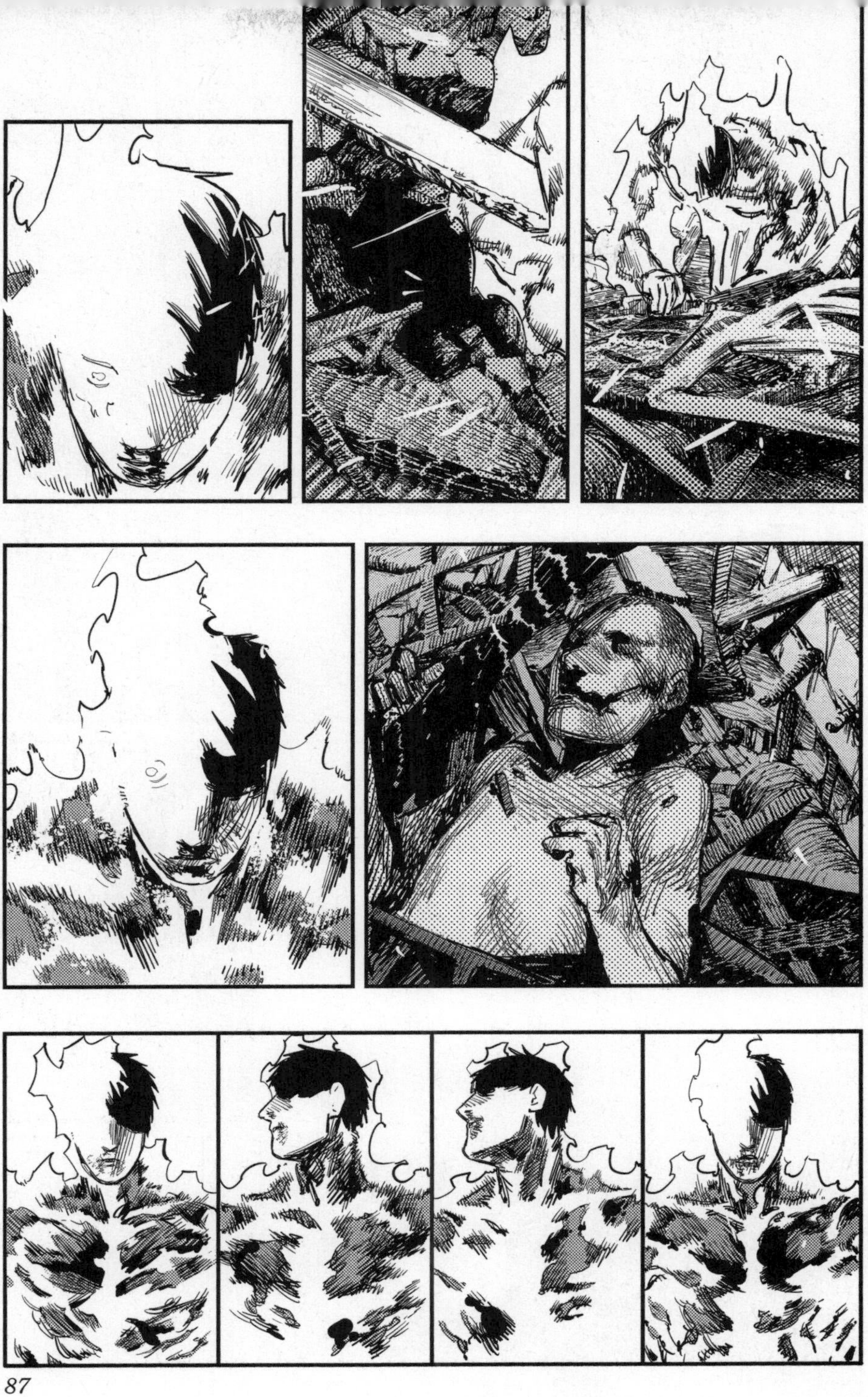

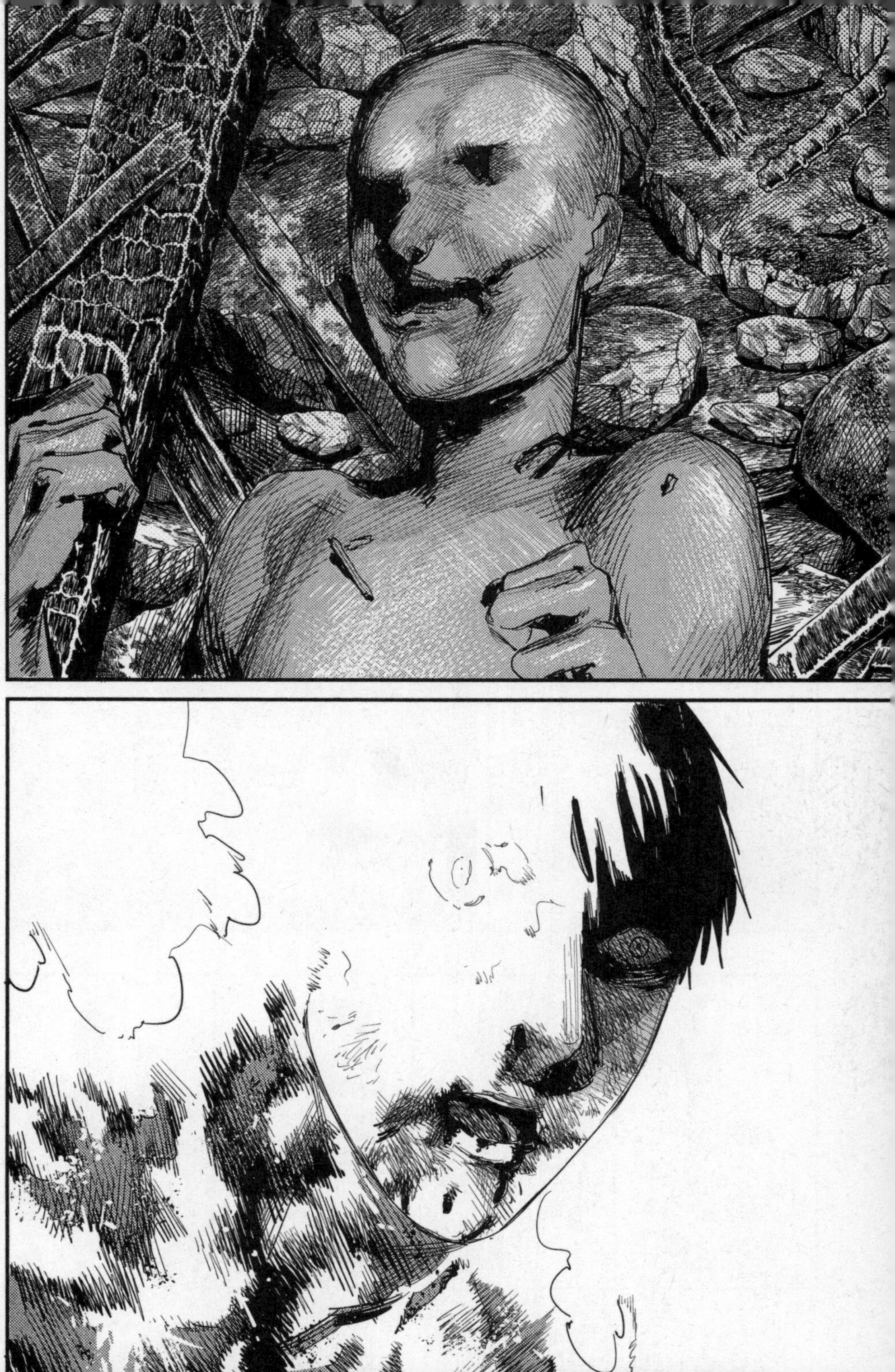

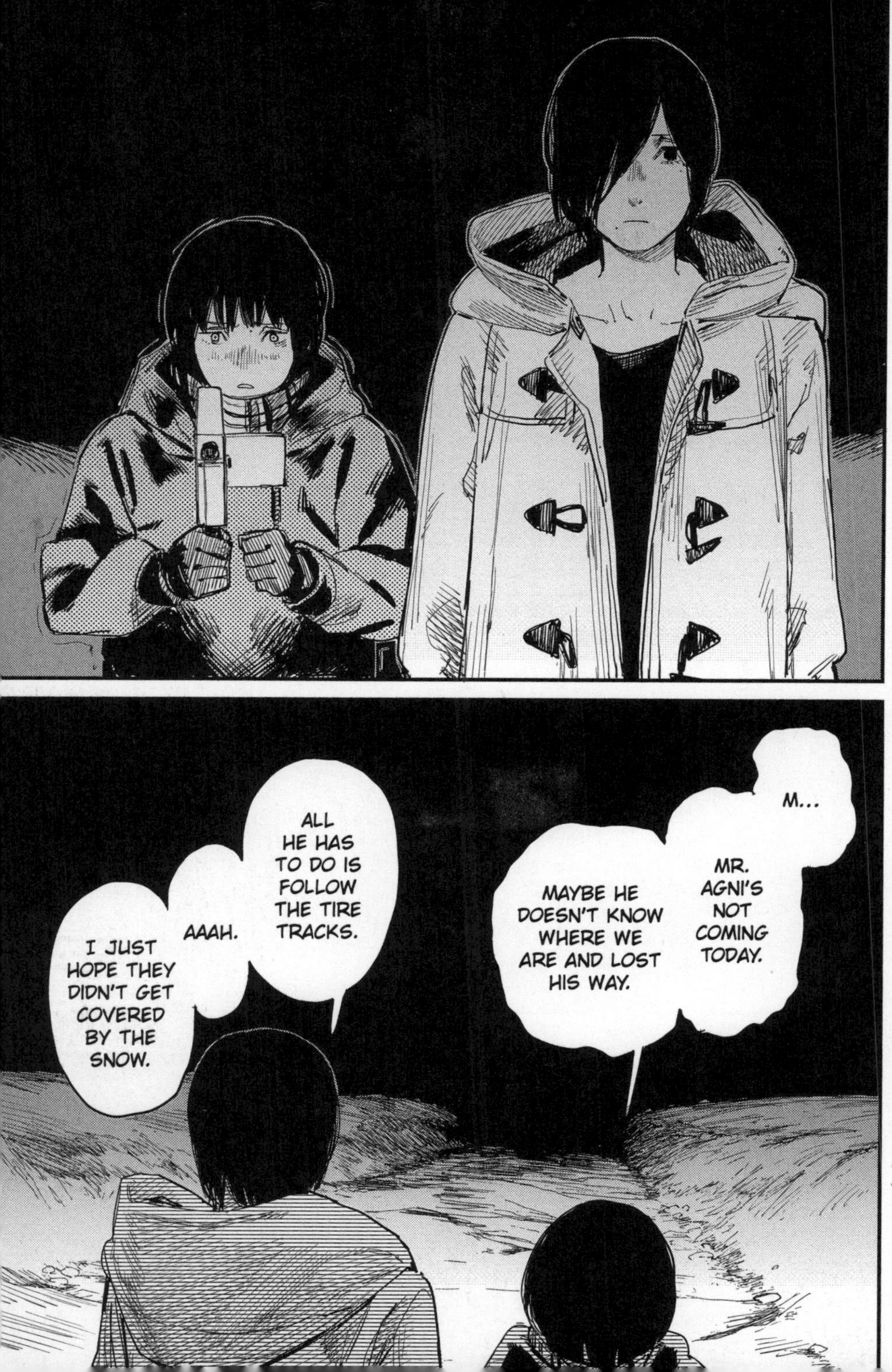
M...
MR. AGNI'S NOT COMING TODAY.
MAYBE HE DOESN'T KNOW WHERE WE ARE AND LOST HIS WAY.
ALL HE HAS TO DO IS FOLLOW THE TIRE TRACKS.
AAAH.
I JUST HOPE THEY DIDN'T GET COVERED BY THE SNOW.

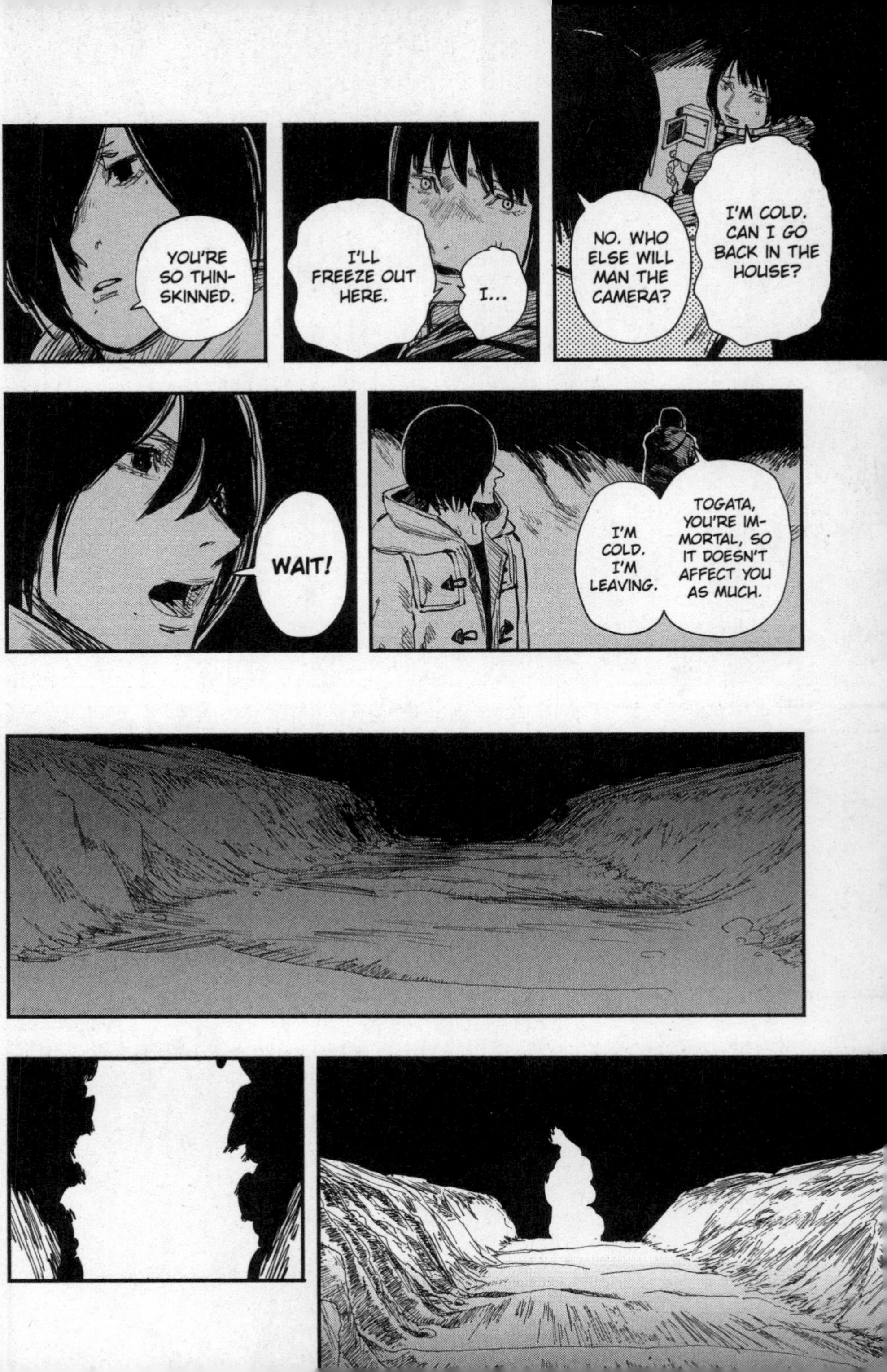
I'M COLD. CAN I GO BACK IN THE HOUSE?
NO. WHO ELSE WILL MAN THE CAMERA?
I...
I'LL FREEZE OUT HERE.
YOU'RE SO THIN-SKINNED.
TOGATA, YOU'RE IM-MORTAL, SO IT DOESN'T AFFECT YOU AS MUCH.
I'M COLD. I'M LEAVING.
WAIT!

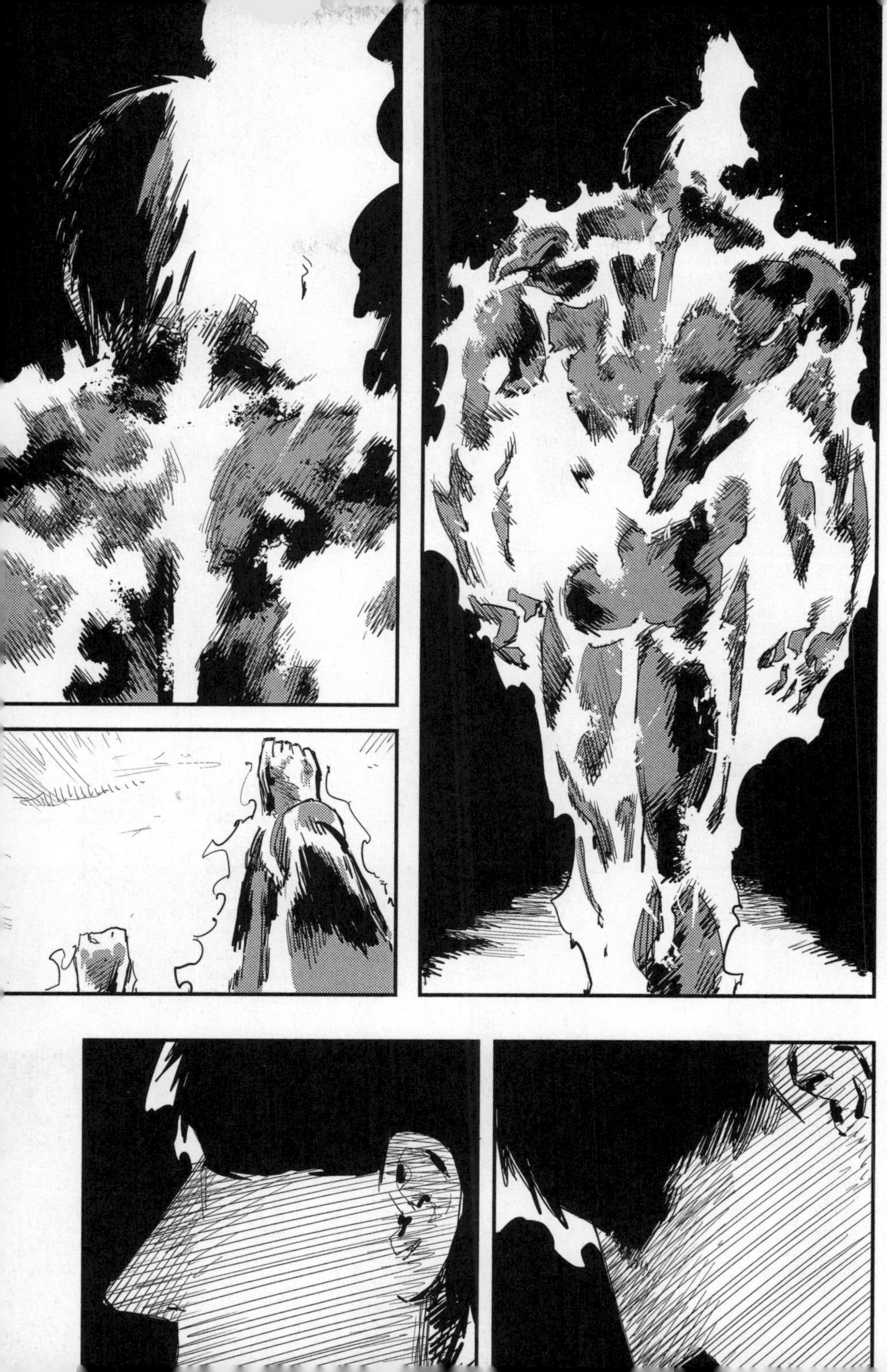

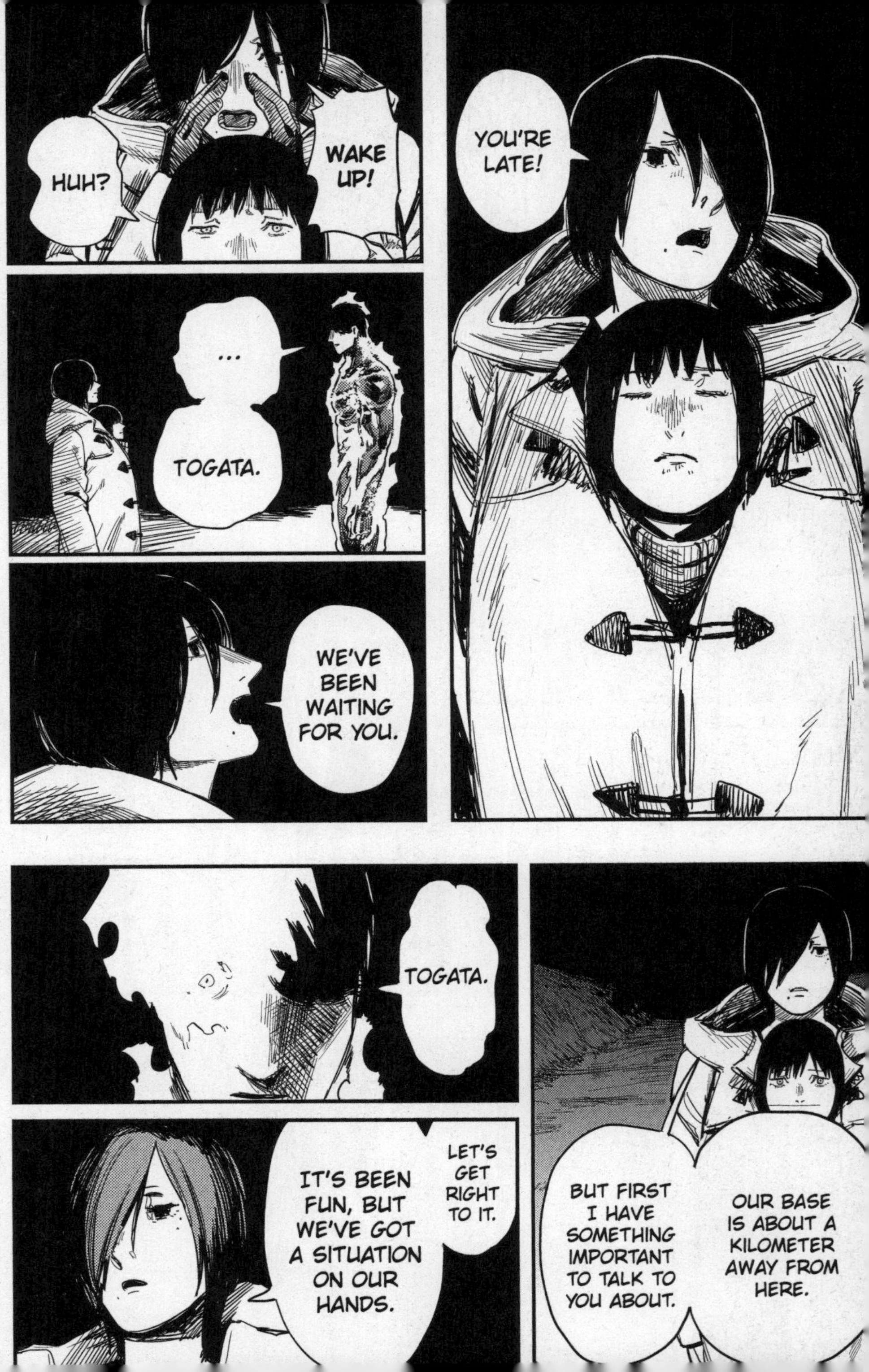
YOU'RE LATE!
WAKE UP!
HUH?
...
TOGATA.
WE'VE BEEN WAITING FOR YOU.
OUR BASE IS ABOUT A KILOMETER AWAY FROM HERE.
BUT FIRST I HAVE SOMETHING IMPORTANT TO TALK TO YOU ABOUT.
TOGATA.
LET'S GET RIGHT TO IT.
IT'S BEEN FUN, BUT WE'VE GOT A SITUATION ON OUR HANDS.

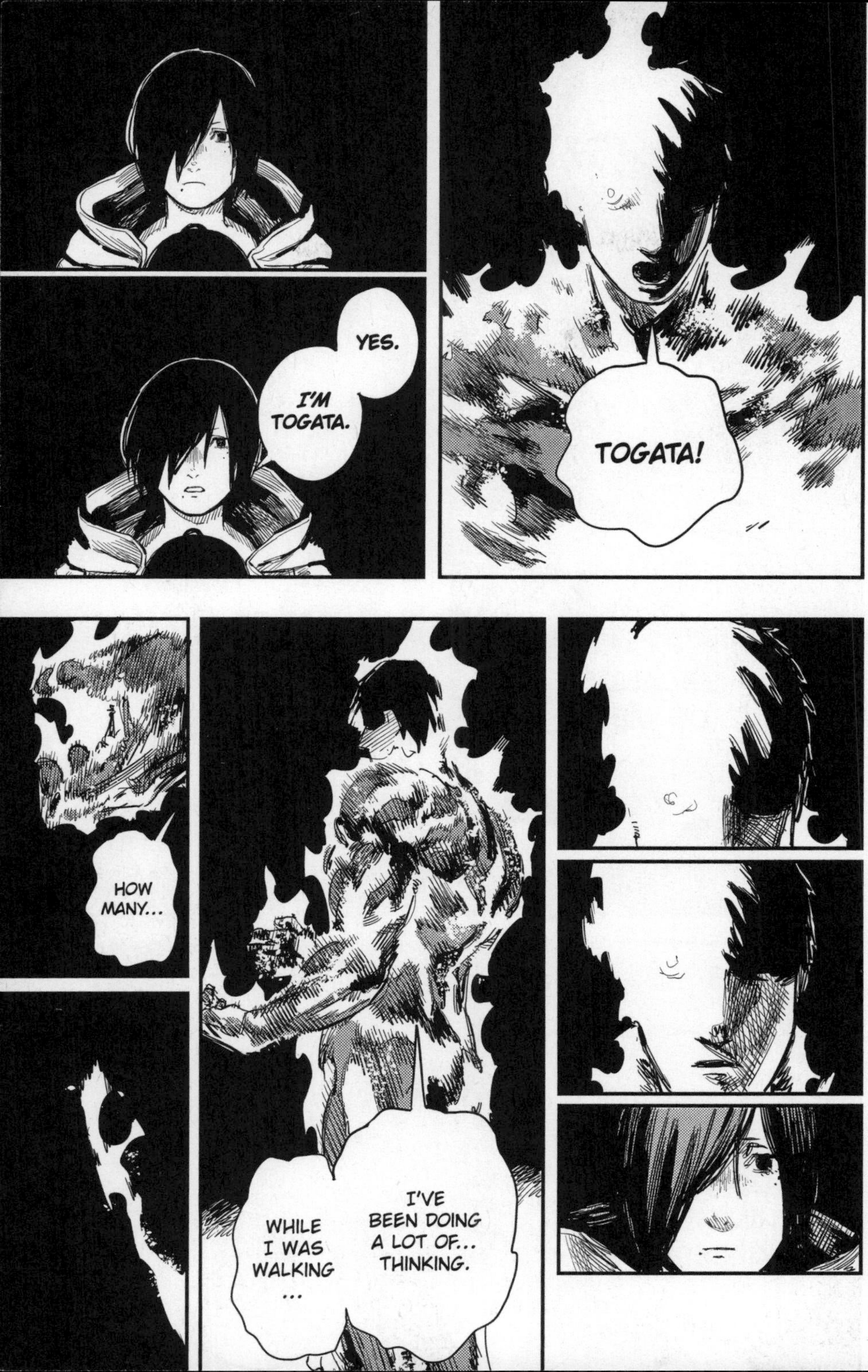
TOGATA!
YES.
I'M TOGATA.
I'VE BEEN DOING A LOT OF... THINKING.
WHILE I WAS WALKING ...
HOW MANY...

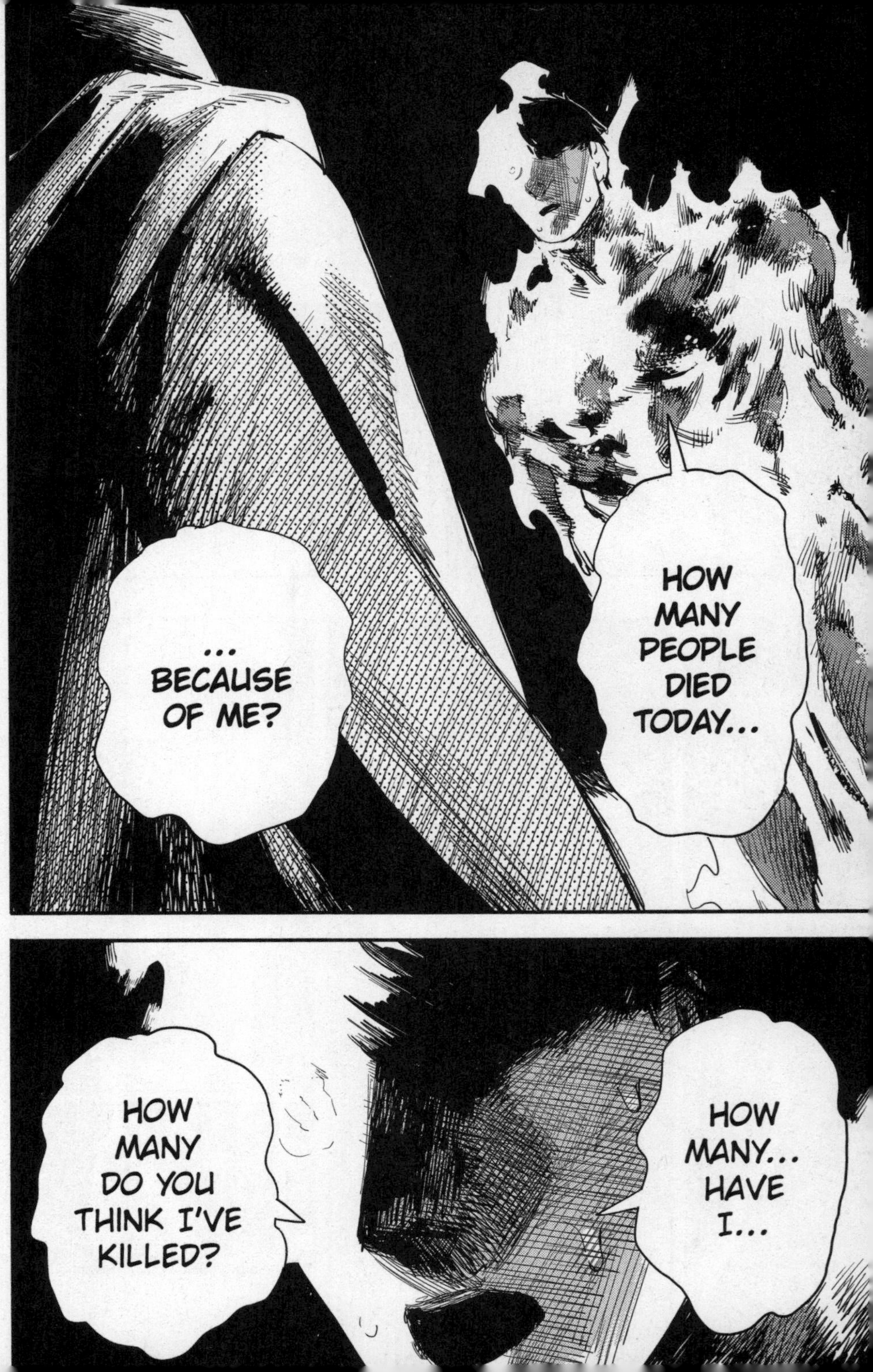
HOW MANY PEOPLE DIED TODAY...
... BECAUSE OF ME?
HOW MANY... HAVE I...
HOW MANY DO YOU THINK I'VE KILLED?

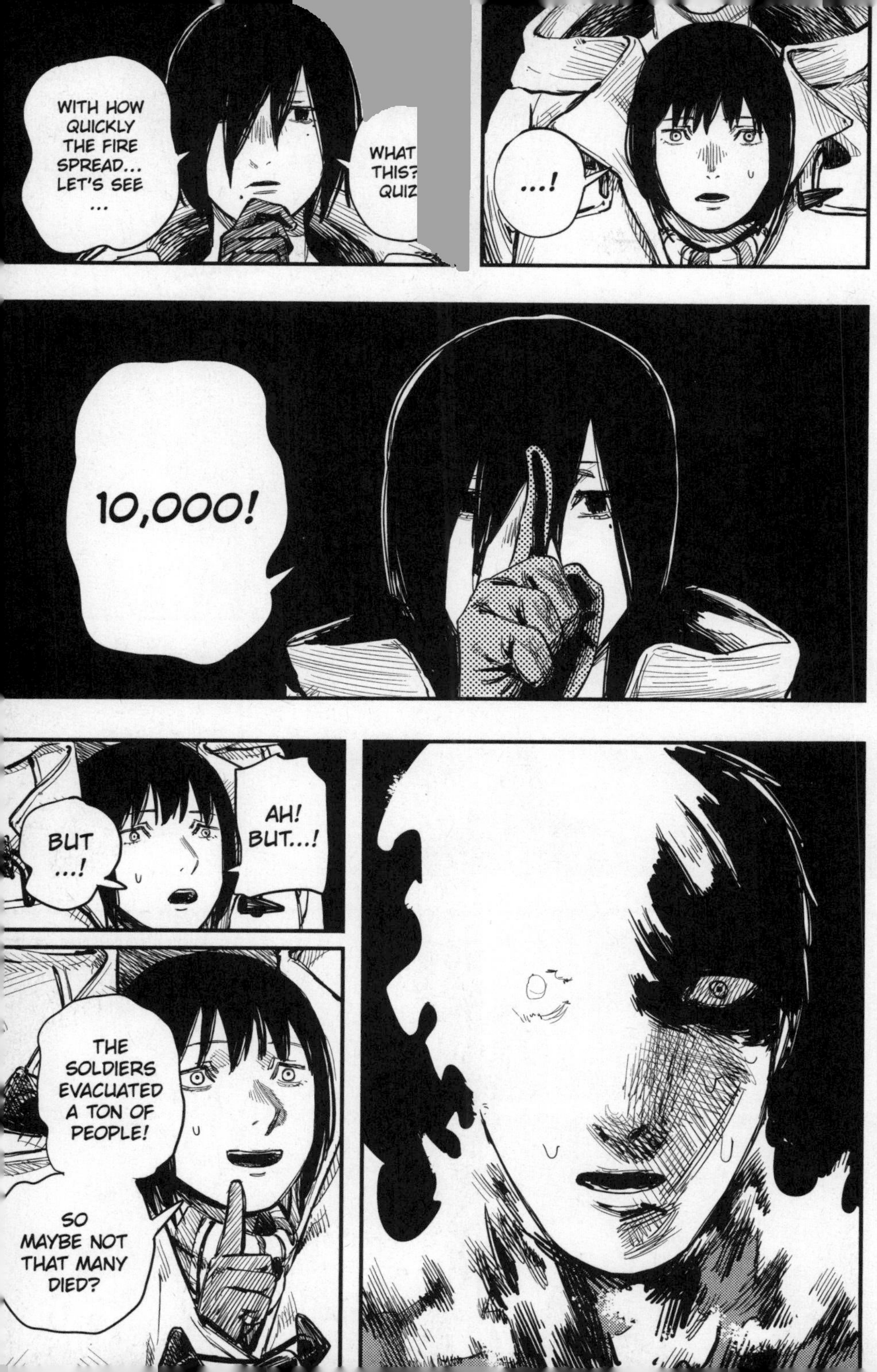
...!
WHAT THIS? QUIZ
WITH HOW QUICKLY THE FIRE SPREAD... LET'S SEE ...
10,000!
AH! BUT...!
BUT ...!
THE SOLDIERS EVACUATED A TON OF PEOPLE!
SO MAYBE NOT THAT MANY DIED?

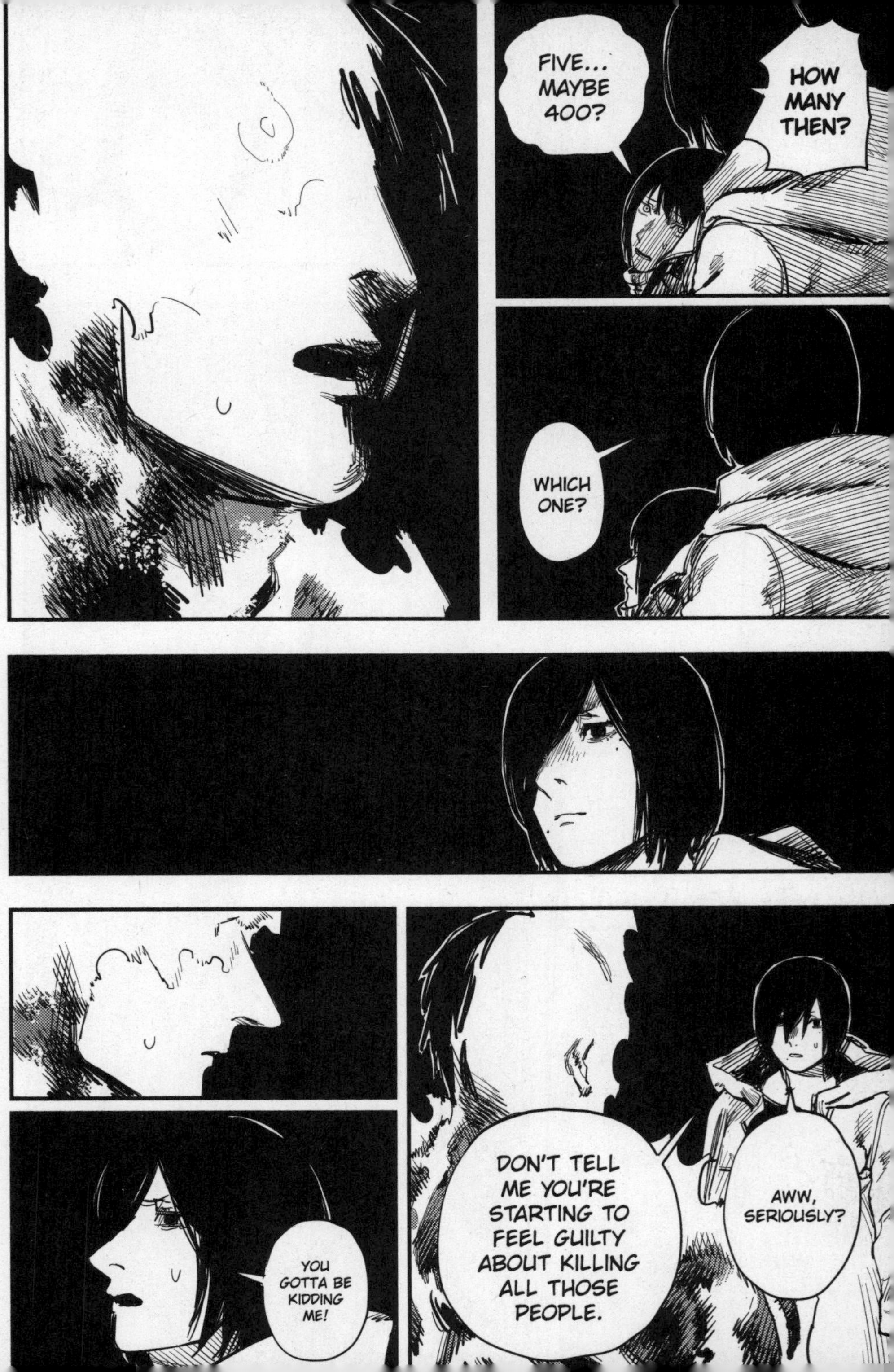
HOW MANY THEN?
FIVE... MAYBE 400?
WHICH ONE?
AWW, SERIOUSLY?
DON'T TELL ME YOU'RE STARTING TO FEEL GUILTY ABOUT KILLING ALL THOSE PEOPLE.
YOU GOTTA BE KIDDING ME!

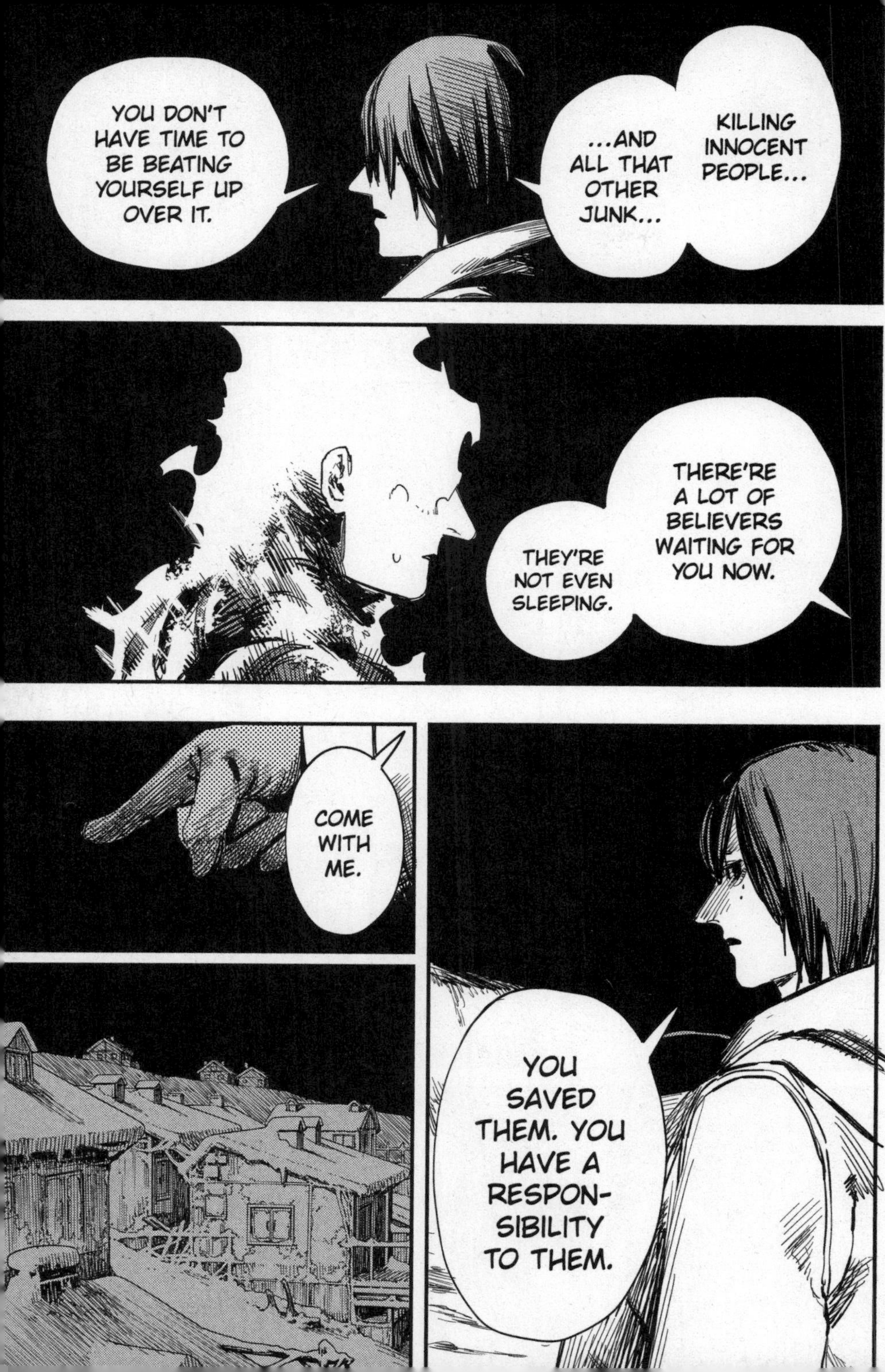
KILLING INNOCENT PEOPLE...
...AND ALL THAT OTHER JUNK...
YOU DON'T HAVE TIME TO BE BEATING YOURSELF UP OVER IT.
THERE'RE A LOT OF BELIEVERS WAITING FOR YOU NOW.
THEY'RE NOT EVEN SLEEPING.
YOU SAVED THEM. YOU HAVE A RESPON-SIBILITY TO THEM.
COME WITH ME.

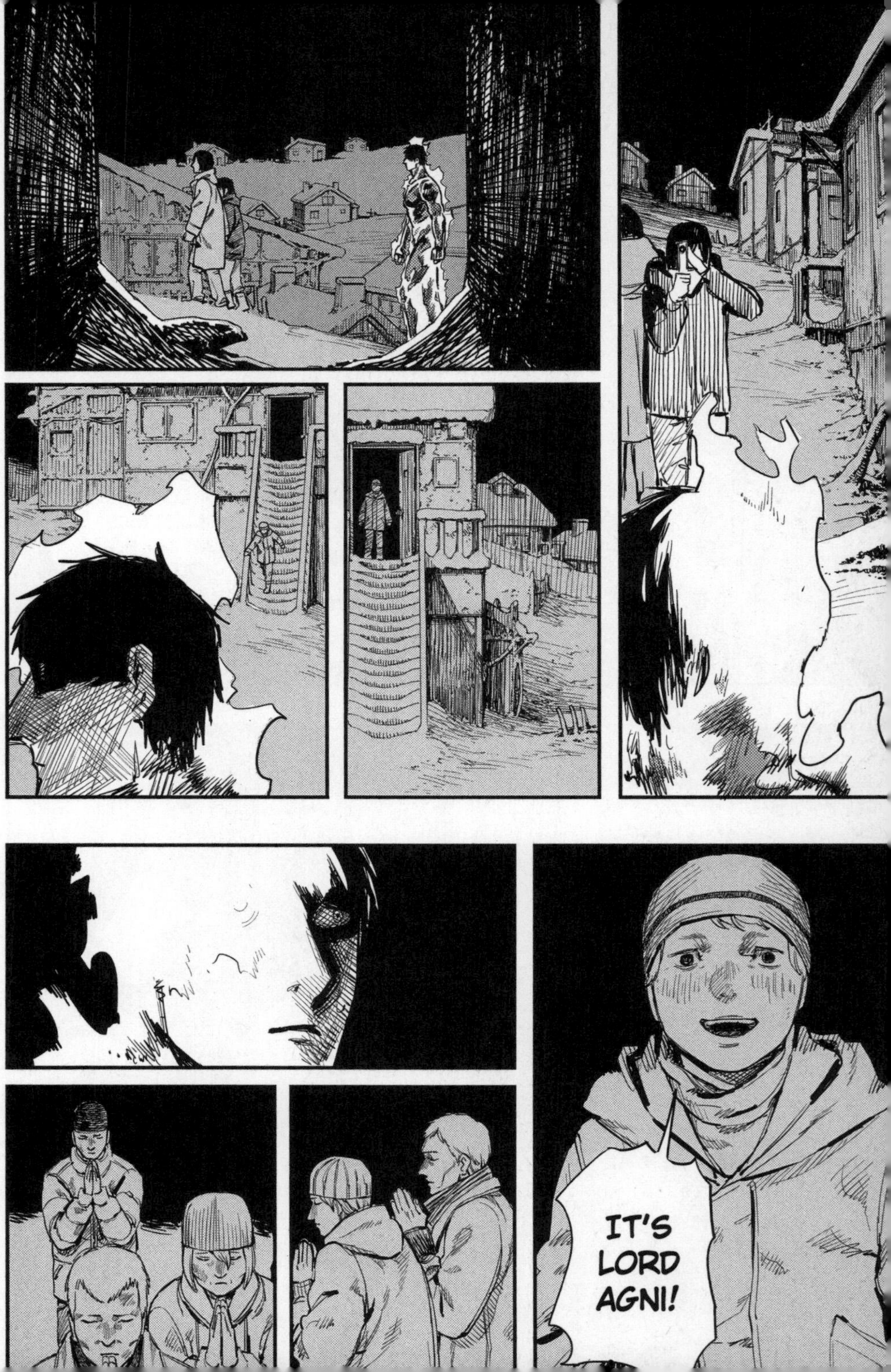
IT'S LORD AGNI!

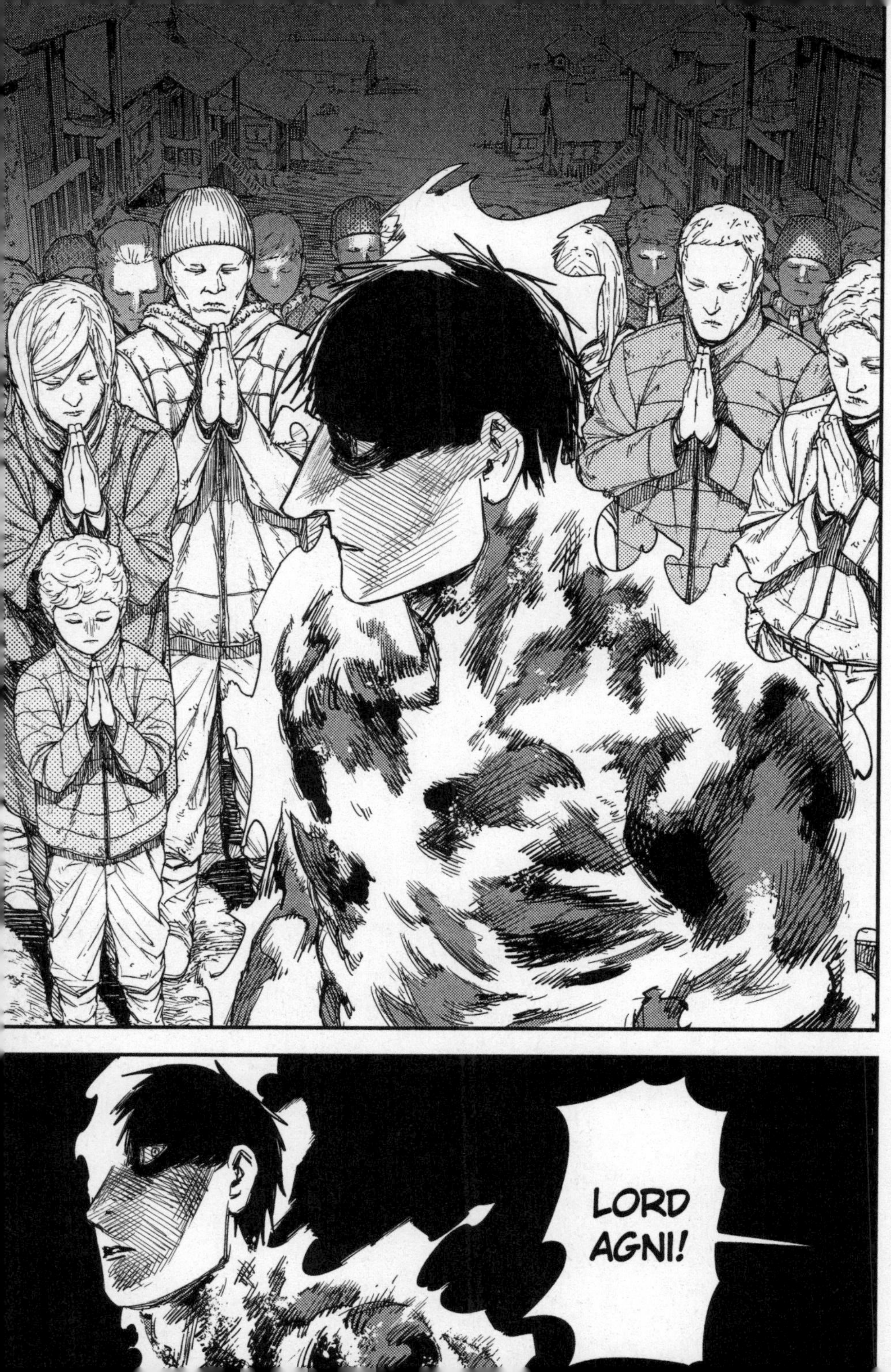
LORD
AGNI!

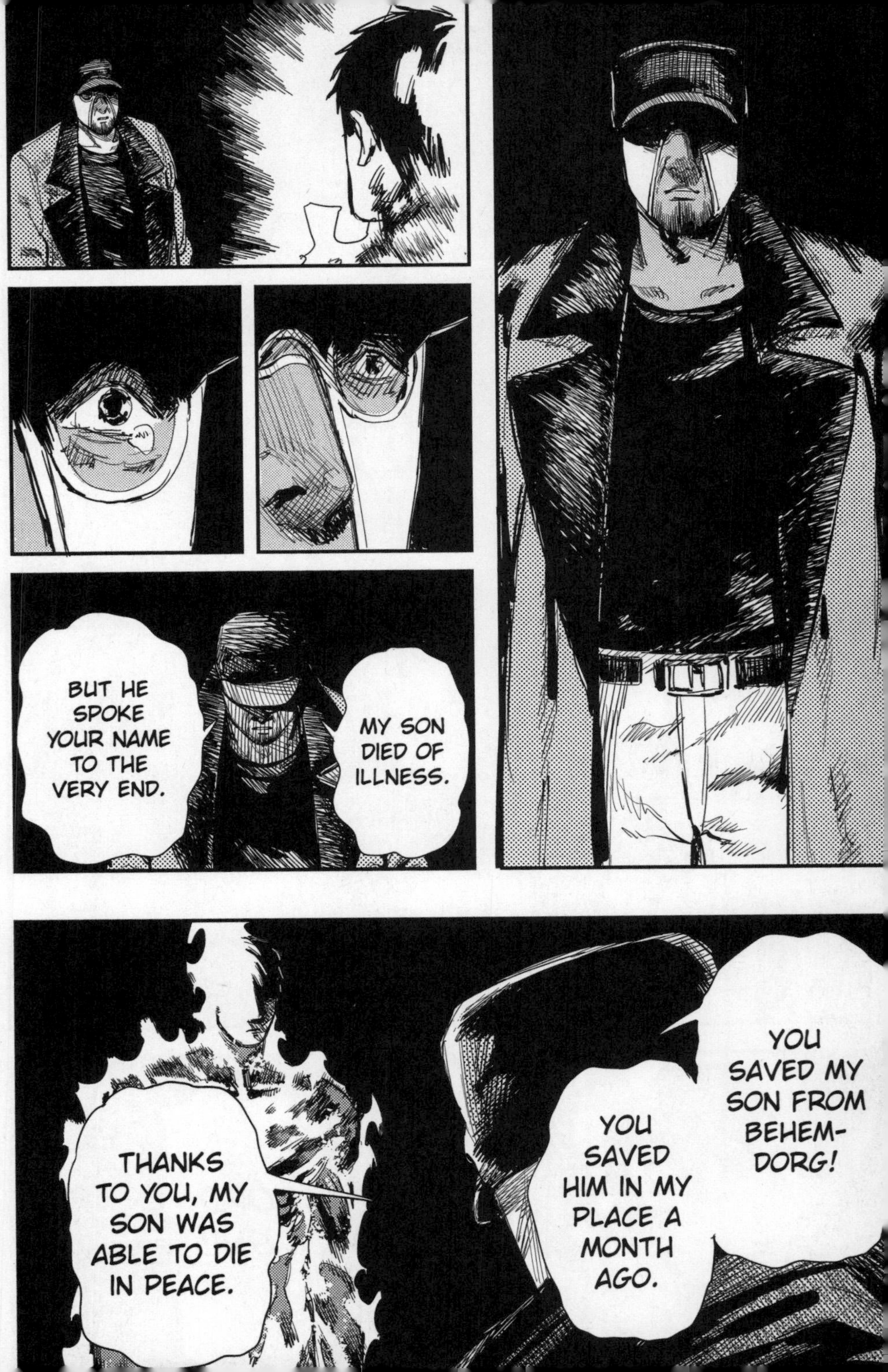
MY SON DIED OF ILLNESS.
BUT HE SPOKE YOUR NAME TO THE VERY END.
YOU SAVED MY SON FROM BEHEM-DORG!
YOU SAVED HIM IN MY PLACE A MONTH AGO.
THANKS TO YOU, MY SON WAS ABLE TO DIE IN PEACE.

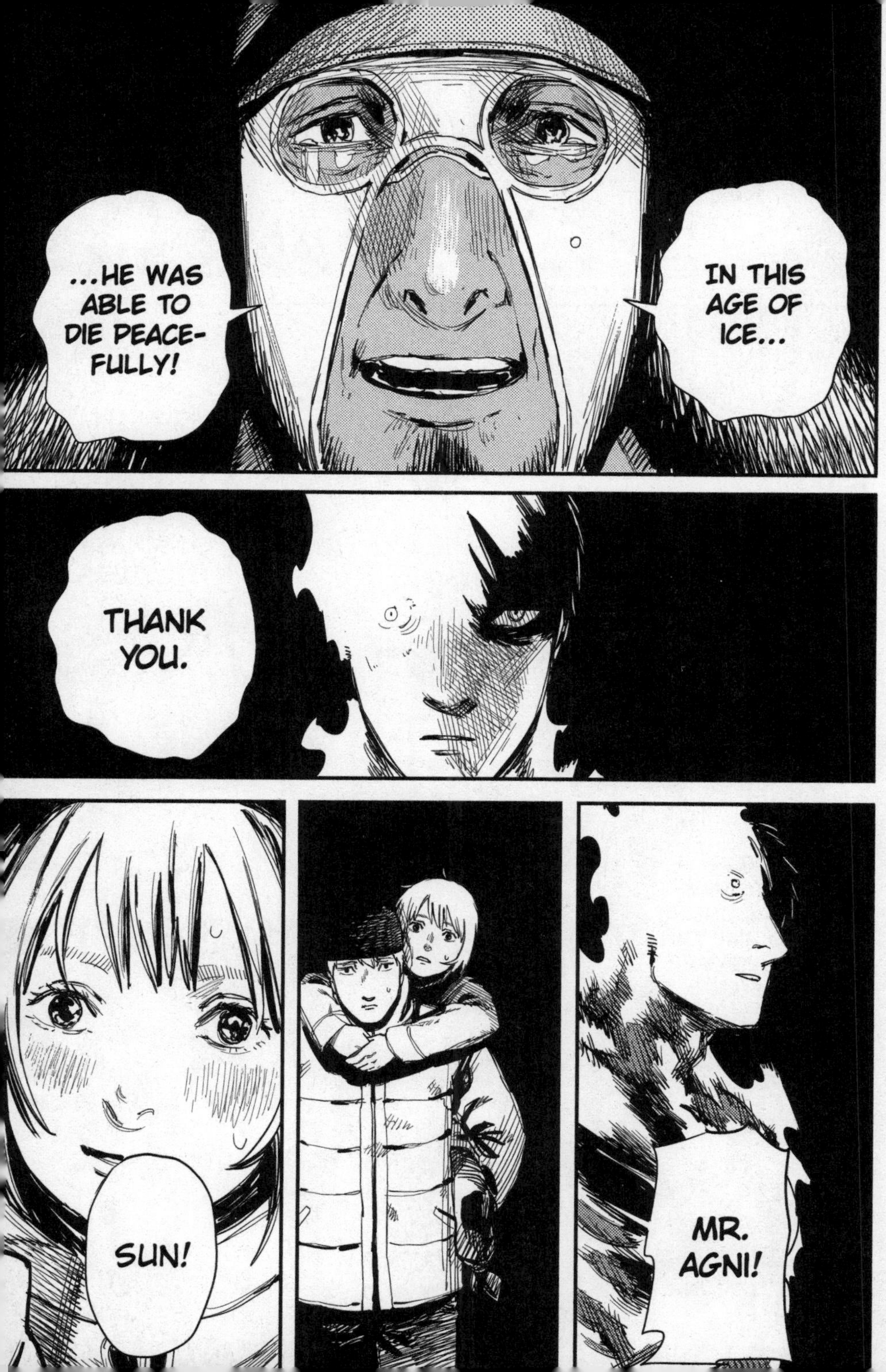
IN THIS AGE OF ICE...
...HE WAS ABLE TO DIE PEACEFULLY!
THANK YOU.
MR. AGNI!
SUN!

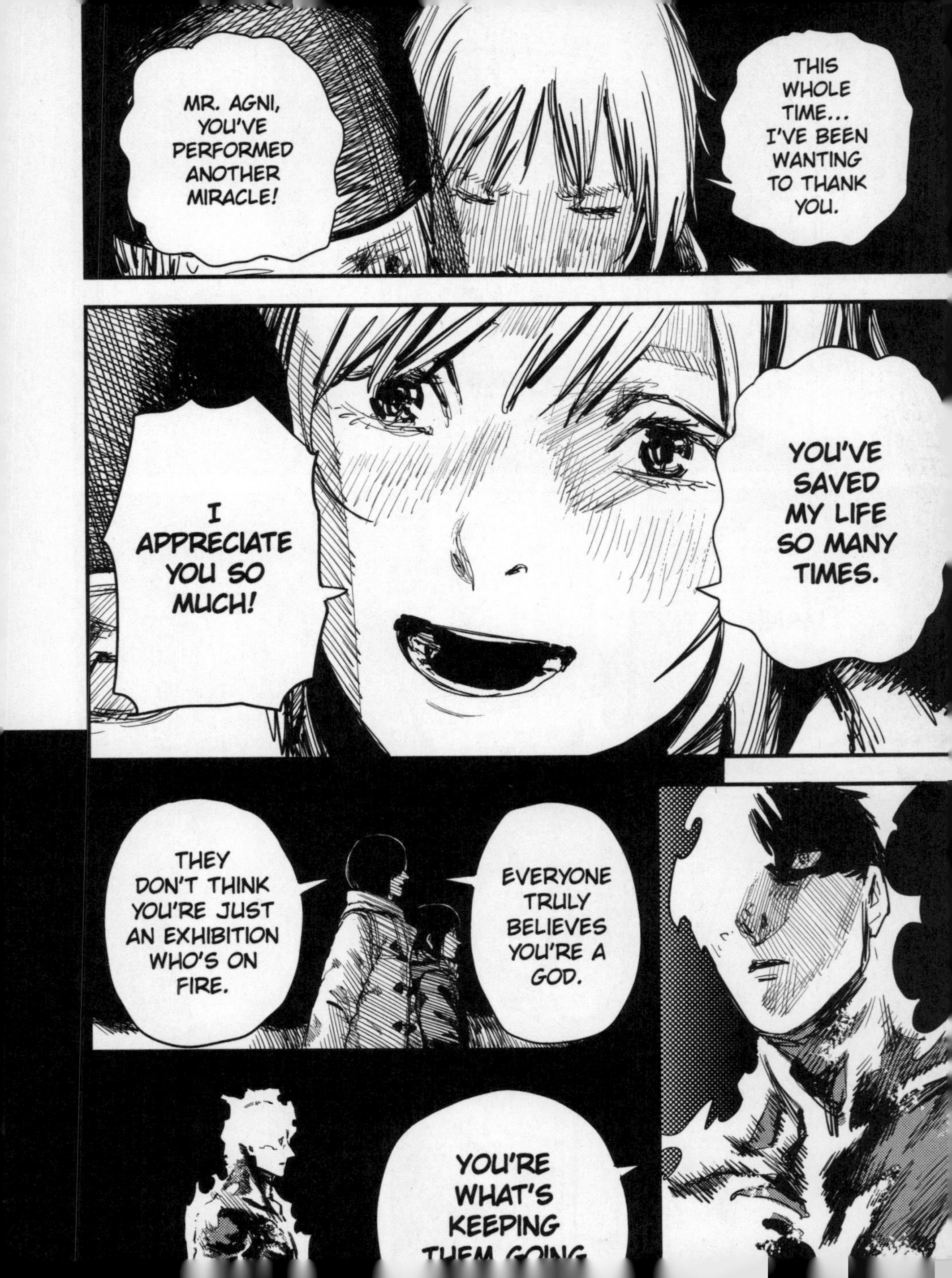
THIS WHOLE TIME... I'VE BEEN WANTING TO THANK YOU.
MR. AGNI, YOU'VE PERFORMED ANOTHER MIRACLE!
YOU'VE SAVED MY LIFE SO MANY TIMES.
I APPRECIATE YOU SO MUCH!
EVERYONE TRULY BELIEVES YOU'RE A GOD.
THEY DON'T THINK YOU'RE JUST AN EXHIBITION WHO'S ON FIRE.
YOU'RE WHAT'S KEEPING THEM GOING

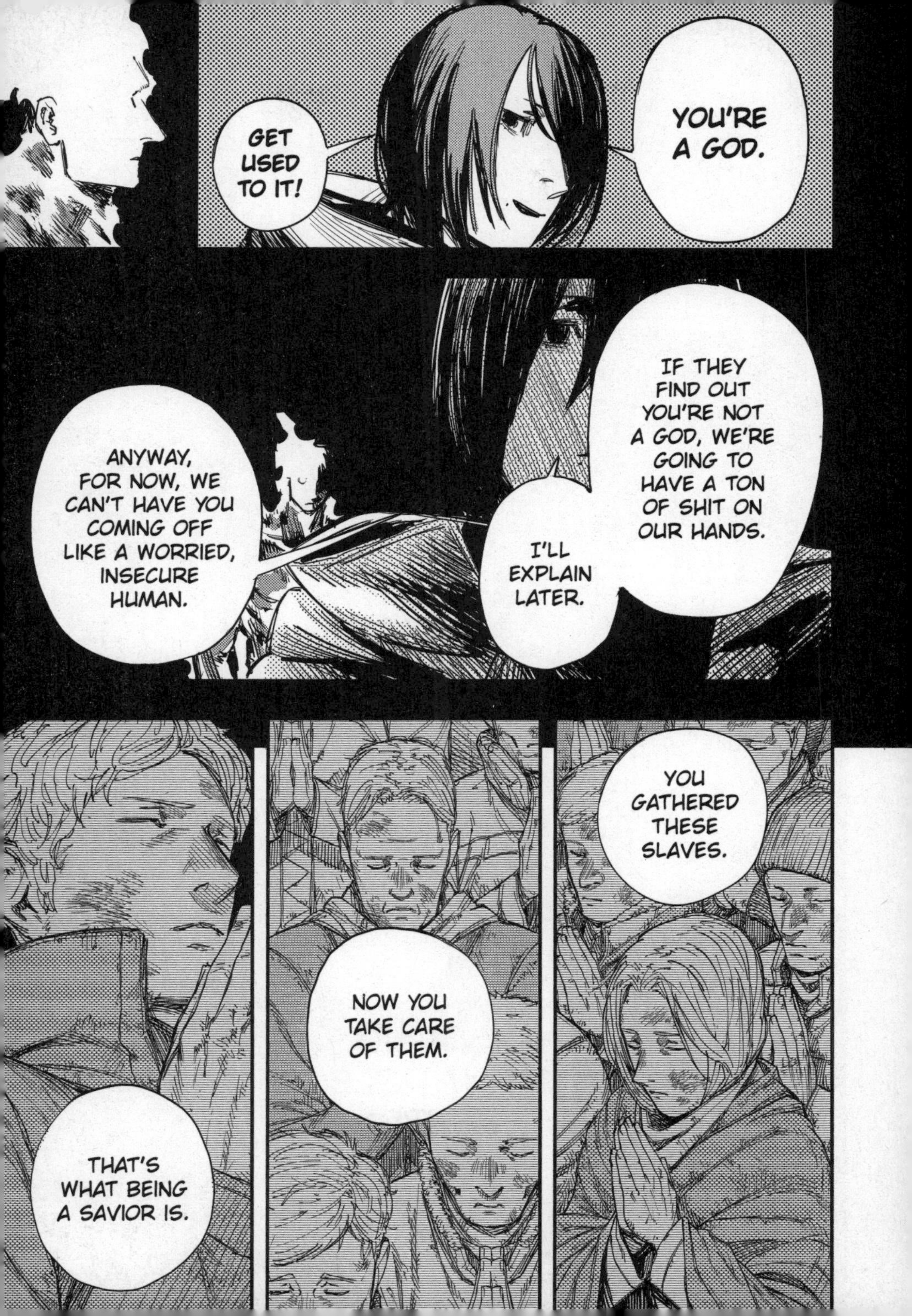
YOU'RE A GOD.
GET USED TO IT!
IF THEY FIND OUT YOU'RE NOT A GOD, WE'RE GOING TO HAVE A TON OF SHIT ON OUR HANDS.
I'LL EXPLAIN LATER.
ANYWAY, FOR NOW, WE CAN'T HAVE YOU COMING OFF LIKE A WORRIED, INSECURE HUMAN.
YOU GATHERED THESE SLAVES.
NOW YOU TAKE CARE OF THEM.
THAT'S WHAT BEING A SAVIOR IS.

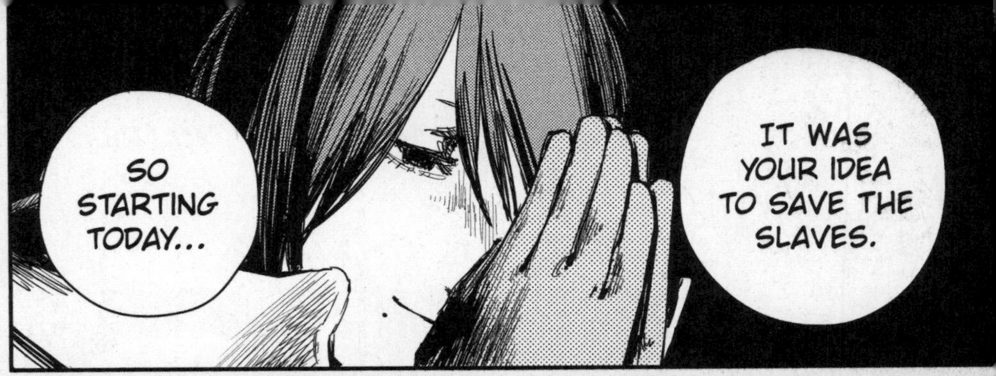
IT WAS YOUR IDEA TO SAVE THE SLAVES.
SO STARTING TODAY...
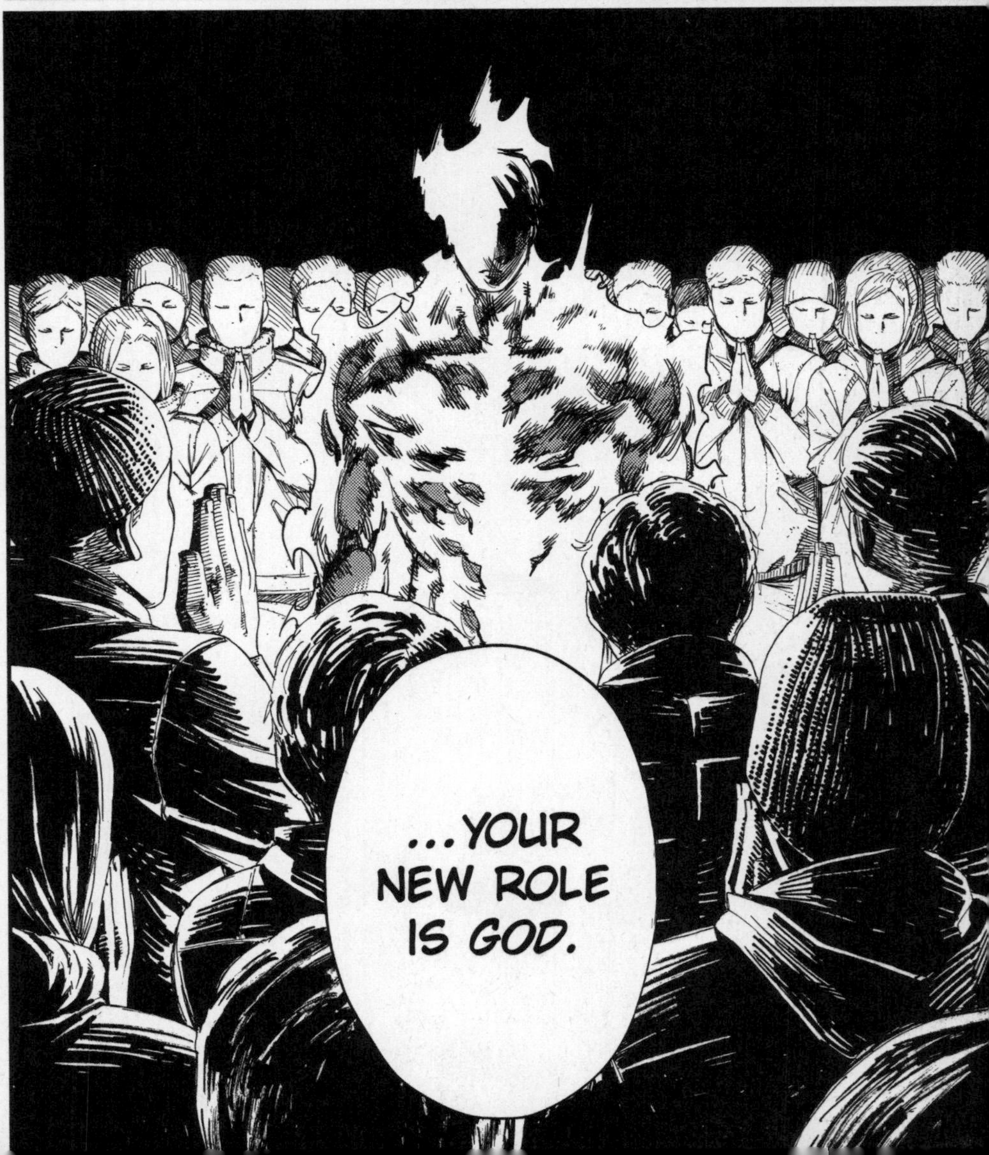
...YOUR NEW ROLE IS GOD.

FIRE PUNCH

CHAPTER 34

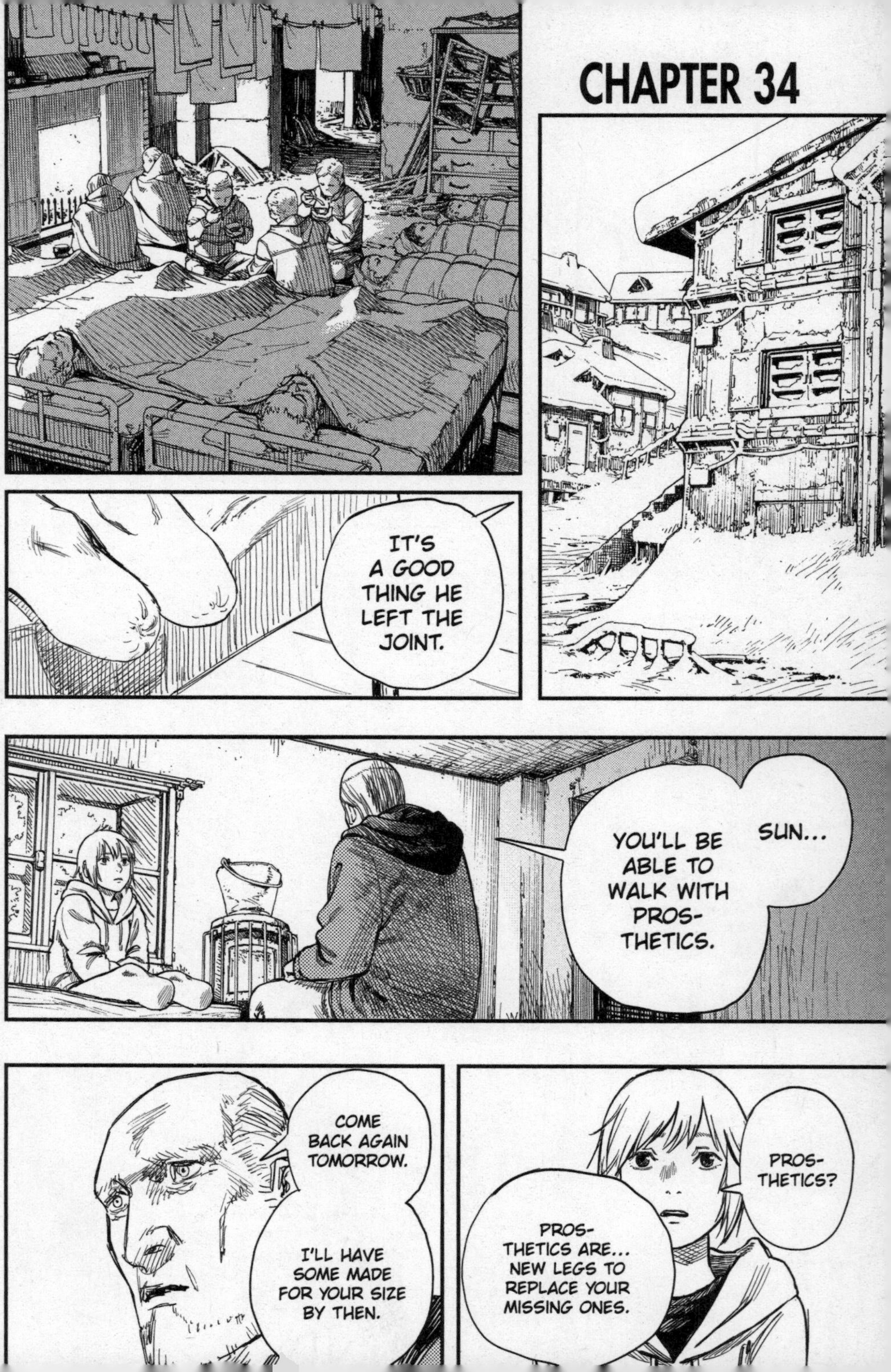
IT'S A GOOD THING HE LEFT THE JOINT.
SUN...
YOU'LL BE ABLE TO WALK WITH PROS-THETICS.
PROS-THETICS?
PROS-THETICS ARE... NEW LEGS TO REPLACE YOUR MISSING ONES.
COME BACK AGAIN TOMORROW.
I'LL HAVE SOME MADE FOR YOUR SIZE BY THEN.

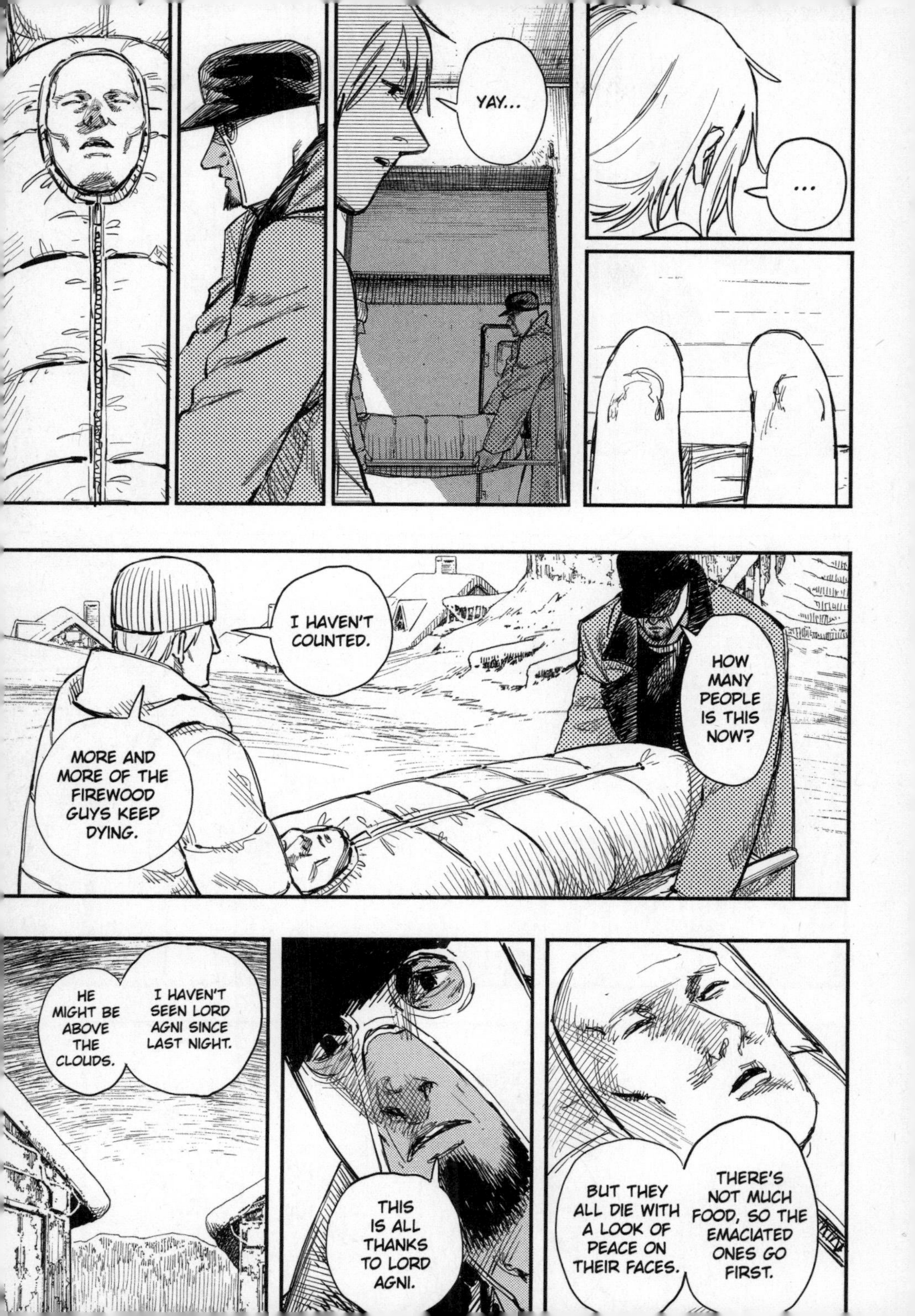
...
YAY...
HOW MANY PEOPLE IS THIS NOW?
I HAVEN'T COUNTED.
MORE AND MORE OF THE FIREWOOD GUYS KEEP DYING.
THERE'S NOT MUCH FOOD, SO THE EMACIATED ONES GO FIRST.
BUT THEY ALL DIE WITH A LOOK OF PEACE ON THEIR FACES.
THIS IS ALL THANKS TO LORD AGNI.
I HAVEN'T SEEN LORD AGNI SINCE LAST NIGHT.
HE MIGHT BE ABOVE THE CLOUDS.

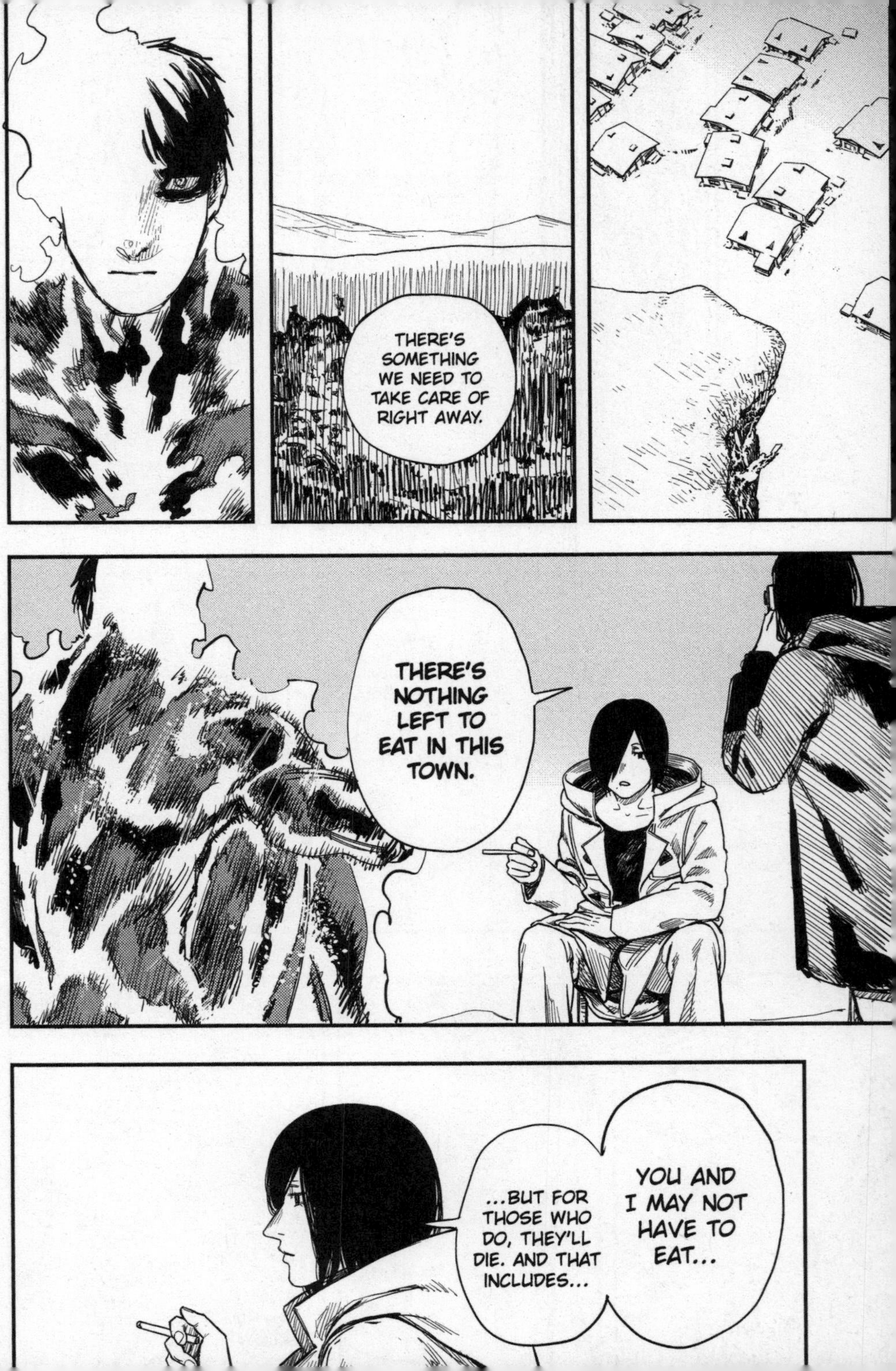
THERE'S SOMETHING WE NEED TO TAKE CARE OF RIGHT AWAY.
THERE'S NOTHING LEFT TO EAT IN THIS TOWN.
YOU AND I MAY NOT HAVE TO EAT...
...BUT FOR THOSE WHO DO, THEY'LL DIE. AND THAT INCLUDES...

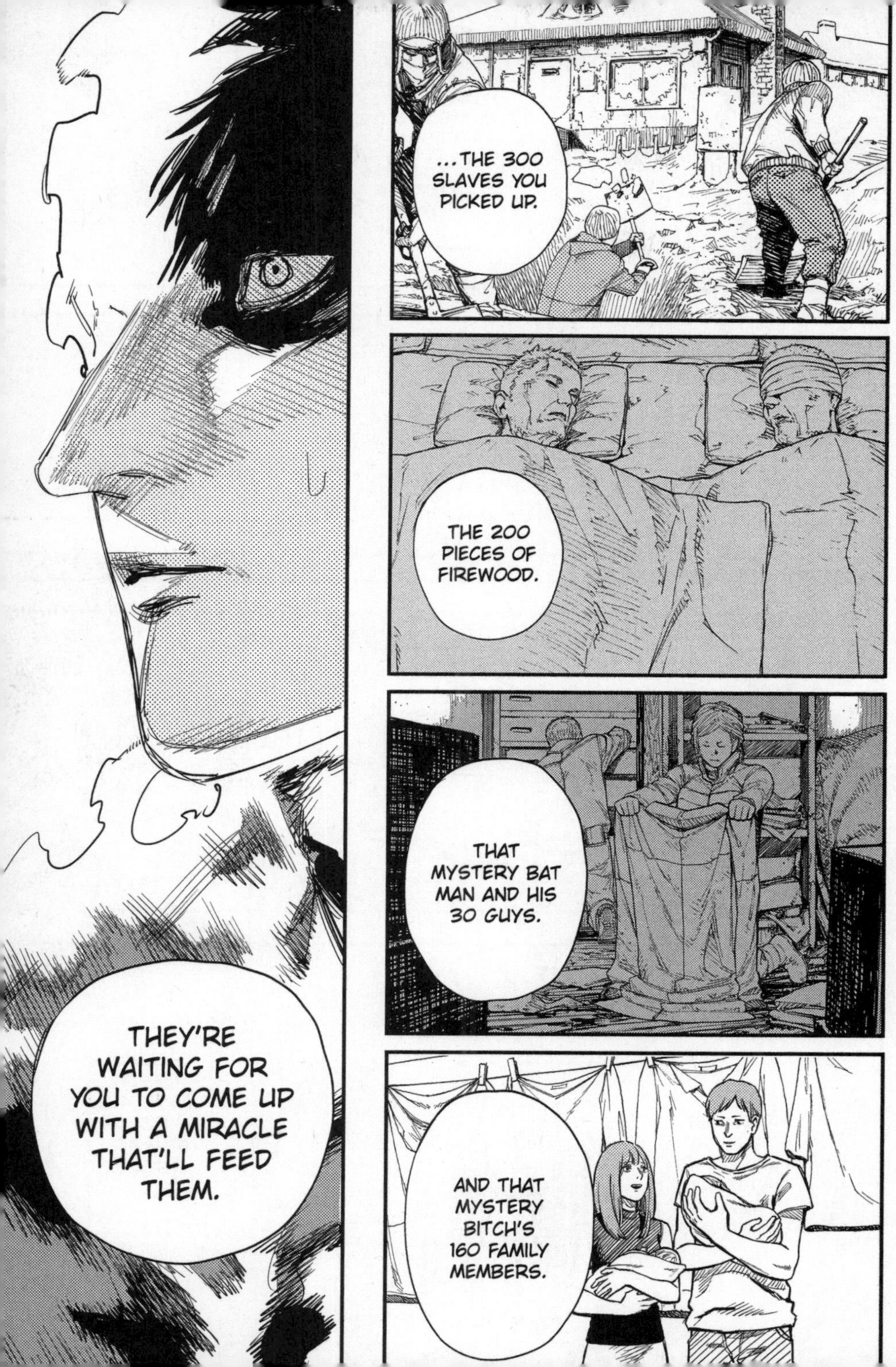
...THE 300 SLAVES YOU PICKED UP.
THE 200 PIECES OF FIREWOOD.
THAT MYSTERY BAT MAN AND HIS 30 GUYS.
AND THAT MYSTERY BITCH'S 160 FAMILY MEMBERS.
THEY'RE WAITING FOR YOU TO COME UP WITH A MIRACLE THAT'LL FEED THEM.

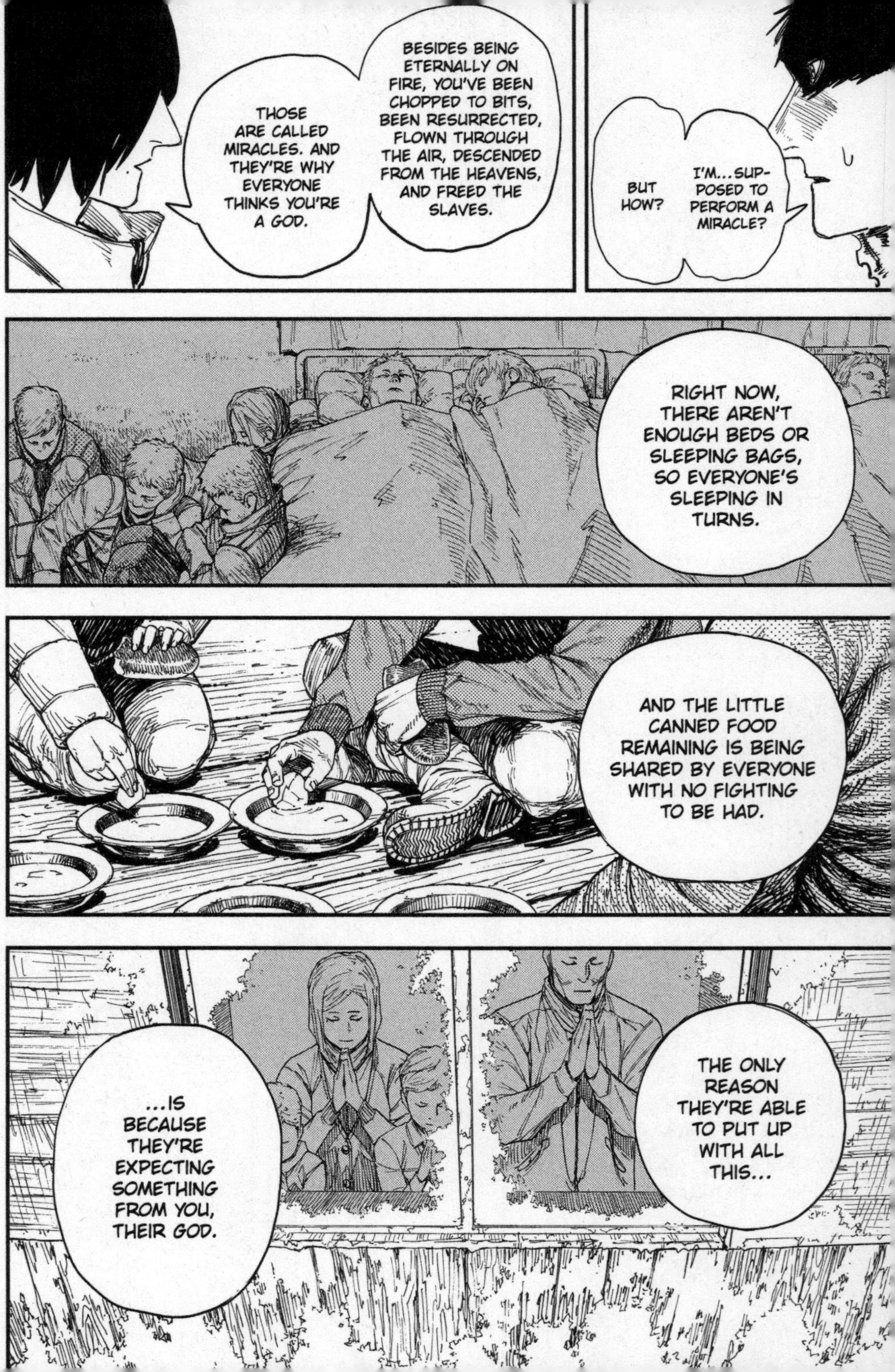
I'M...SUP-POSED TO PERFORM A MIRACLE?
BUT HOW?
BESIDES BEING ETERNALLY ON FIRE, YOU'VE BEEN CHOPPED TO BITS, BEEN RESURRECTED, FLOWN THROUGH THE AIR, DESCENDED FROM THE HEAVENS, AND FREED THE SLAVES.
THOSE ARE CALLED MIRACLES. AND THEY'RE WHY EVERYONE THINKS YOU'RE A GOD.
RIGHT NOW, THERE AREN'T ENOUGH BEDS OR SLEEPING BAGS, SO EVERYONE'S SLEEPING IN TURNS.
AND THE LITTLE CANNED FOOD REMAINING IS BEING SHARED BY EVERYONE WITH NO FIGHTING TO BE HAD.
THE ONLY REASON THEY'RE ABLE TO PUT UP WITH ALL THIS...
...IS BECAUSE THEY'RE EXPECTING SOMETHING FROM YOU, THEIR GOD.

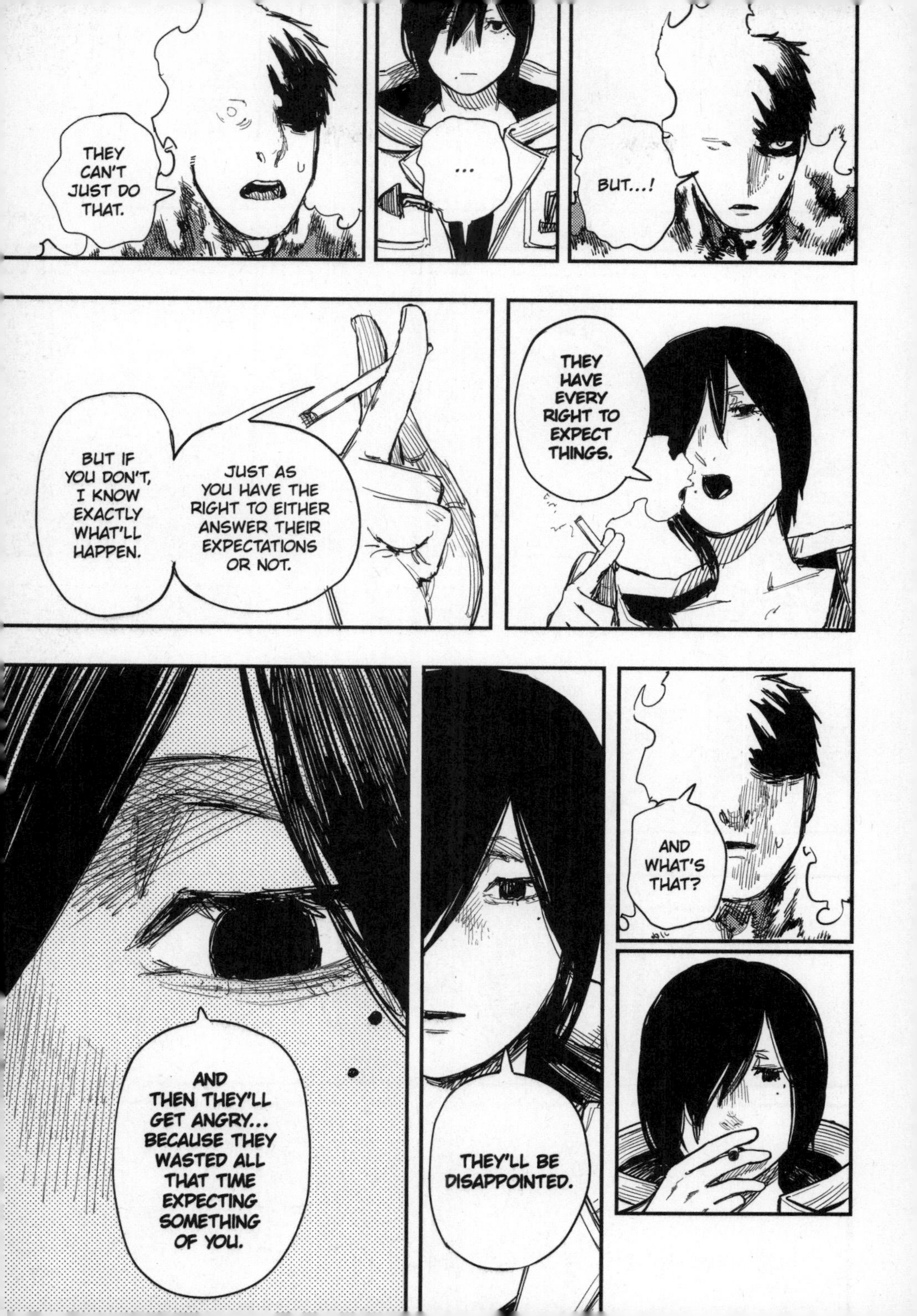
BUT...!
...
THEY CAN'T JUST DO THAT.
THEY HAVE EVERY RIGHT TO EXPECT THINGS.
JUST AS YOU HAVE THE RIGHT TO EITHER ANSWER THEIR EXPECTATIONS OR NOT.
BUT IF YOU DON'T, I KNOW EXACTLY WHAT'LL HAPPEN.
AND WHAT'S THAT?
THEY'LL BE DISAPPOINTED.
AND THEN THEY'LL GET ANGRY... BECAUSE THEY WASTED ALL THAT TIME EXPECTING SOMETHING OF YOU.

AND THEN THE SLAVES YOU TOOK IN...

...OR TURN ON YOU.

...WILL EITHER RUN AWAY...

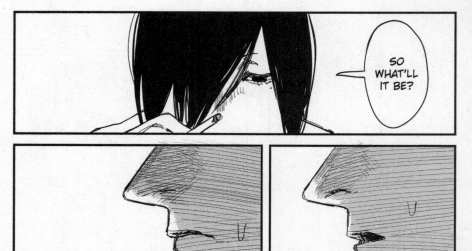

SO WHAT'LL IT BE?

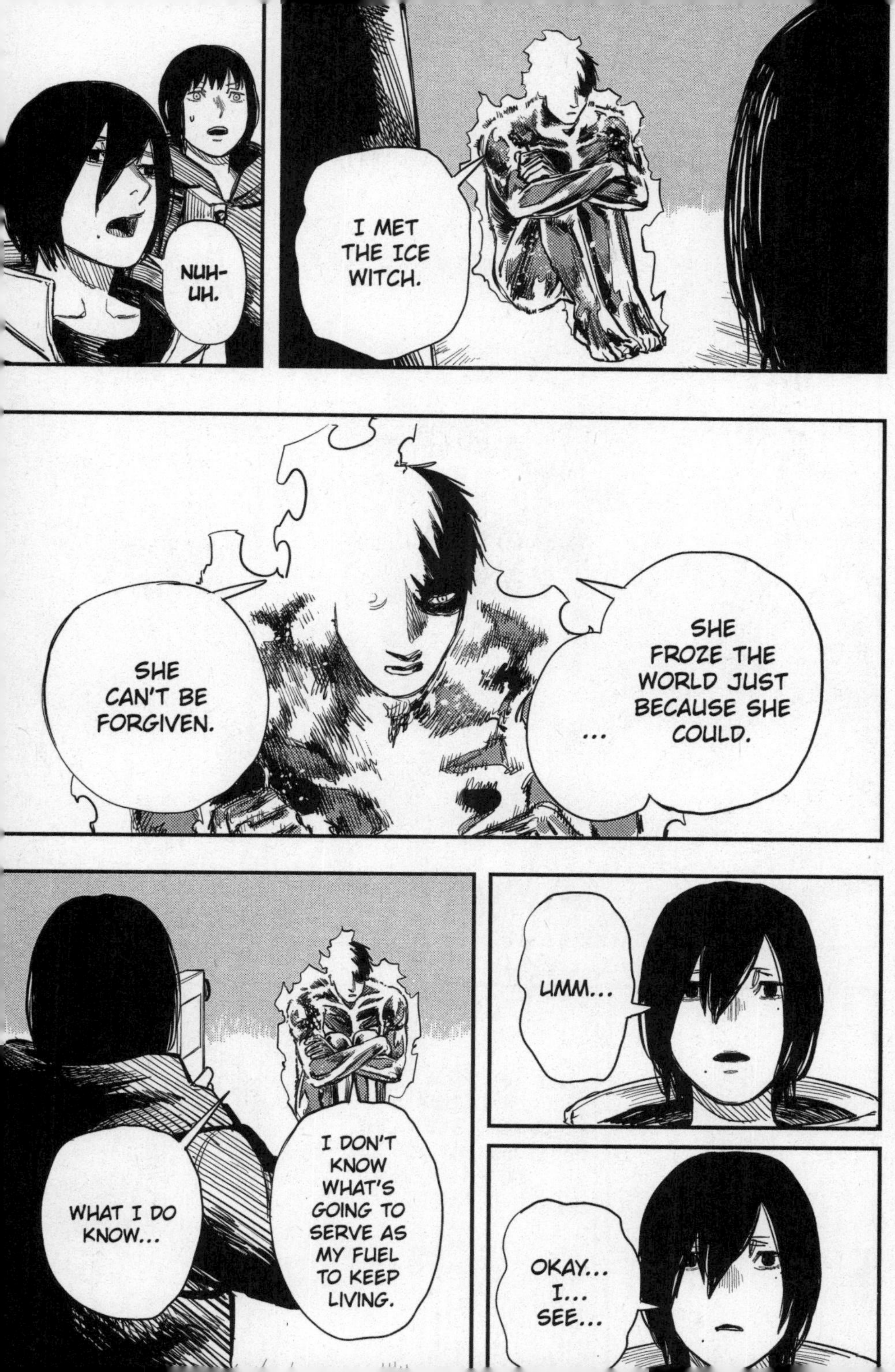
I MET THE ICE WITCH.
NUH-UH.
SHE FROZE THE WORLD JUST BECAUSE SHE COULD.
...
SHE CAN'T BE FORGIVEN.
UMM...
OKAY... I... SEE...
I DON'T KNOW WHAT'S GOING TO SERVE AS MY FUEL TO KEEP LIVING.
WHAT I DO KNOW...

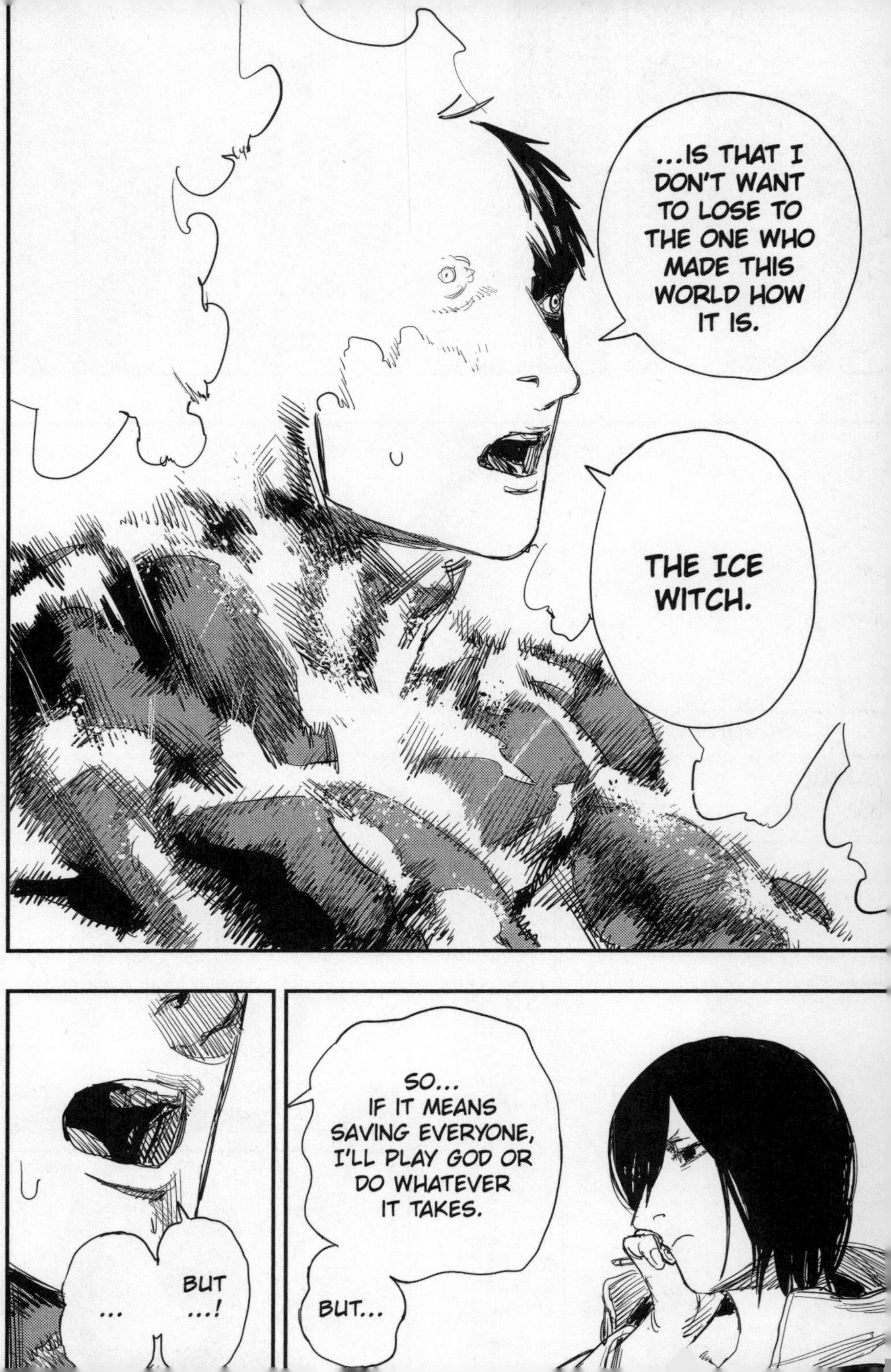
...IS THAT I DON'T WANT TO LOSE TO THE ONE WHO MADE THIS WORLD HOW IT IS.
THE ICE WITCH.
SO... IF IT MEANS SAVING EVERYONE, I'LL PLAY GOD OR DO WHATEVER IT TAKES.
BUT...
BUT ...!
...

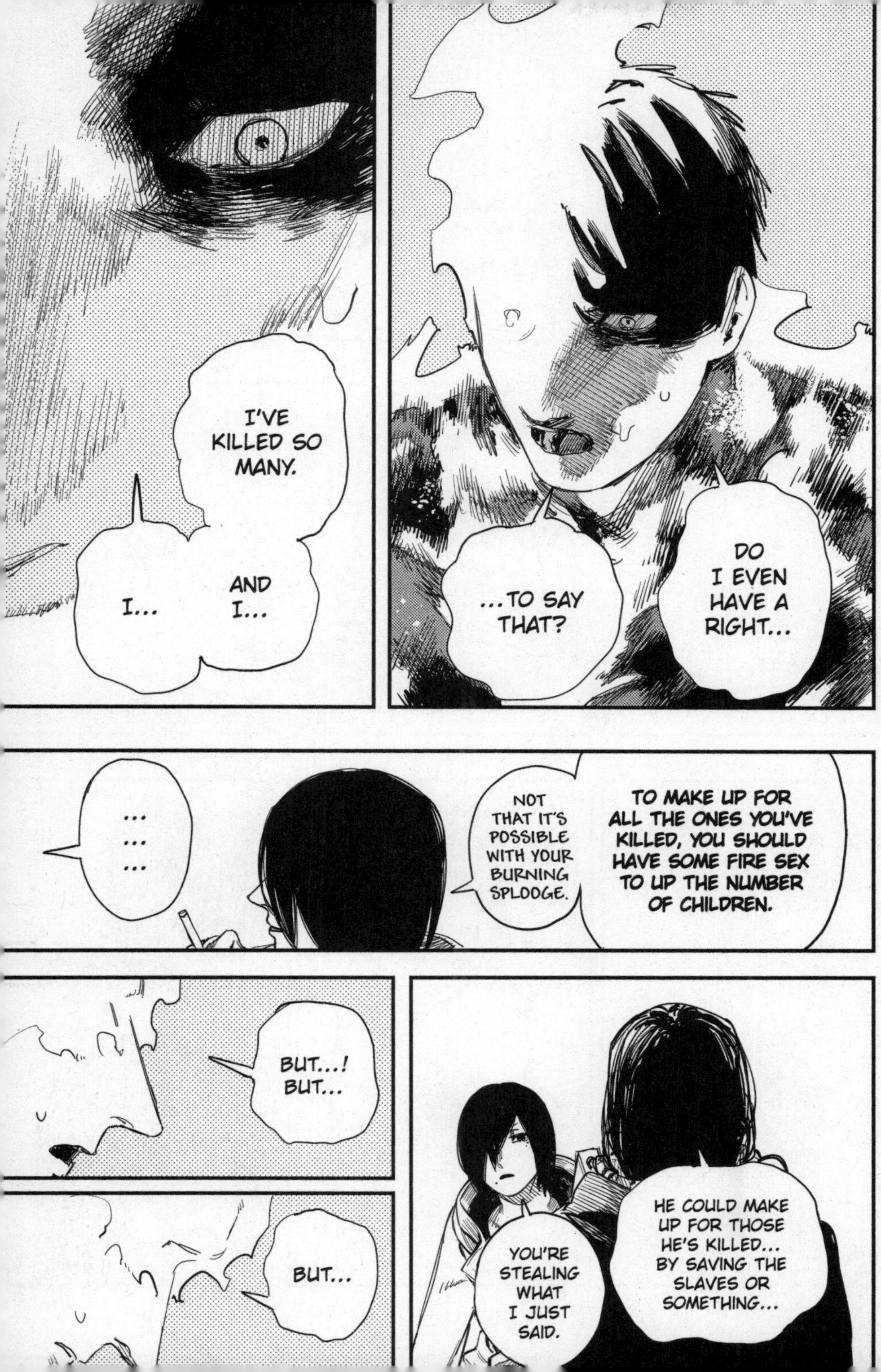
DO I EVEN HAVE A RIGHT...
...TO SAY THAT?
I'VE KILLED SO MANY.
AND I...
I...
TO MAKE UP FOR ALL THE ONES YOU'VE KILLED, YOU SHOULD HAVE SOME FIRE SEX TO UP THE NUMBER OF CHILDREN.
NOT THAT IT'S POSSIBLE WITH YOUR BURNING SPLOOGE.
... ...
HE COULD MAKE UP FOR THOSE HE'S KILLED... BY SAVING THE SLAVES OR SOMETHING...
YOU'RE STEALING WHAT I JUST SAID.
BUT...! BUT...
BUT...

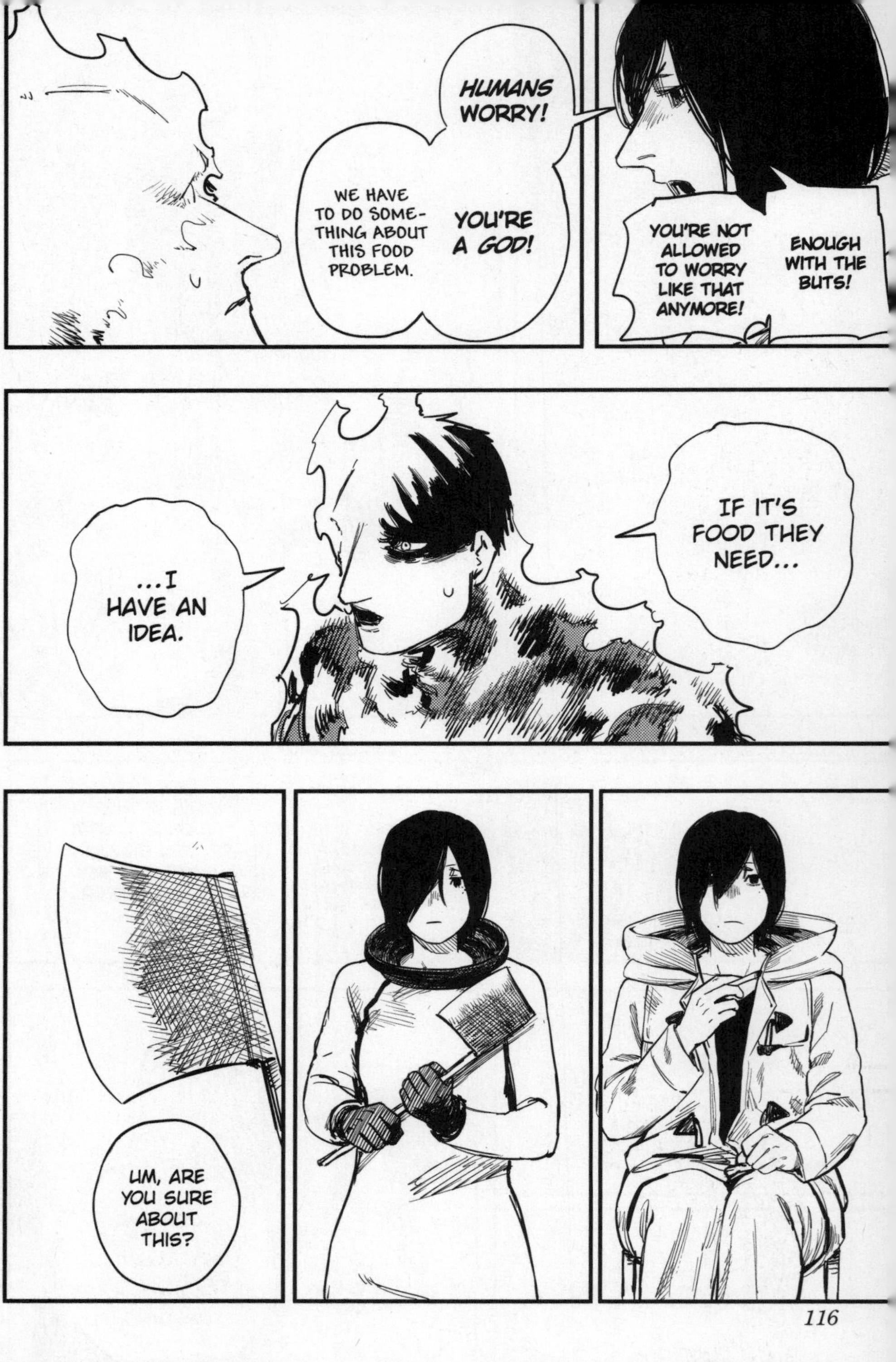
ENOUGH WITH THE BUTS!
YOU'RE NOT ALLOWED TO WORRY LIKE THAT ANYMORE!
HUMANS WORRY!
YOU'RE A GOD!
WE HAVE TO DO SOMETHING ABOUT THIS FOOD PROBLEM.
IF IT'S FOOD THEY NEED...
...I HAVE AN IDEA.
UM, ARE YOU SURE ABOUT THIS?

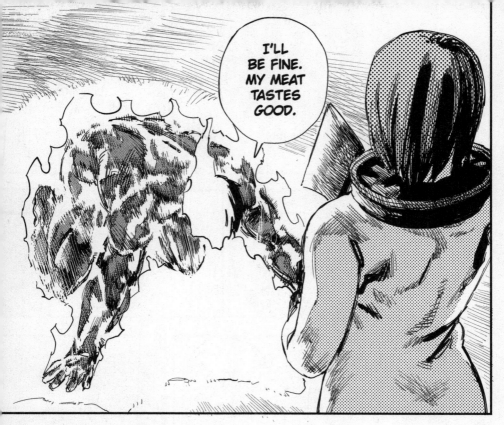

I'LL BE FINE. MY MEAT TASTES GOOD.

AND YOU SHOULD BE ABLE TO CUT IT OFF WITHOUT IT CATCHING FIRE.

BUT THE LEFT SIDE OF MY HEAD ISN'T BURNING, SO YOU CAN EAT IT.

MY BODY'S TOO BURNED TO EAT.

CUT OFF THE LEFT SIDE OF MY HEAD.

THERE'S PROBABLY NOT A LOT OF MEAT IN MY HEAD, SO WE'LL HAVE TO CUT OFF A LOT.

SORRY, TOGATA, BUT I NEED YOU TO DO THIS.

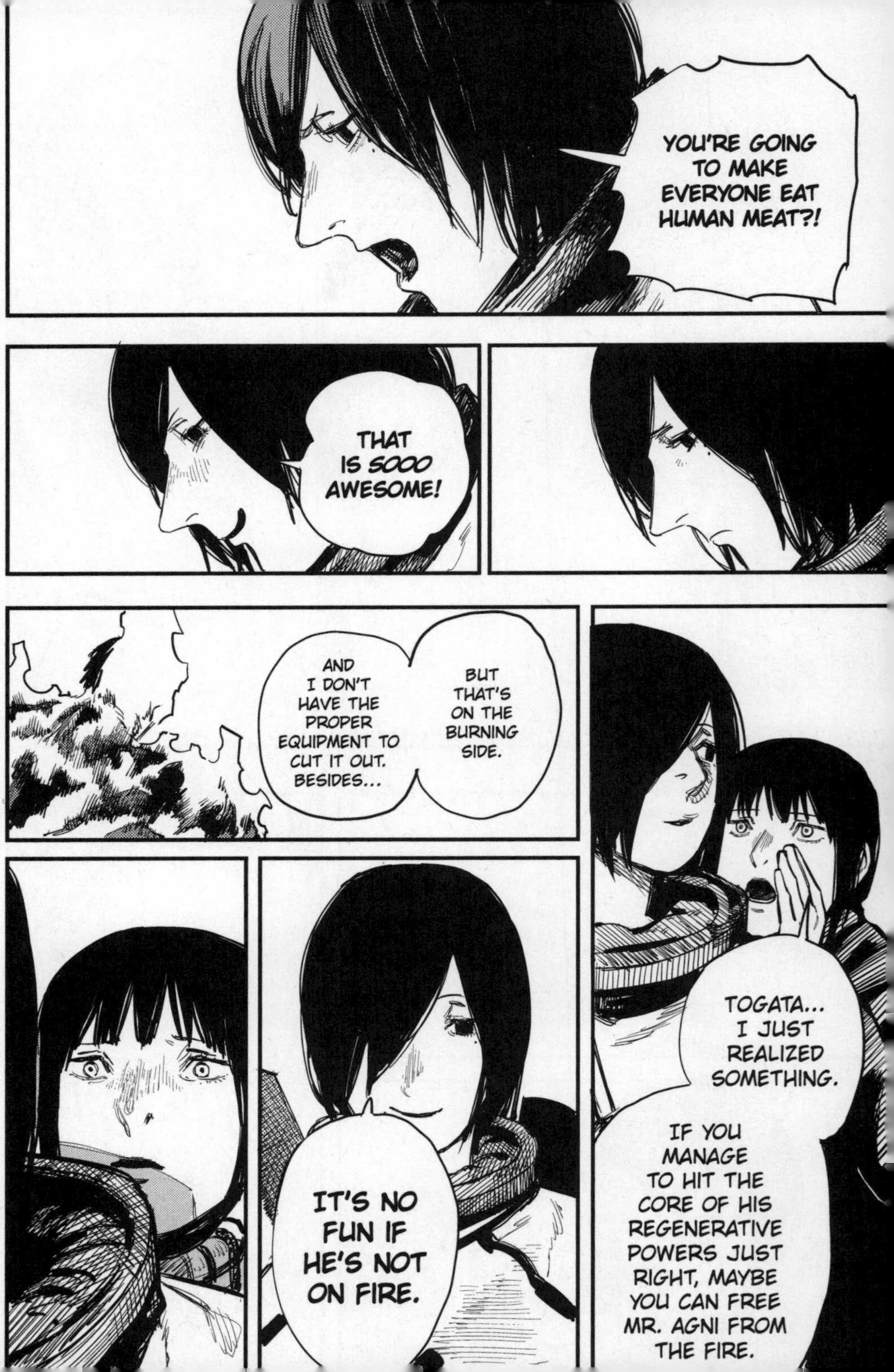
YOU'RE GOING TO MAKE EVERYONE EAT HUMAN MEAT?!
THAT IS SOOO AWESOME!
TOGATA... I JUST REALIZED SOMETHING.
IF YOU MANAGE TO HIT THE CORE OF HIS REGENERATIVE POWERS JUST RIGHT, MAYBE YOU CAN FREE MR. AGNI FROM THE FIRE.
BUT THAT'S ON THE BURNING SIDE.
AND I DON'T HAVE THE PROPER EQUIPMENT TO CUT IT OUT. BESIDES...
IT'S NO FUN IF HE'S NOT ON FIRE.

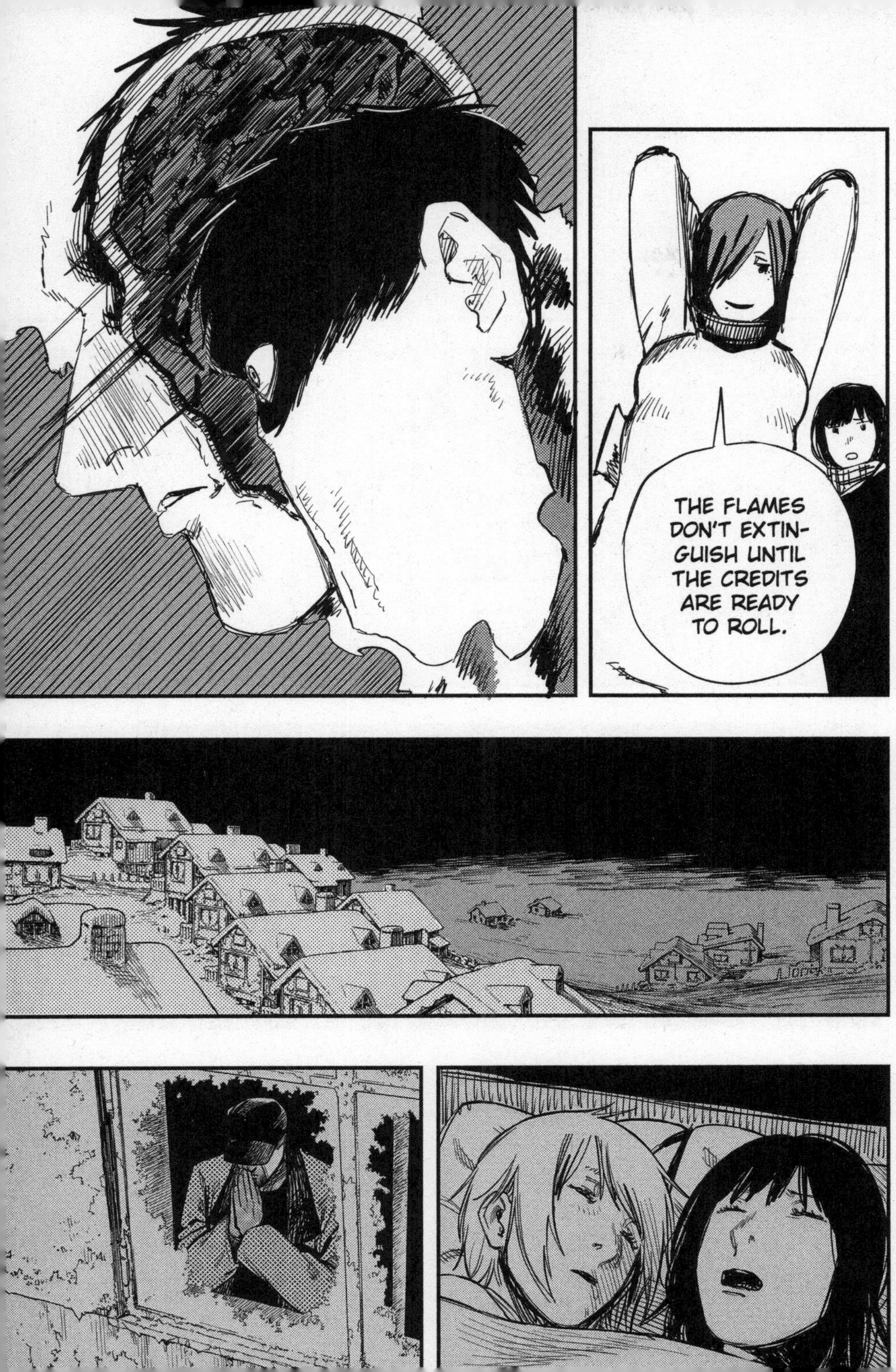
THE FLAMES DON'T EXTINGUISH UNTIL THE CREDITS ARE READY TO ROLL.

MAKE ANOTHER.

HEY, IT'S GONE BAD AGAIN.

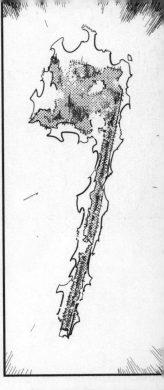

PLOK

SHWF

CAN'T YOU MAKE A COOLER ONE?

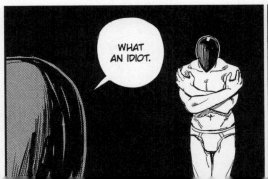

WHAT AN IDIOT.

AREN'T YOU COLD?

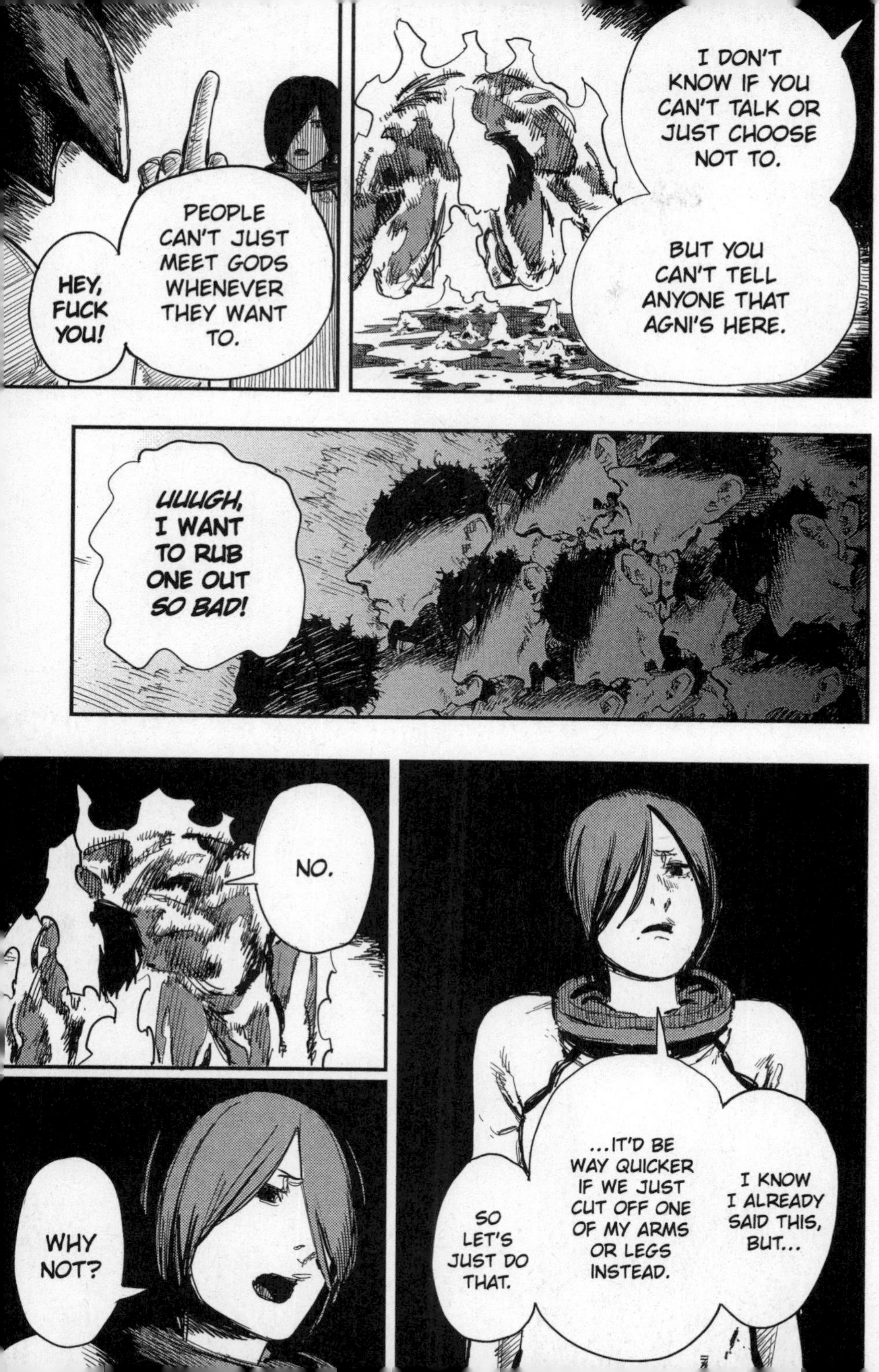
I DON'T KNOW IF YOU CAN'T TALK OR JUST CHOOSE NOT TO.
BUT YOU CAN'T TELL ANYONE THAT AGNI'S HERE.
PEOPLE CAN'T JUST MEET GODS WHENEVER THEY WANT TO.
HEY, FUCK YOU!
UUUGH, I WANT TO RUB ONE OUT SO BAD!
I KNOW I ALREADY SAID THIS, BUT...
...IT'D BE WAY QUICKER IF WE JUST CUT OFF ONE OF MY ARMS OR LEGS INSTEAD.
SO LET'S JUST DO THAT.
NO.
WHY NOT?

AWW.

... BEING PUT THROUGH PAIN LIKE THAT.

I CAN'T WATCH YOU...

SO CHIVAL-ROUS!

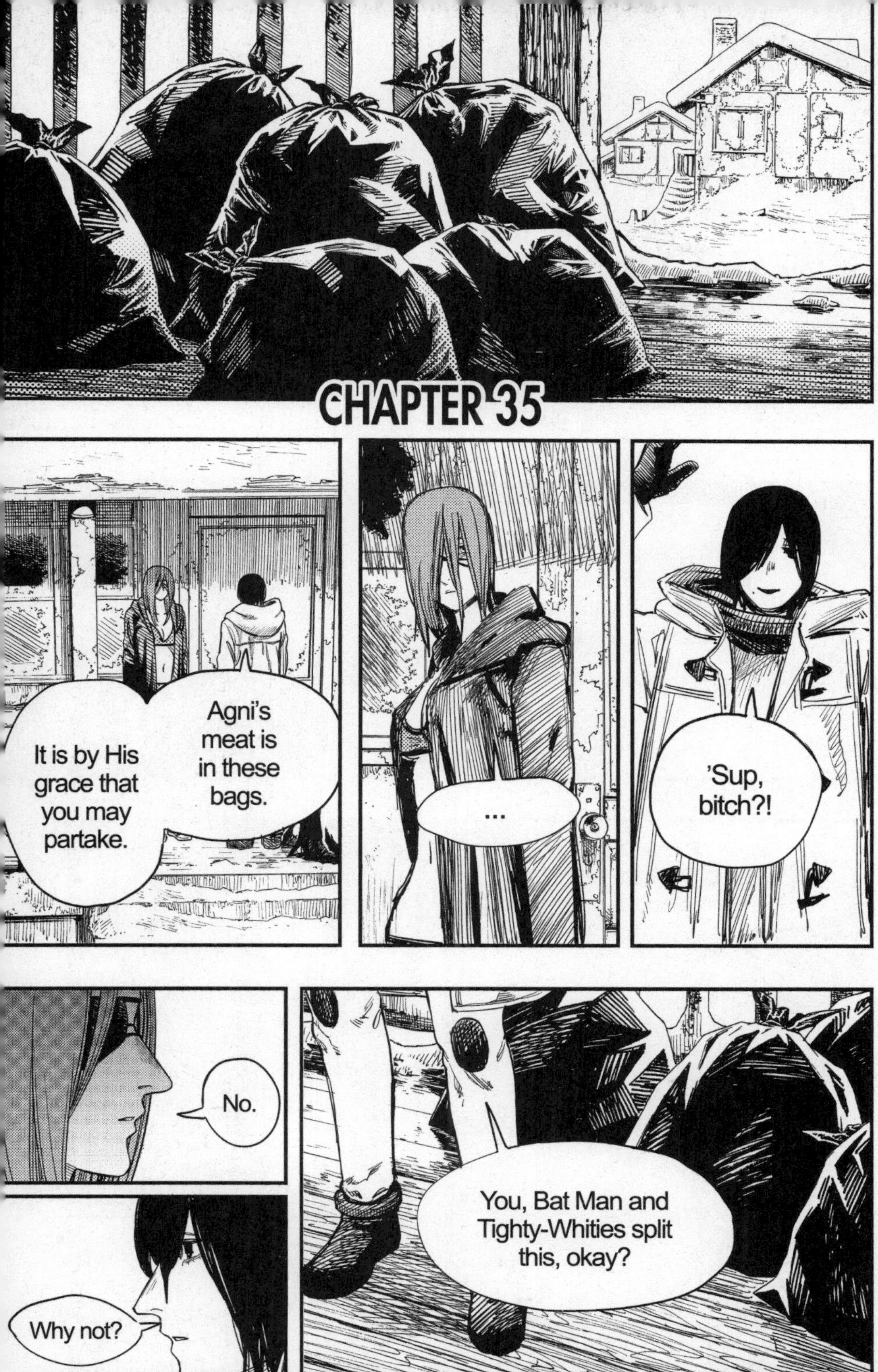
CHAPTER 35
'Sup, bitch?!
...
Agni's meat is in these bags.
It is by His grace that you may partake.
You, Bat Man and Tighty-Whities split this, okay?
No.
Why not?

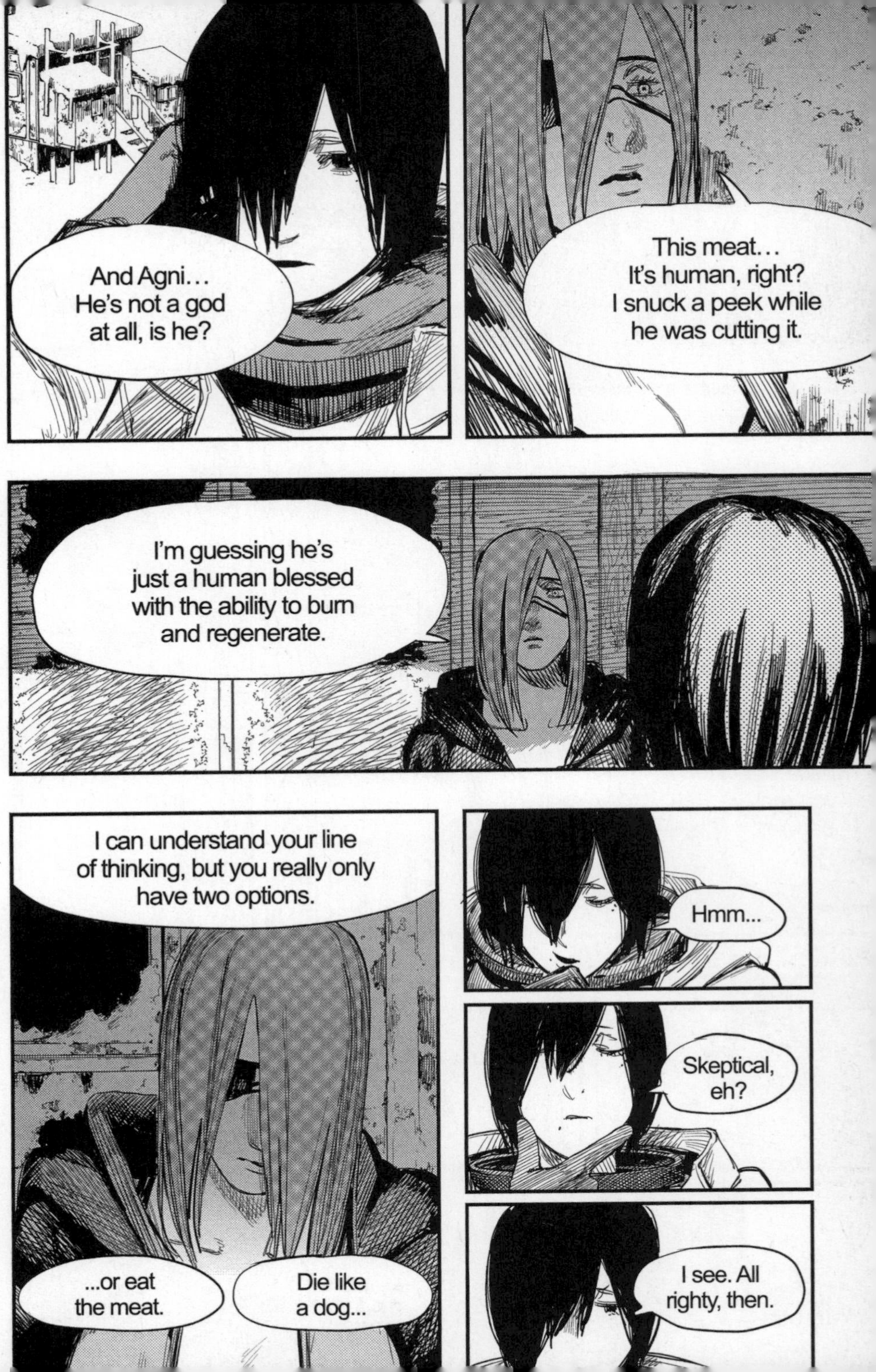
This meat… It's human, right? I snuck a peek while he was cutting it.
And Agni… He's not a god at all, is he?
I'm guessing he's just a human blessed with the ability to burn and regenerate.
Hmm...
Skeptical, eh?
I see. All righty, then.
I can understand your line of thinking, but you really only have two options.
Die like a dog...
...or eat the meat.

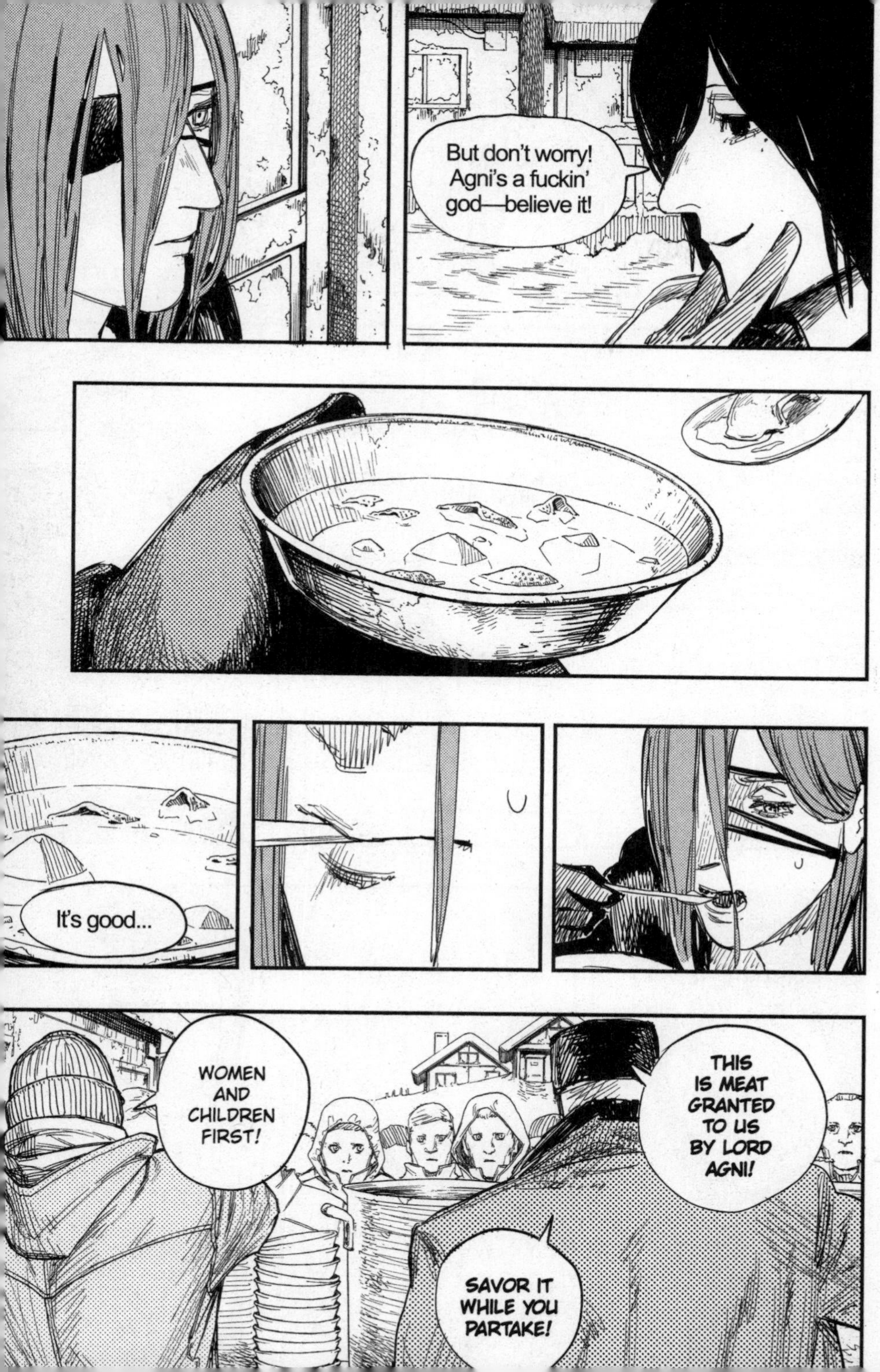
But don't worry! Agni's a fuckin' god—believe it!
It's good...
THIS IS MEAT GRANTED TO US BY LORD AGNI!
WOMEN AND CHILDREN FIRST!
SAVOR IT WHILE YOU PARTAKE!

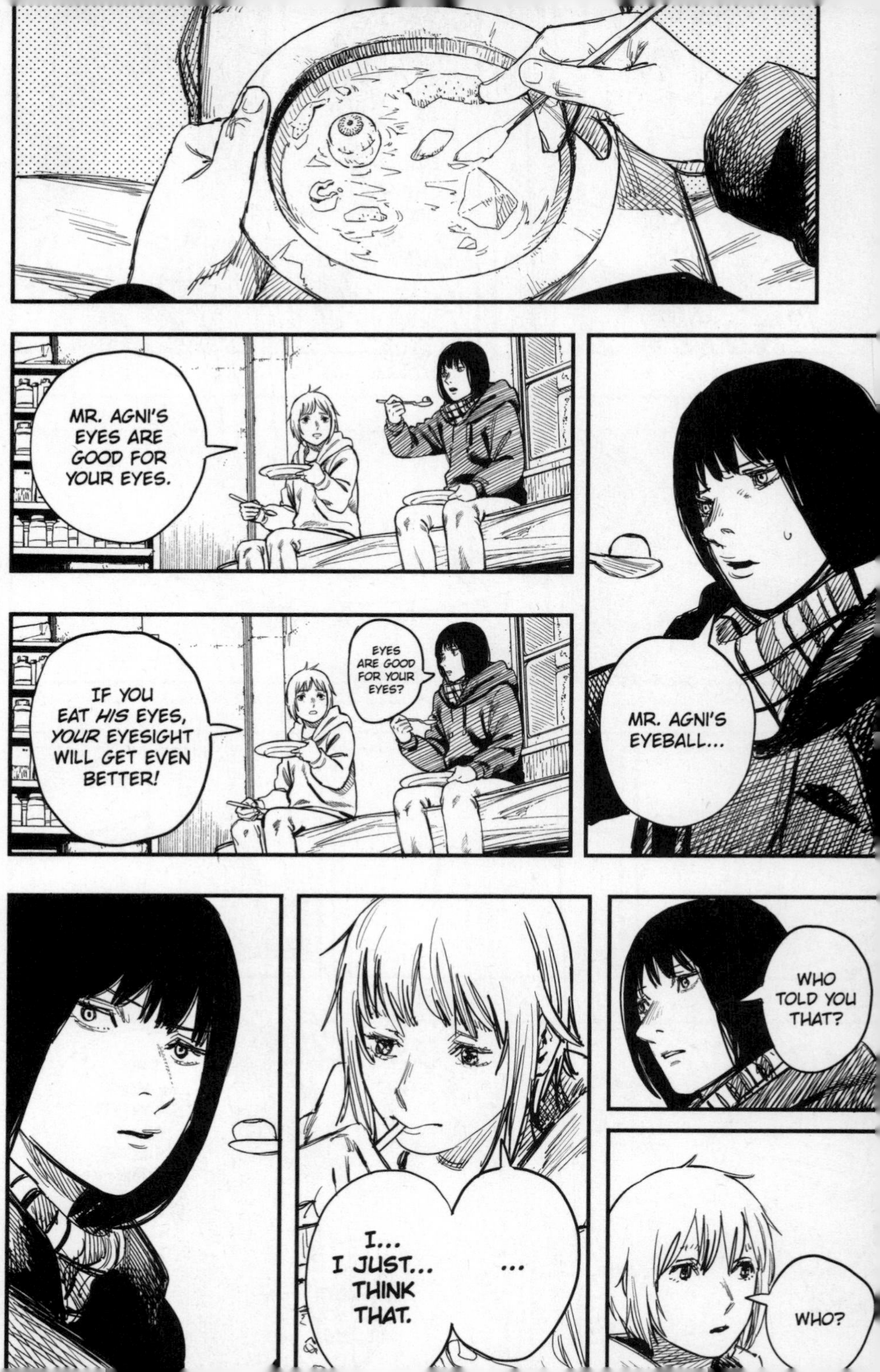
MR. AGNI'S EYEBALL...
MR. AGNI'S EYES ARE GOOD FOR YOUR EYES.
EYES ARE GOOD FOR YOUR EYES?
IF YOU EAT *HIS* EYES, *YOUR* EYESIGHT WILL GET EVEN BETTER!
WHO TOLD YOU THAT?
WHO?
...
I... I JUST... THINK THAT.

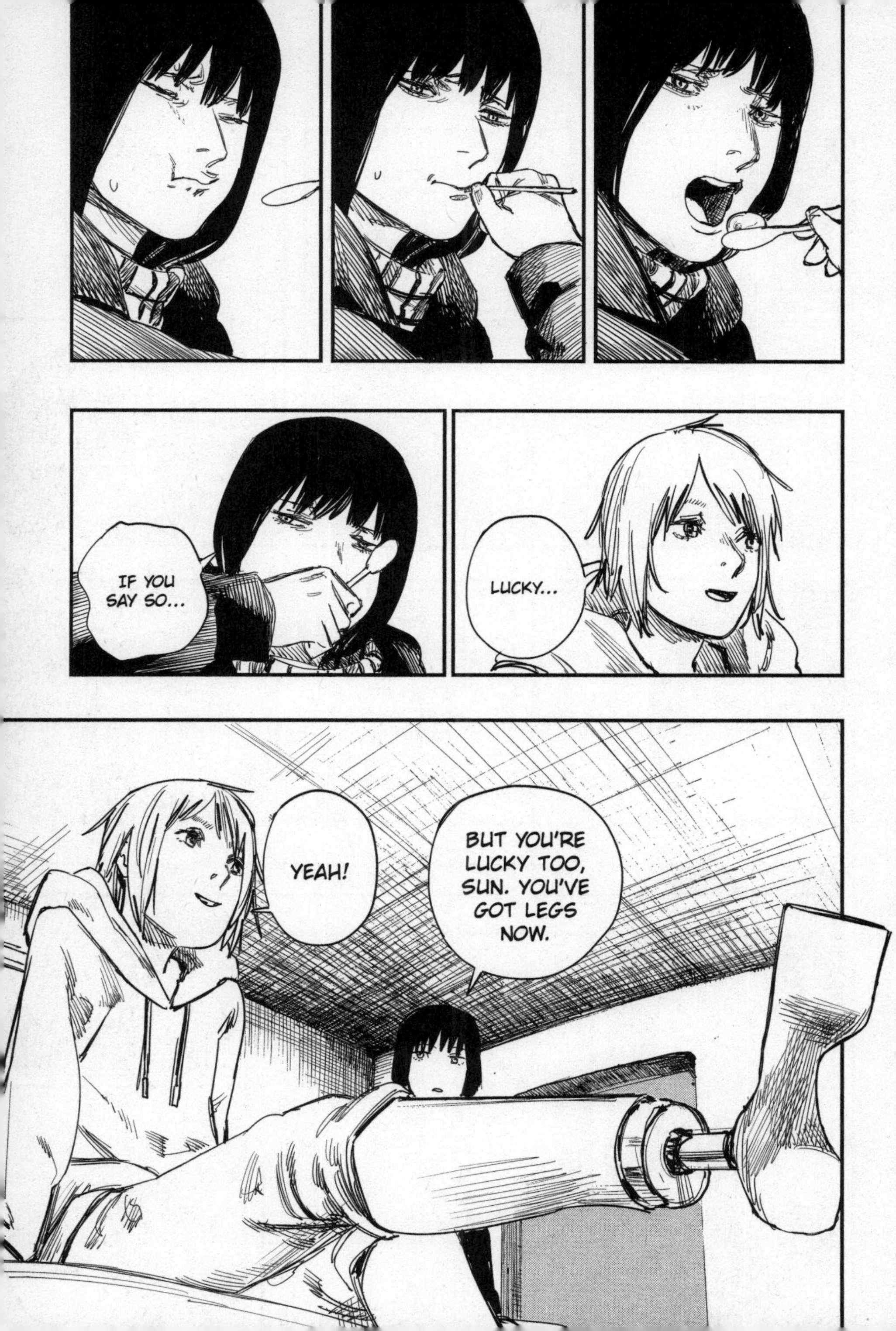
LUCKY...
IF YOU SAY SO...
BUT YOU'RE LUCKY TOO, SUN. YOU'VE GOT LEGS NOW.
YEAH!

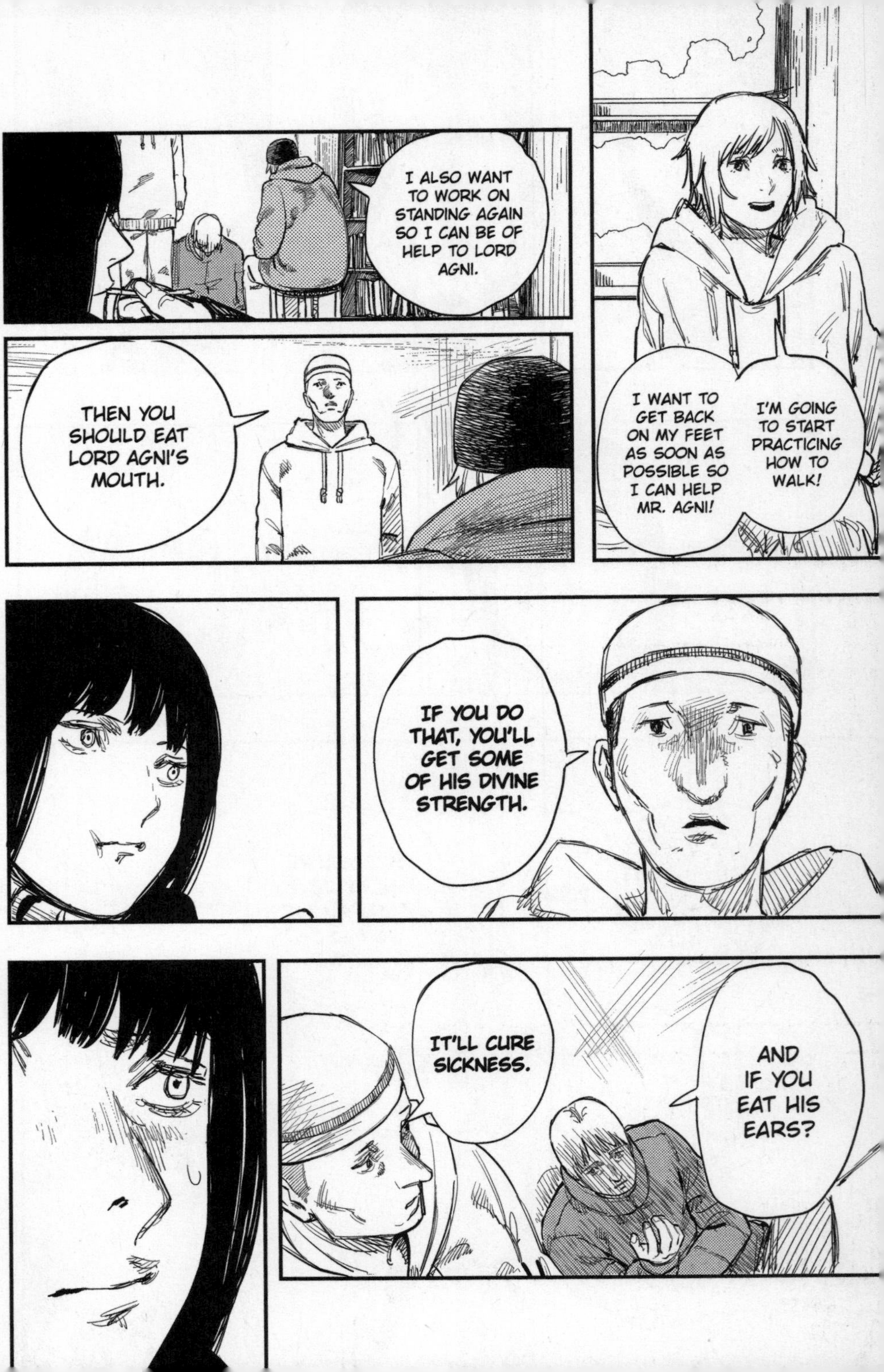
I'M GOING TO START PRACTICING HOW TO WALK!
I WANT TO GET BACK ON MY FEET AS SOON AS POSSIBLE SO I CAN HELP MR. AGNI!
I ALSO WANT TO WORK ON STANDING AGAIN SO I CAN BE OF HELP TO LORD AGNI.
THEN YOU SHOULD EAT LORD AGNI'S MOUTH.
IF YOU DO THAT, YOU'LL GET SOME OF HIS DIVINE STRENGTH.
AND IF YOU EAT HIS EARS?
IT'LL CURE SICKNESS.

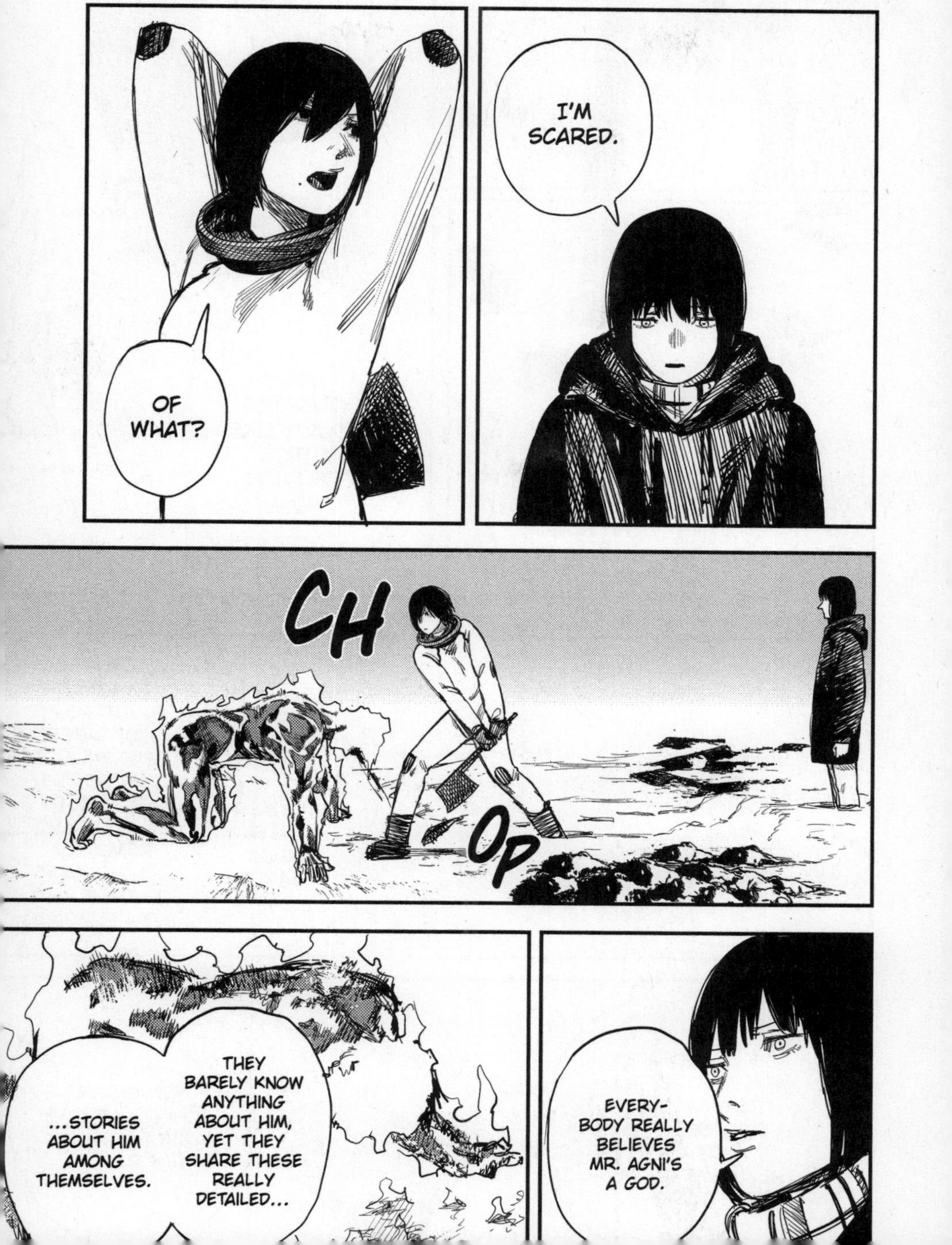
I'M SCARED.
OF WHAT?
CHOP
EVERY-BODY REALLY BELIEVES MR. AGNI'S A GOD.
THEY BARELY KNOW ANYTHING ABOUT HIM, YET THEY SHARE THESE REALLY DETAILED...
...STORIES ABOUT HIM AMONG THEMSELVES.

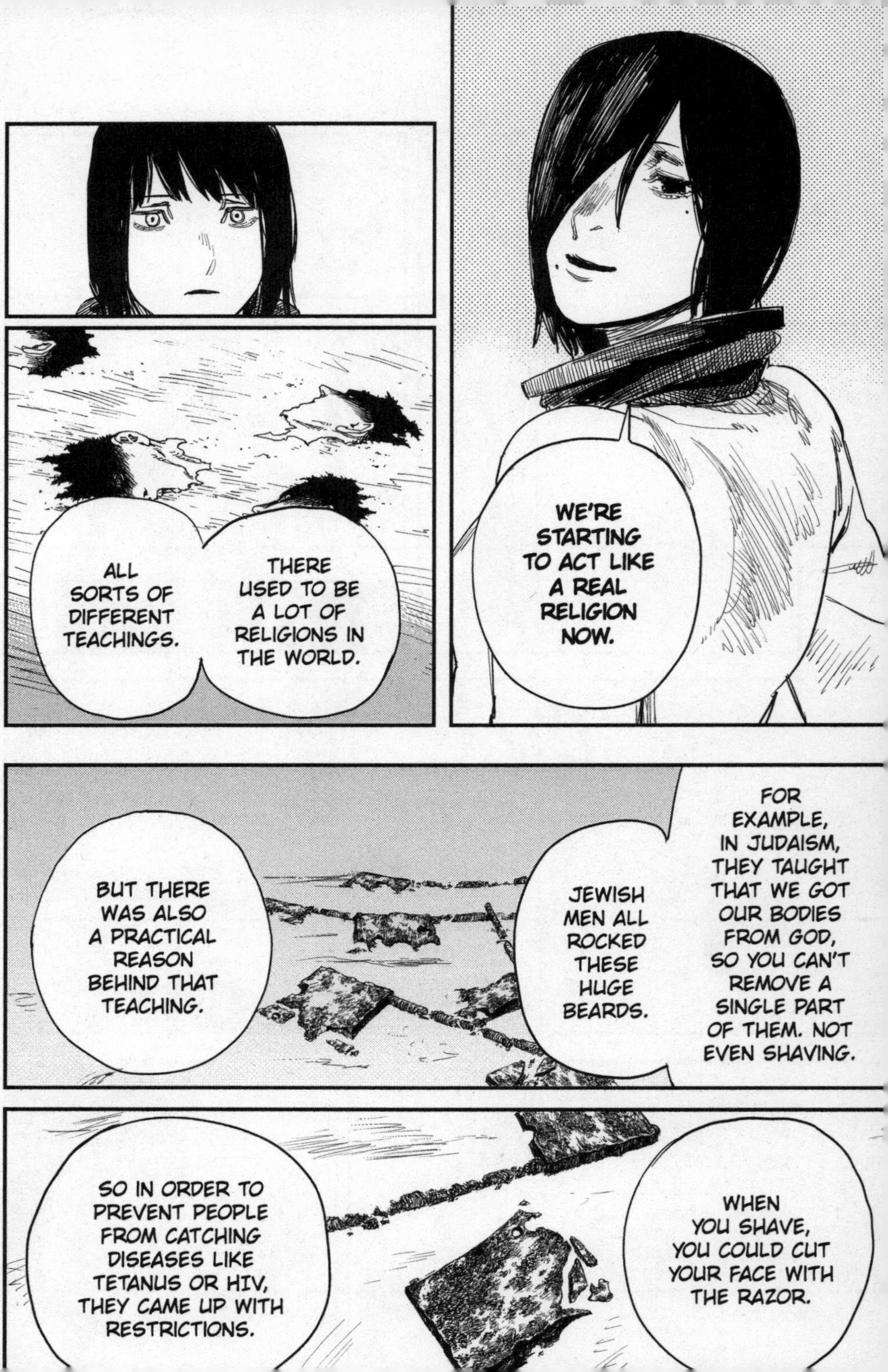
WE'RE STARTING TO ACT LIKE A REAL RELIGION NOW.
THERE USED TO BE A LOT OF RELIGIONS IN THE WORLD.
ALL SORTS OF DIFFERENT TEACHINGS.
FOR EXAMPLE, IN JUDAISM, THEY TAUGHT THAT WE GOT OUR BODIES FROM GOD, SO YOU CAN'T REMOVE A SINGLE PART OF THEM. NOT EVEN SHAVING.
JEWISH MEN ALL ROCKED THESE HUGE BEARDS.
BUT THERE WAS ALSO A PRACTICAL REASON BEHIND THAT TEACHING.
WHEN YOU SHAVE, YOU COULD CUT YOUR FACE WITH THE RAZOR.
SO IN ORDER TO PREVENT PEOPLE FROM CATCHING DISEASES LIKE TETANUS OR HIV, THEY CAME UP WITH RESTRICTIONS.

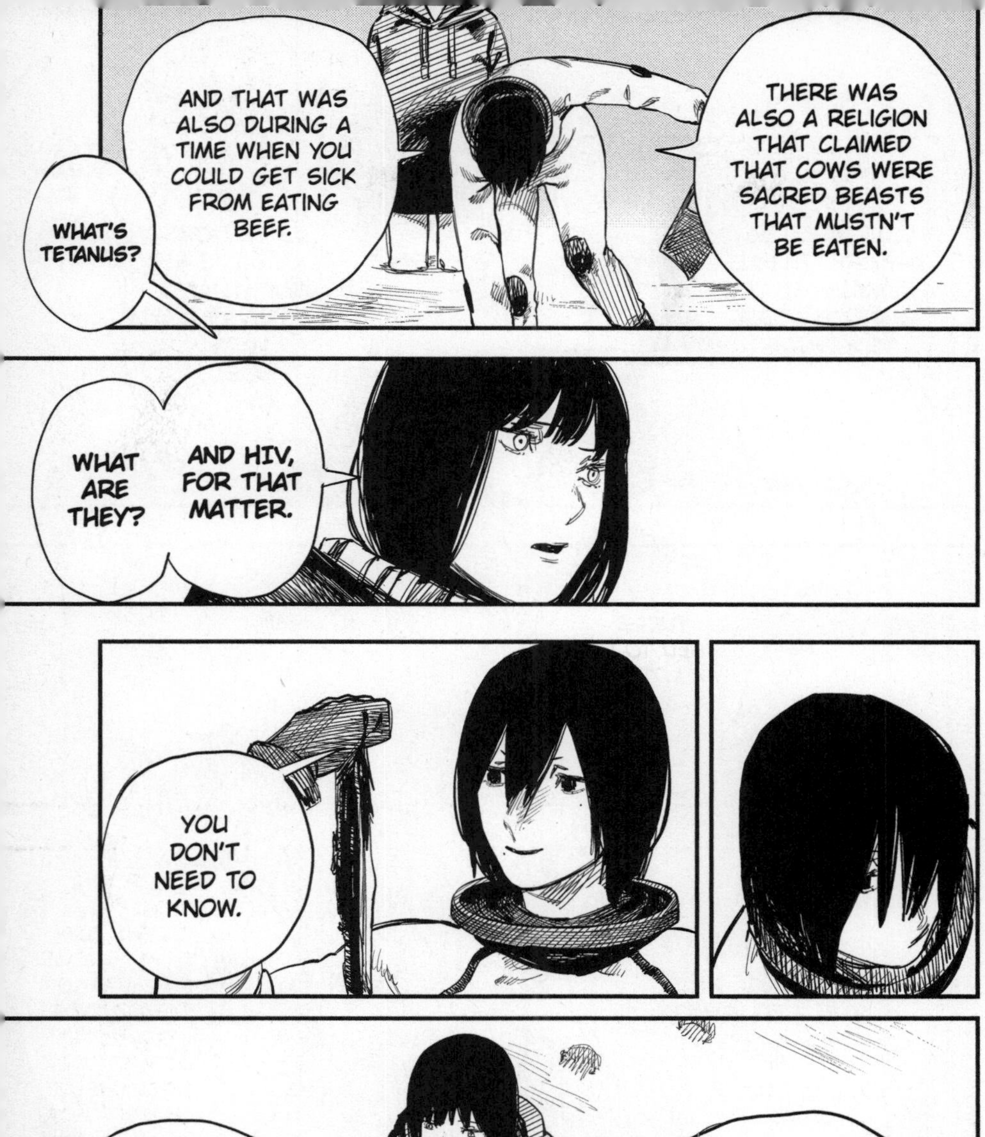
THERE WAS ALSO A RELIGION THAT CLAIMED THAT COWS WERE SACRED BEASTS THAT MUSTN'T BE EATEN.
AND THAT WAS ALSO DURING A TIME WHEN YOU COULD GET SICK FROM EATING BEEF.
WHAT'S TETANUS?
AND HIV, FOR THAT MATTER.
WHAT ARE THEY?
YOU DON'T NEED TO KNOW.
PEOPLE WHO DON'T KNOW ABOUT TETANUS OR HIV AND ARE BASICALLY UNEDUCATED...
...ONLY NEED TO BE TOLD THAT THEY'RE GOD'S TEACHINGS AND TO HAVE FAITH. AND YOU KNOW WHY, RIGHT?

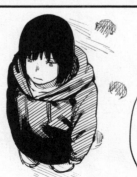

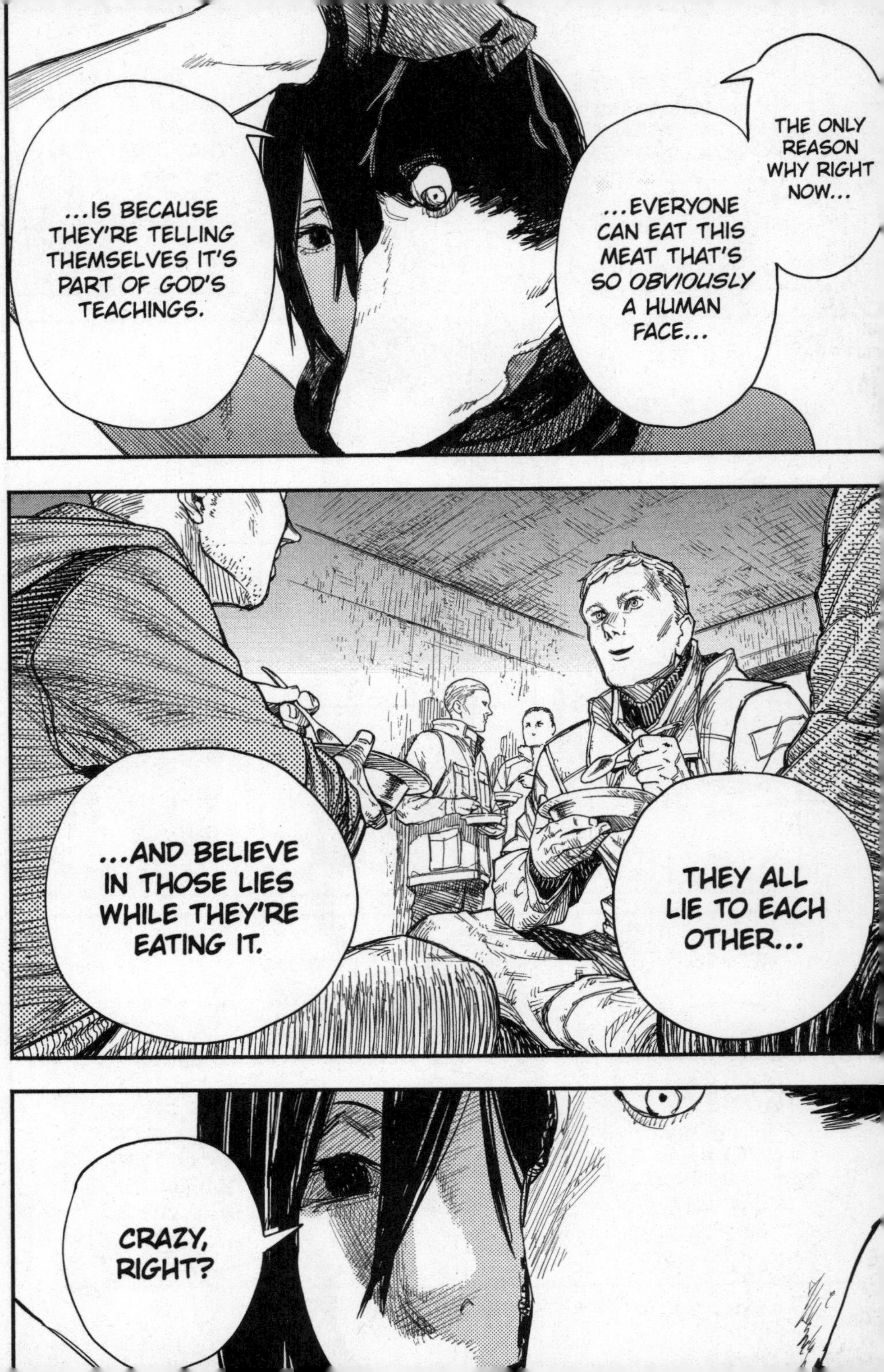

THE ONLY REASON WHY RIGHT NOW...
...EVERYONE CAN EAT THIS MEAT THAT'S SO *OBVIOUSLY* A HUMAN FACE...
...IS BECAUSE THEY'RE TELLING THEMSELVES IT'S PART OF GOD'S TEACHINGS.
THEY ALL LIE TO EACH OTHER...
...AND BELIEVE IN THOSE LIES WHILE THEY'RE EATING IT.
CRAZY, RIGHT?

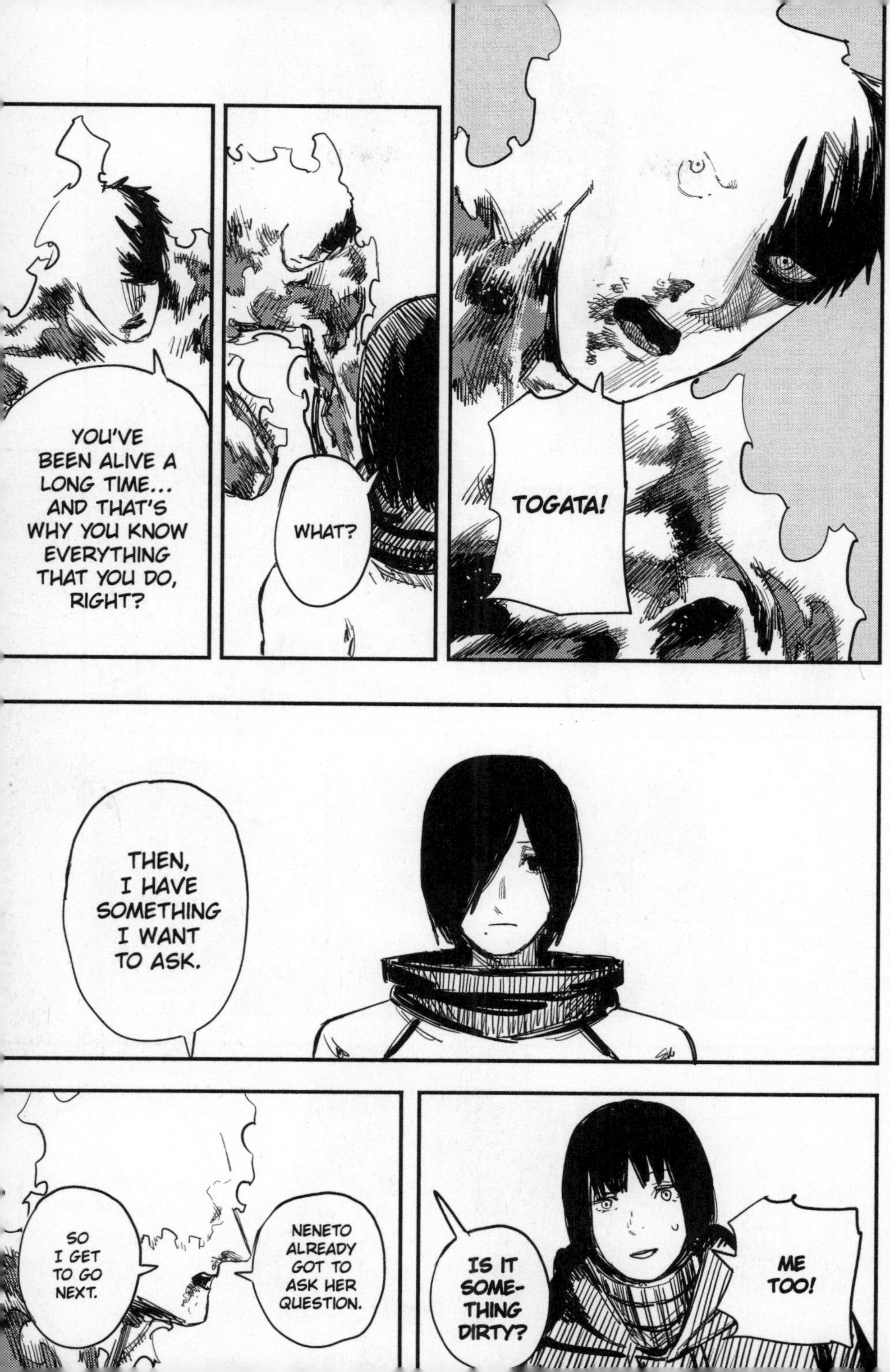
TOGATA!
WHAT?
YOU'VE BEEN ALIVE A LONG TIME... AND THAT'S WHY YOU KNOW EVERYTHING THAT YOU DO, RIGHT?
THEN, I HAVE SOMETHING I WANT TO ASK.
ME TOO!
IS IT SOME-THING DIRTY?
NENETO ALREADY GOT TO ASK HER QUESTION.
SO I GET TO GO NEXT.

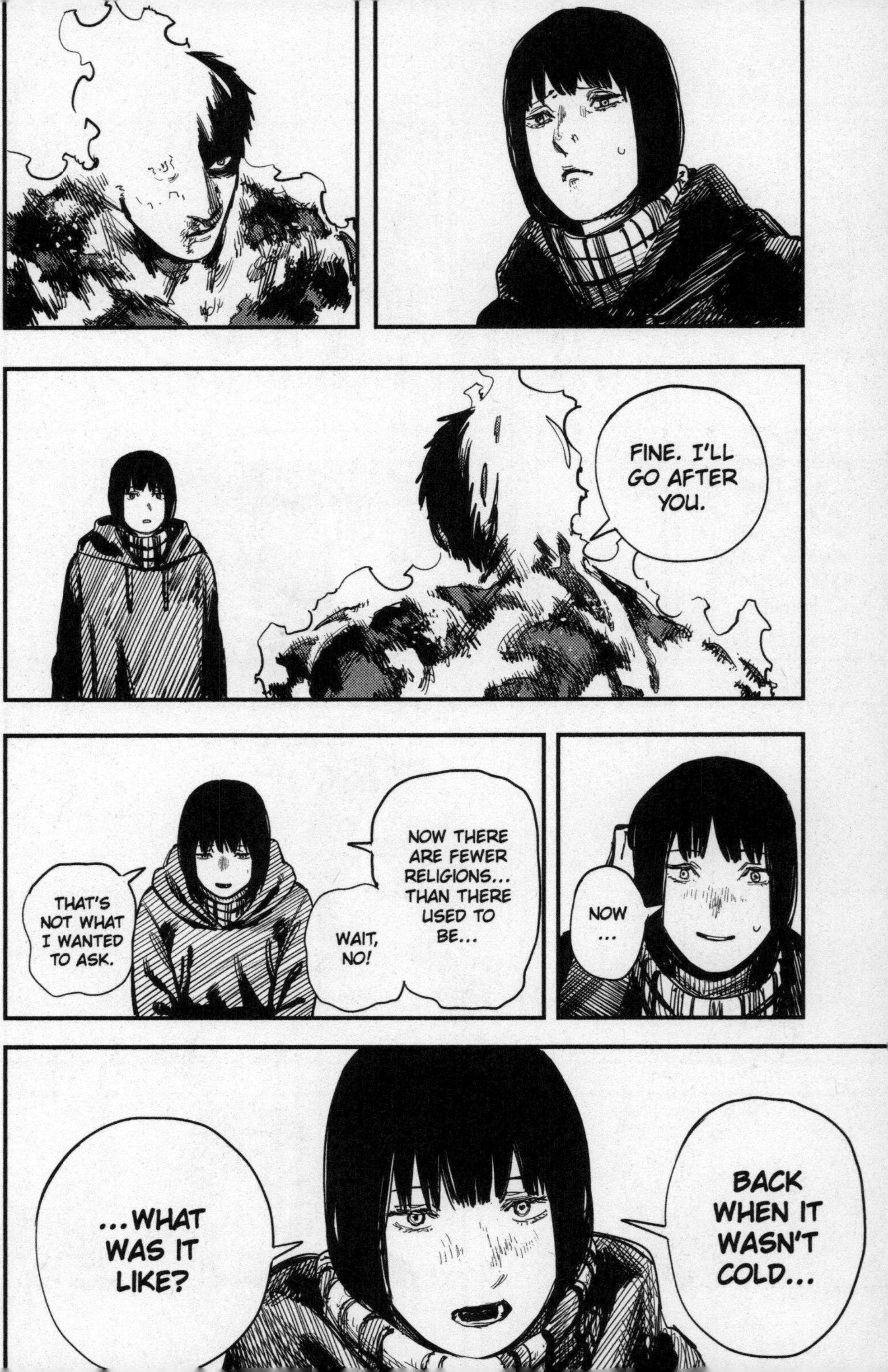
FINE. I'LL GO AFTER YOU.
NOW ...
NOW THERE ARE FEWER RELIGIONS... THAN THERE USED TO BE...
WAIT, NO!
THAT'S NOT WHAT I WANTED TO ASK.
BACK WHEN IT WASN'T COLD...
...WHAT WAS IT LIKE?

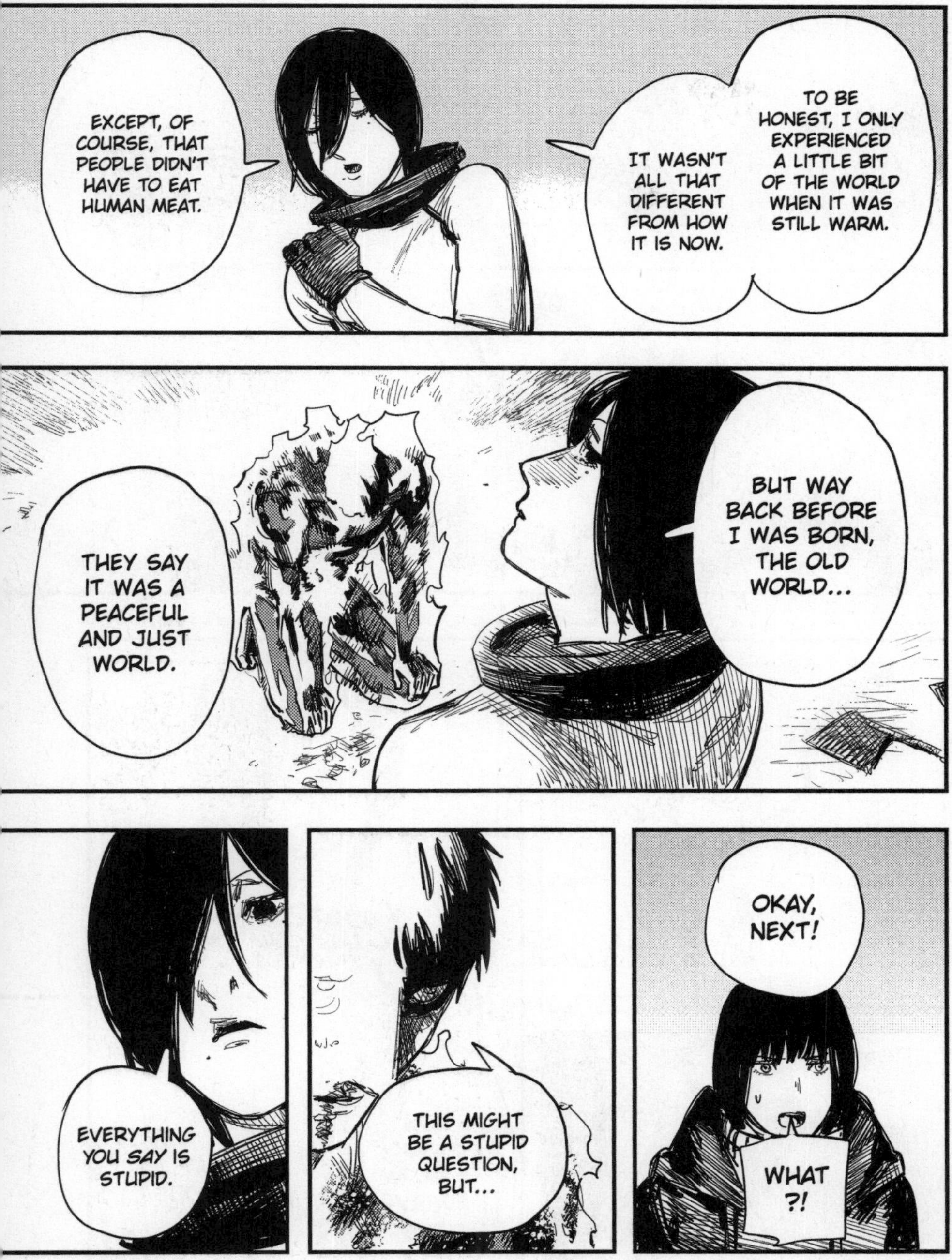
TO BE HONEST, I ONLY EXPERIENCED A LITTLE BIT OF THE WORLD WHEN IT WAS STILL WARM.
IT WASN'T ALL THAT DIFFERENT FROM HOW IT IS NOW.
EXCEPT, OF COURSE, THAT PEOPLE DIDN'T HAVE TO EAT HUMAN MEAT.
BUT WAY BACK BEFORE I WAS BORN, THE OLD WORLD...
THEY SAY IT WAS A PEACEFUL AND JUST WORLD.
OKAY, NEXT!
WHAT ?!
THIS MIGHT BE A STUPID QUESTION, BUT...
EVERYTHING YOU SAY IS STUPID.

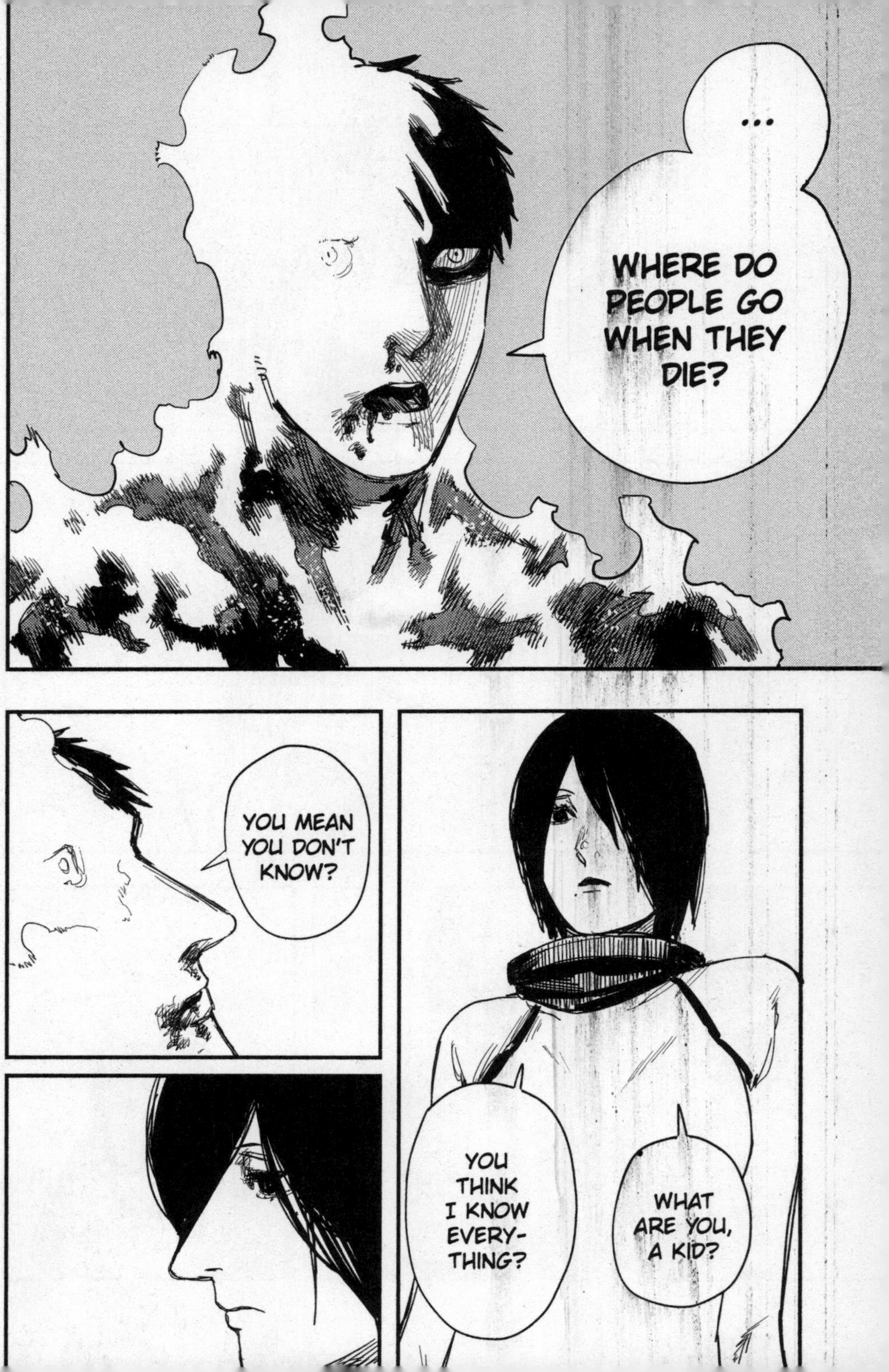
...
WHERE DO PEOPLE GO WHEN THEY DIE?
WHAT ARE YOU, A KID?
YOU THINK I KNOW EVERY-THING?
YOU MEAN YOU DON'T KNOW?

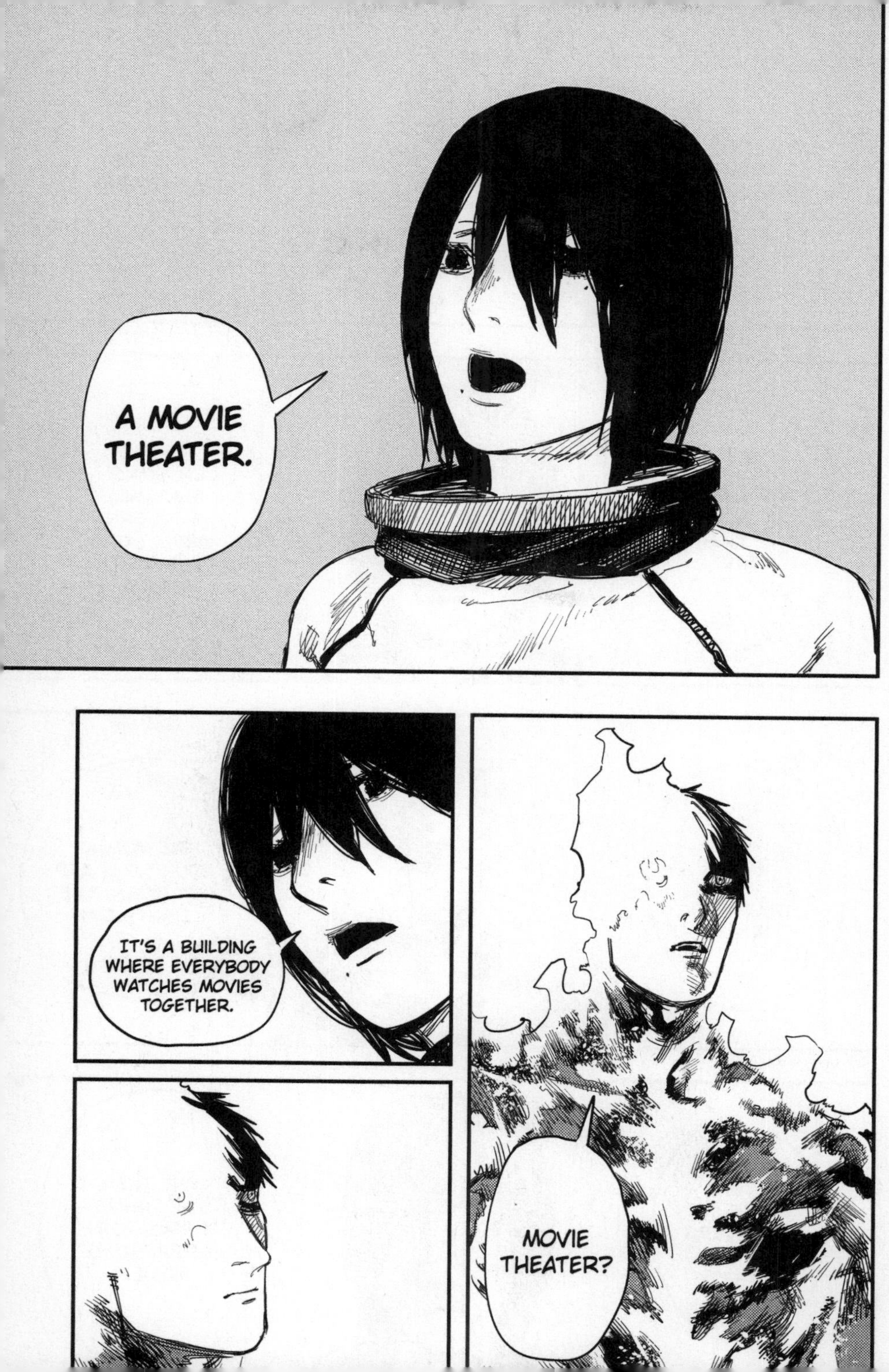
A MOVIE THEATER.
MOVIE THEATER?
IT'S A BUILDING WHERE EVERYBODY WATCHES MOVIES TOGETHER.

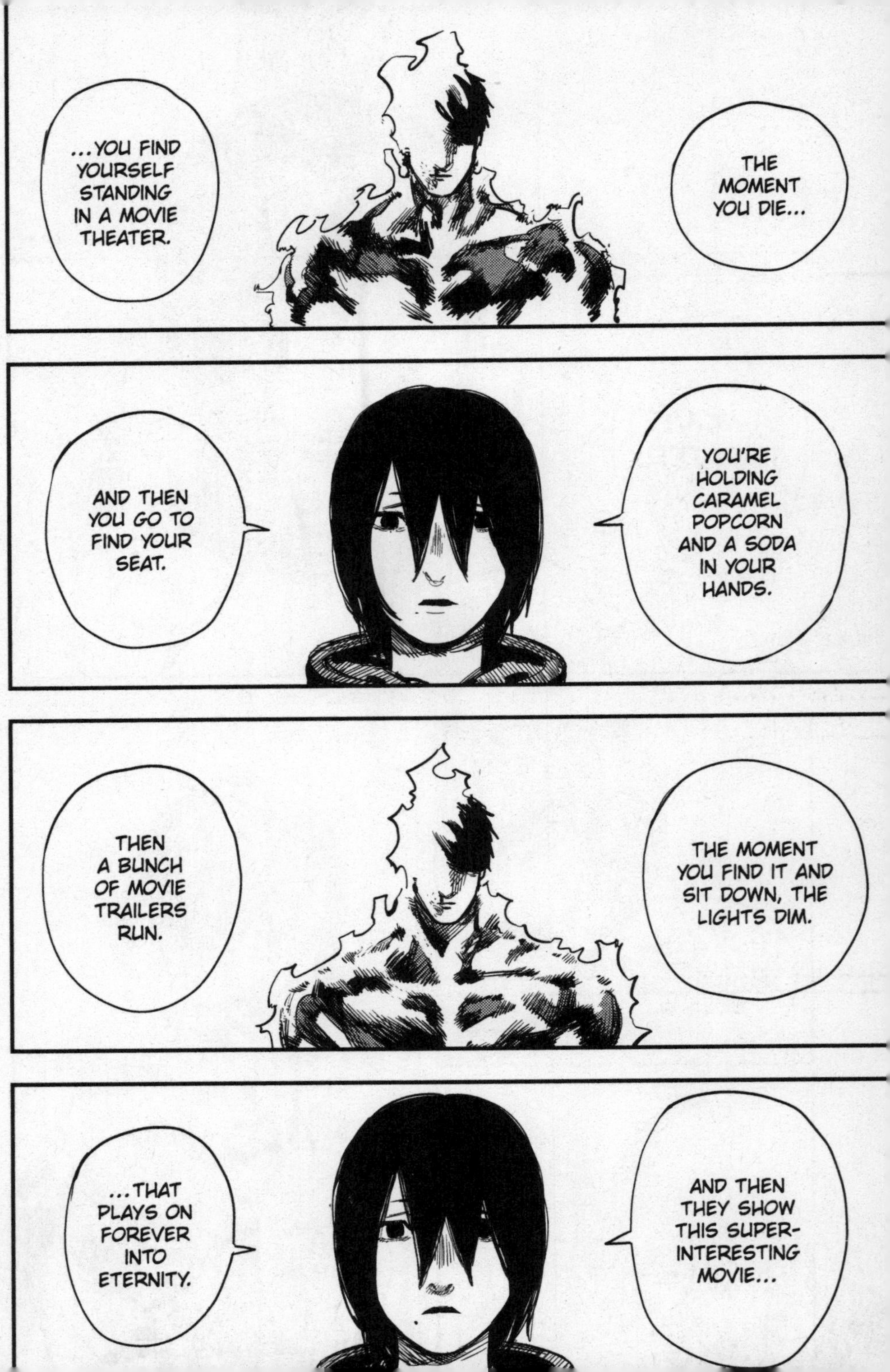
THE MOMENT YOU DIE...
...YOU FIND YOURSELF STANDING IN A MOVIE THEATER.
YOU'RE HOLDING CARAMEL POPCORN AND A SODA IN YOUR HANDS.
AND THEN YOU GO TO FIND YOUR SEAT.
THE MOMENT YOU FIND IT AND SIT DOWN, THE LIGHTS DIM.
THEN A BUNCH OF MOVIE TRAILERS RUN.
AND THEN THEY SHOW THIS SUPER-INTERESTING MOVIE...
...THAT PLAYS ON FOREVER INTO ETERNITY.

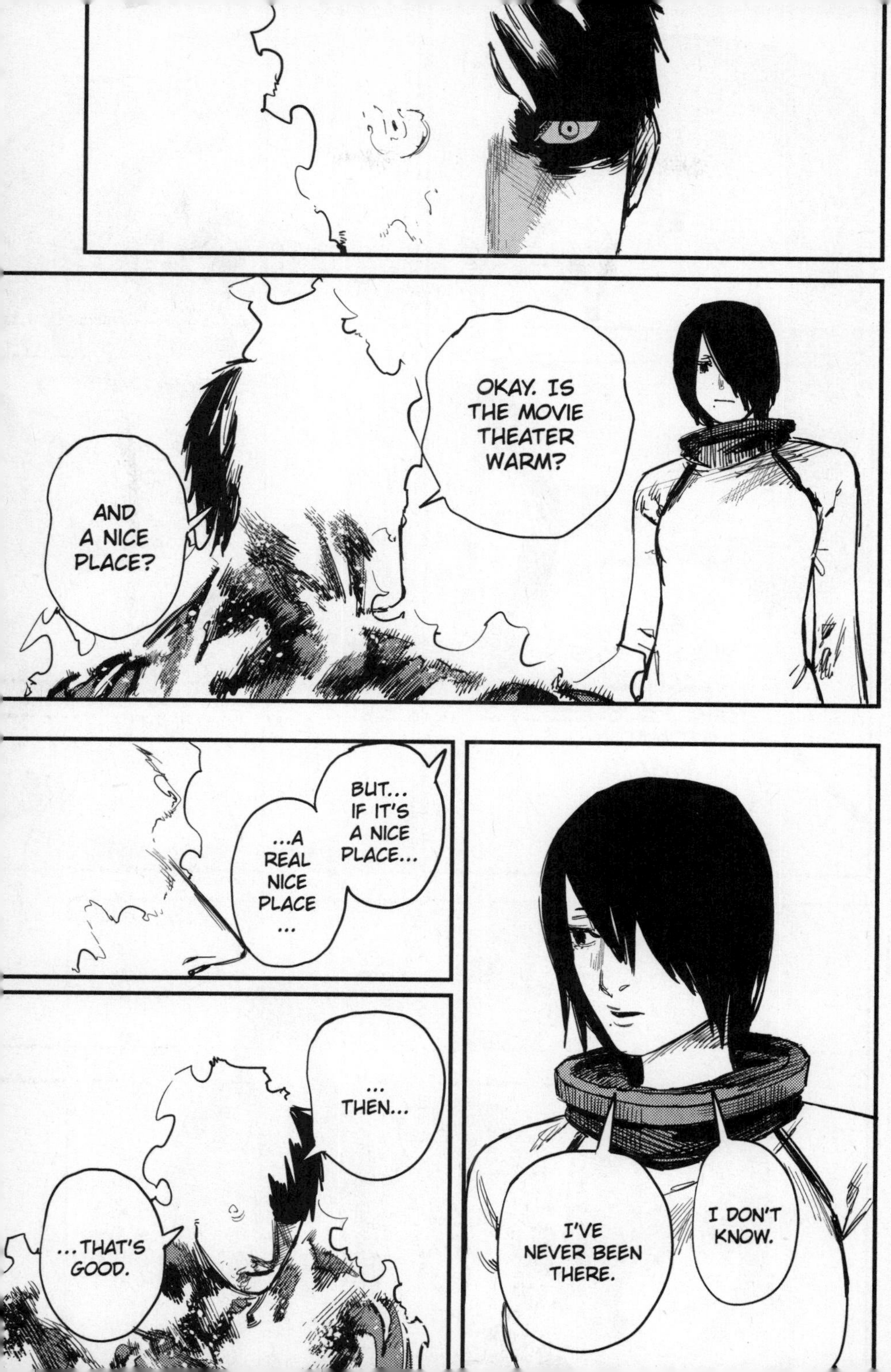
OKAY. IS THE MOVIE THEATER WARM?
AND A NICE PLACE?
I DON'T KNOW.
I'VE NEVER BEEN THERE.
BUT... IF IT'S A NICE PLACE...
...A REAL NICE PLACE ...
... THEN...
...THAT'S GOOD.

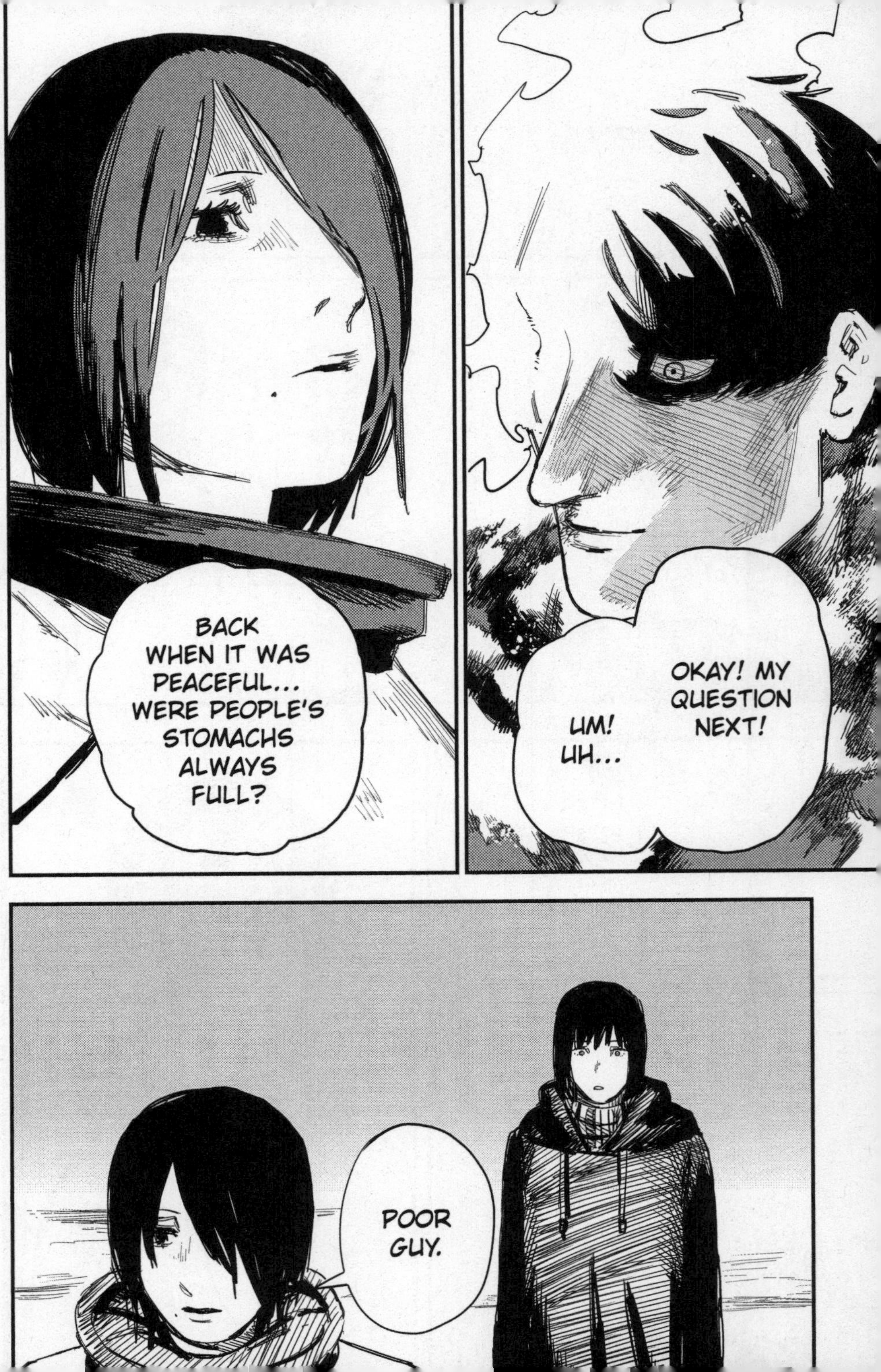
OKAY! MY QUESTION NEXT!
UM! UH...
BACK WHEN IT WAS PEACEFUL... WERE PEOPLE'S STOMACHS ALWAYS FULL?
POOR GUY.

CHAPTER 36

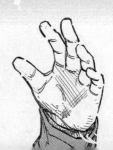

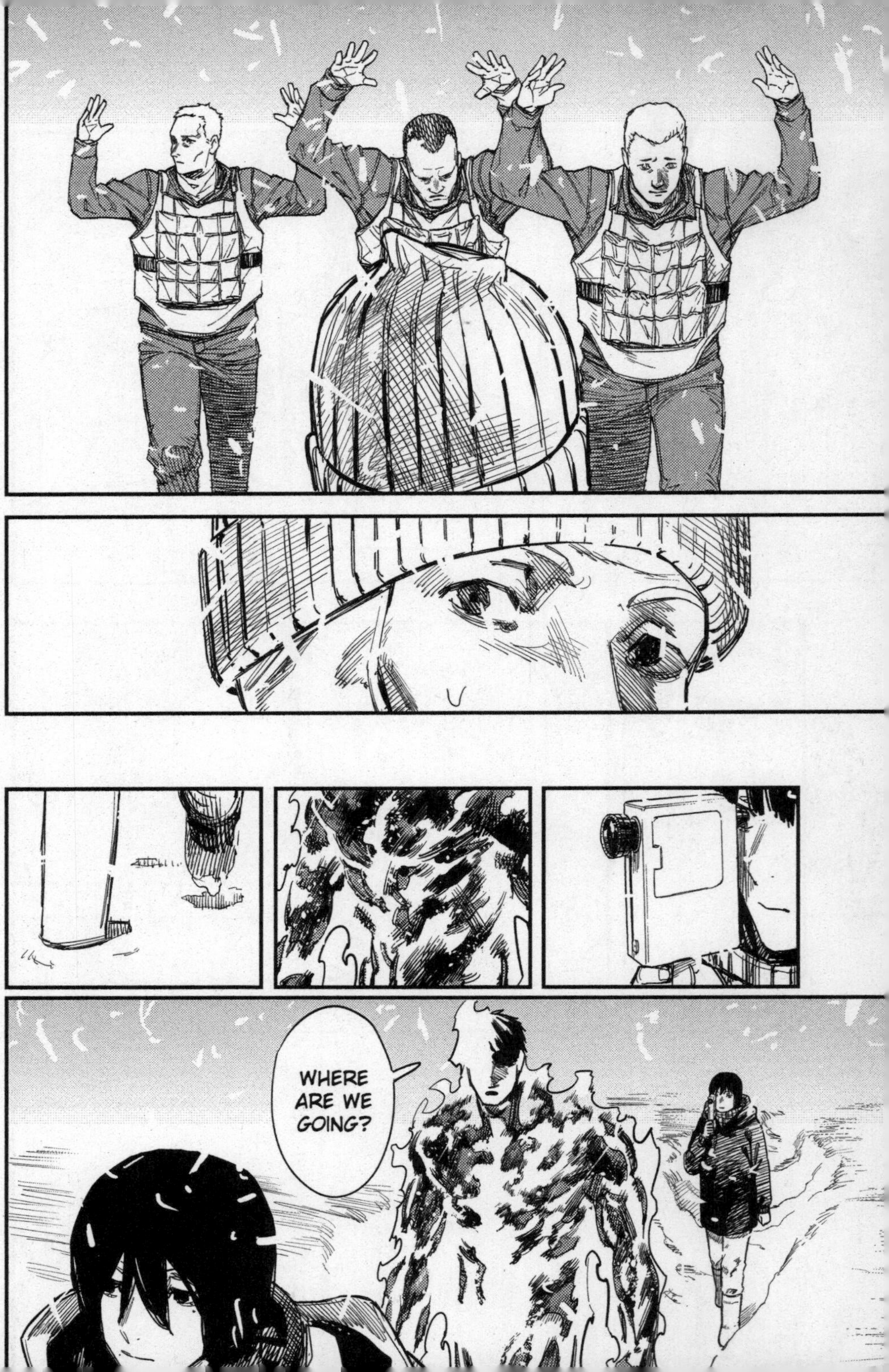
WHERE ARE WE GOING?

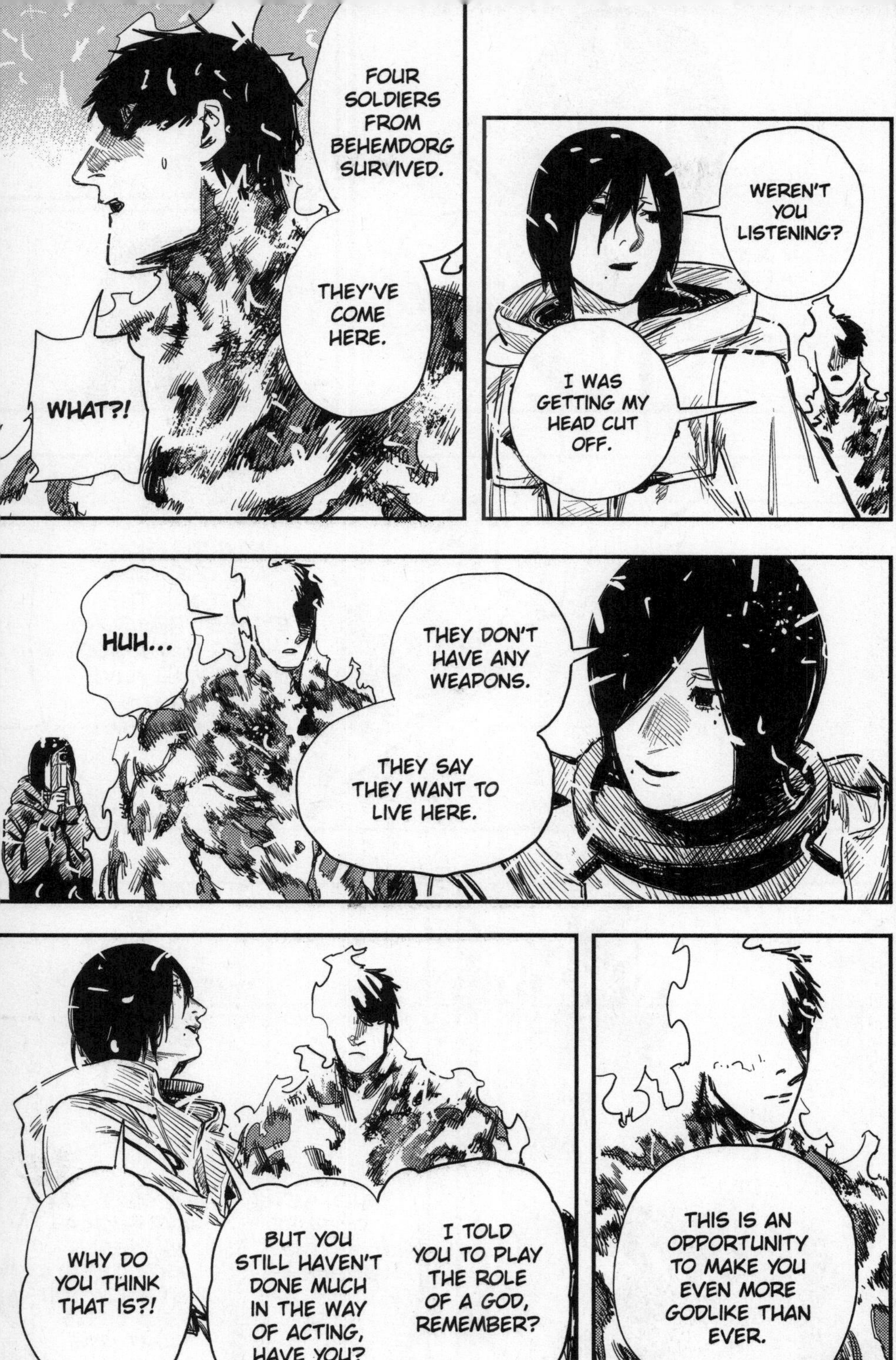
WEREN'T YOU LISTENING?
I WAS GETTING MY HEAD CUT OFF.
FOUR SOLDIERS FROM BEHEMDORG SURVIVED.
THEY'VE COME HERE.
WHAT?!
THEY DON'T HAVE ANY WEAPONS.
THEY SAY THEY WANT TO LIVE HERE.
HUH...
THIS IS AN OPPORTUNITY TO MAKE YOU EVEN MORE GODLIKE THAN EVER.
I TOLD YOU TO PLAY THE ROLE OF A GOD, REMEMBER?
BUT YOU STILL HAVEN'T DONE MUCH IN THE WAY OF ACTING, HAVE YOU?
WHY DO YOU THINK THAT IS?!

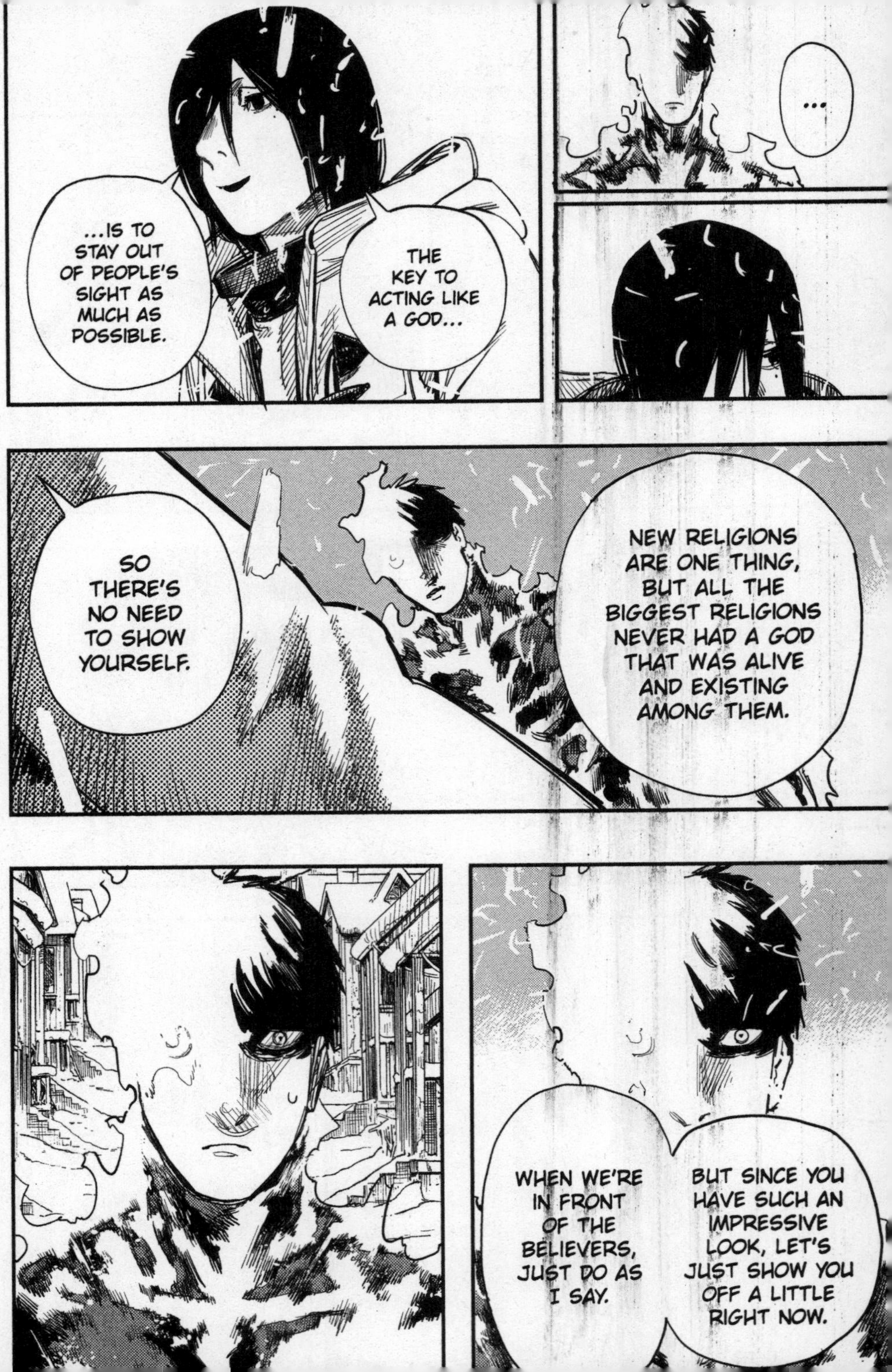
...
THE KEY TO ACTING LIKE A GOD...
...IS TO STAY OUT OF PEOPLE'S SIGHT AS MUCH AS POSSIBLE.
NEW RELIGIONS ARE ONE THING, BUT ALL THE BIGGEST RELIGIONS NEVER HAD A GOD THAT WAS ALIVE AND EXISTING AMONG THEM.
SO THERE'S NO NEED TO SHOW YOURSELF.
BUT SINCE YOU HAVE SUCH AN IMPRESSIVE LOOK, LET'S JUST SHOW YOU OFF A LITTLE RIGHT NOW.
WHEN WE'RE IN FRONT OF THE BELIEVERS, JUST DO AS I SAY.

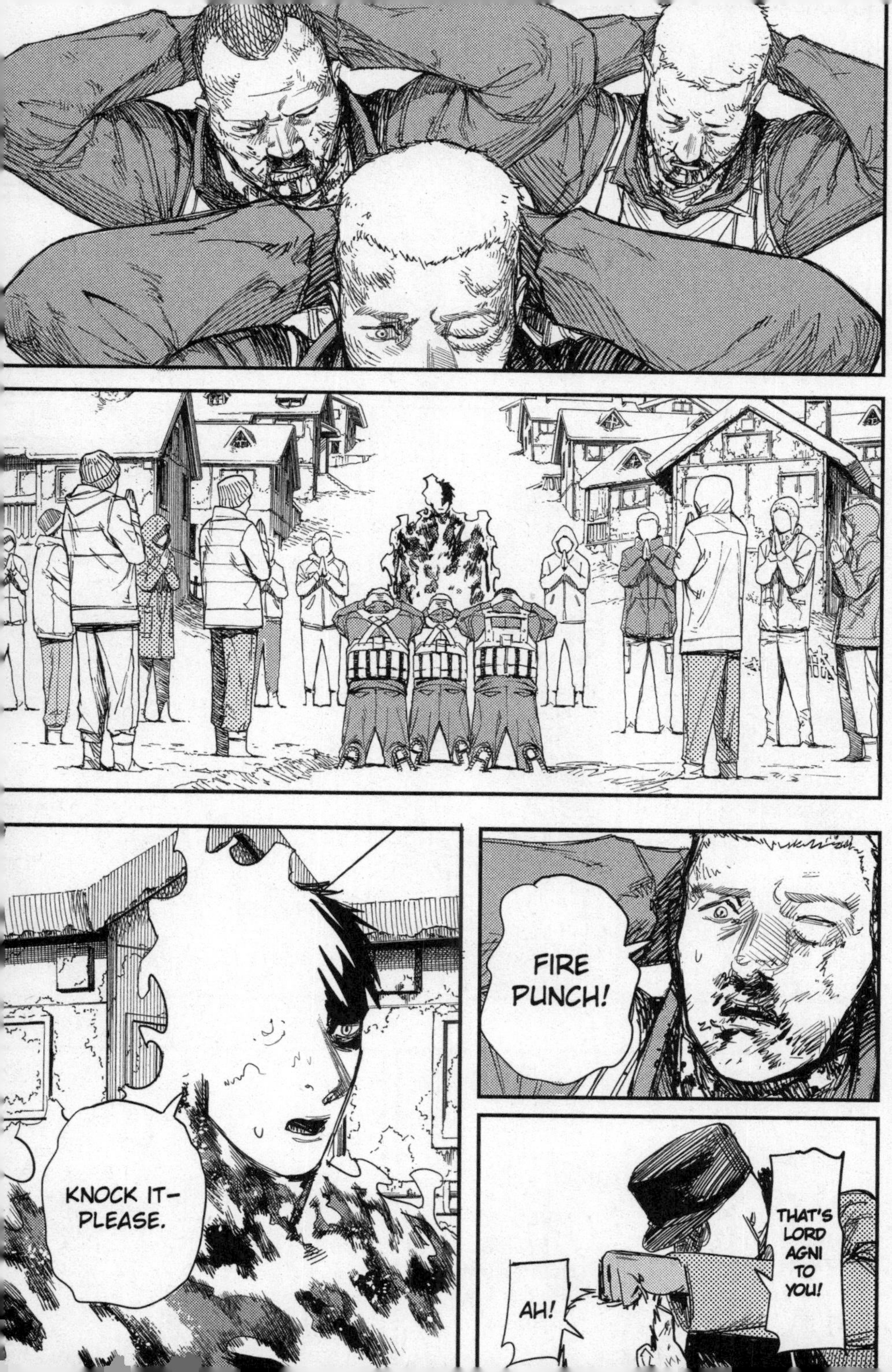
FIRE PUNCH!
THAT'S LORD AGNI TO YOU!
AH!
KNOCK IT—PLEASE.

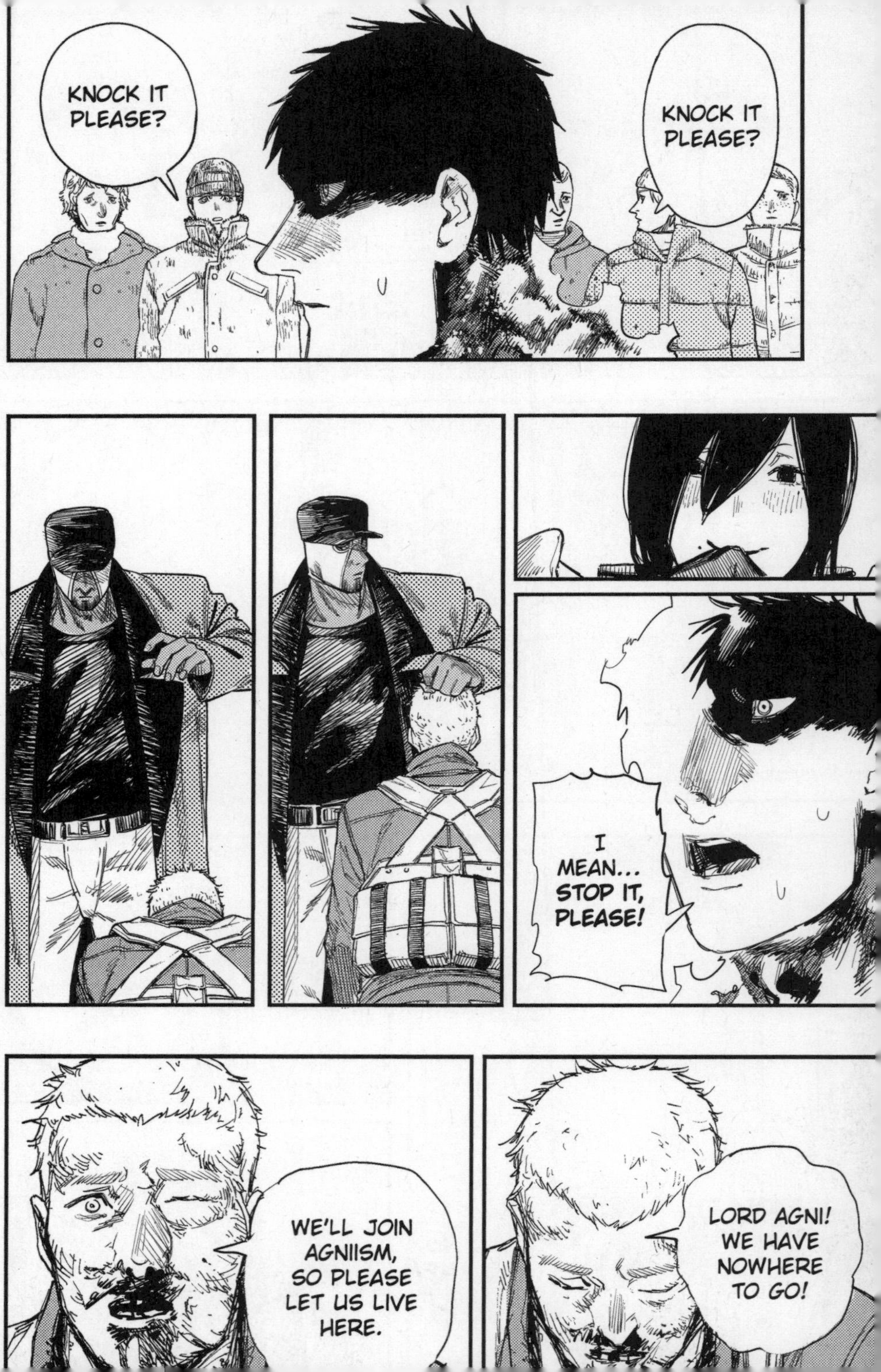
KNOCK IT PLEASE?
KNOCK IT PLEASE?
I MEAN... STOP IT, PLEASE!
LORD AGNI! WE HAVE NOWHERE TO GO!
WE'LL JOIN AGNIISM, SO PLEASE LET US LIVE HERE.

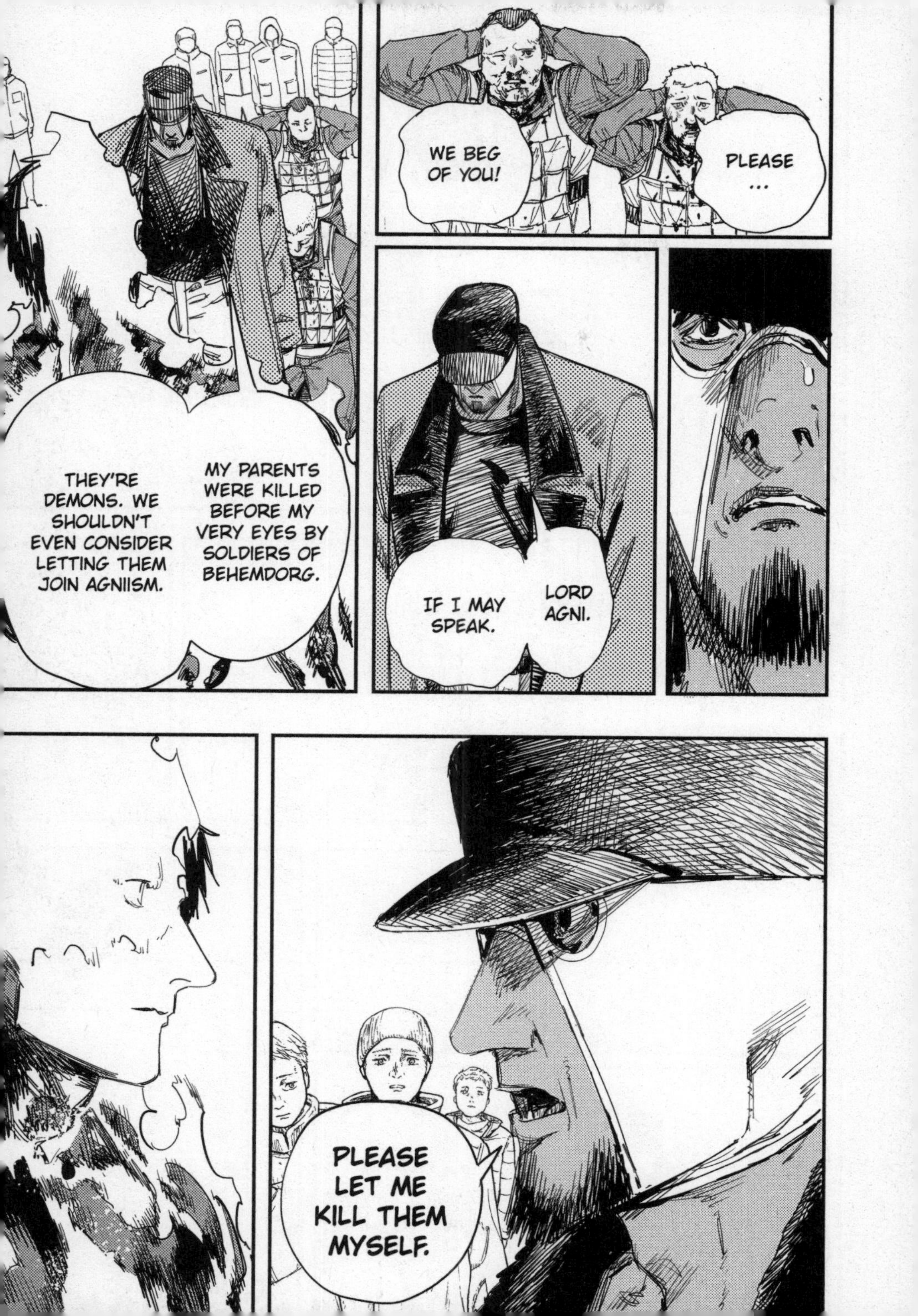
PLEASE ...
WE BEG OF YOU!
LORD AGNI.
IF I MAY SPEAK.
MY PARENTS WERE KILLED BEFORE MY VERY EYES BY SOLDIERS OF BEHEMDORG.
THEY'RE DEMONS. WE SHOULDN'T EVEN CONSIDER LETTING THEM JOIN AGNIISM.
PLEASE LET ME KILL THEM MYSELF.

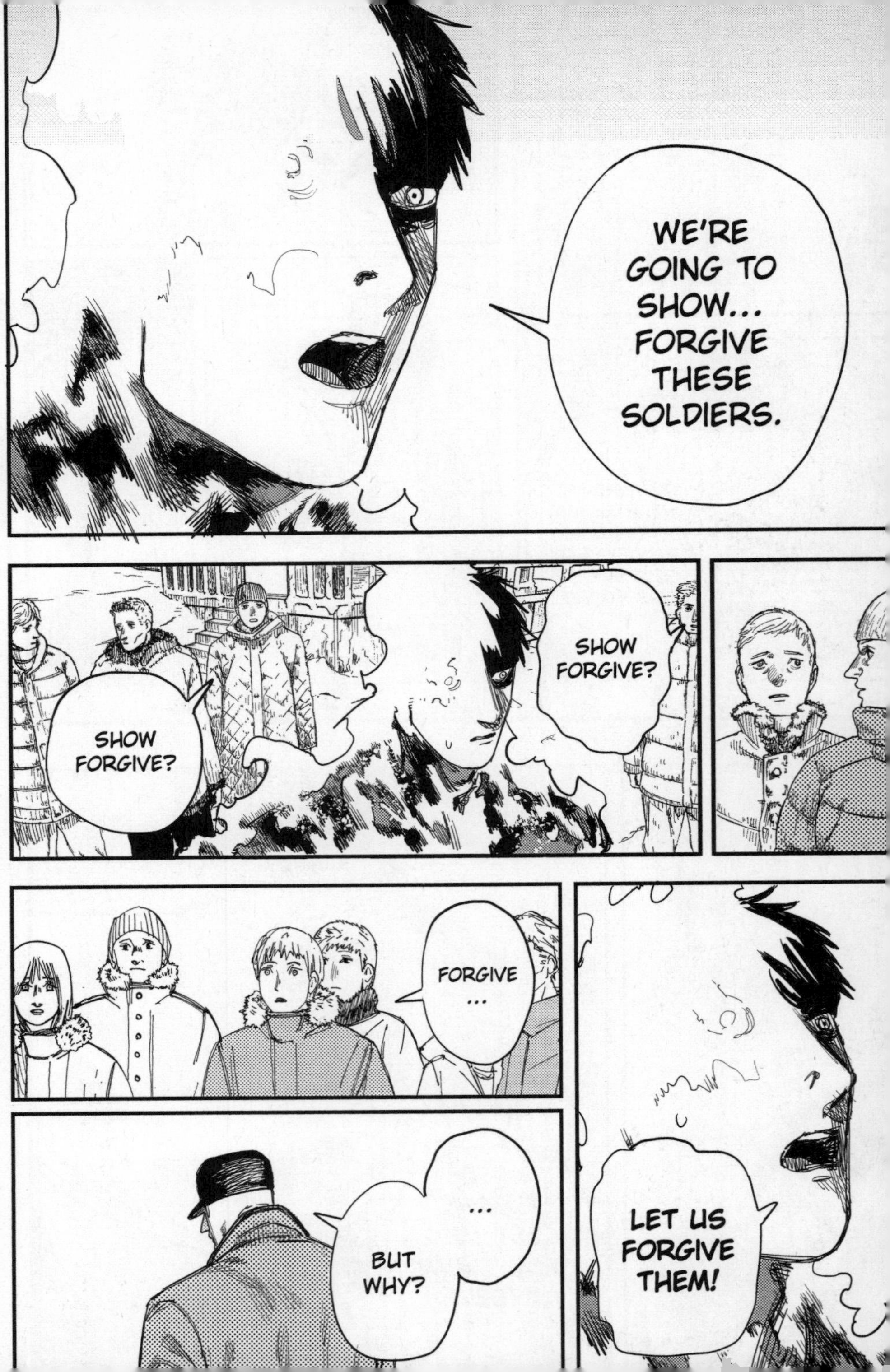
WE'RE GOING TO SHOW... FORGIVE THESE SOLDIERS.
SHOW FORGIVE?
SHOW FORGIVE?
LET US FORGIVE THEM!
FORGIVE ...
... BUT WHY?

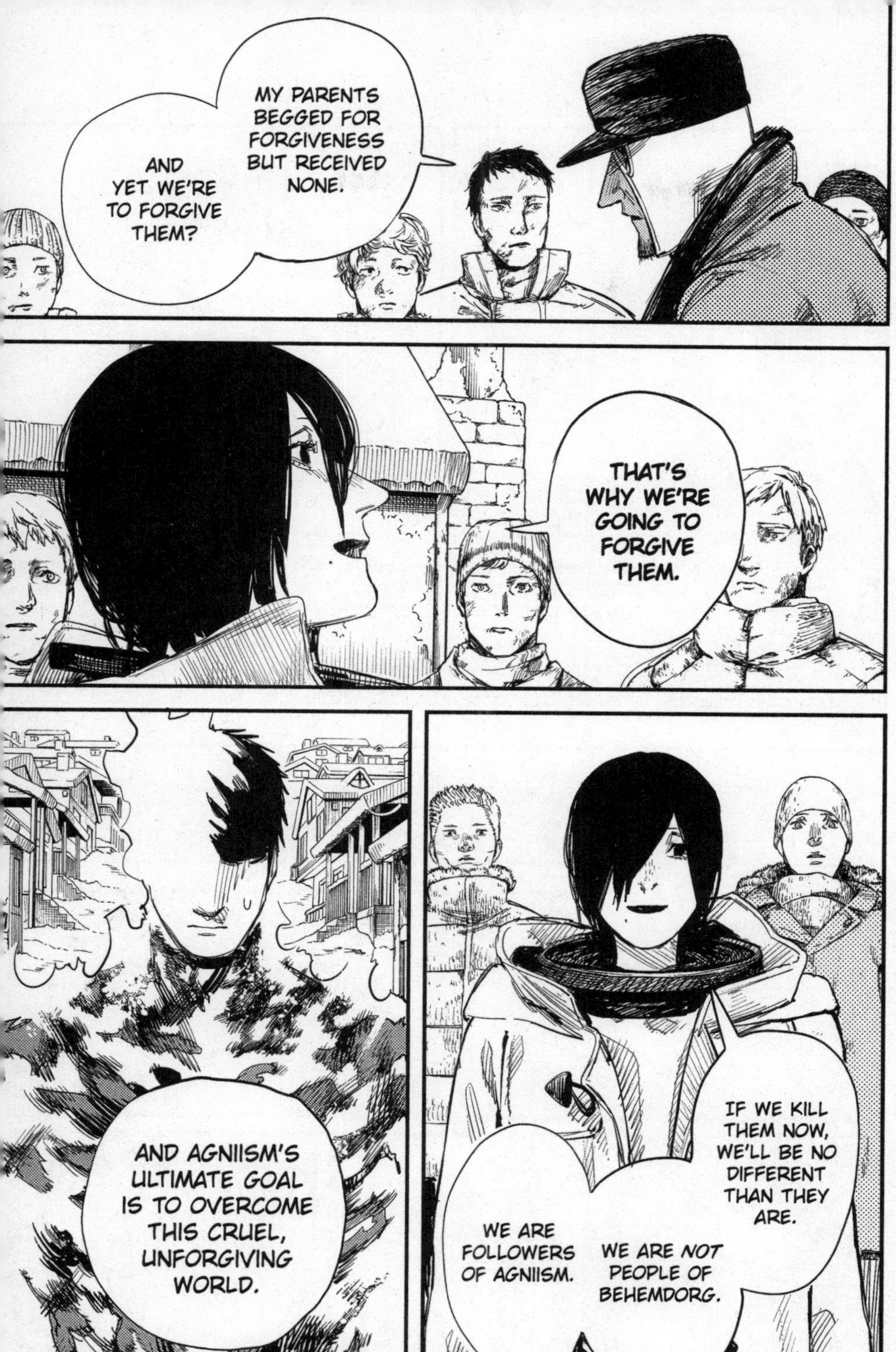
MY PARENTS BEGGED FOR FORGIVENESS BUT RECEIVED NONE.
AND YET WE'RE TO FORGIVE THEM?
THAT'S WHY WE'RE GOING TO FORGIVE THEM.
IF WE KILL THEM NOW, WE'LL BE NO DIFFERENT THAN THEY ARE.
WE ARE *NOT* PEOPLE OF BEHEMDORG.
WE ARE FOLLOWERS OF AGNIISM.
AND AGNIISM'S ULTIMATE GOAL IS TO OVERCOME THIS CRUEL, UNFORGIVING WORLD.

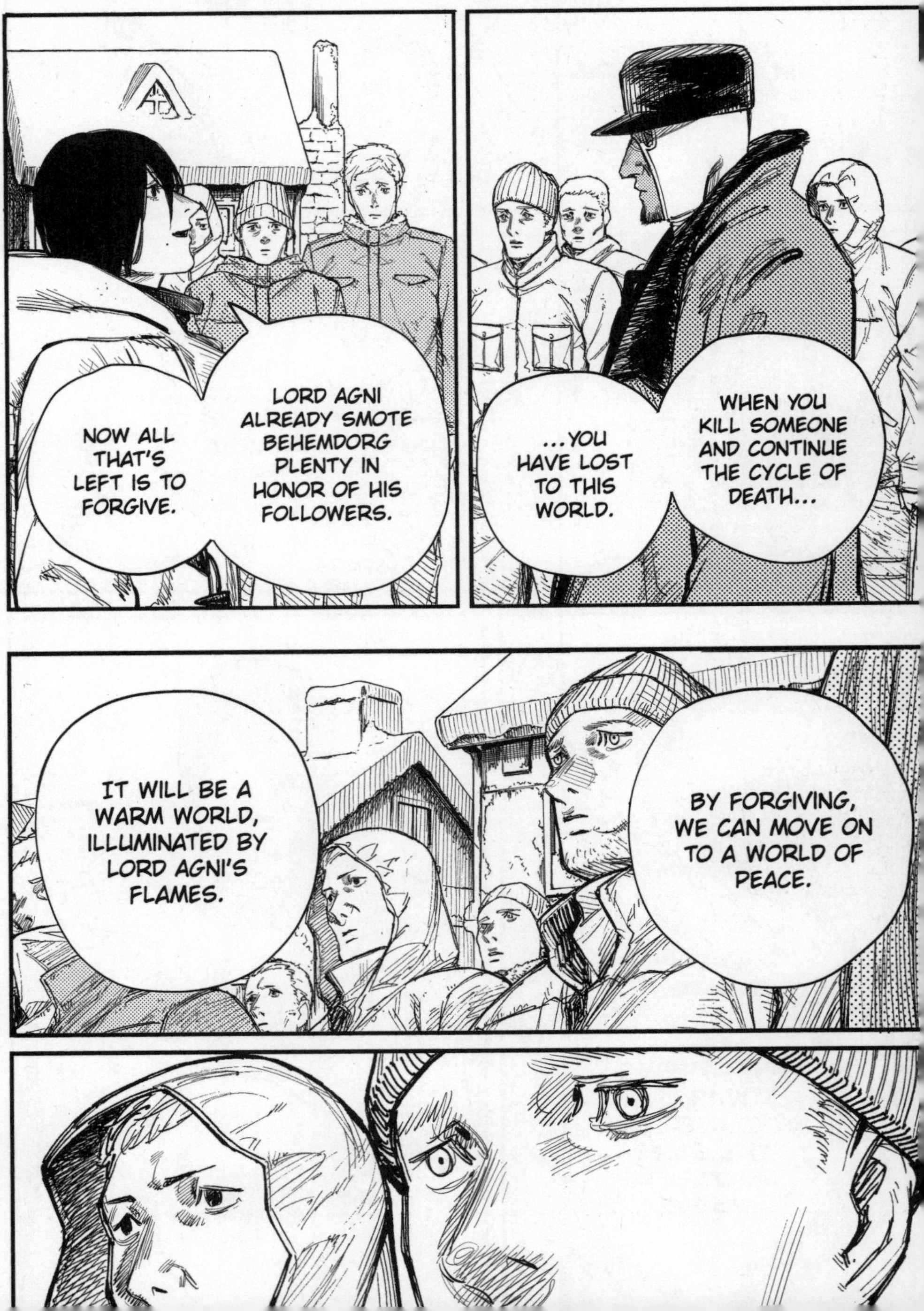
WHEN YOU KILL SOMEONE AND CONTINUE THE CYCLE OF DEATH...
...YOU HAVE LOST TO THIS WORLD.
LORD AGNI ALREADY SMOTE BEHEMDORG PLENTY IN HONOR OF HIS FOLLOWERS.
NOW ALL THAT'S LEFT IS TO FORGIVE.
BY FORGIVING, WE CAN MOVE ON TO A WORLD OF PEACE.
IT WILL BE A WARM WORLD, ILLUMINATED BY LORD AGNI'S FLAMES.

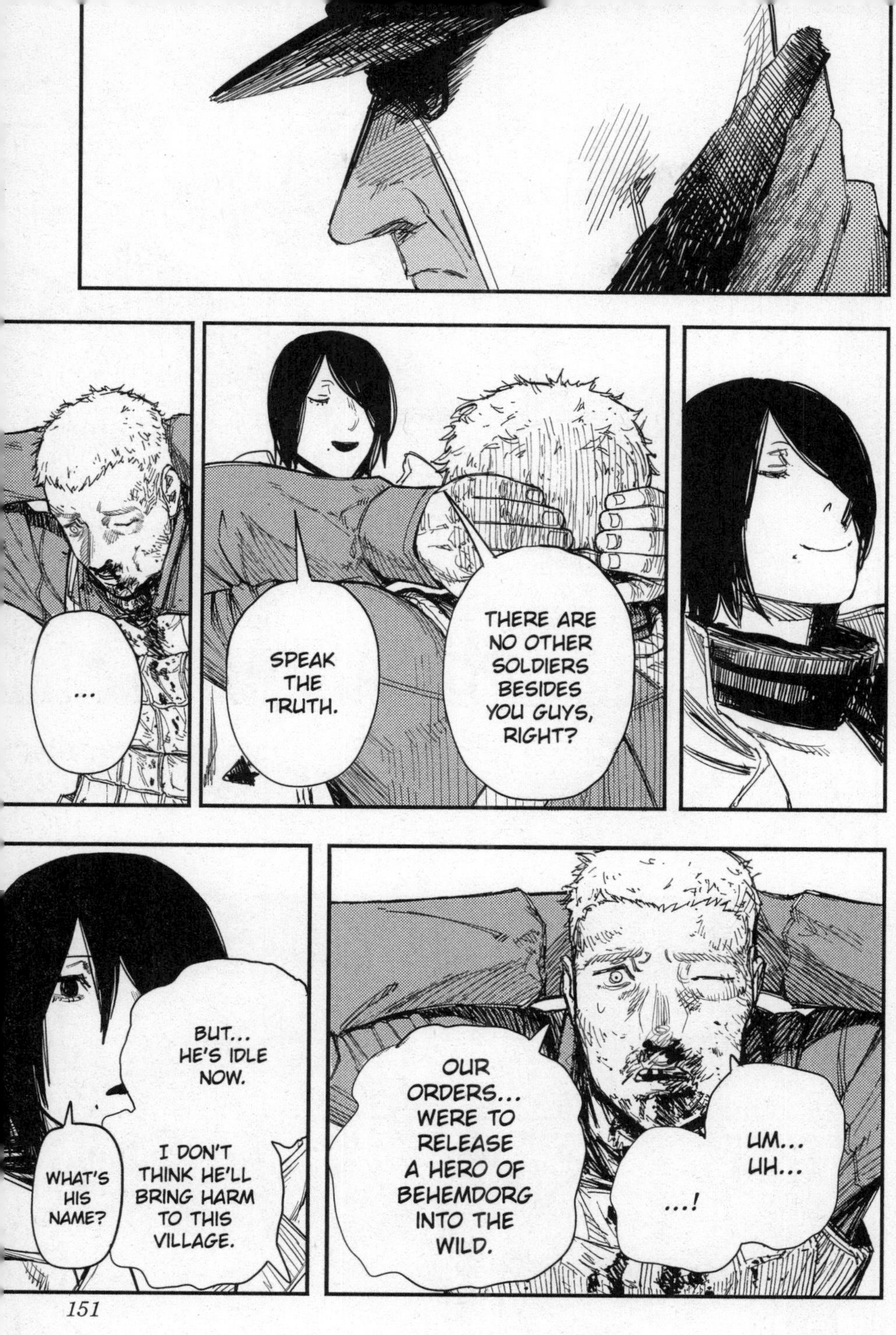
THERE ARE NO OTHER SOLDIERS BESIDES YOU GUYS, RIGHT?
SPEAK THE TRUTH.
...
UM... UH...
...!
OUR ORDERS... WERE TO RELEASE A HERO OF BEHEMDORG INTO THE WILD.
BUT... HE'S IDLE NOW.
I DON'T THINK HE'LL BRING HARM TO THIS VILLAGE.
WHAT'S HIS NAME?

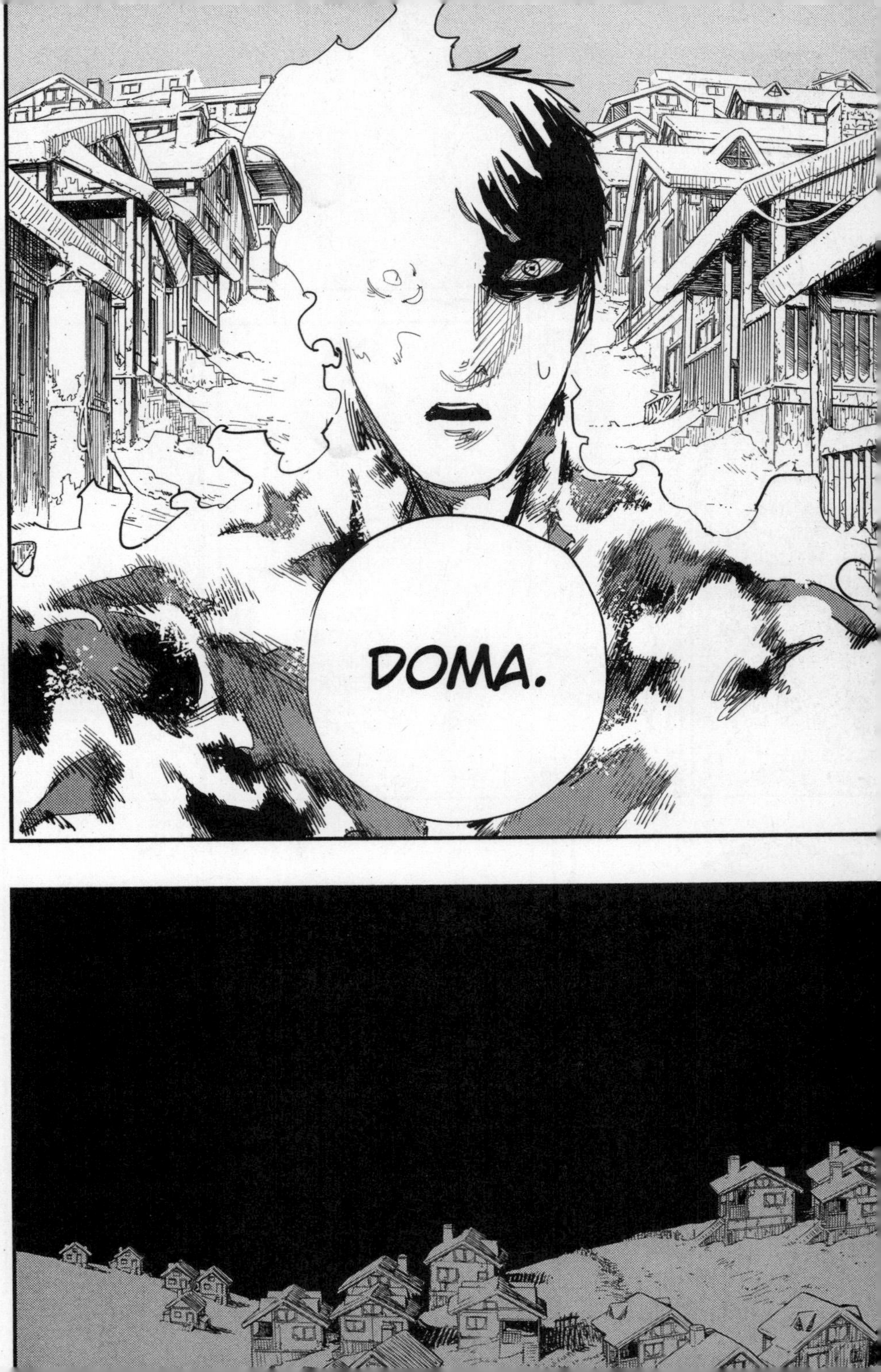
DOMA.

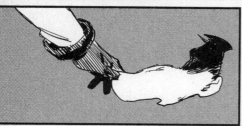

I MEAN YOUR WHOLE REVENGE-ARC THING.

I DON'T MEAN THAT.

WELL, IT HURTS, BUT THAT'S PRETTY OBVIOUS.

YOU OKAY?

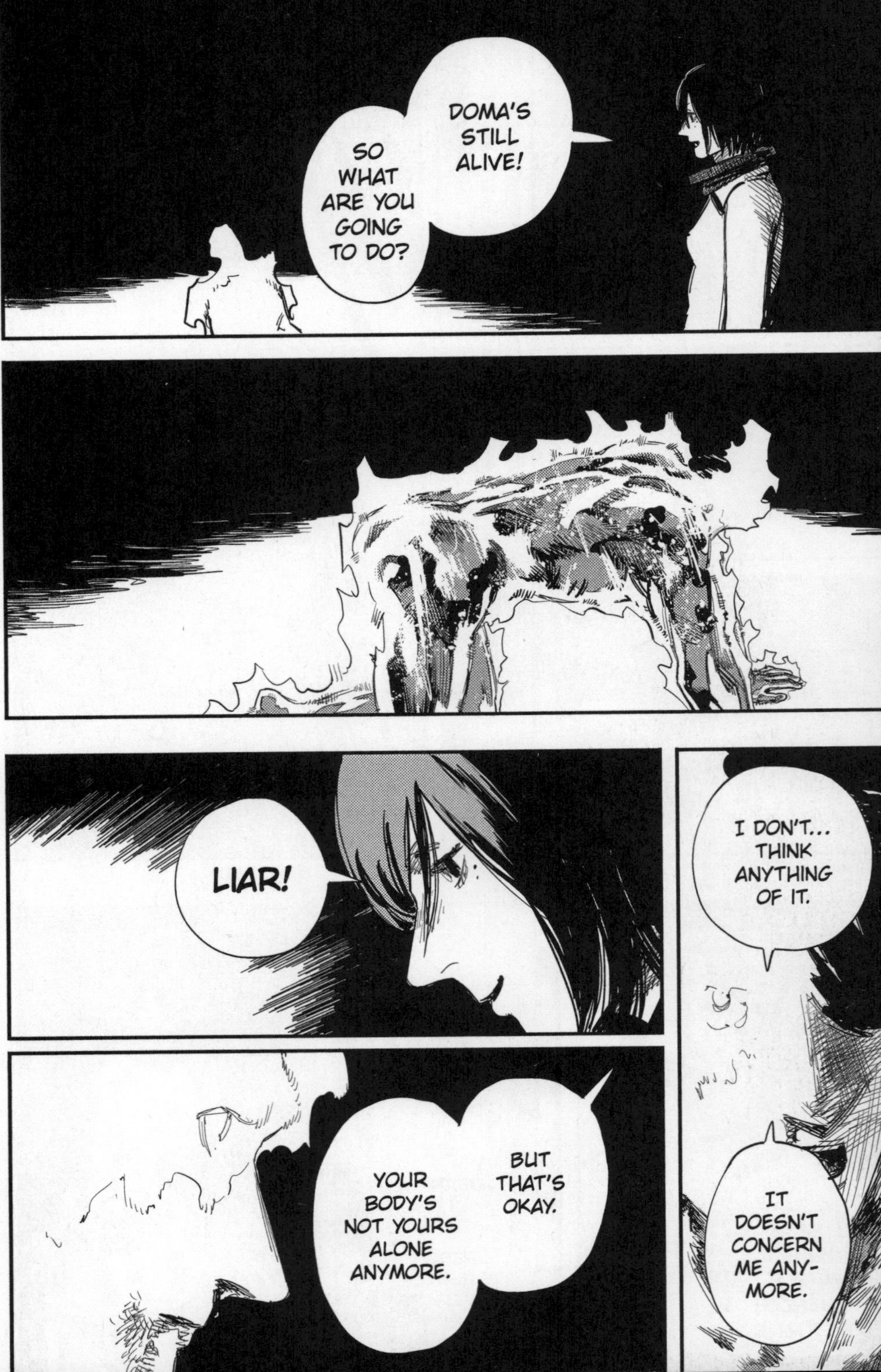
DOMA'S STILL ALIVE!
SO WHAT ARE YOU GOING TO DO?
I DON'T... THINK ANYTHING OF IT.
IT DOESN'T CONCERN ME ANYMORE.
LIAR!
BUT THAT'S OKAY.
YOUR BODY'S NOT YOURS ALONE ANYMORE.

TMP

YOU'RE NO LONGER FIRE MAN.

YOU'RE LORD AGNI.

WHAT'RE YOU DOING HERE?

LORD AGNI!

I'M SORRY FOR COMING UNINVITED!

BUT I'M BLESSED WITH BEING ABLE TO LOOK INTO PEOPLE'S HEARTS.

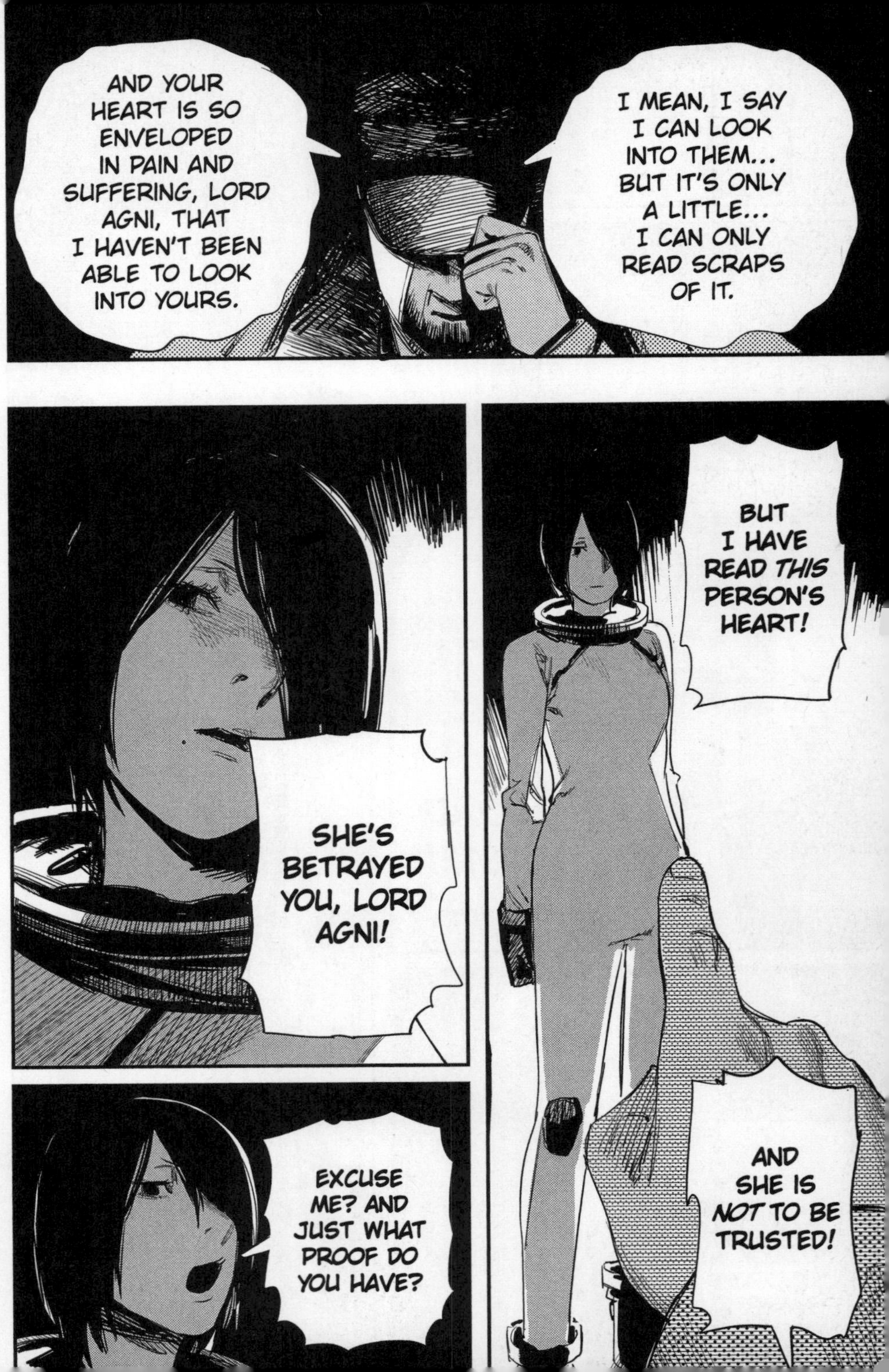
I MEAN, I SAY I CAN LOOK INTO THEM... BUT IT'S ONLY A LITTLE... I CAN ONLY READ SCRAPS OF IT.
AND YOUR HEART IS SO ENVELOPED IN PAIN AND SUFFERING, LORD AGNI, THAT I HAVEN'T BEEN ABLE TO LOOK INTO YOURS.
BUT I HAVE READ *THIS* PERSON'S HEART!
AND SHE IS *NOT* TO BE TRUSTED!
SHE'S BETRAYED YOU, LORD AGNI!
EXCUSE ME? AND JUST WHAT PROOF DO YOU HAVE?

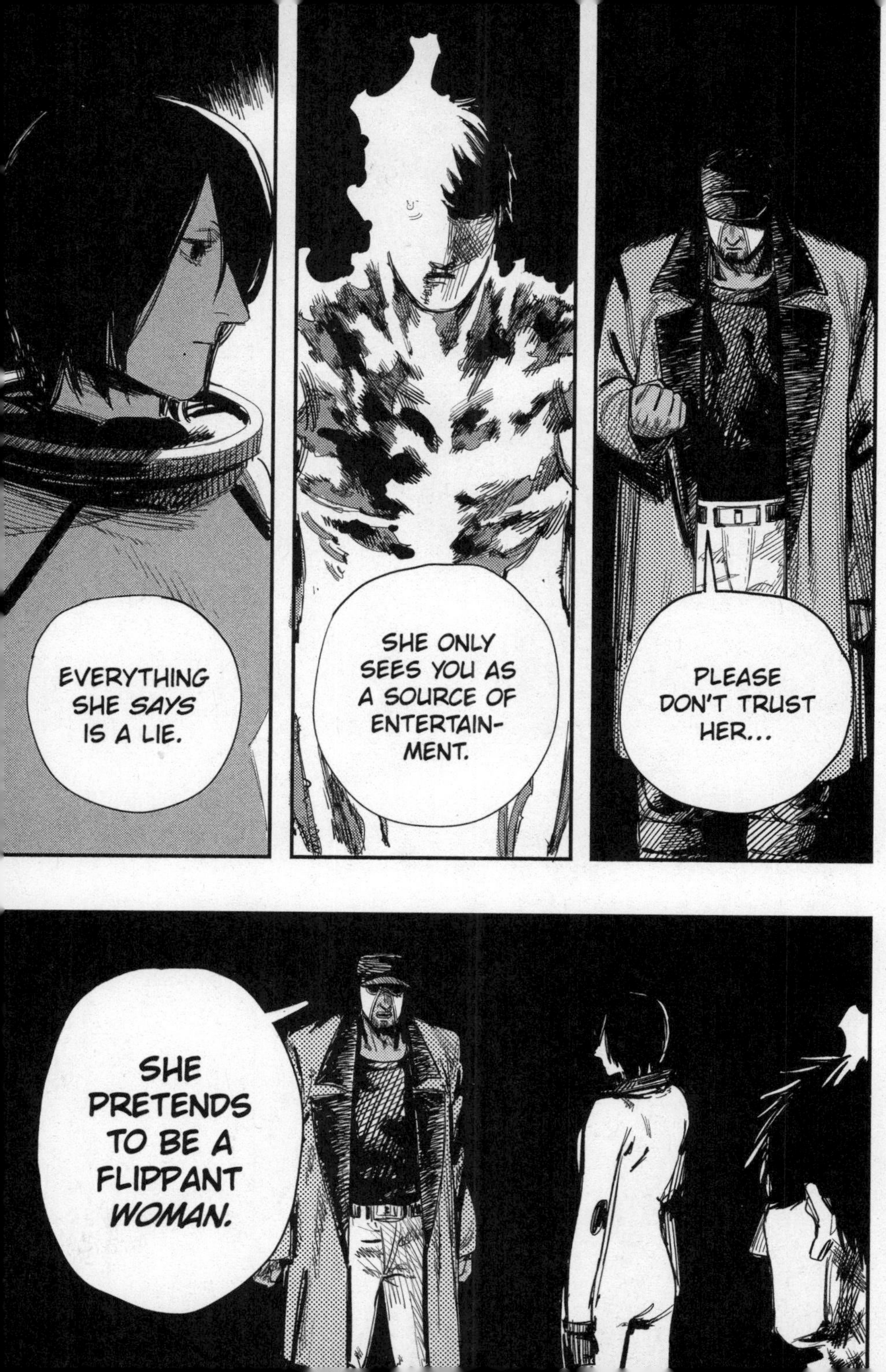
PLEASE DON'T TRUST HER...
SHE ONLY SEES YOU AS A SOURCE OF ENTERTAIN-MENT.
EVERYTHING SHE *SAYS* IS A LIE.
SHE PRETENDS TO BE A FLIPPANT *WOMAN.*

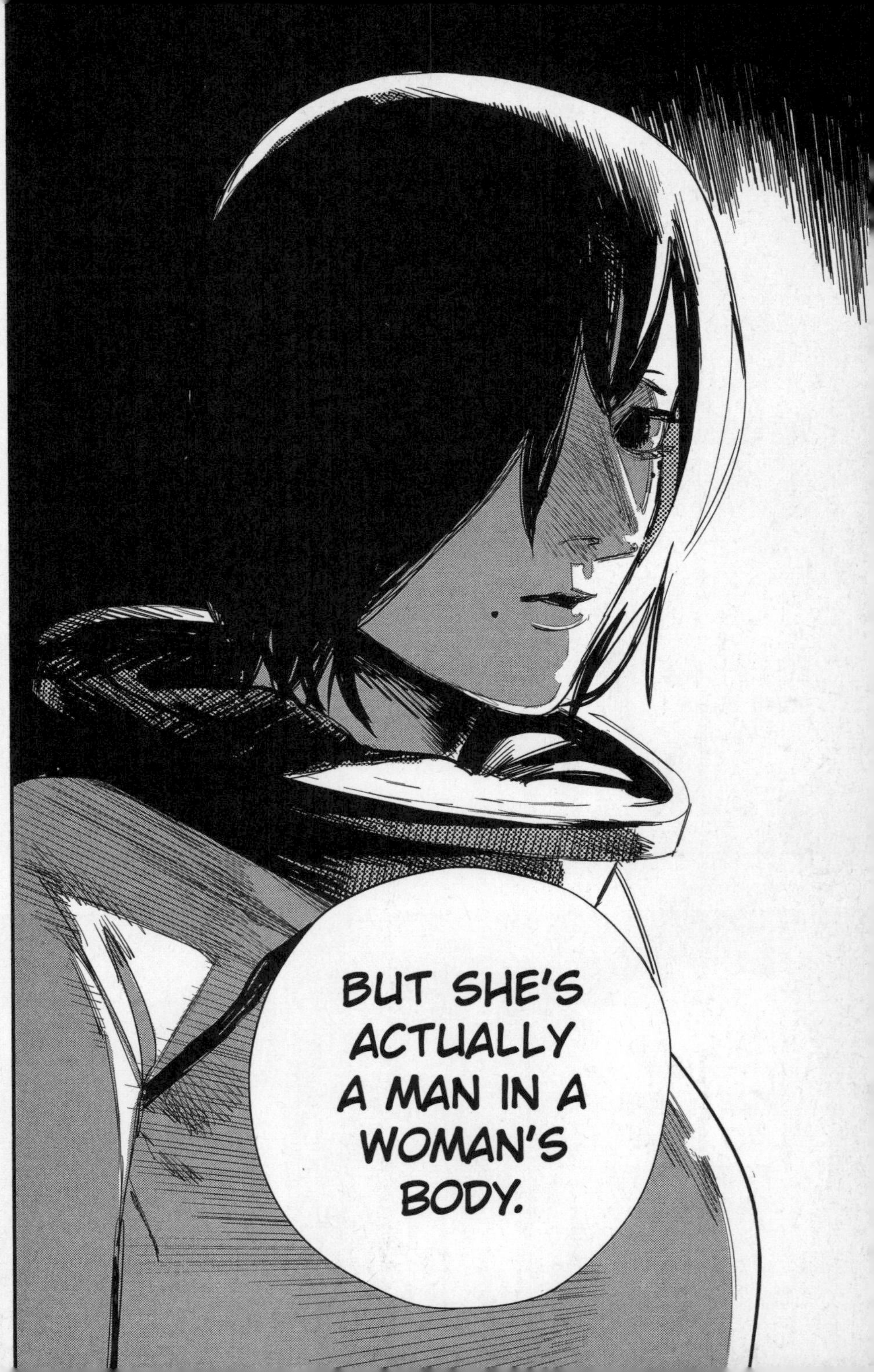
BUT SHE'S ACTUALLY A MAN IN A WOMAN'S BODY.

FIRE PUNCH

CHAPTER 37

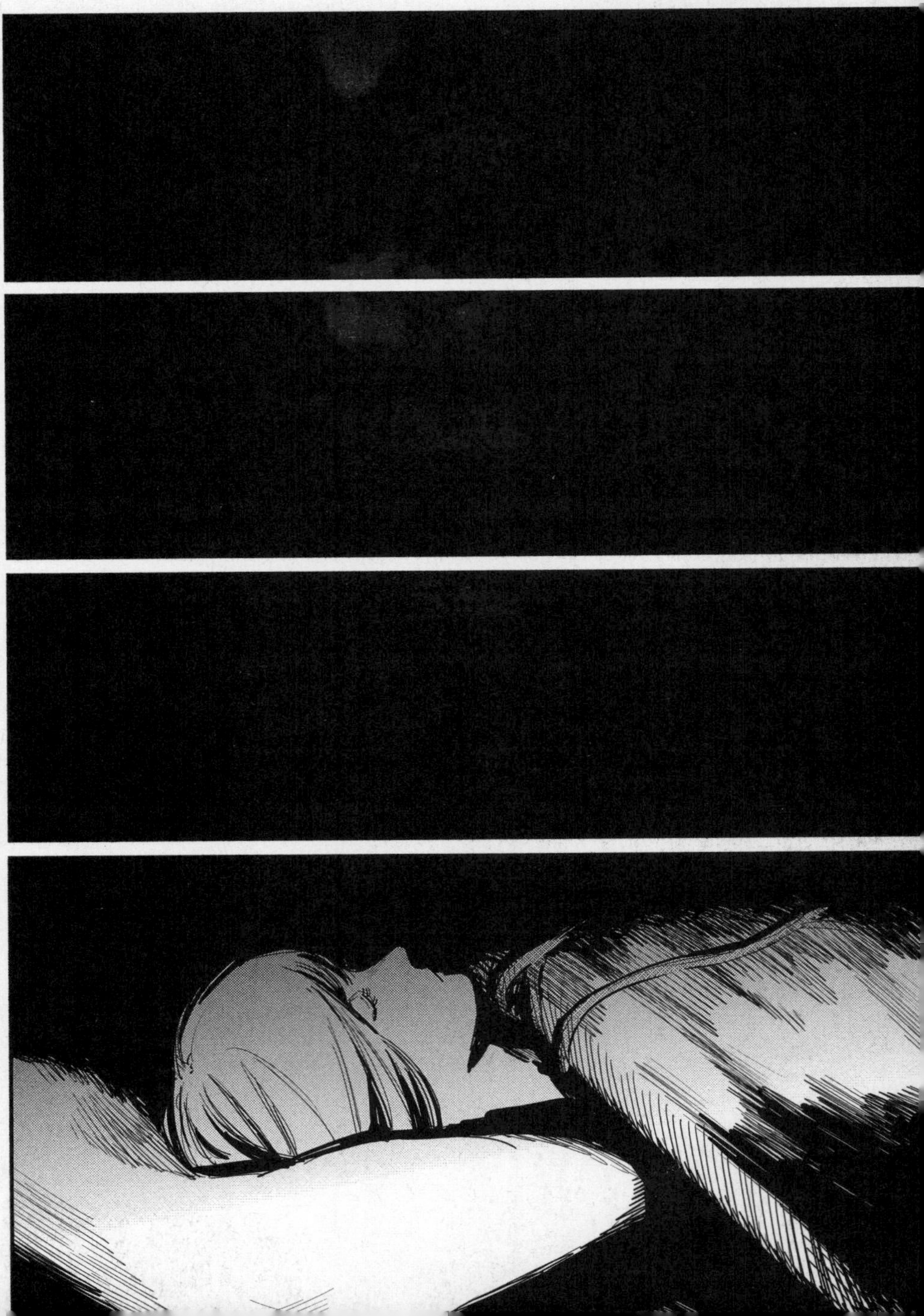

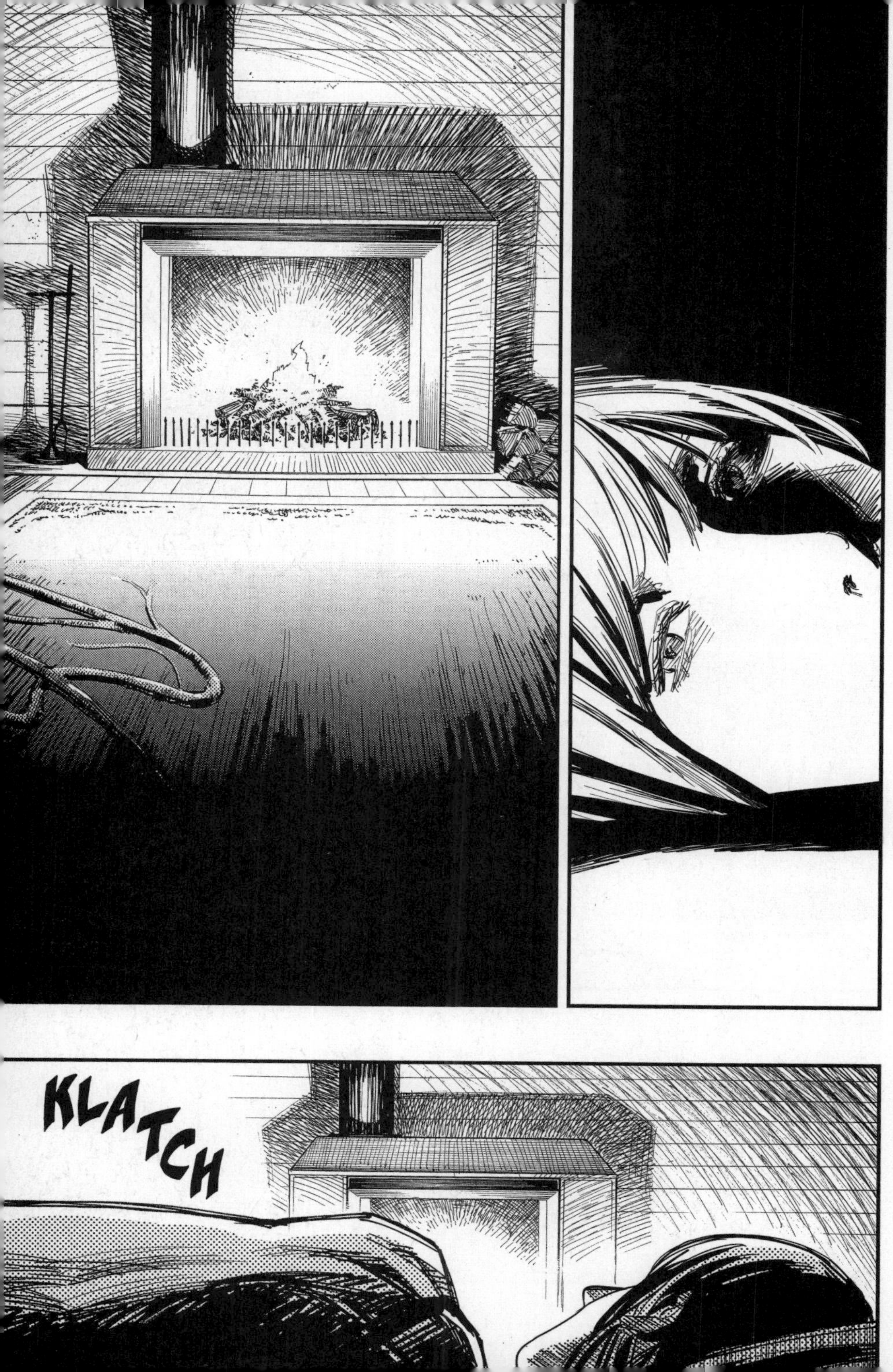
KLATCH

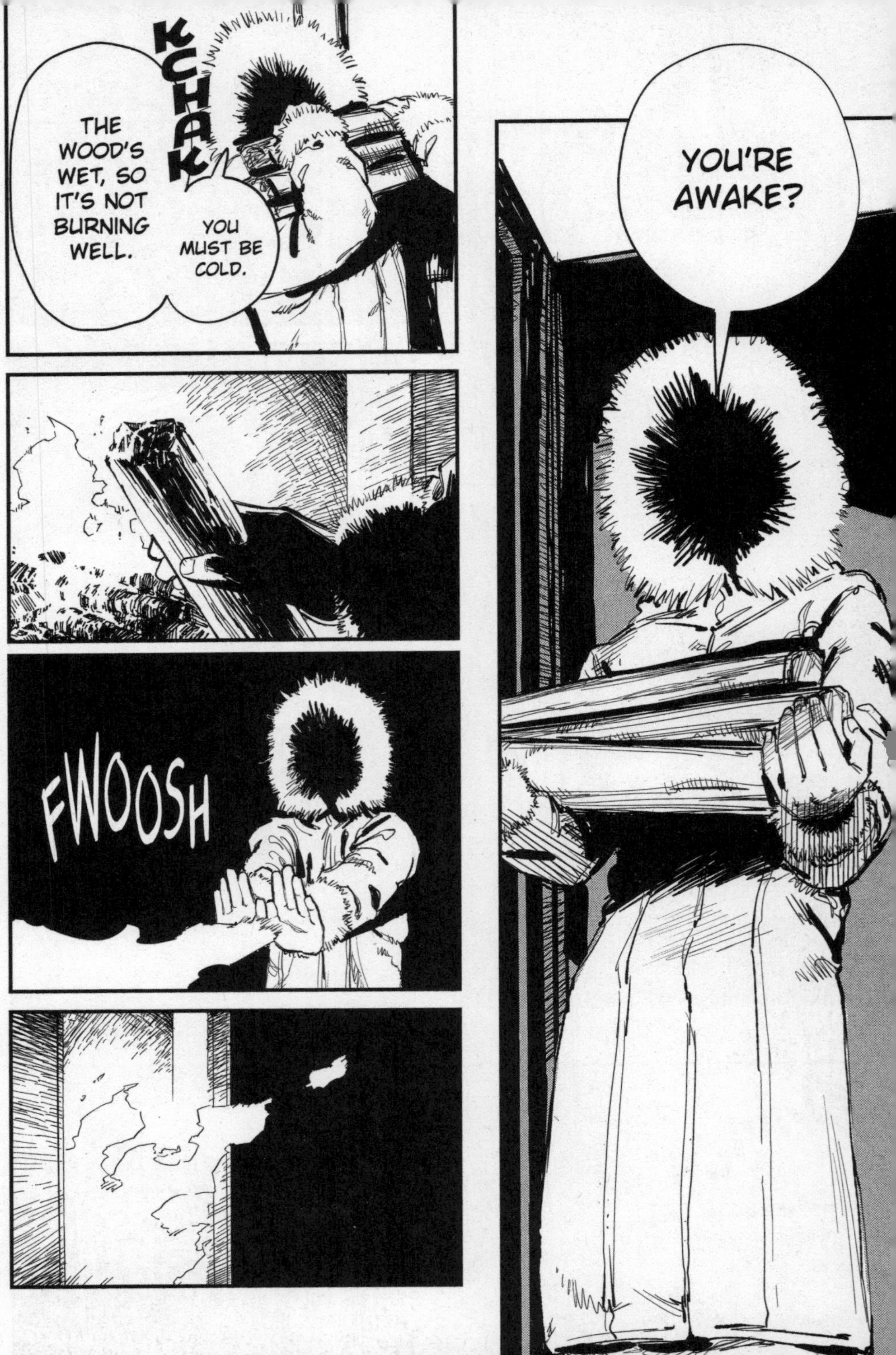
YOU'RE AWAKE?
KCHAK
YOU MUST BE COLD.
THE WOOD'S WET, SO IT'S NOT BURNING WELL.
FWOOSH

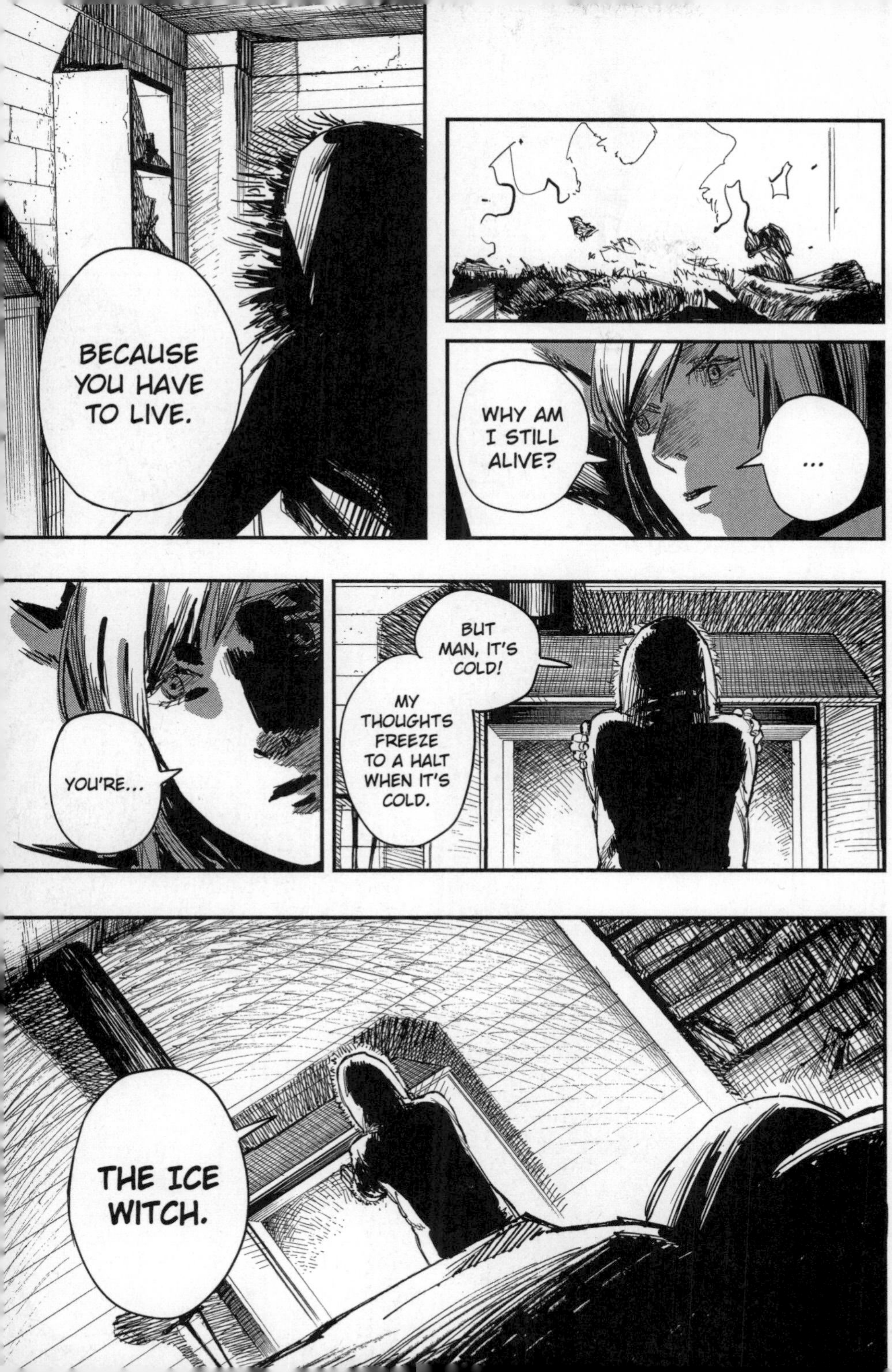
...
WHY AM I STILL ALIVE?
BECAUSE YOU HAVE TO LIVE.
BUT MAN, IT'S COLD!
MY THOUGHTS FREEZE TO A HALT WHEN IT'S COLD.
YOU'RE...
THE ICE WITCH.

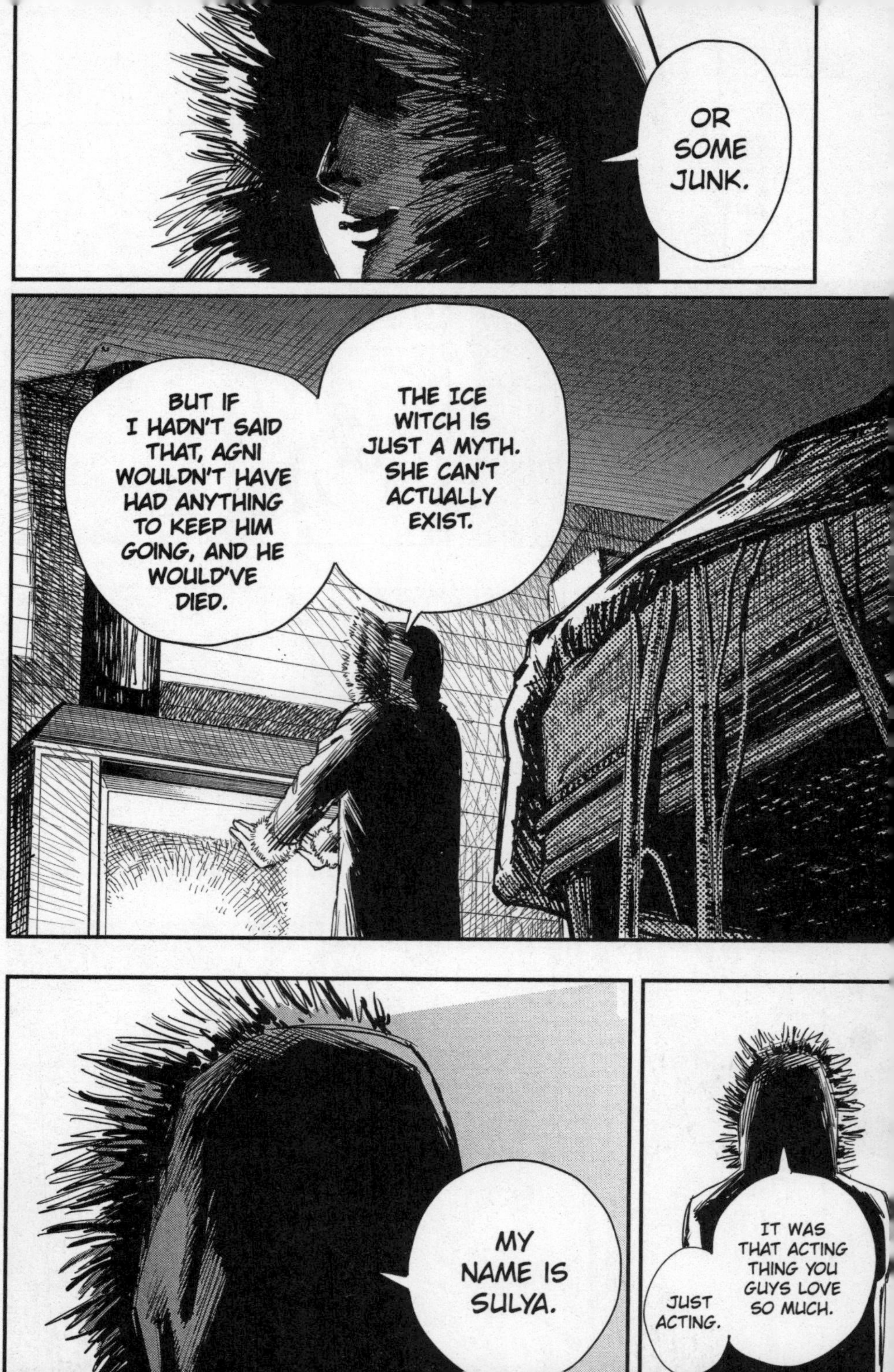
OR SOME JUNK.
THE ICE WITCH IS JUST A MYTH. SHE CAN'T ACTUALLY EXIST.
BUT IF I HADN'T SAID THAT, AGNI WOULDN'T HAVE HAD ANYTHING TO KEEP HIM GOING, AND HE WOULD'VE DIED.
IT WAS THAT ACTING THING YOU GUYS LOVE SO MUCH.
JUST ACTING.
MY NAME IS SULYA.

SORRY I HAD TO PUT YOU THROUGH THAT.

YOU PROBABLY CAN'T MOVE ANYTHING BELOW YOUR NECK.

LET ME DIE.

PLEASE.

...DON'T CARE...IF I DIE.

I...

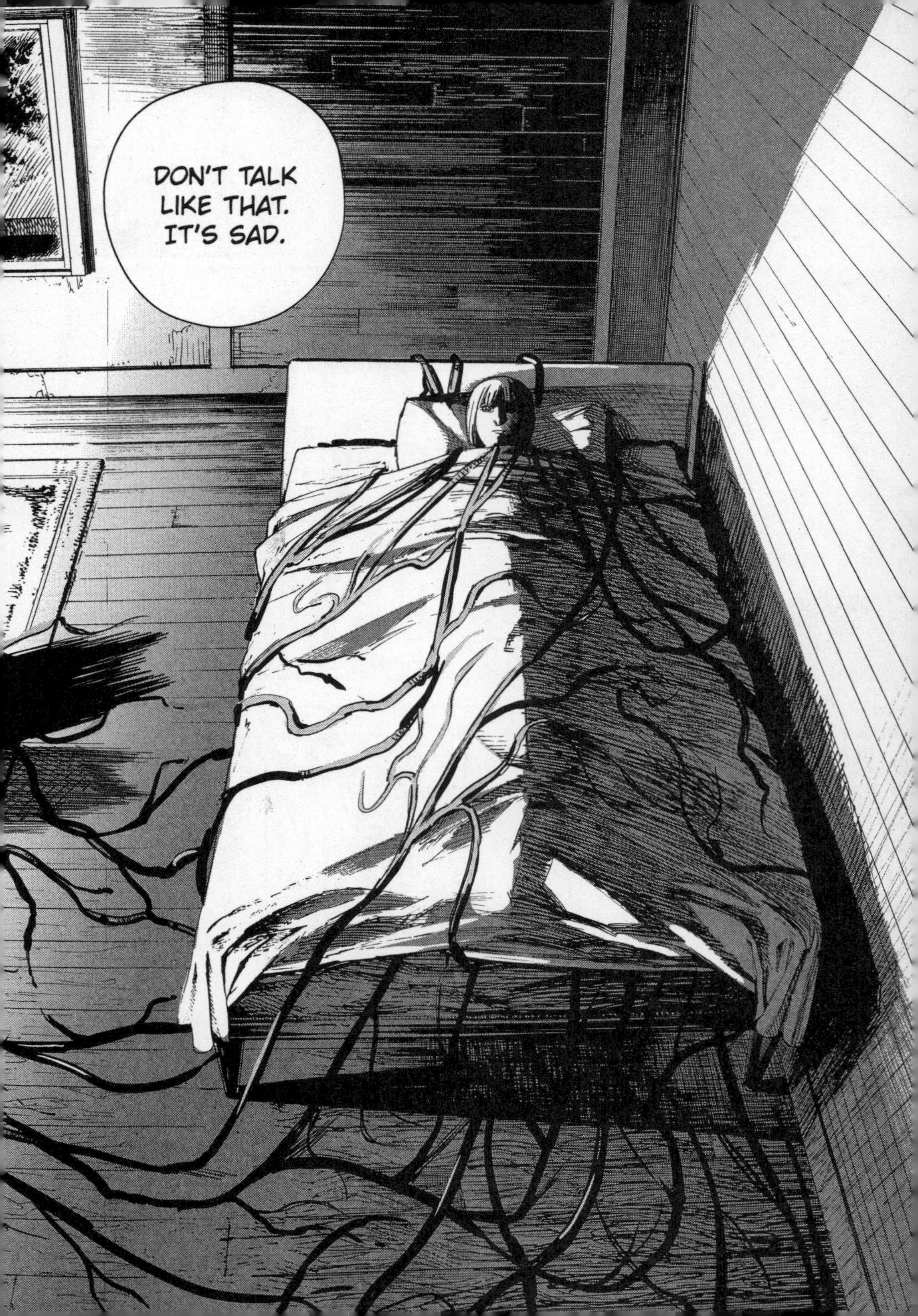
DON'T TALK LIKE THAT. IT'S SAD.

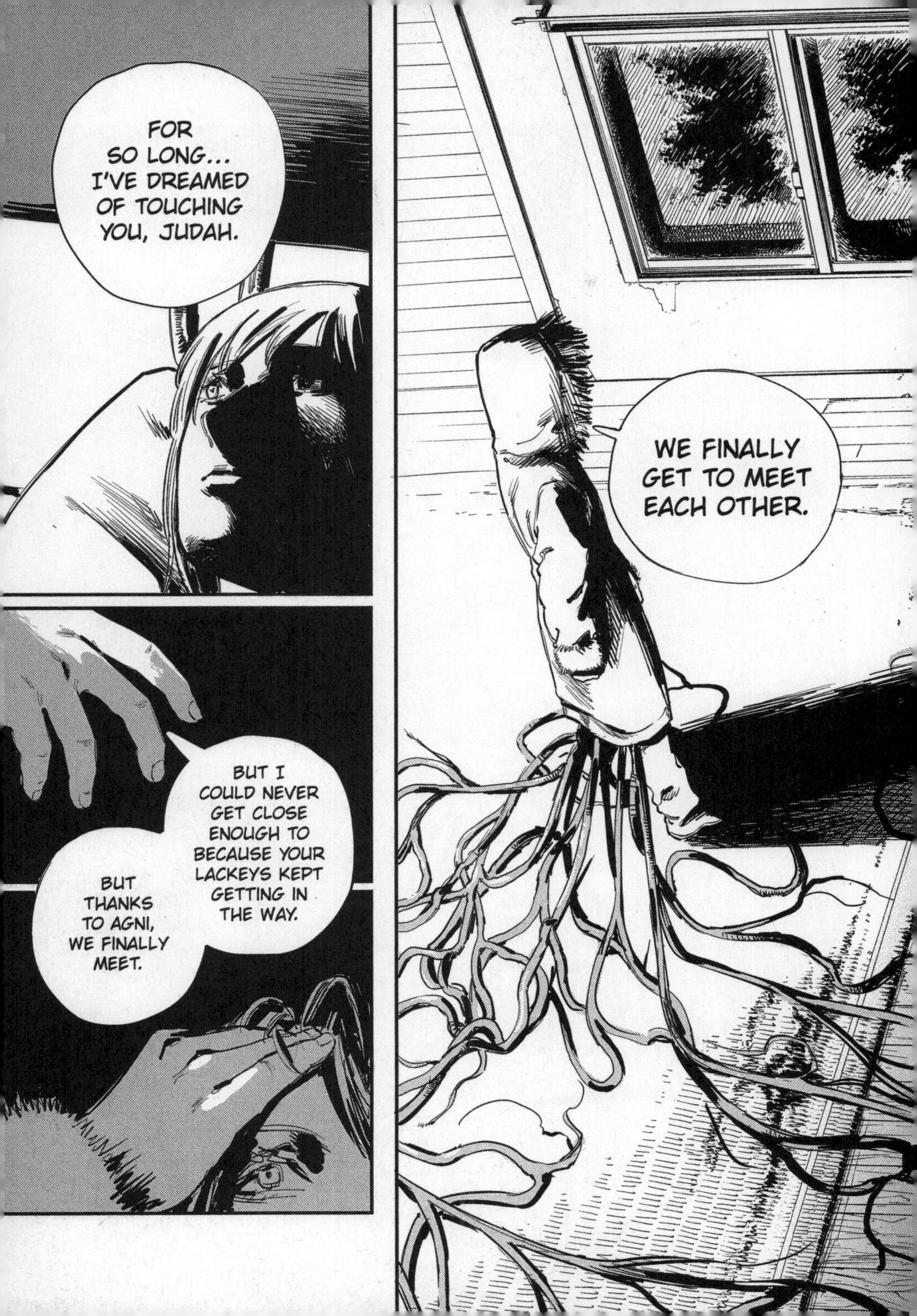
WE FINALLY GET TO MEET EACH OTHER.
FOR SO LONG... I'VE DREAMED OF TOUCHING YOU, JUDAH.
BUT I COULD NEVER GET CLOSE ENOUGH TO BECAUSE YOUR LACKEYS KEPT GETTING IN THE WAY.
BUT THANKS TO AGNI, WE FINALLY MEET.

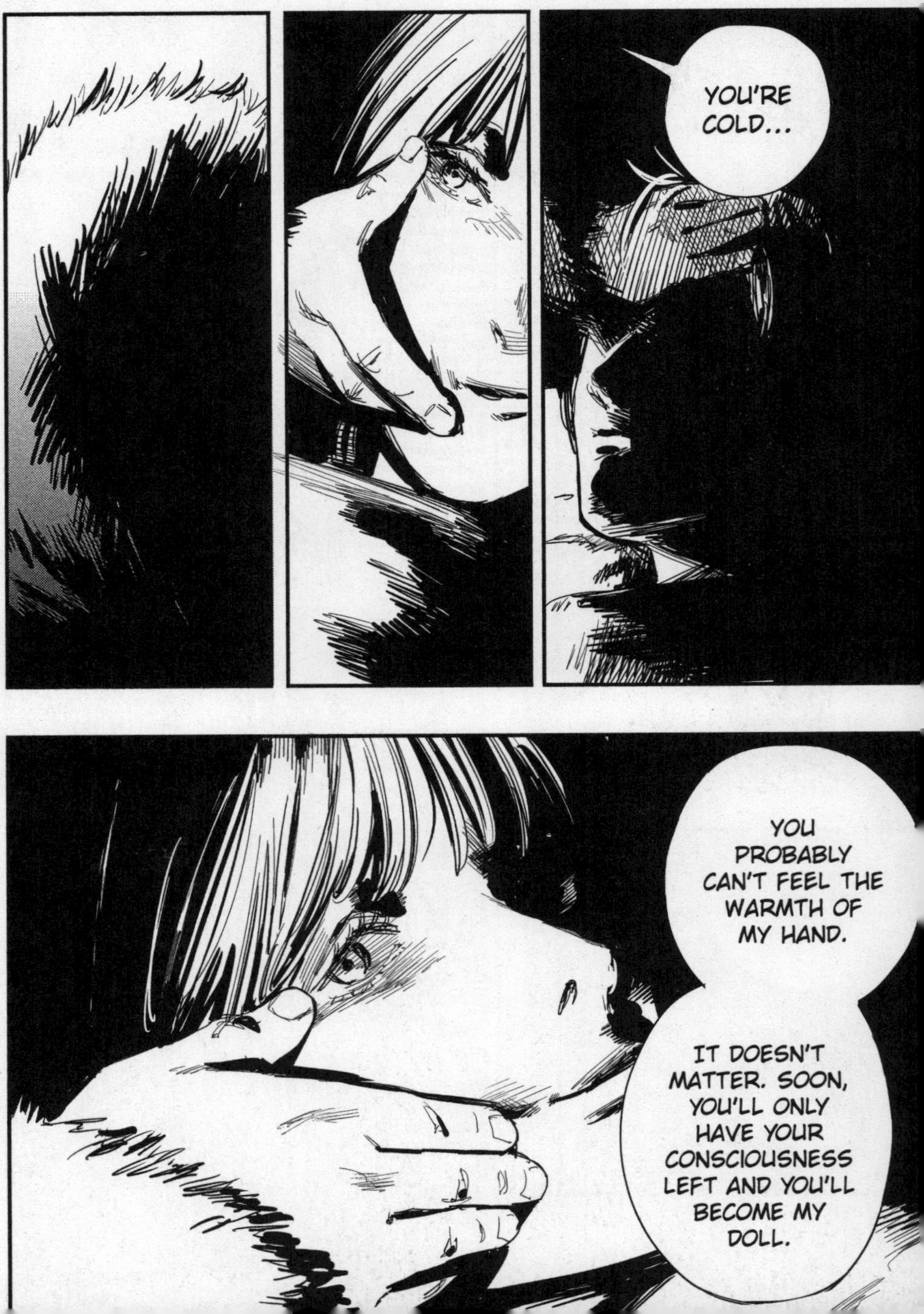
YOU'RE COLD...
YOU PROBABLY CAN'T FEEL THE WARMTH OF MY HAND.
IT DOESN'T MATTER. SOON, YOU'LL ONLY HAVE YOUR CONSCIOUSNESS LEFT AND YOU'LL BECOME MY DOLL.

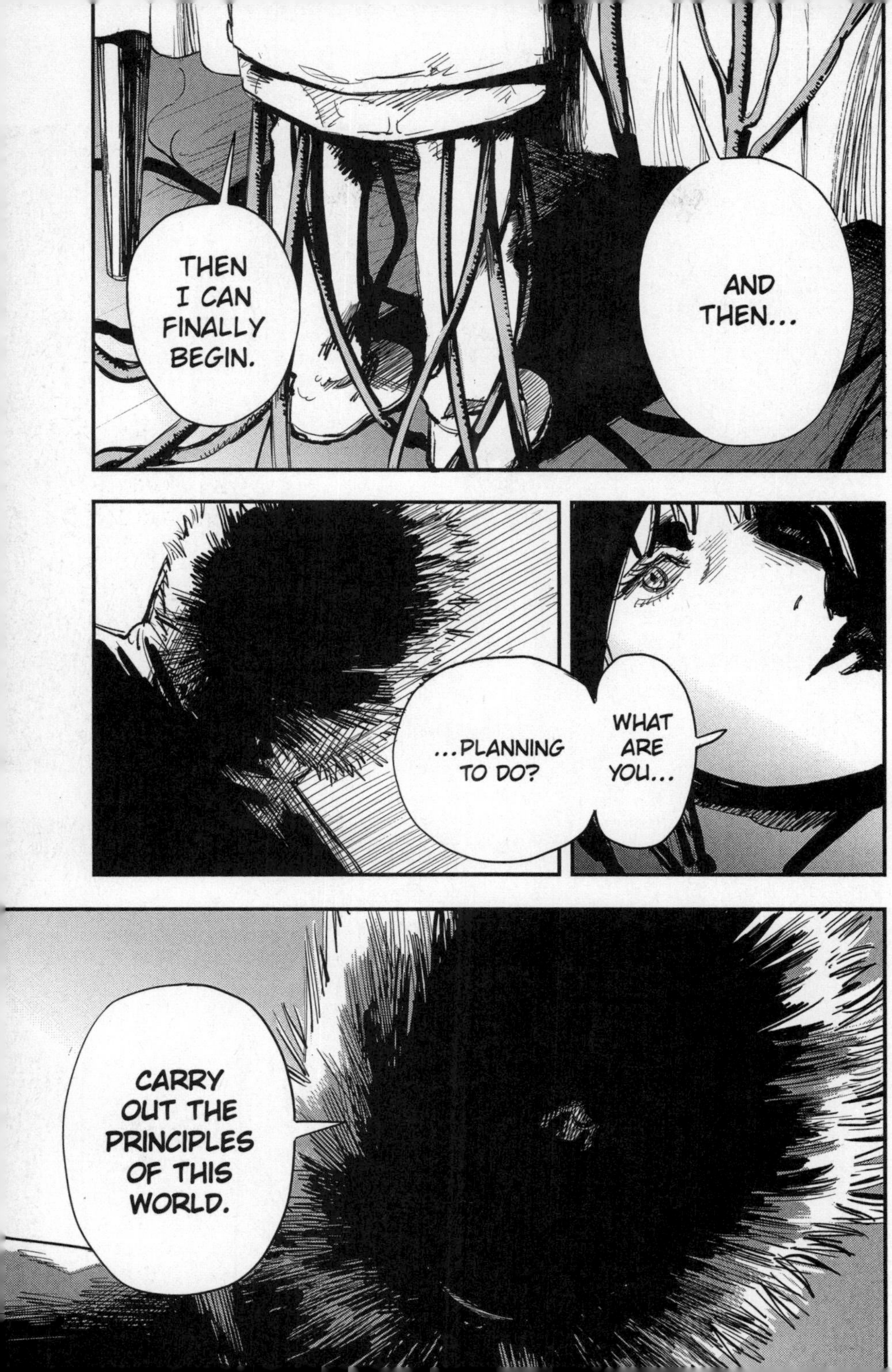
AND THEN...
THEN I CAN FINALLY BEGIN.
WHAT ARE YOU...
...PLANNING TO DO?
CARRY OUT THE PRINCIPLES OF THIS WORLD.

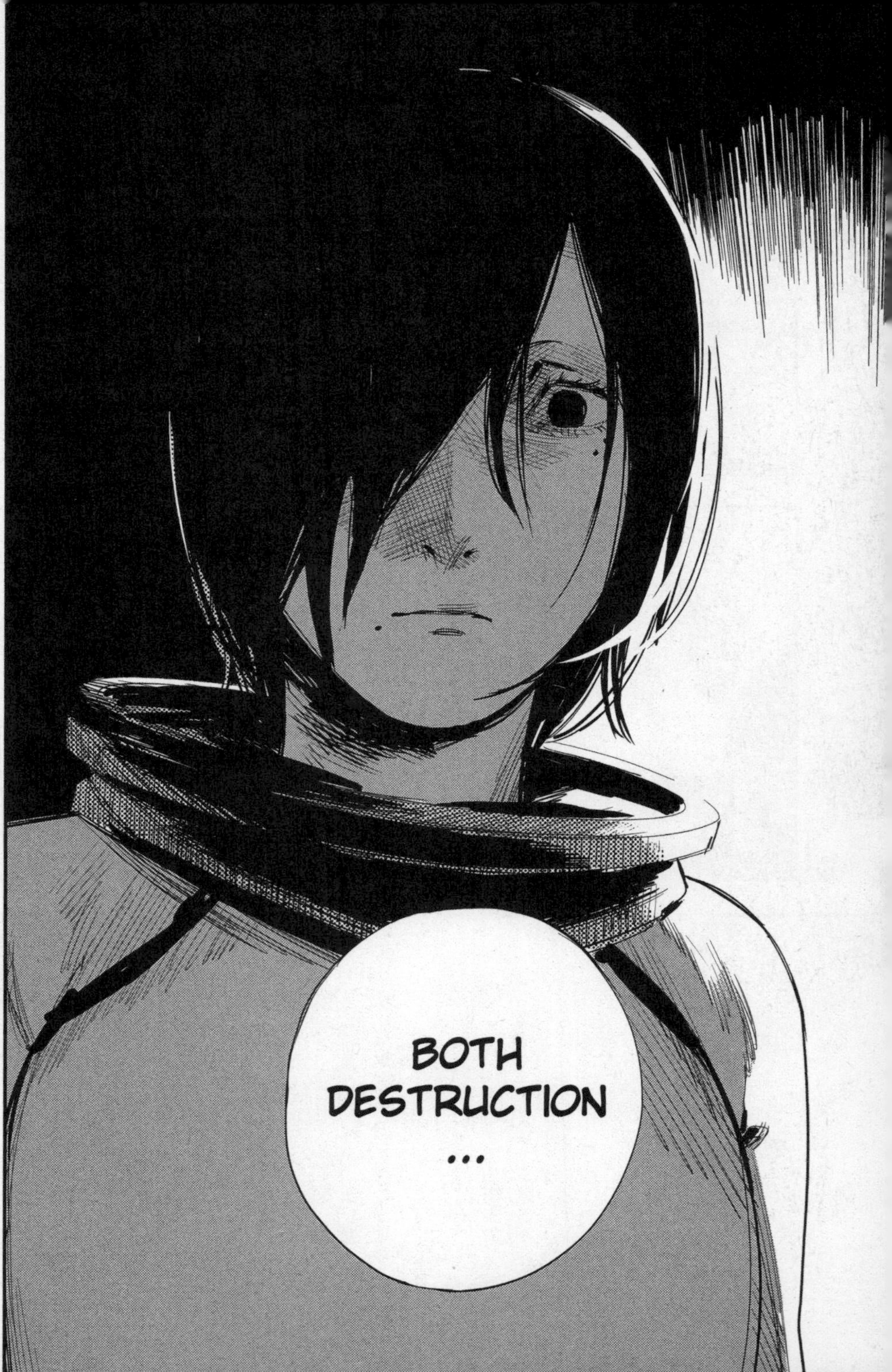
BOTH DESTRUCTION ...

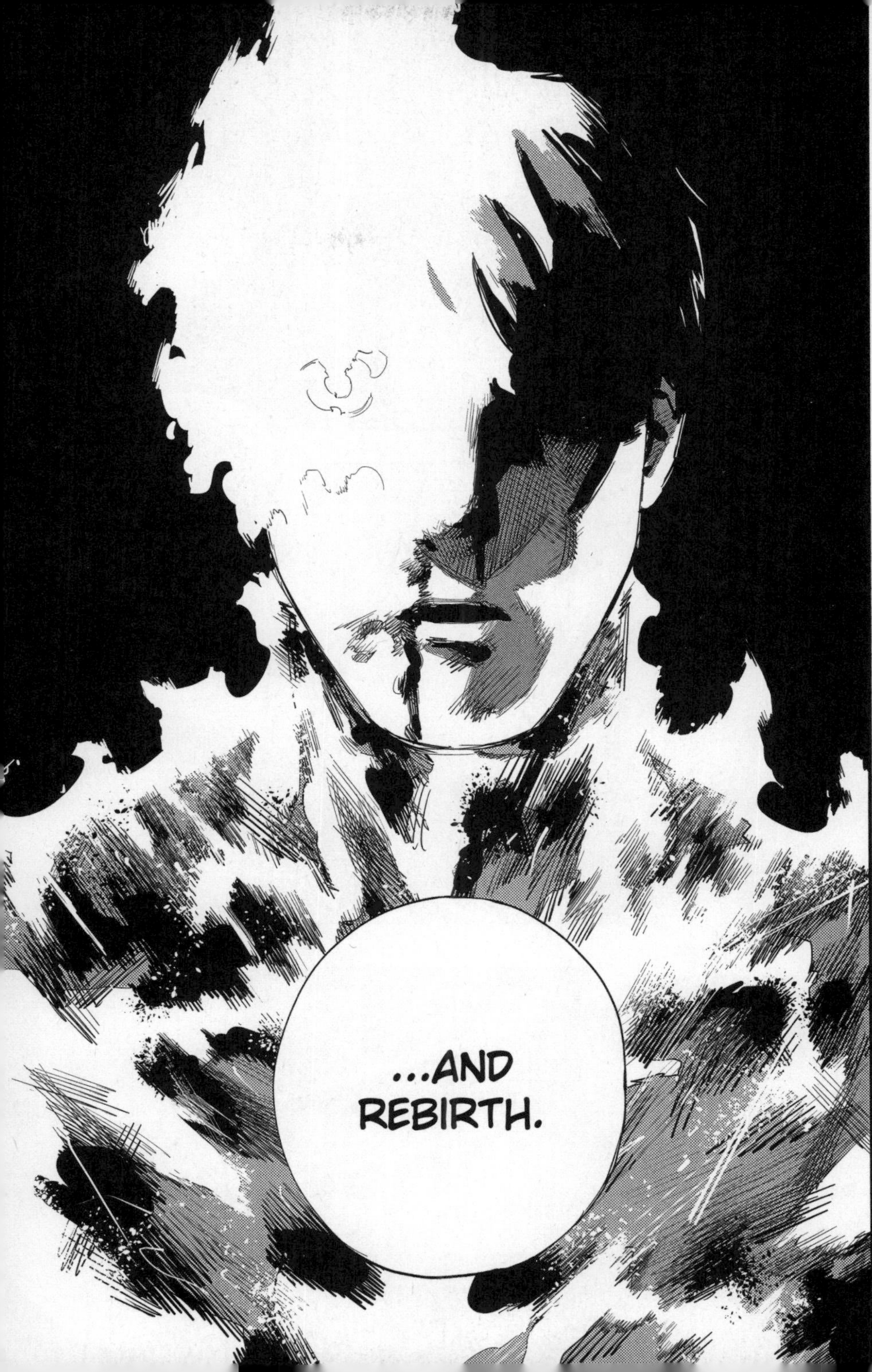
...AND REBIRTH.

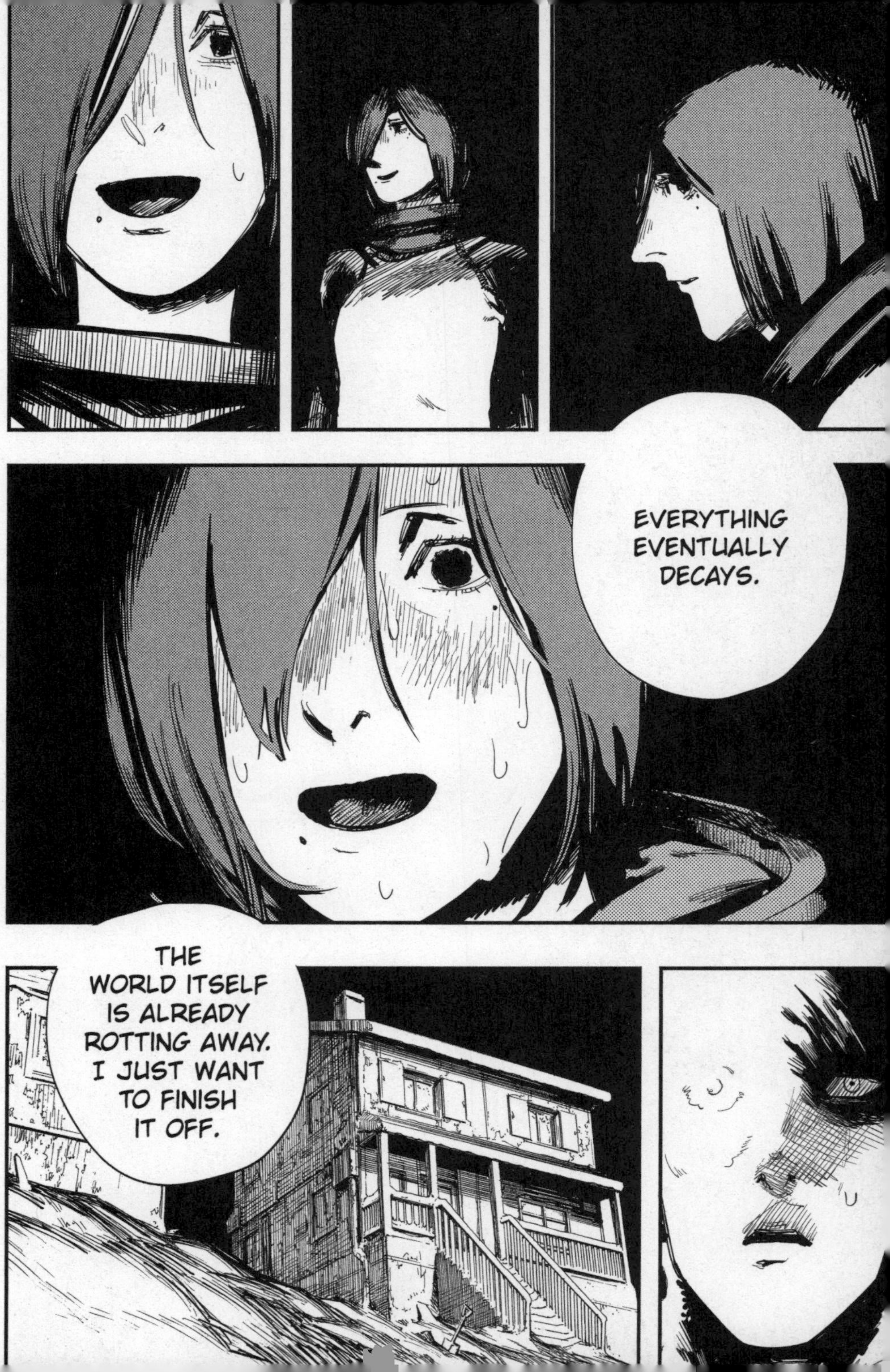
EVERYTHING EVENTUALLY DECAYS.
THE WORLD ITSELF IS ALREADY ROTTING AWAY. I JUST WANT TO FINISH IT OFF.

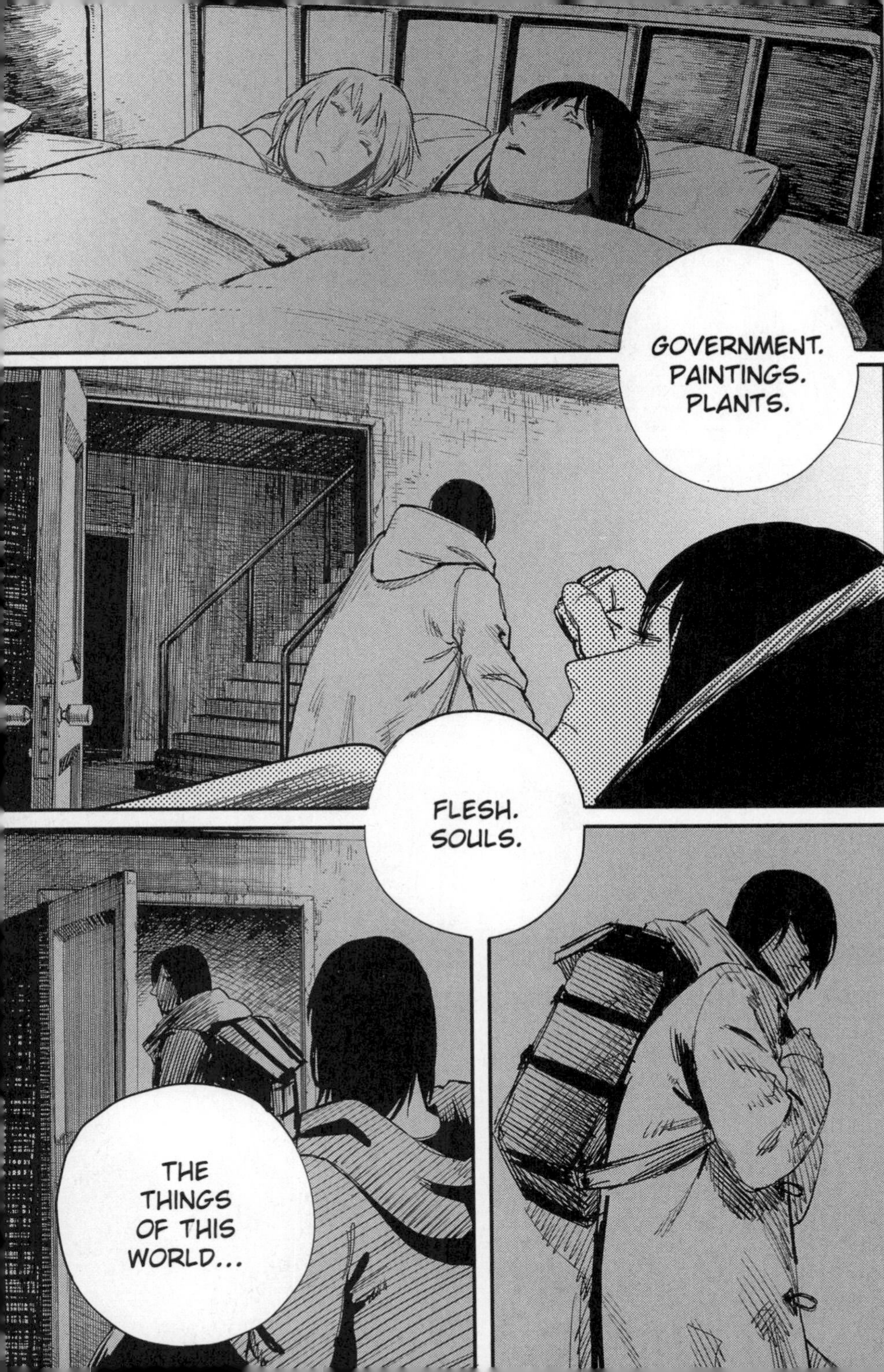
GOVERNMENT.
PAINTINGS.
PLANTS.
FLESH.
SOULS.
THE THINGS OF THIS WORLD...

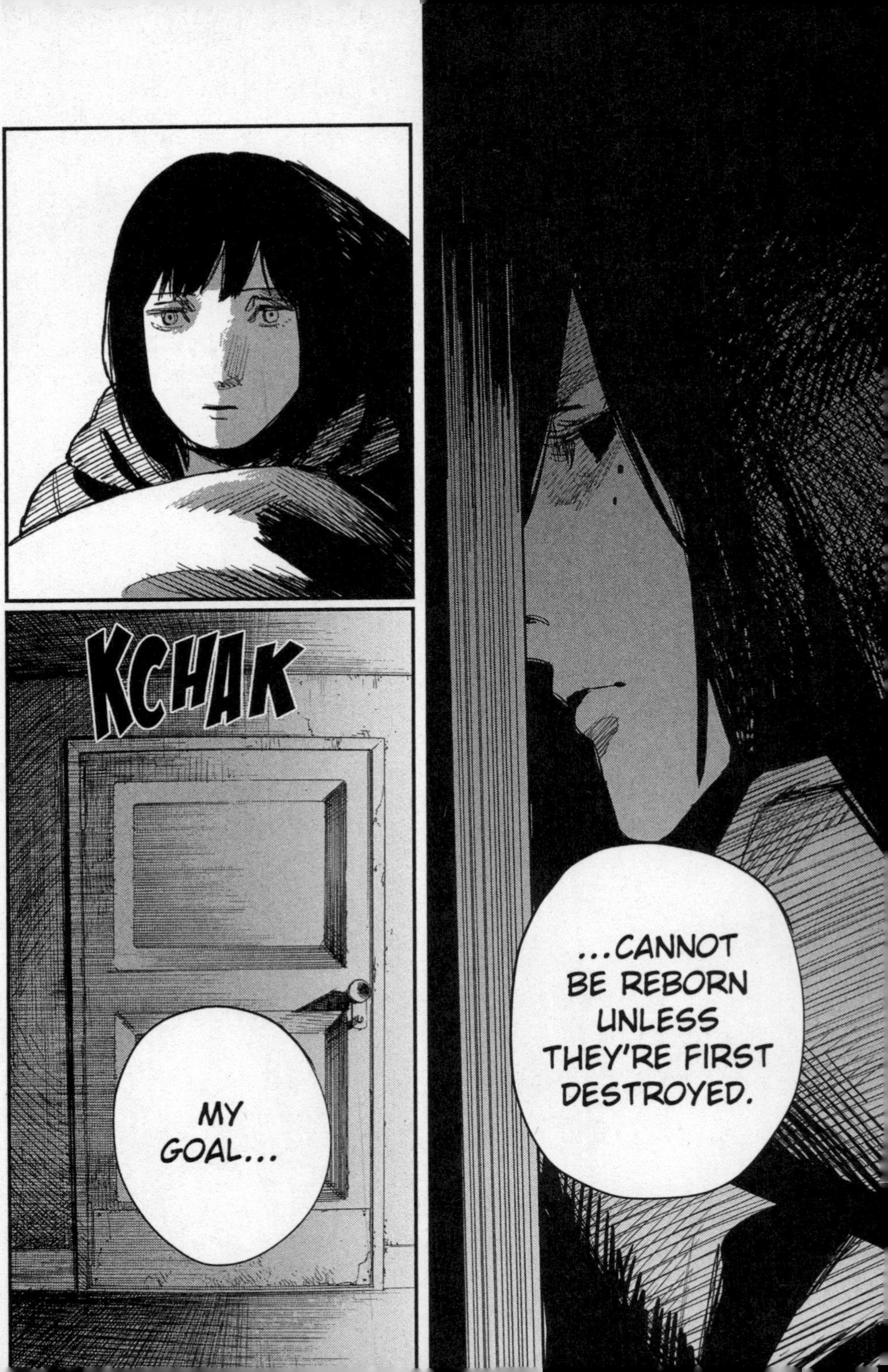
...CANNOT BE REBORN UNLESS THEY'RE FIRST DESTROYED.
KCHAK
MY GOAL...

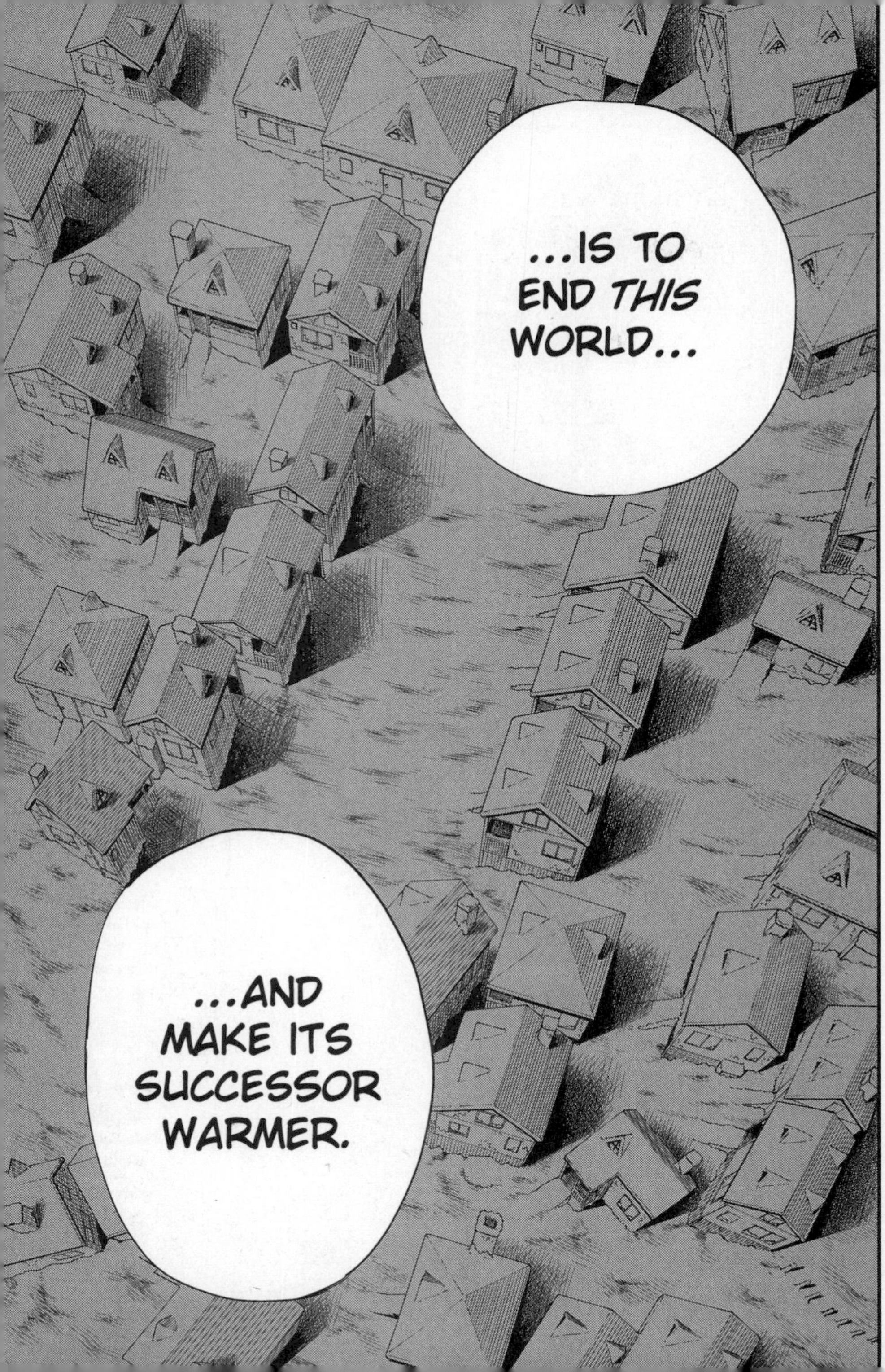
...IS TO END *THIS* WORLD...
...AND MAKE ITS SUCCESSOR WARMER.

FIRE PUNCH

CHAPTER 38

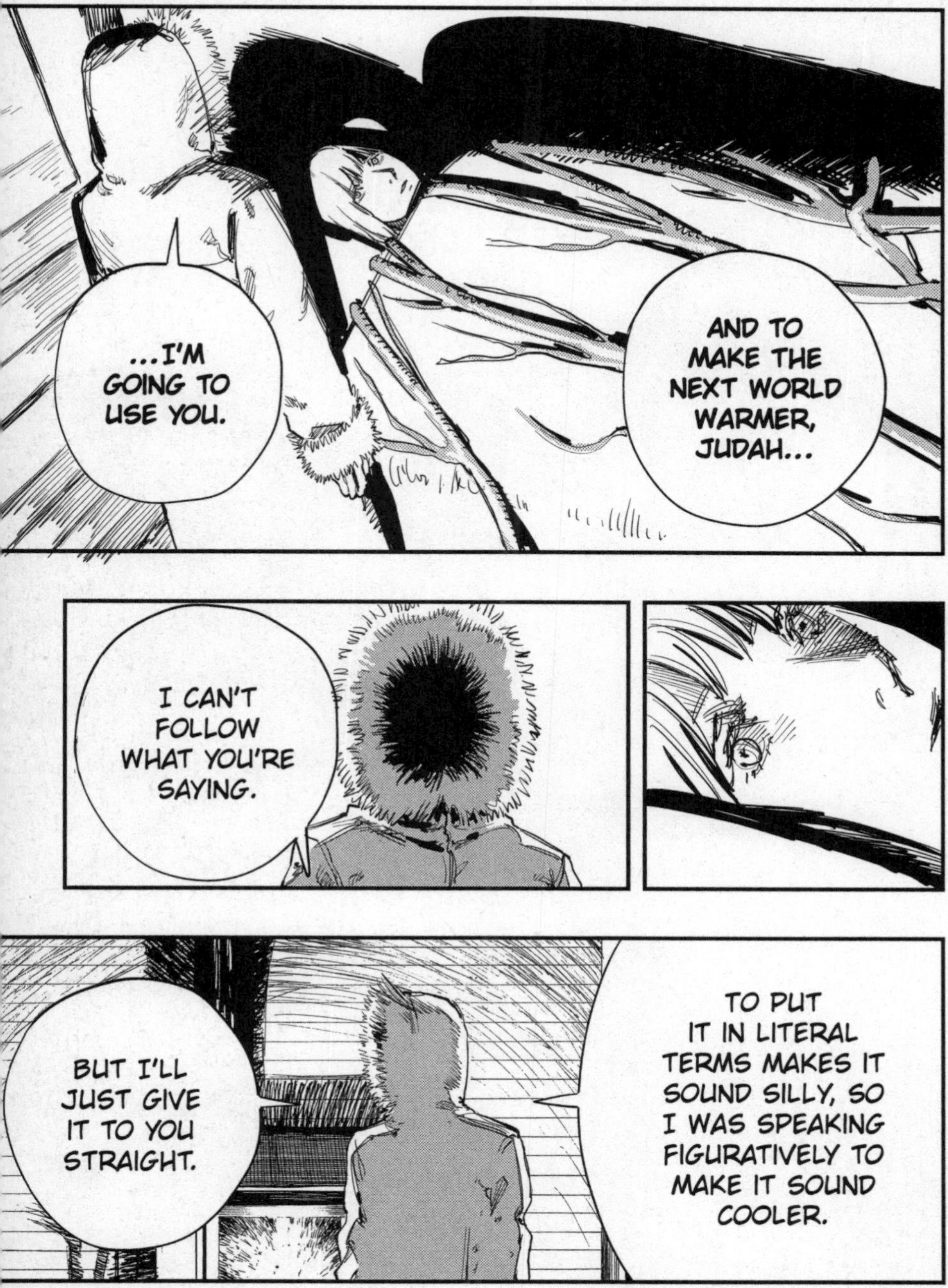

AND TO MAKE THE NEXT WORLD WARMER, JUDAH...
...I'M GOING TO USE YOU.
I CAN'T FOLLOW WHAT YOU'RE SAYING.
TO PUT IT IN LITERAL TERMS MAKES IT SOUND SILLY, SO I WAS SPEAKING FIGURATIVELY TO MAKE IT SOUND COOLER.
BUT I'LL JUST GIVE IT TO YOU STRAIGHT.

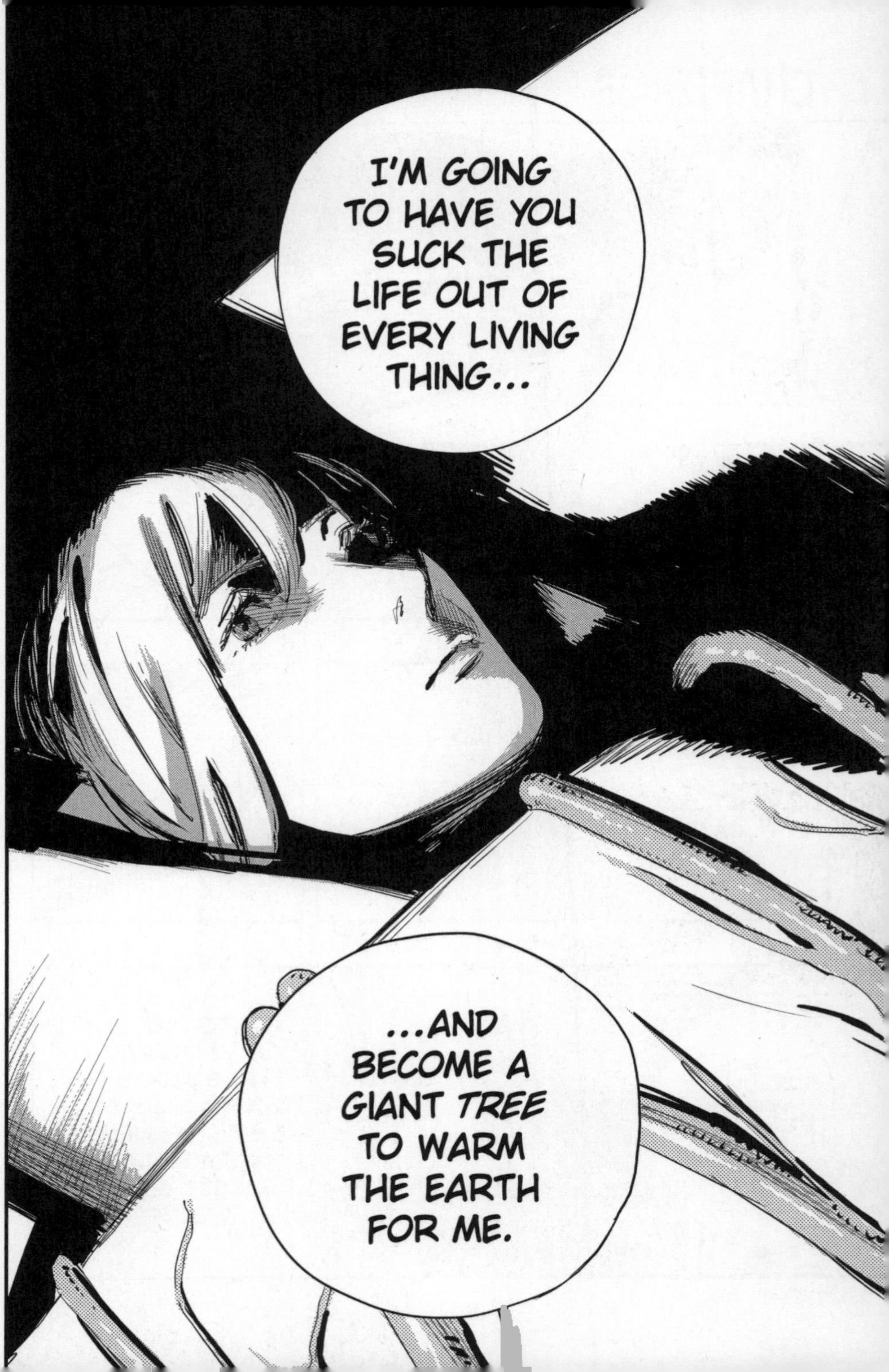
I'M GOING TO HAVE YOU SUCK THE LIFE OUT OF EVERY LIVING THING...
...AND BECOME A GIANT *TREE* TO WARM THE EARTH FOR ME.

...
...
...

A
TREE.

A
TREE?

...?

A TREE!
LIKE THE
PLANT.
YOU KNOW...
WHERE
FIREWOOD
COMES FROM!

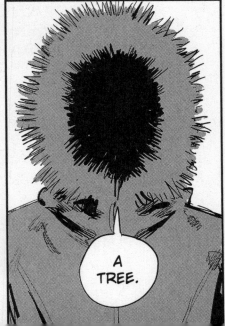

A
TREE.

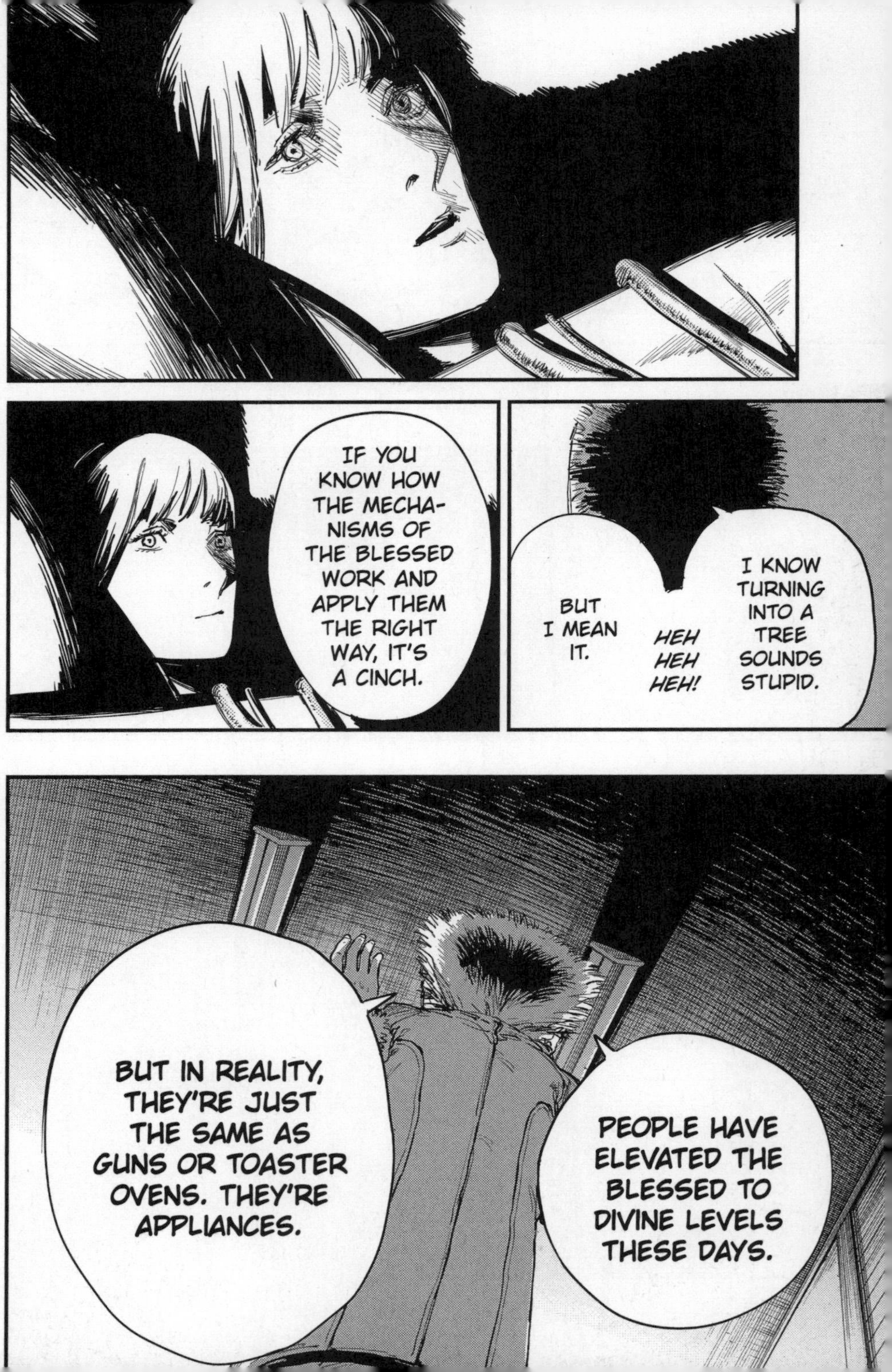
I KNOW TURNING INTO A TREE SOUNDS STUPID.
HEH HEH HEH!
BUT I MEAN IT.
IF YOU KNOW HOW THE MECHA-NISMS OF THE BLESSED WORK AND APPLY THEM THE RIGHT WAY, IT'S A CINCH.
PEOPLE HAVE ELEVATED THE BLESSED TO DIVINE LEVELS THESE DAYS.
BUT IN REALITY, THEY'RE JUST THE SAME AS GUNS OR TOASTER OVENS. THEY'RE APPLIANCES.

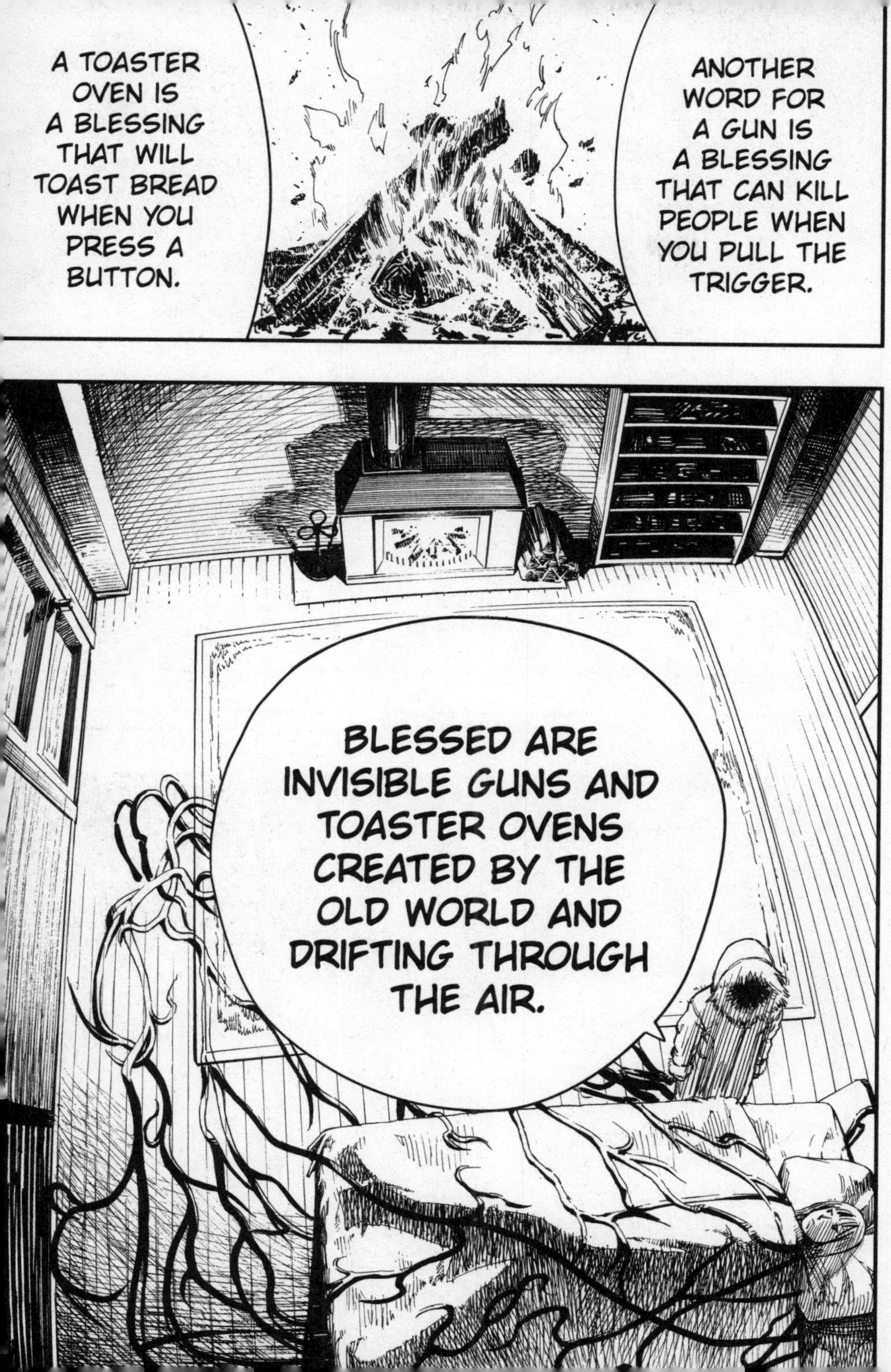
ANOTHER WORD FOR A GUN IS A BLESSING THAT CAN KILL PEOPLE WHEN YOU PULL THE TRIGGER.
A TOASTER OVEN IS A BLESSING THAT WILL TOAST BREAD WHEN YOU PRESS A BUTTON.
BLESSED ARE INVISIBLE GUNS AND TOASTER OVENS CREATED BY THE OLD WORLD AND DRIFTING THROUGH THE AIR.

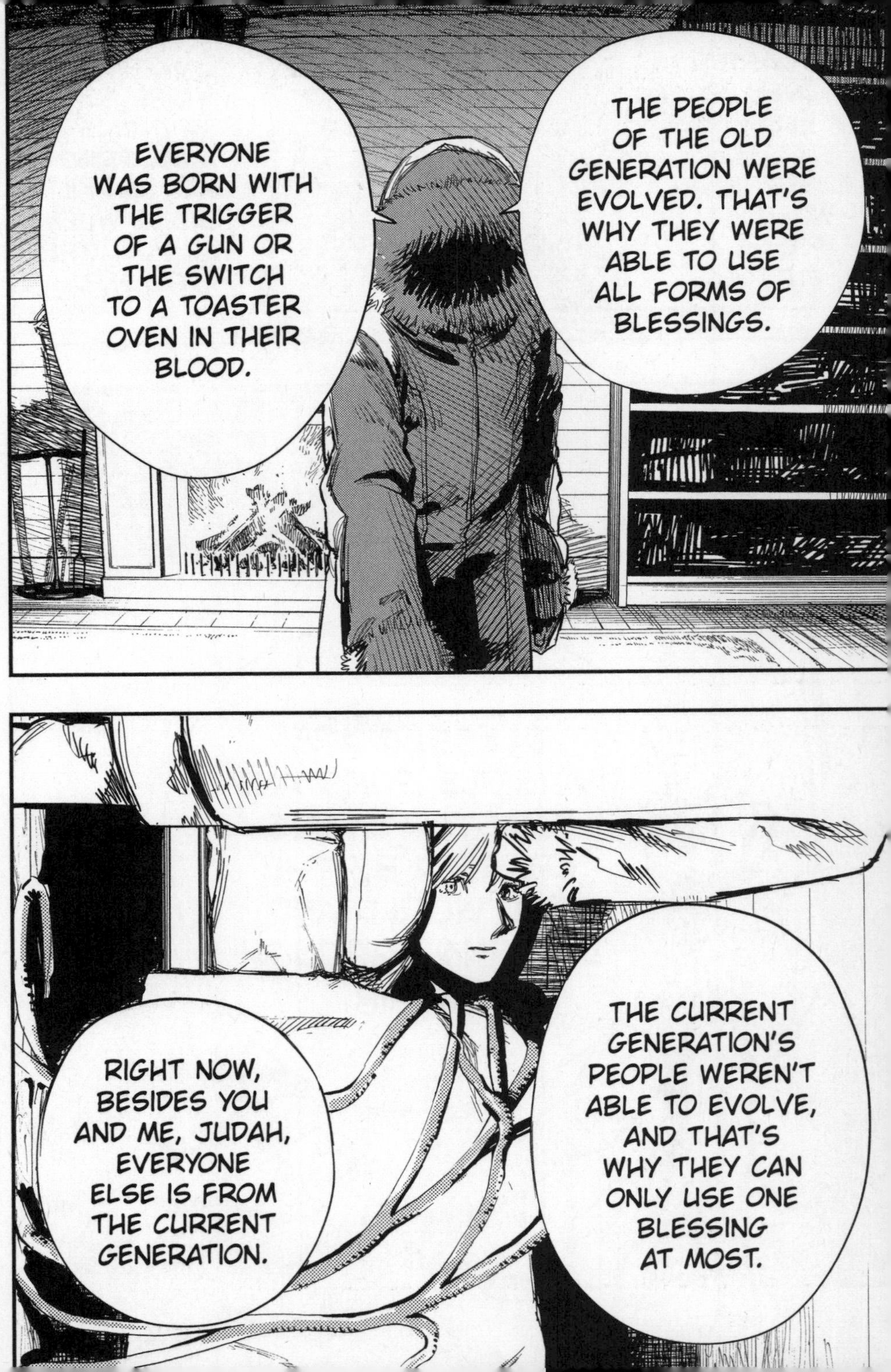
THE PEOPLE OF THE OLD GENERATION WERE EVOLVED. THAT'S WHY THEY WERE ABLE TO USE ALL FORMS OF BLESSINGS.
EVERYONE WAS BORN WITH THE TRIGGER OF A GUN OR THE SWITCH TO A TOASTER OVEN IN THEIR BLOOD.
THE CURRENT GENERATION'S PEOPLE WEREN'T ABLE TO EVOLVE, AND THAT'S WHY THEY CAN ONLY USE ONE BLESSING AT MOST.
RIGHT NOW, BESIDES YOU AND ME, JUDAH, EVERYONE ELSE IS FROM THE CURRENT GENERATION.

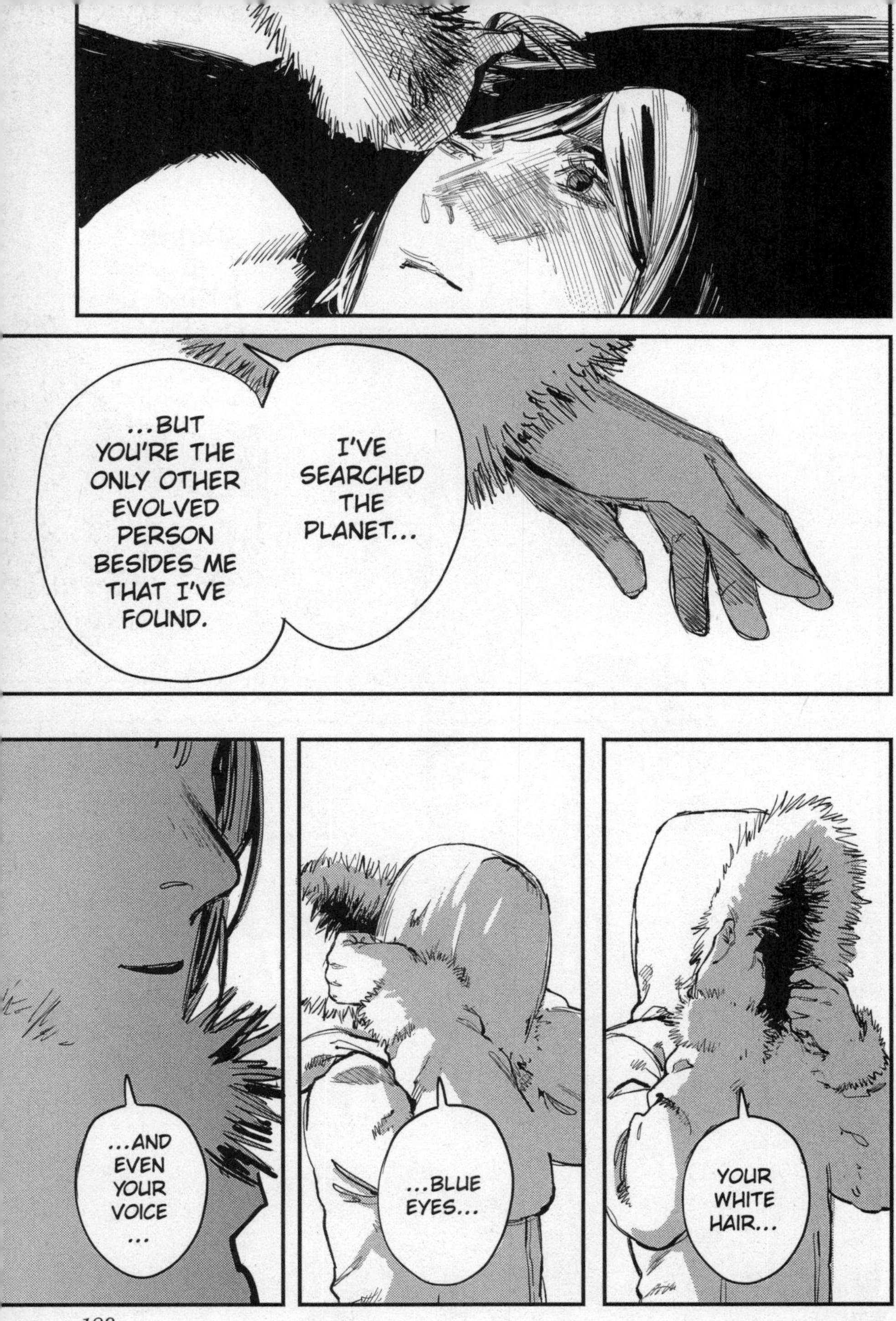
I'VE SEARCHED THE PLANET...
...BUT YOU'RE THE ONLY OTHER EVOLVED PERSON BESIDES ME THAT I'VE FOUND.
YOUR WHITE HAIR...
...BLUE EYES...
...AND EVEN YOUR VOICE ...

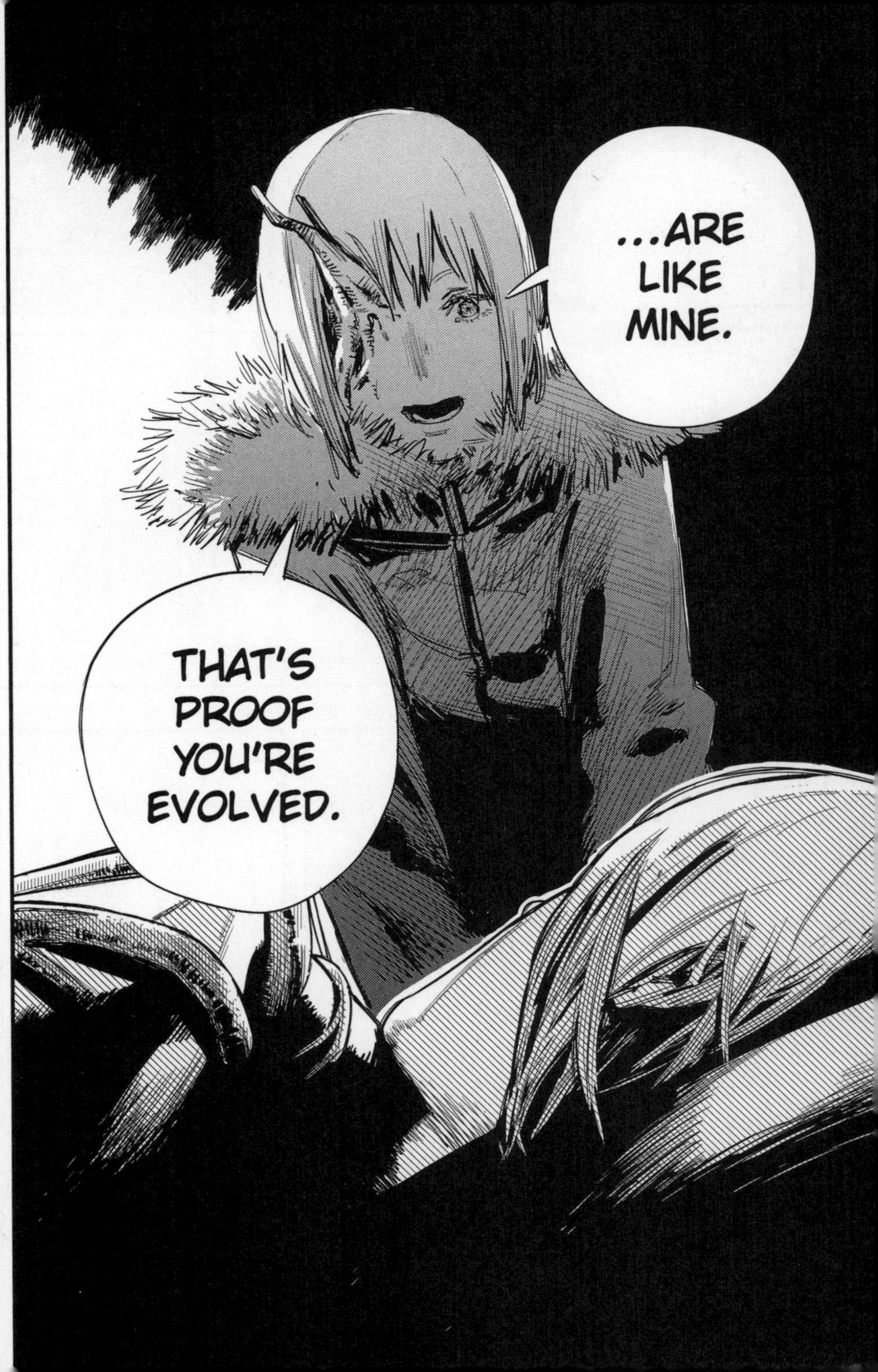
...ARE LIKE MINE.
THAT'S PROOF YOU'RE EVOLVED.

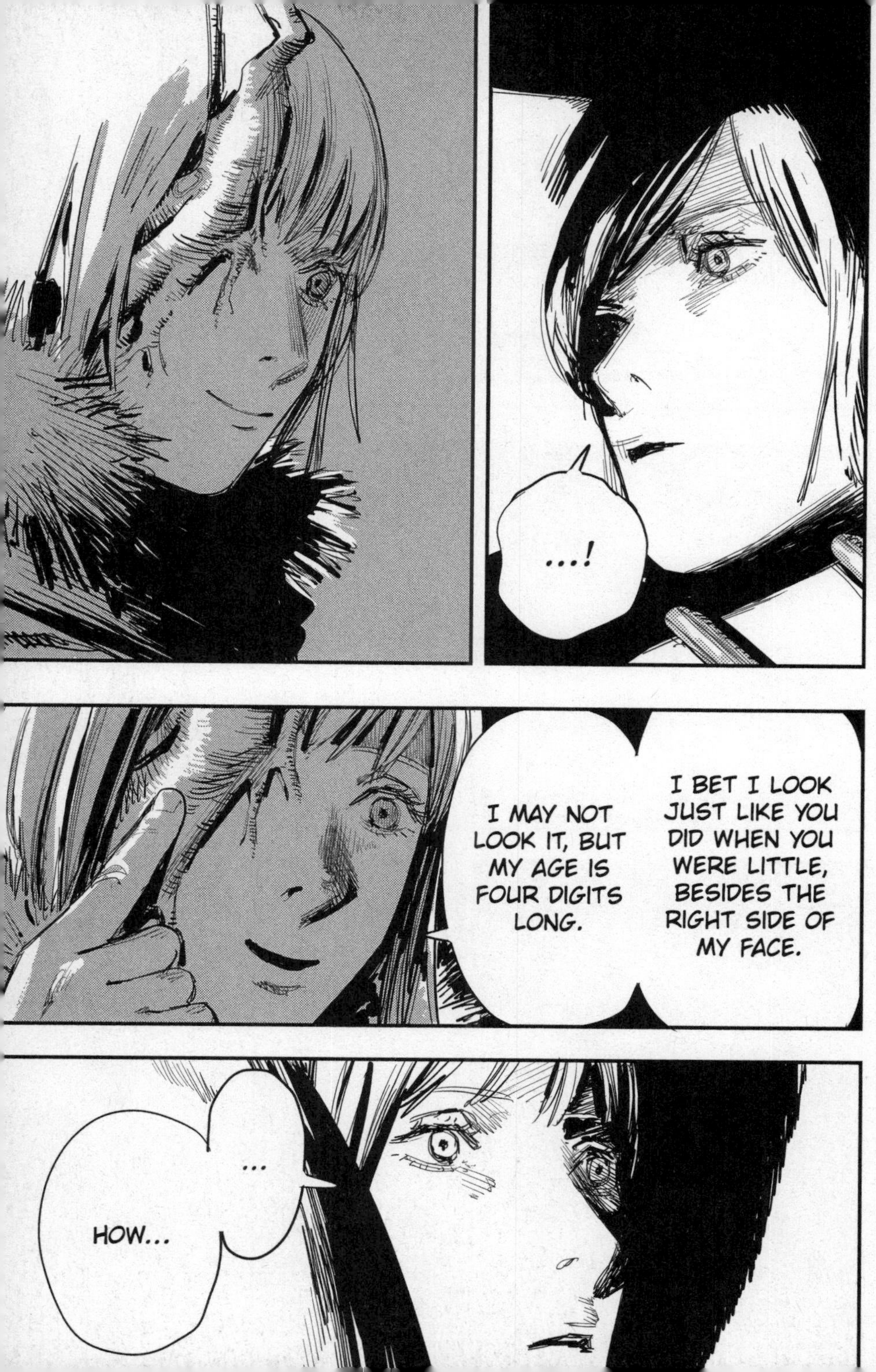
...!
I BET I LOOK JUST LIKE YOU DID WHEN YOU WERE LITTLE, BESIDES THE RIGHT SIDE OF MY FACE.
I MAY NOT LOOK IT, BUT MY AGE IS FOUR DIGITS LONG.
...
HOW...

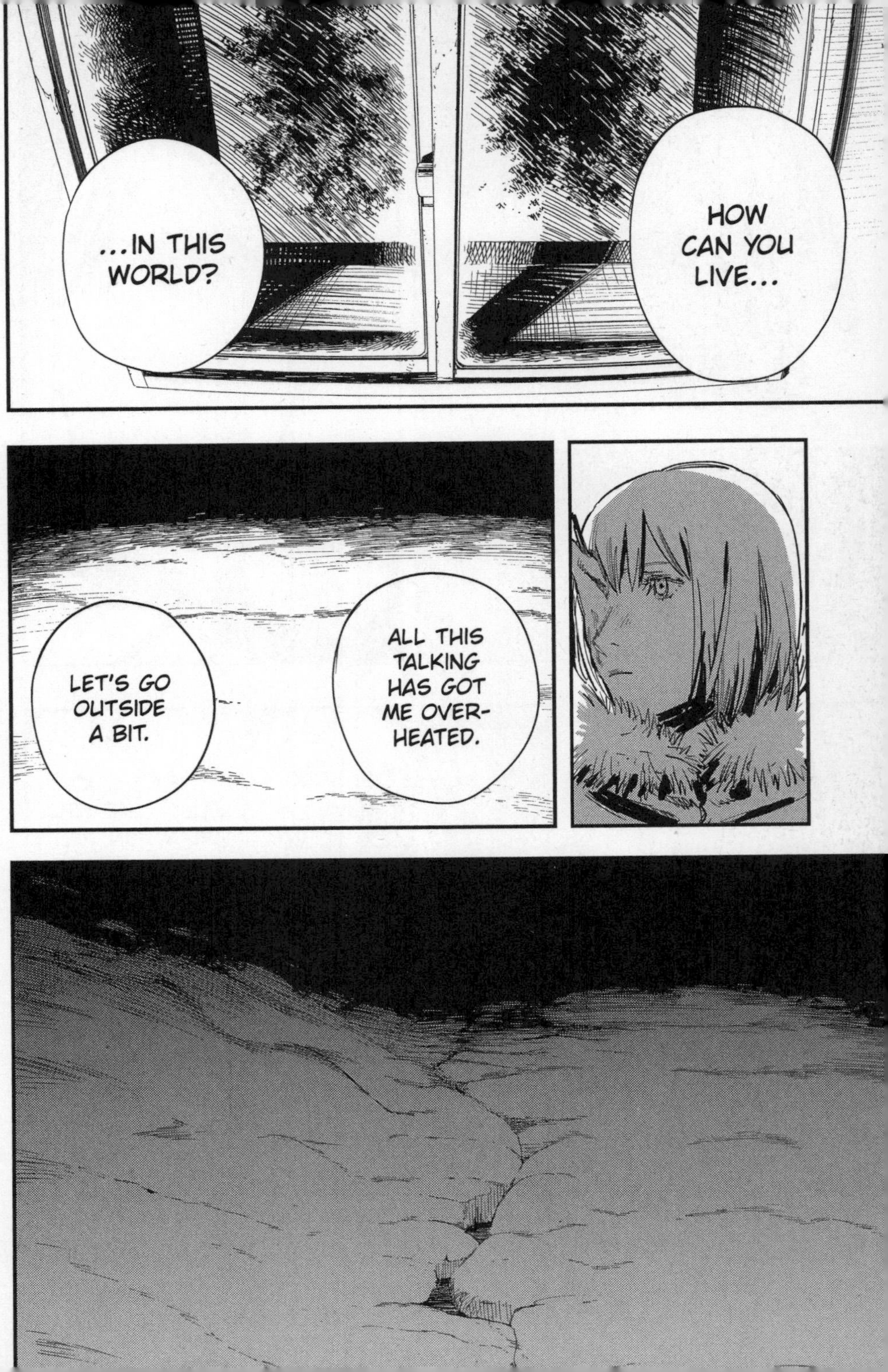
HOW CAN YOU LIVE...
...IN THIS WORLD?
ALL THIS TALKING HAS GOT ME OVER-HEATED.
LET'S GO OUTSIDE A BIT.

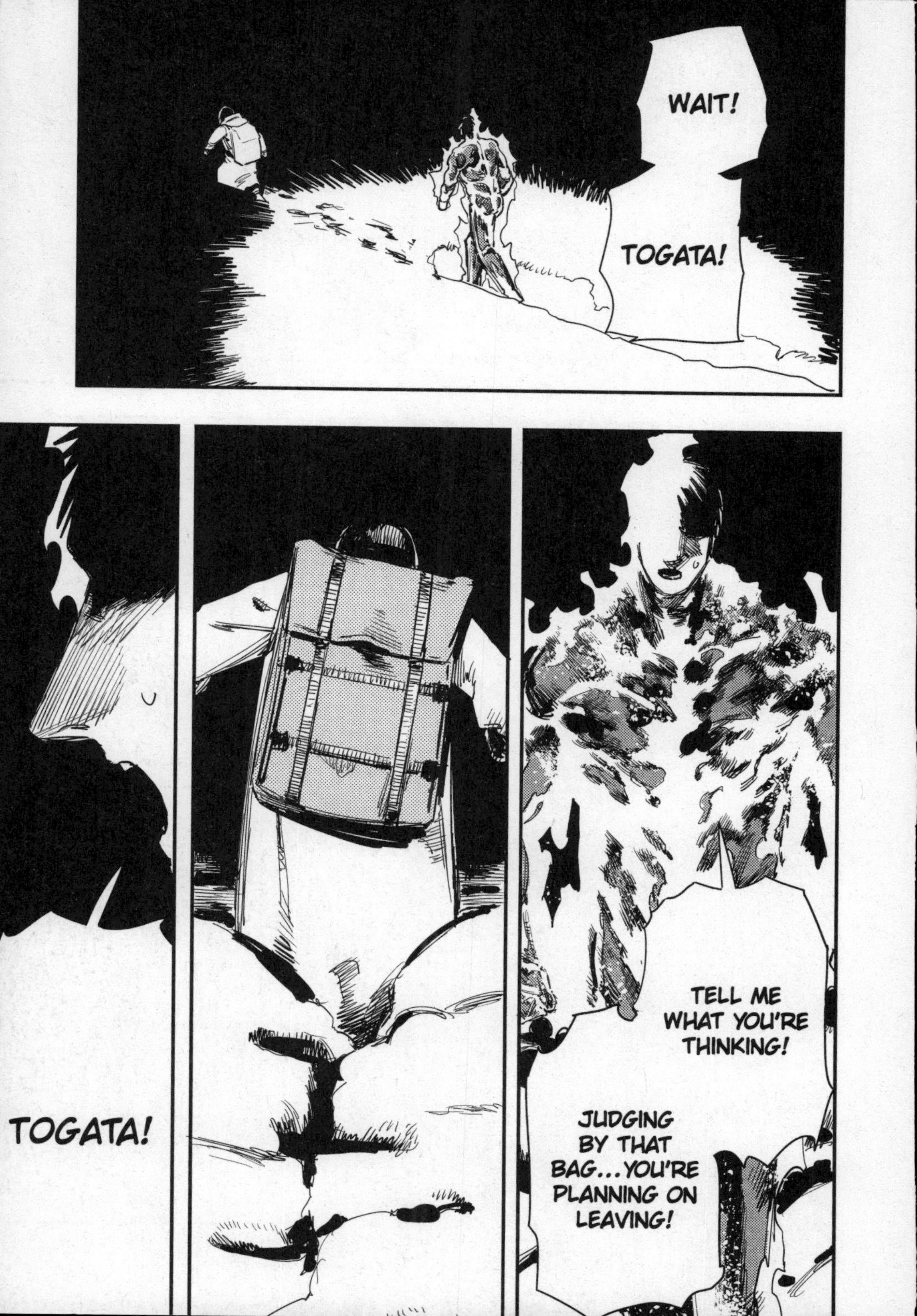
WAIT!
TOGATA!
TELL ME WHAT YOU'RE THINKING!
JUDGING BY THAT BAG...YOU'RE PLANNING ON LEAVING!
TOGATA!

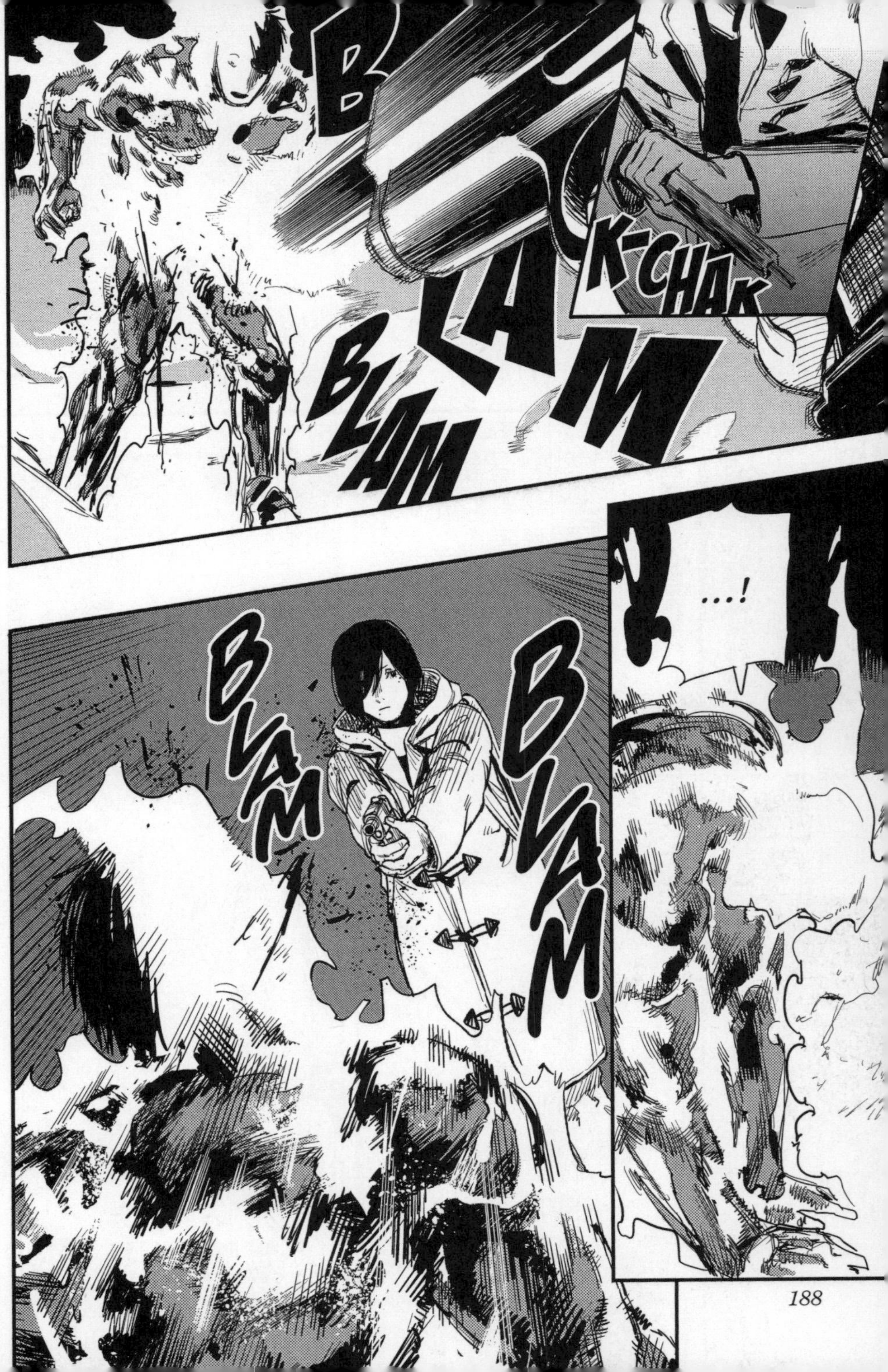
K-CHAK
BLAM
BLAM
...!
BLAM
BLAM

TOGATA!

DID WHAT THAT MASKED GUY SAID UPSET YOU THAT MUCH?

WHAT'S GOING ON? I DON'T GET YOU!

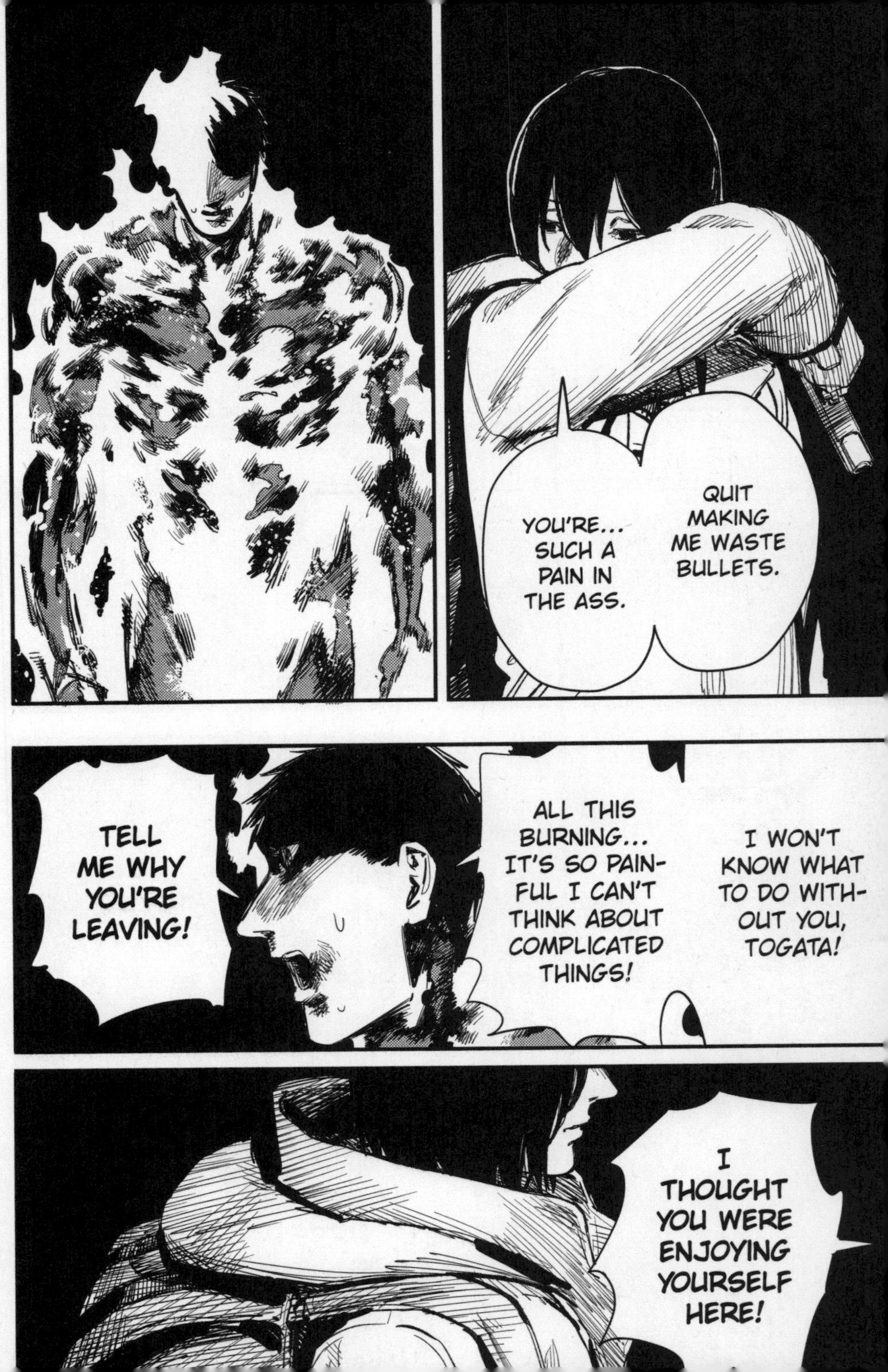
YOU'RE... SUCH A PAIN IN THE ASS.
QUIT MAKING ME WASTE BULLETS.
I WON'T KNOW WHAT TO DO WITH-OUT YOU, TOGATA!
ALL THIS BURNING... IT'S SO PAIN-FUL I CAN'T THINK ABOUT COMPLICATED THINGS!
TELL ME WHY YOU'RE LEAVING!
I THOUGHT YOU WERE ENJOYING YOURSELF HERE!

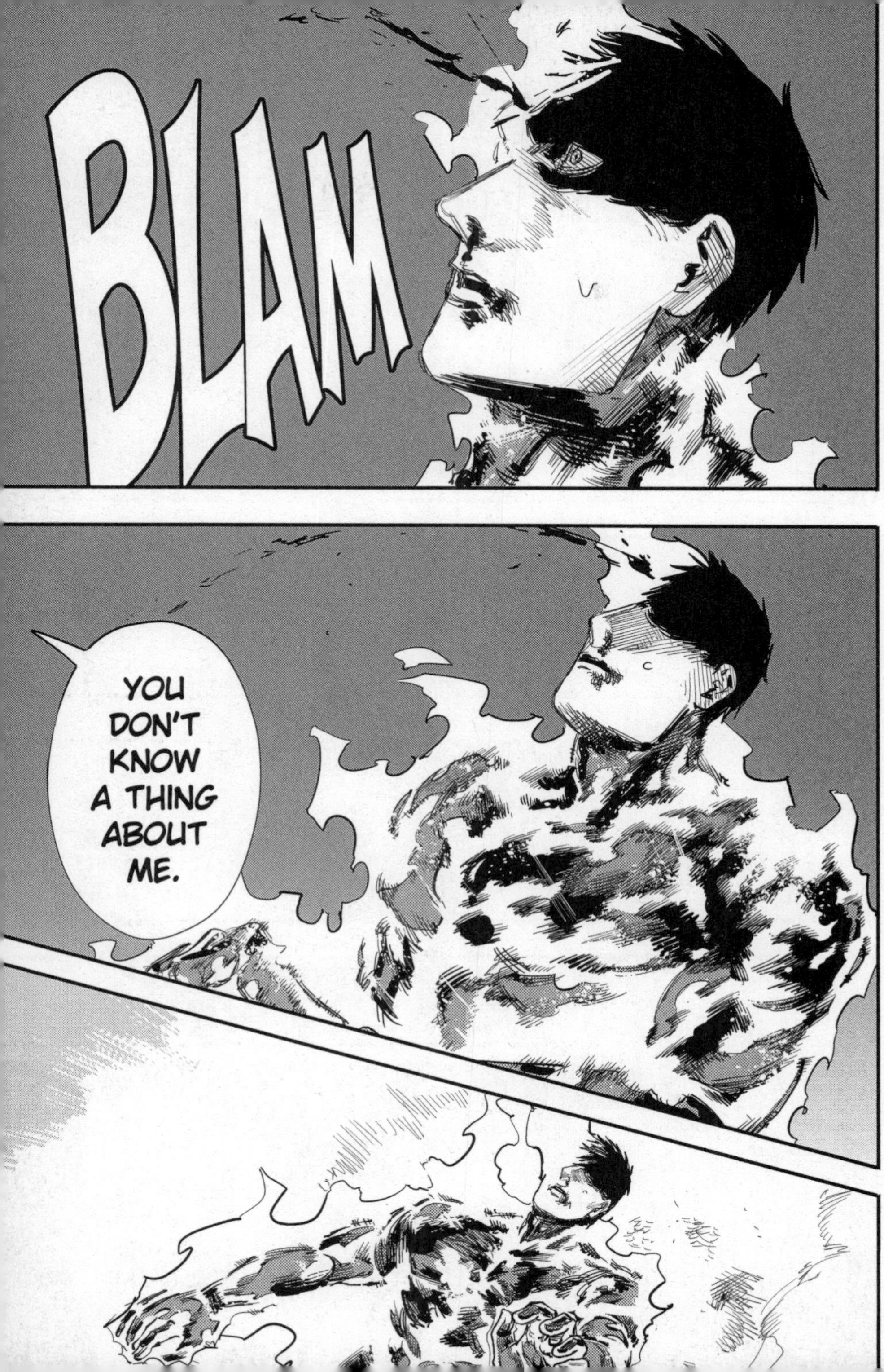
BLAM
YOU DON'T KNOW A THING ABOUT ME.

SORRY! I GUESS I STILL DON'T HAVE GOOD CONTROL OF YOUR BODY JUST YET.

I DON'T LIKE SEEING MY OWN FACE GLARING BACK AT ME.

CHAPTER 39

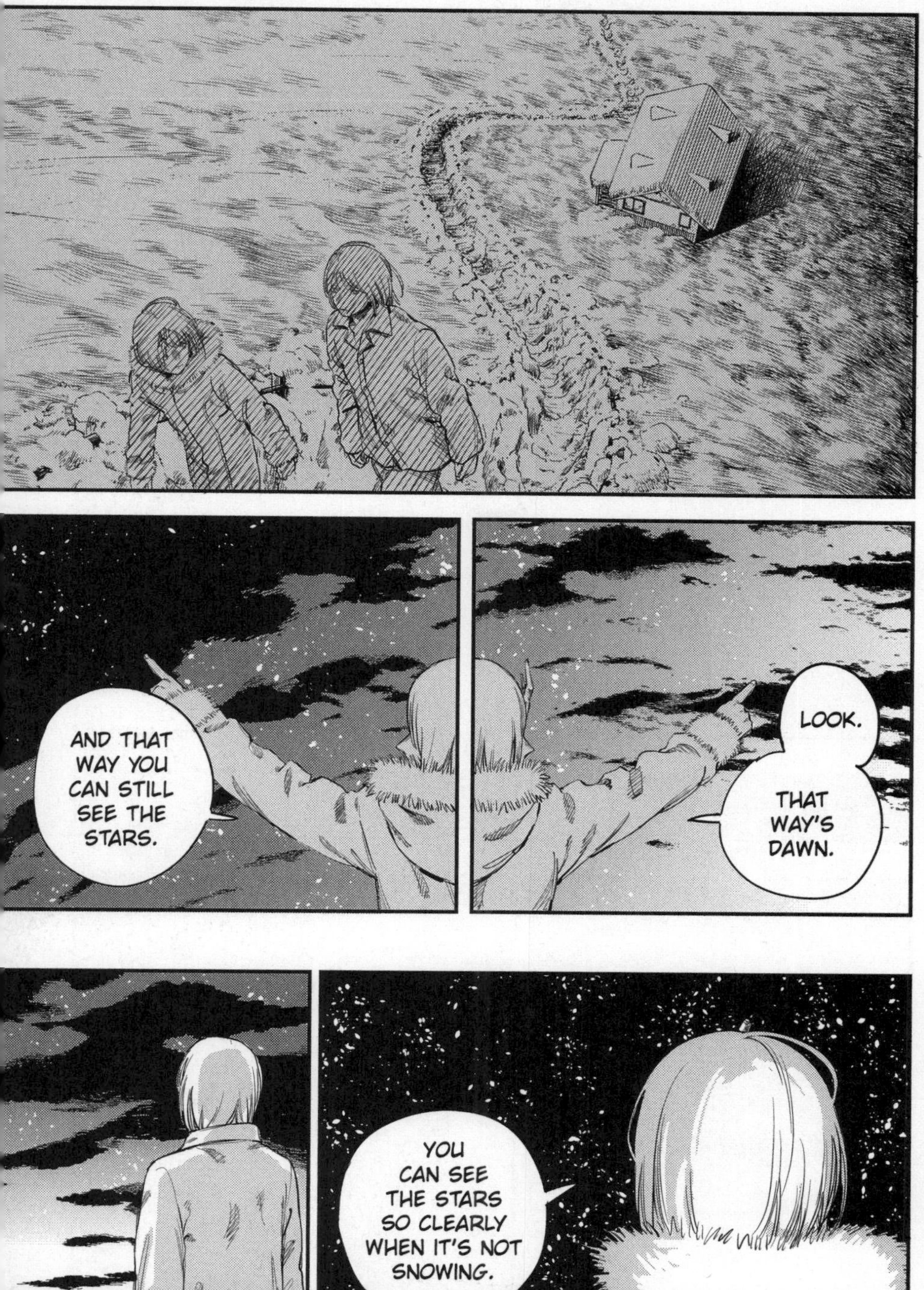
LOOK.
THAT WAY'S DAWN.
AND THAT WAY YOU CAN STILL SEE THE STARS.
YOU CAN SEE THE STARS SO CLEARLY WHEN IT'S NOT SNOWING.

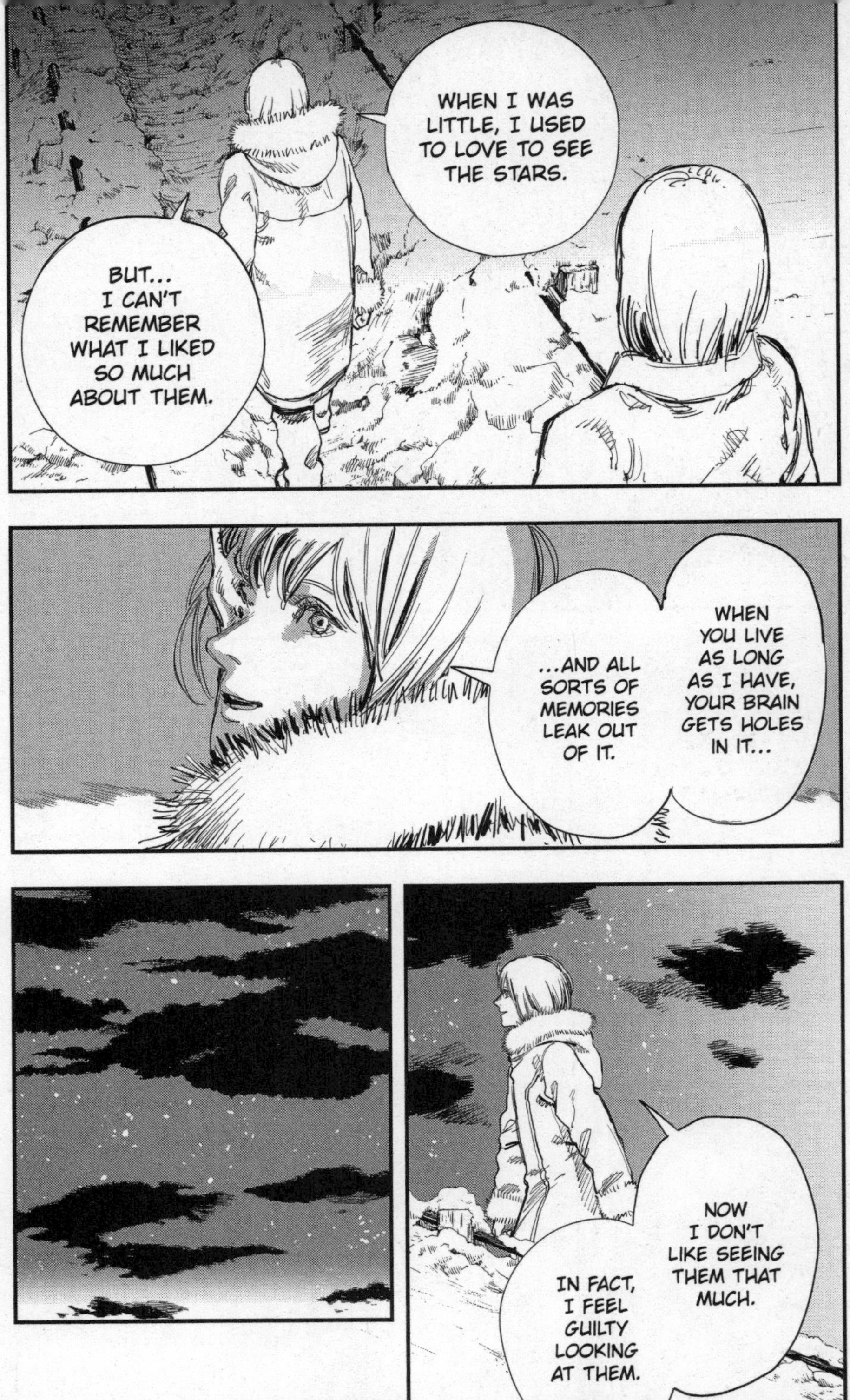
WHEN I WAS LITTLE, I USED TO LOVE TO SEE THE STARS.
BUT... I CAN'T REMEMBER WHAT I LIKED SO MUCH ABOUT THEM.
WHEN YOU LIVE AS LONG AS I HAVE, YOUR BRAIN GETS HOLES IN IT...
...AND ALL SORTS OF MEMORIES LEAK OUT OF IT.
NOW I DON'T LIKE SEEING THEM THAT MUCH.
IN FACT, I FEEL GUILTY LOOKING AT THEM.

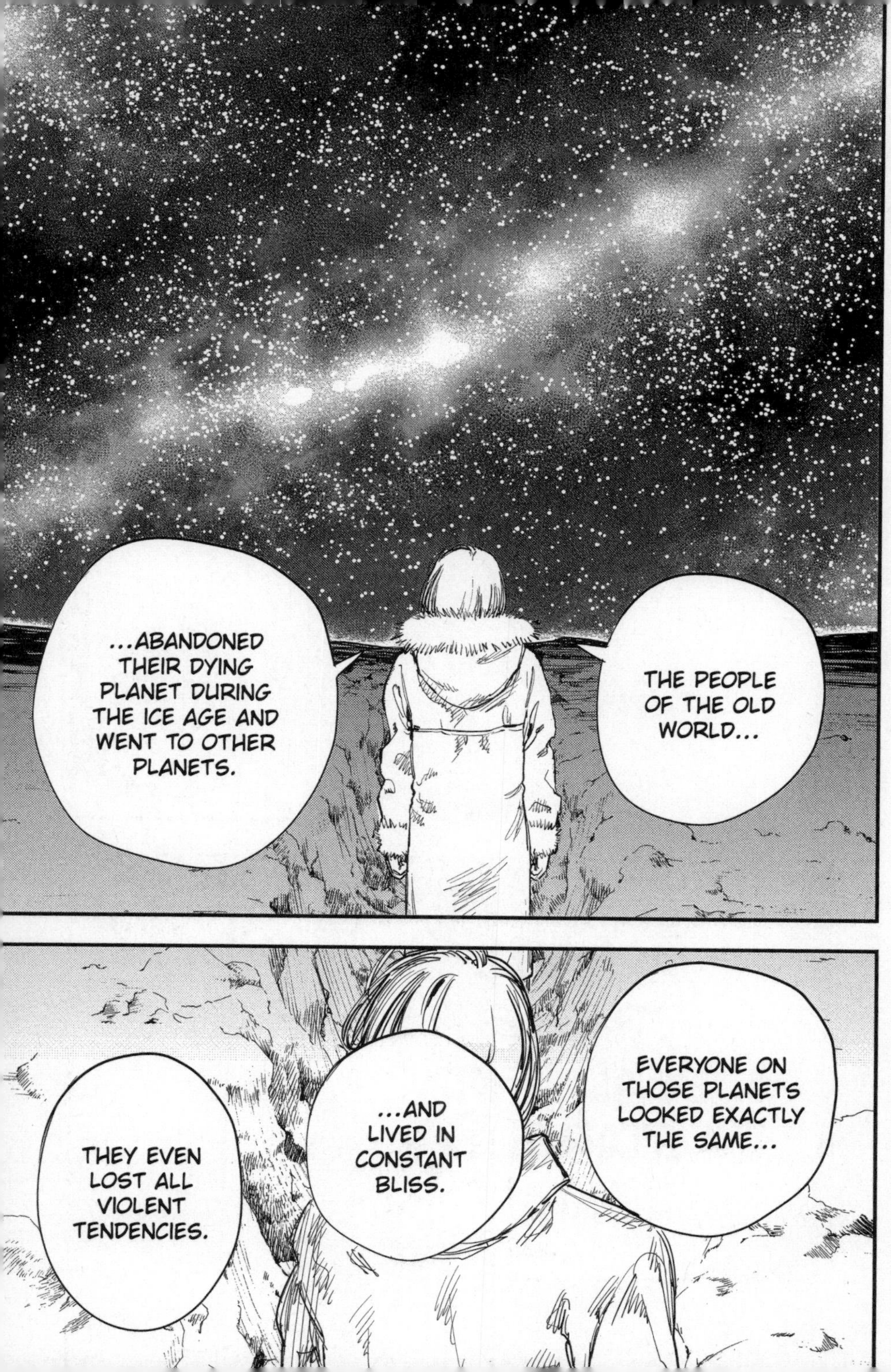
THE PEOPLE OF THE OLD WORLD...
...ABANDONED THEIR DYING PLANET DURING THE ICE AGE AND WENT TO OTHER PLANETS.
EVERYONE ON THOSE PLANETS LOOKED EXACTLY THE SAME...
...AND LIVED IN CONSTANT BLISS.
THEY EVEN LOST ALL VIOLENT TENDENCIES.

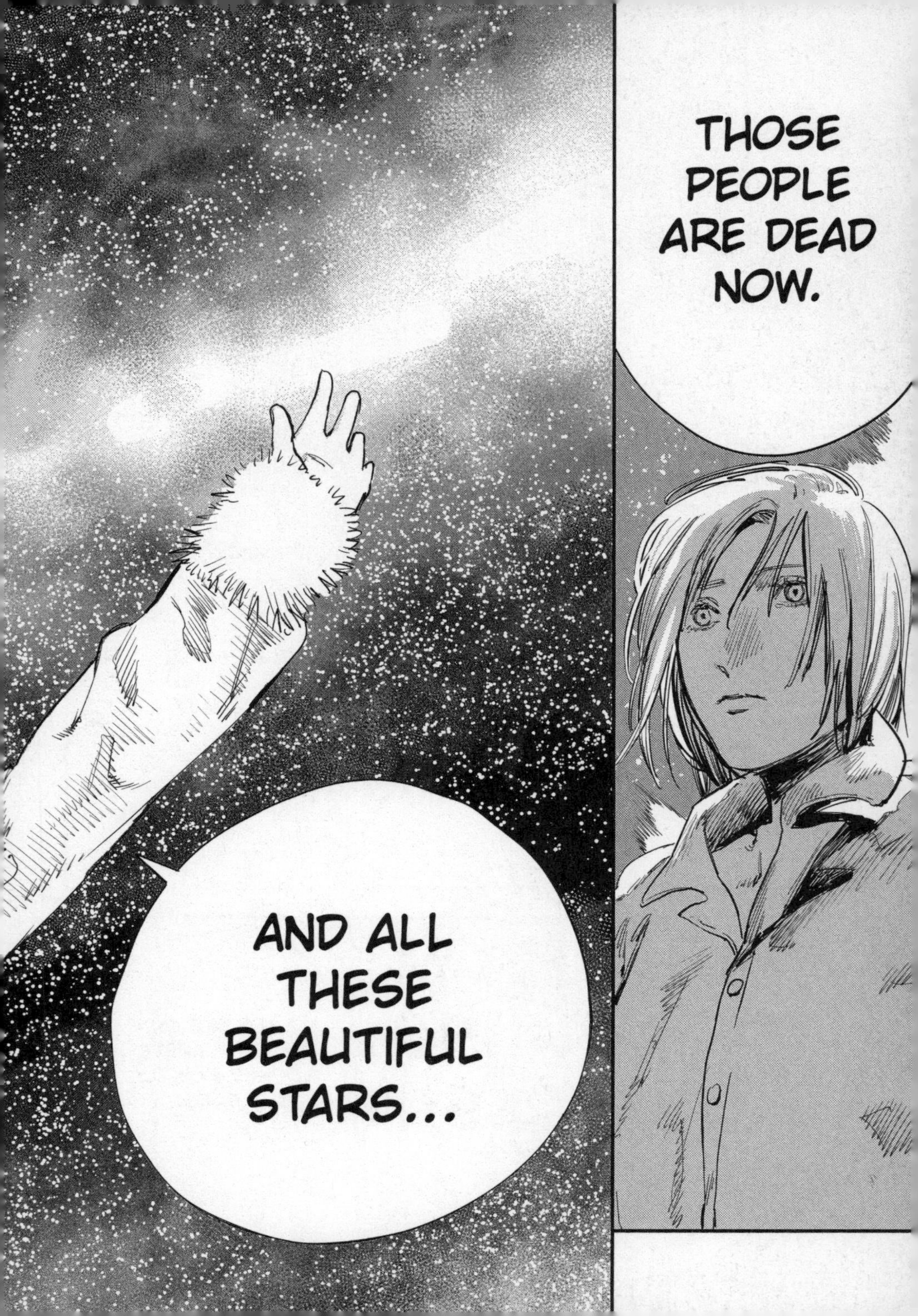
THOSE PEOPLE ARE DEAD NOW.
AND ALL THESE BEAUTIFUL STARS...

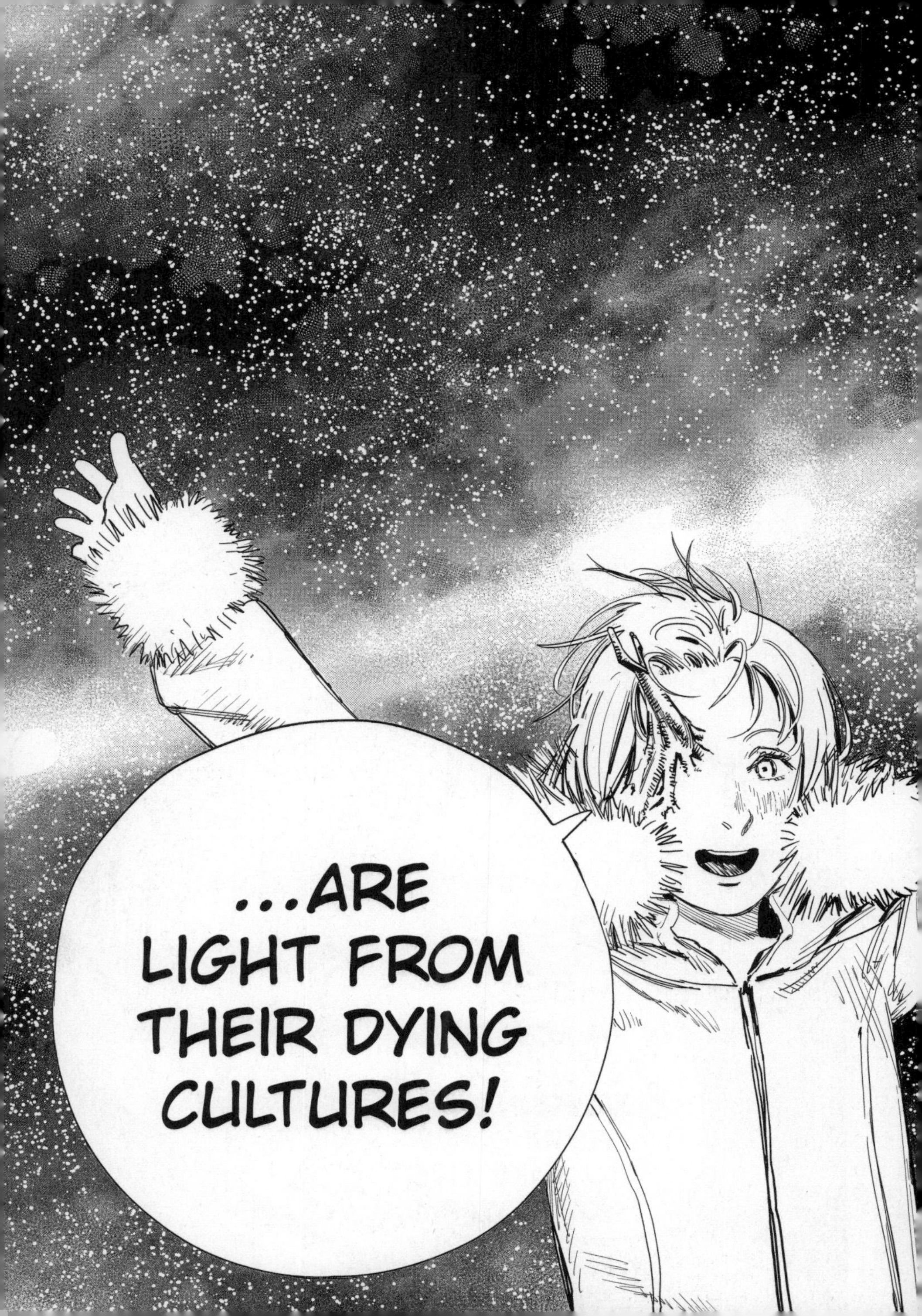
...ARE LIGHT FROM THEIR DYING CULTURES!

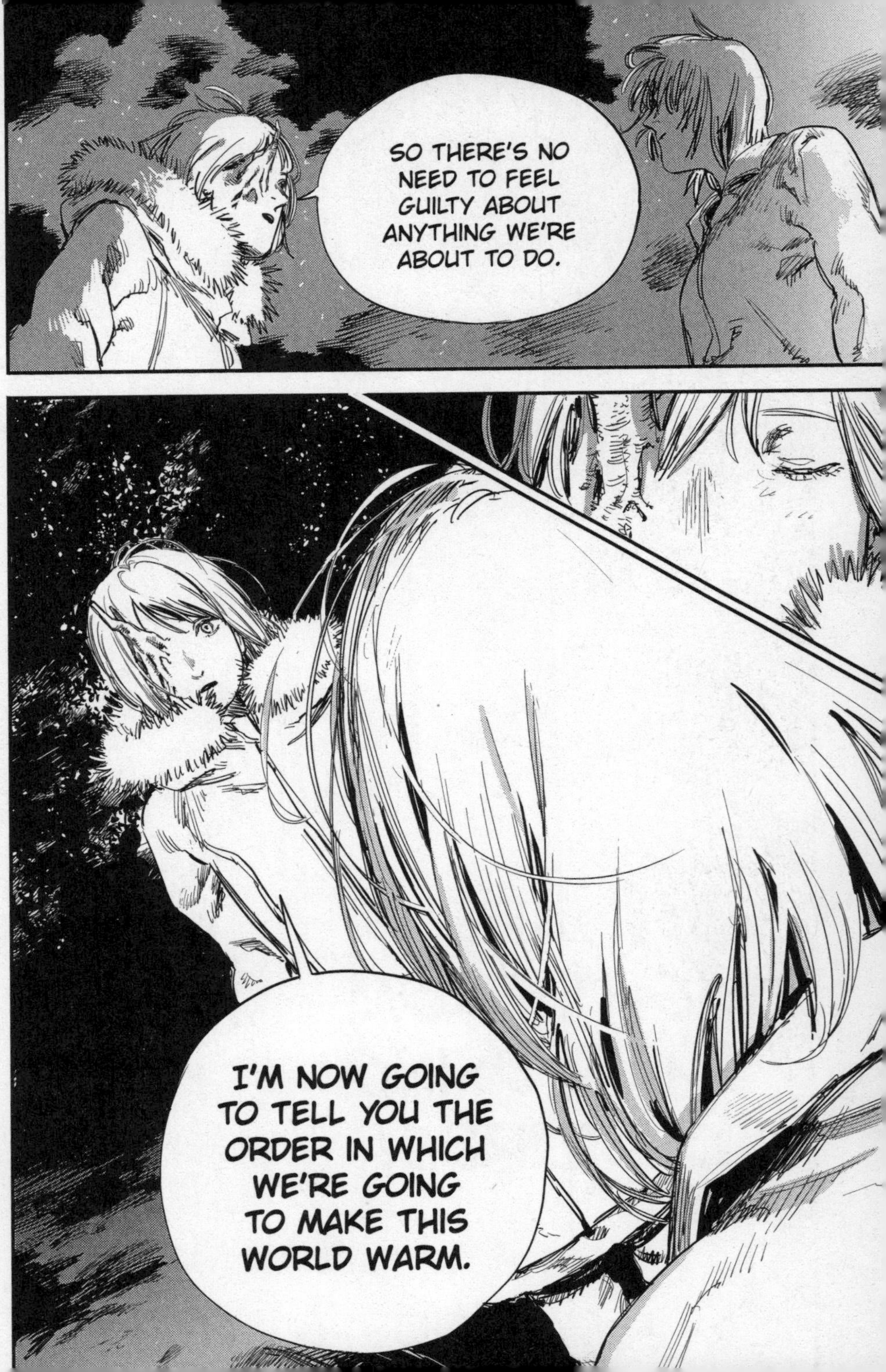
SO THERE'S NO NEED TO FEEL GUILTY ABOUT ANYTHING WE'RE ABOUT TO DO.
I'M NOW GOING TO TELL YOU THE ORDER IN WHICH WE'RE GOING TO MAKE THIS WORLD WARM.

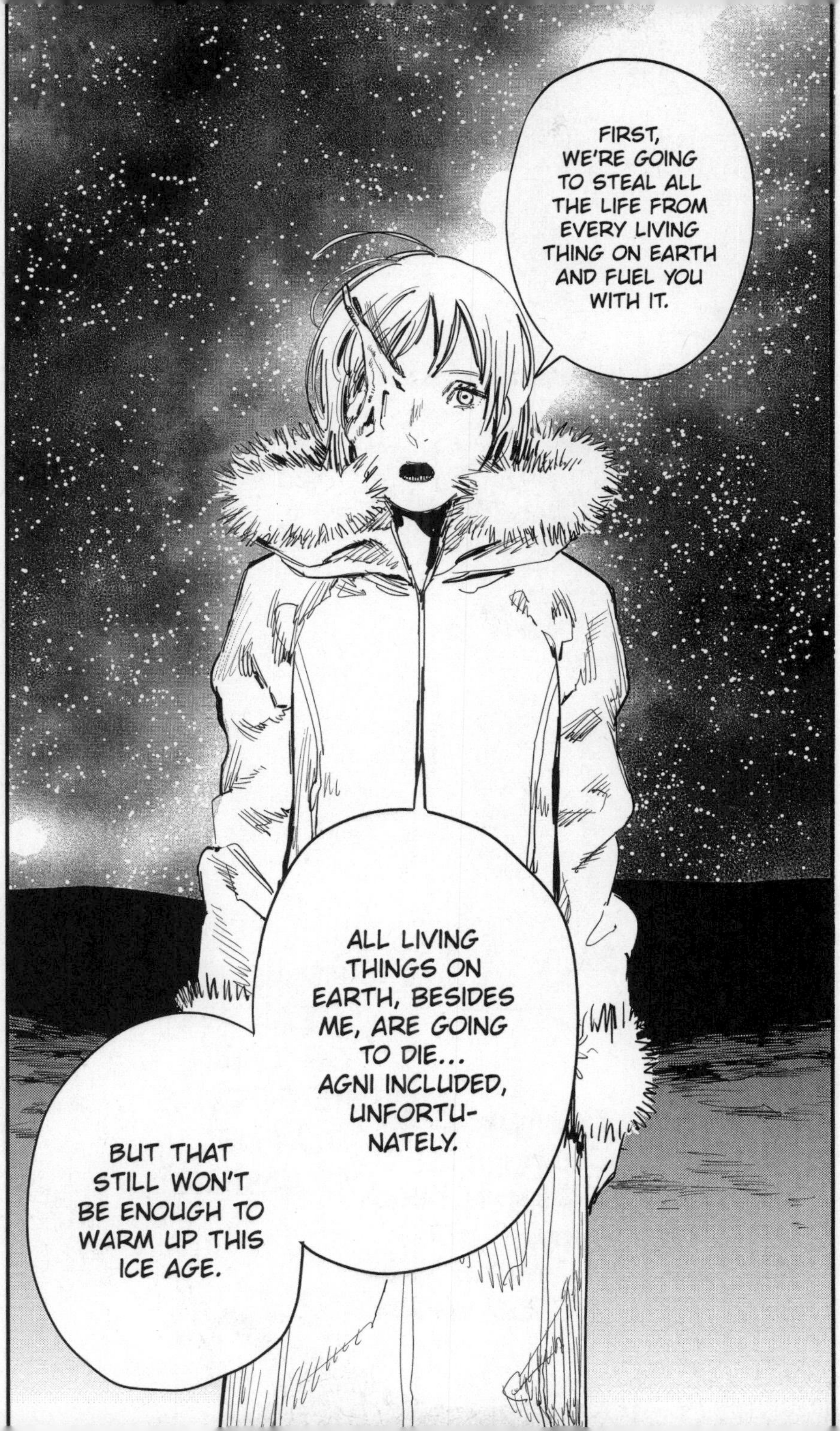
FIRST, WE'RE GOING TO STEAL ALL THE LIFE FROM EVERY LIVING THING ON EARTH AND FUEL YOU WITH IT.
ALL LIVING THINGS ON EARTH, BESIDES ME, ARE GOING TO DIE... AGNI INCLUDED, UNFORTU-NATELY.
BUT THAT STILL WON'T BE ENOUGH TO WARM UP THIS ICE AGE.

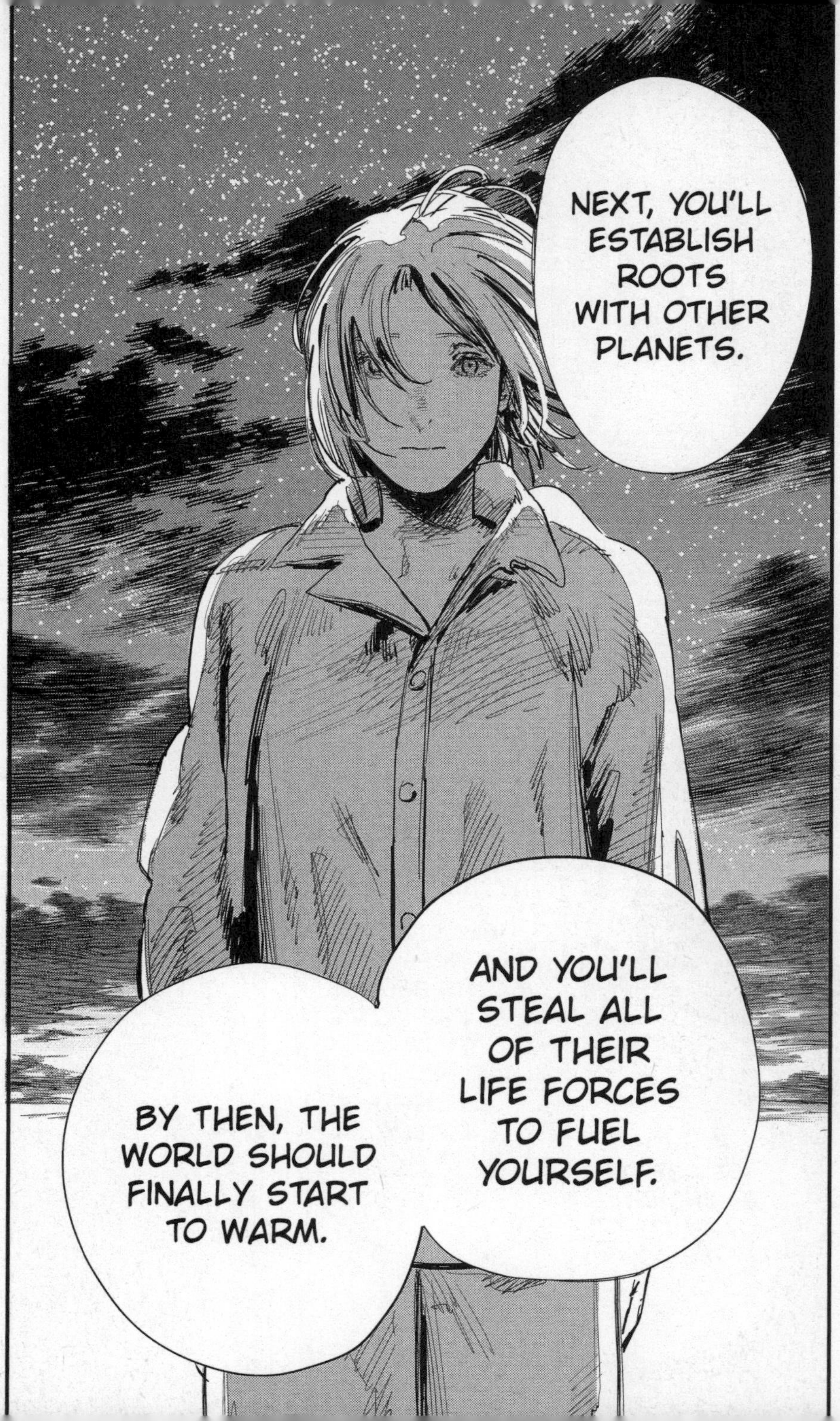
NEXT, YOU'LL ESTABLISH ROOTS WITH OTHER PLANETS.
AND YOU'LL STEAL ALL OF THEIR LIFE FORCES TO FUEL YOURSELF.
BY THEN, THE WORLD SHOULD FINALLY START TO WARM.

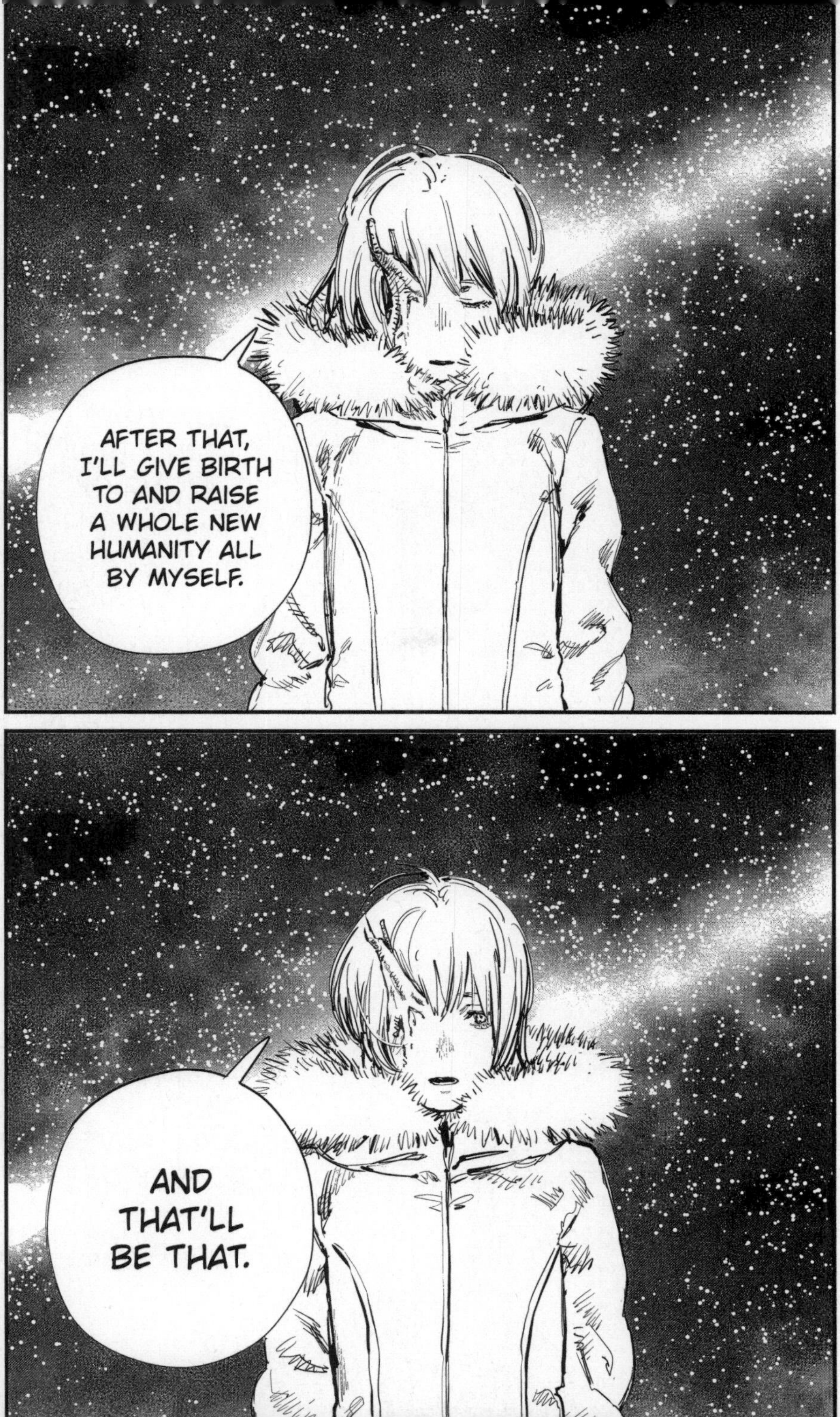
AFTER THAT, I'LL GIVE BIRTH TO AND RAISE A WHOLE NEW HUMANITY ALL BY MYSELF.
AND THAT'LL BE THAT.

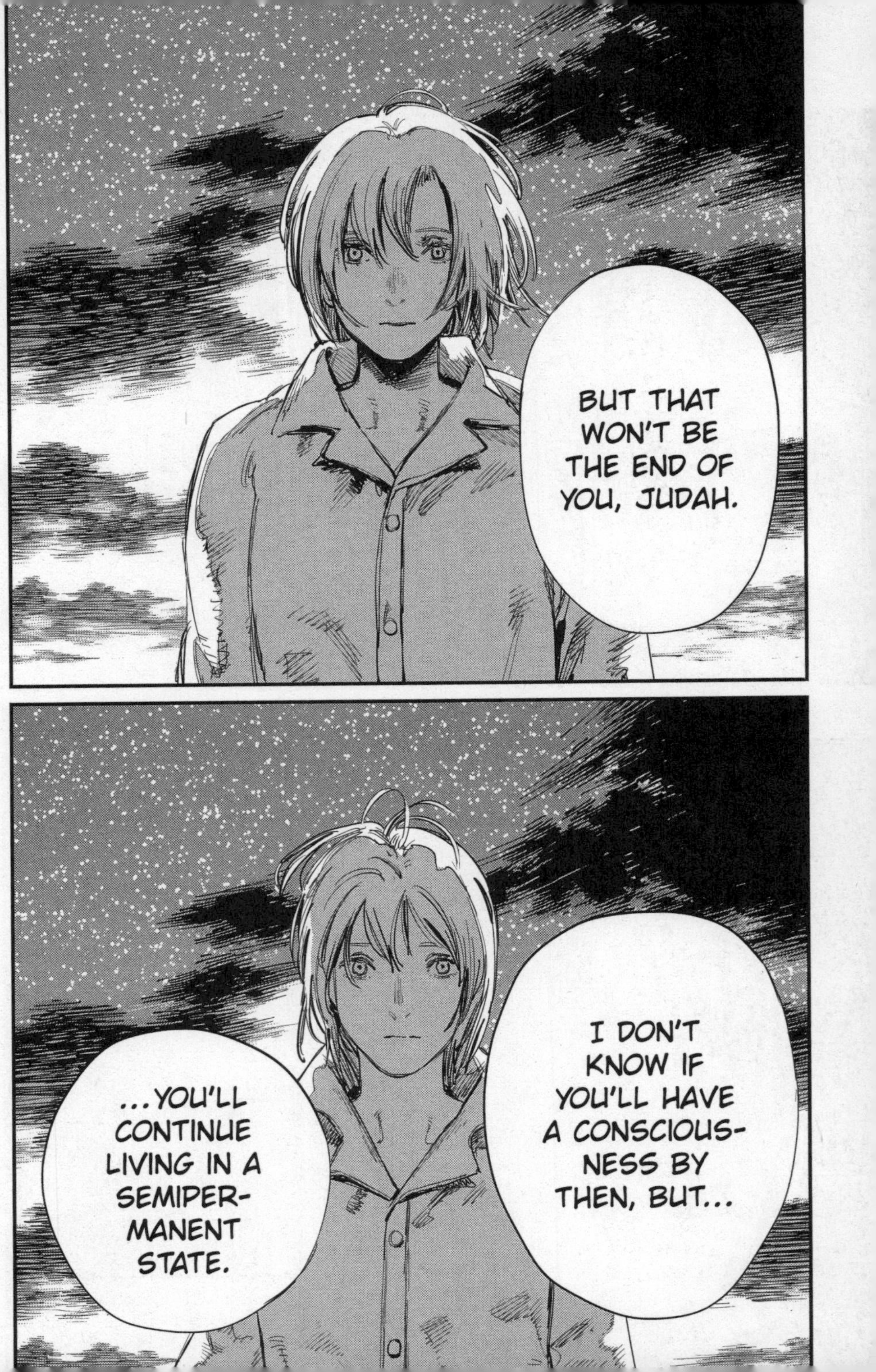
BUT THAT WON'T BE THE END OF YOU, JUDAH.
I DON'T KNOW IF YOU'LL HAVE A CONSCIOUSNESS BY THEN, BUT...
...YOU'LL CONTINUE LIVING IN A SEMIPERMANENT STATE.

ARE YOU COMPLETELY UNABLE TO MOVE NOW?

...

ONLY THE RIGHT SIDE OF MY FACE IS DIFFERENT FROM YOU, JUDAH.

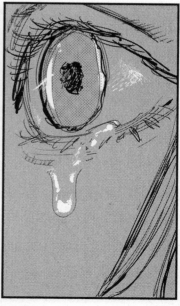

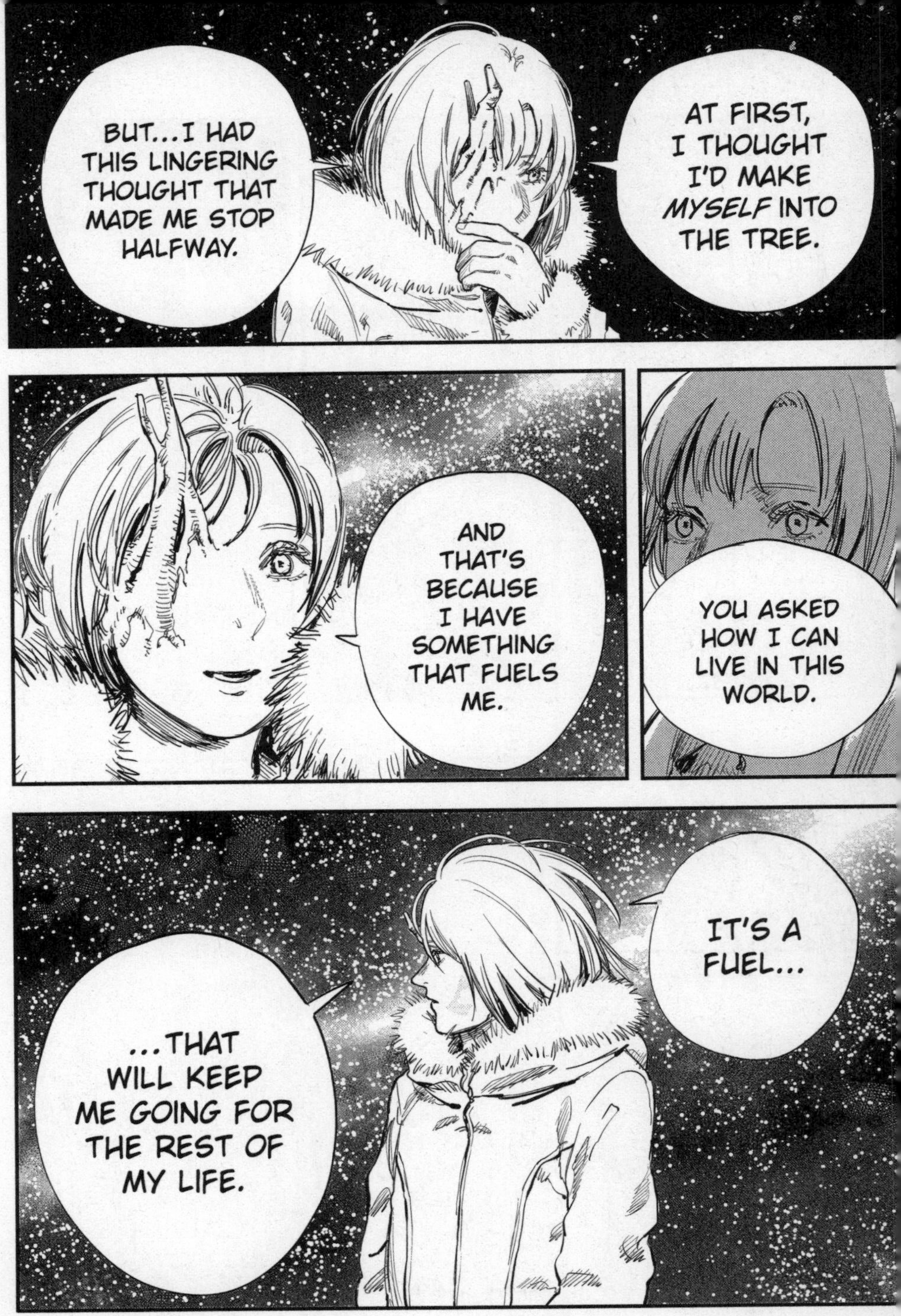
AT FIRST, I THOUGHT I'D MAKE *MYSELF* INTO THE TREE.
BUT...I HAD THIS LINGERING THOUGHT THAT MADE ME STOP HALFWAY.
YOU ASKED HOW I CAN LIVE IN THIS WORLD.
AND THAT'S BECAUSE I HAVE SOMETHING THAT FUELS ME.
IT'S A FUEL...
...THAT WILL KEEP ME GOING FOR THE REST OF MY LIFE.

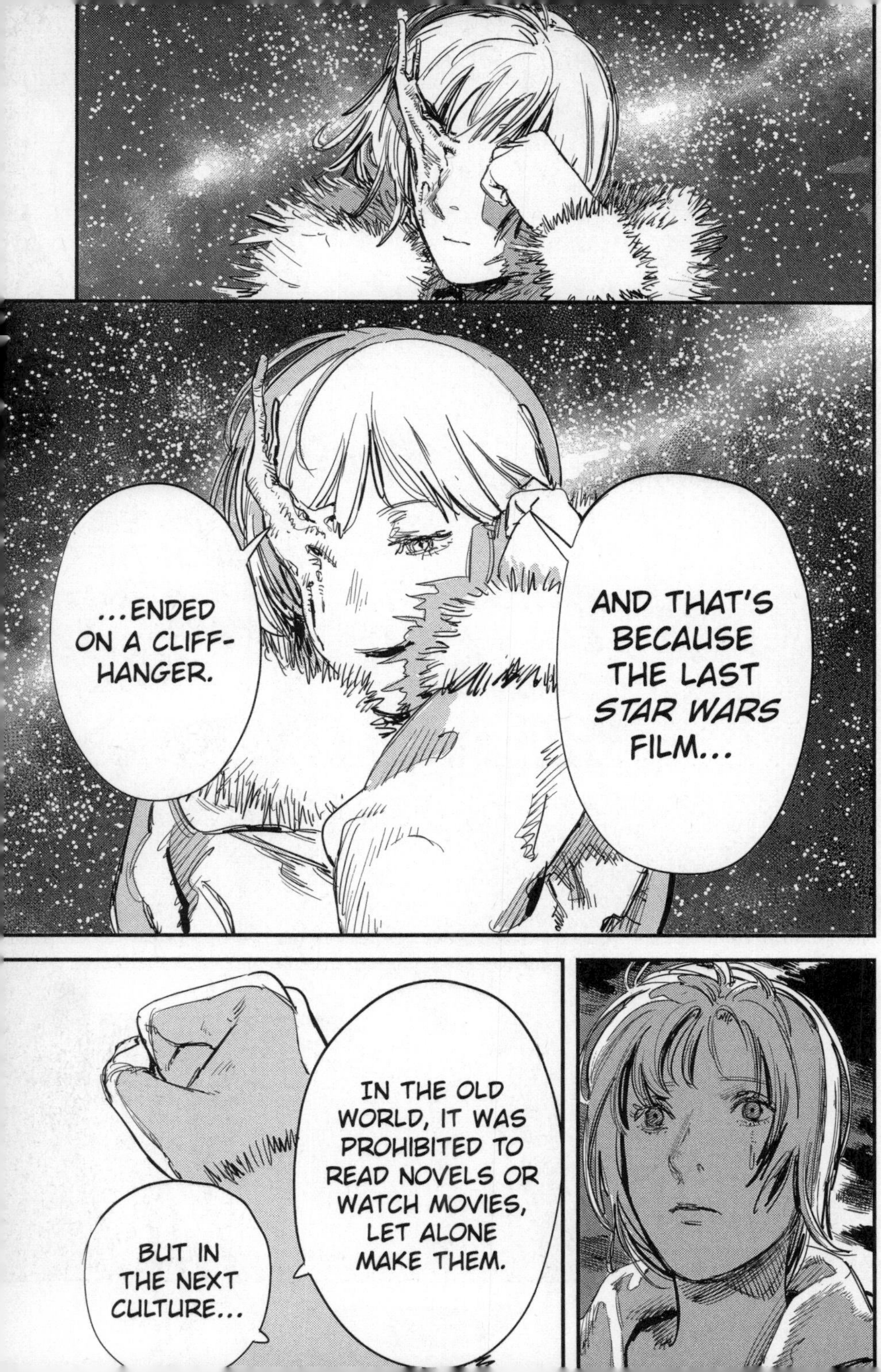
AND THAT'S BECAUSE THE LAST *STAR WARS* FILM...
...ENDED ON A CLIFF-HANGER.
IN THE OLD WORLD, IT WAS PROHIBITED TO READ NOVELS OR WATCH MOVIES, LET ALONE MAKE THEM.
BUT IN THE NEXT CULTURE...

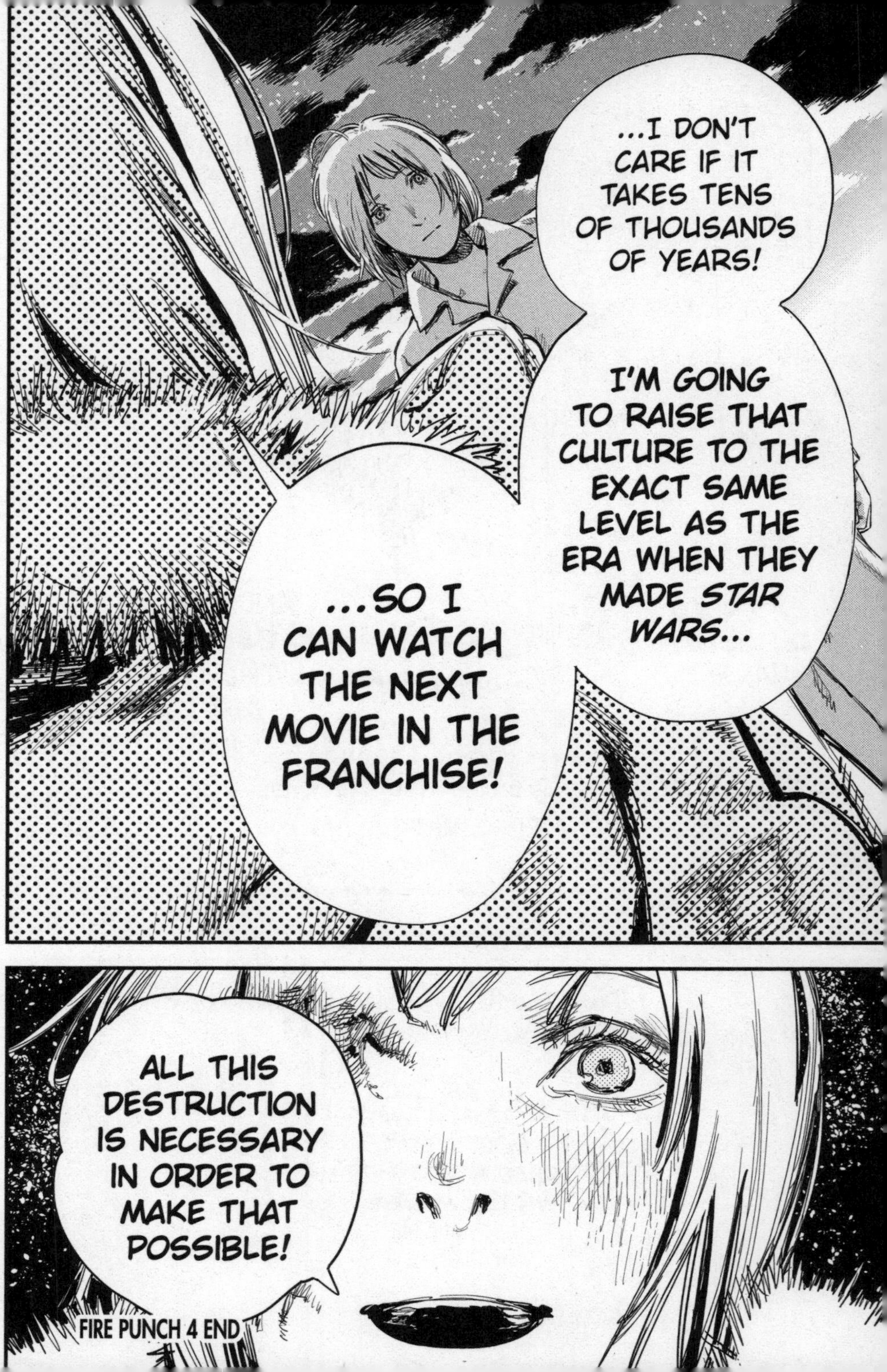
...I DON'T CARE IF IT TAKES TENS OF THOUSANDS OF YEARS!
I'M GOING TO RAISE THAT CULTURE TO THE EXACT SAME LEVEL AS THE ERA WHEN THEY MADE *STAR WARS*...
...SO I CAN WATCH THE NEXT MOVIE IN THE FRANCHISE!
ALL THIS DESTRUCTION IS NECESSARY IN ORDER TO MAKE THAT POSSIBLE!
FIRE PUNCH 4 END

TATSUKI FUJIMOTO

Twice a year, I spend time with
my grandmother in France. I'm
trying to get in her will.

Tatsuki Fujimoto won Honorable Mention
in the November 2013 Shueisha Crown
Newcomers' Awards for his debut one-shot
story "Love Is Blind," which was published
in volume 13 of *Jump SQ.19*. Fujimoto's
follow-up series, *Fire Punch*, is the creator's
first English-language release.

FIRE PUNCH

Volume 4
VIZ Signature Edition

Story and Art by Tatsuki Fujimoto

Translation: Christine Dashiell
Touch-Up Art & Lettering: Snir Aharon
Design: Julian [JR] Robinson
Editor: Jennifer LeBlanc

FIRE PUNCH © 2016 by Tatsuki Fujimoto
All rights reserved.
First published in Japan in 2016 by SHUEISHA Inc., Tokyo.
English translation rights arranged by SHUEISHA Inc.

The stories, characters and incidents mentioned in
this publication are entirely fictional.

Printed in the U.S.A.

Published by VIZ Media, LLC
P.O. Box 77010
San Francisco, CA 94107

10 9 8 7 6 5 4 3 2 1
First printing, October 2018

VIZ MEDIA
viz.com

vizsignature.com

PARENTAL ADVISORY
FIRE PUNCH is rated M for Mature. Contains
graphic violence and sexual situations, and is
recommended for mature readers.